The Internation
Harvester Compa

The International Harvester Company

A History of the Founding Families and Their Machines

CHAIM M. ROSENBERG

McFarland & Company, Inc., Publishers

Jefferson, North Carolina

ALSO BY CHAIM M. ROSENBERG
AND FROM MCFARLAND

*The Loyalist Conscience: Principled Opposition
to the American Revolution* (2018)

*Losing America, Conquering India: Lord Cornwallis
and the Remaking of the British Empire* (2017)

Child Labor in America: A History (2013)

Frontispiece: **Cyrus Hall McCormick (Library of Congress).**

All images with a WHS image identification number in the caption are used
with the permission of the Wisconsin Historical Society, wisconsinhistory.org.

LIBRARY OF CONGRESS CATALOGUING-IN-PUBLICATION DATA

Names: Rosenberg, Chaim M., author.
Title: The International Harvester Company : a history of the founding
families and their machines / Chaim M. Rosenberg.
Description: Jefferson, North Carolina : McFarland & Company, Inc.,
Publishers, 2019 | Includes bibliographical references and index.
Identifiers: LCCN 2019013952 | ISBN 9781476677095
(paperback. : acid free paper) ∞
Subjects: LCSH: International Harvester Company. |
McCormick, Cyrus Hall, 1809–1884. | Deering, William, 1826–1913 |
Agricultural machinery—United States—History.
Classification: LCC HD9486.U6 I795 2019 | DDC 338.7/63130973—dc23
LC record available at https://lccn.loc.gov/2019013952

BRITISH LIBRARY CATALOGUING DATA ARE AVAILABLE

ISBN (print) 978-1-4766-7709-5
ISBN (ebook) 978-1-4766-3606-1

Front cover images: Three McCormick harvester machines pulled
by a Mogul 25-hp tractor in 1912; a boy is leaning against a stack of grain
in the foreground (Wisconsin Historical Society Image ID 44843).
Portraits clockwise: Katharine Dexter McCormick (Library of Congress);
Cyrus Hall McCormick, Jr. (Library of Congress); Charles Deering (author collection);
Nancy "Nettie" Fowler McCormick (Wisconsin Historical Society Image ID 8385);
William Deering at age 76 years (Wisconsin Historical Society Image ID 24794)

Printed in the United States of America

McFarland & Company, Inc., Publishers
Box 611, Jefferson, North Carolina 28640
www.mcfarlandpub.com

For the next generation,
Michal, Isla and Noam

Acknowledgments

I would like to thank David Rosenberg and Derek Lamb as helpful and non-complaining technical advisers. Robert Manewith helped with the chapter on Robert Rutherford McCormick. My thanks to staff of the special collections, Cudahy Library, Loyola University in Chicago for access to the Leander Hamilton Collection. Thanks to the Newberry Library for access to the Chauncey Brooks McCormick papers. My deep thanks go to Tom Clark and Vaughn Allen, indefatigable historians of Navistar, Inc., the successor to the International Harvester Company. I am immensely grateful to Navistar, Inc., and the International Truck Intellectual Property Company for permission to select and reproduce in this book images from the company's vast and distinguished collection. The photographs of Robert R. McCormick came from the collection of the First Division Museum, Wheaton, Illinois. Northwestern University Archives and Vizcaya Museum and Gardens gave me permission to use images from their collections. Images indicated with a WHS number are used with the permission of the Wisconsin Historical Society, wisconsin-history.org. Other images come from the collections of the Library of Congress, Museums Victoria, and Wikimedia Commons. A number of the images come from my private collection of period postcards and brochures. Above all else, I thank my wife Dawn who has supported me to research and write yet another book.

Table of Contents

Preface

Since ancient times farmers have used animals to pull their wooden plows to turn the soil for planting. Reaping grains by the heavy sweat of the brow, using sickle or scythe, continued for many centuries until Cyrus Hall McCormick departed the hills of Virginia to manufacture his mechanical harvester in Chicago.

With a population of 20,000, Chicago in 1847 was on the cusp of fantastic growth with the opening of the railroad to Galena, the Illinois & Michigan Canal linking the Great Lakes to the Mississippi River and the Gulf of Mexico, and the arrival of the first telegram. Joined by his younger brothers William and Leander, McCormick set up a factory to build the horse-powered Virginia Reaper that revolutionized farming and greatly expanded the acreage for grains to feed the nation's fast growing human population as well as its animal stock. The McCormick reaper's success at the 1851 Crystal Palace Fair in London expanded sales worldwide. "The reaper is to the North what slavery is to the South," declared Edwin M. Stanton, secretary of war, in 1861. During the Civil War the mechanical reaper released many farmers to join the army and fight to save the Union and end slavery. Before the mechanical reaper, two-thirds of Americans worked on the land. Machinery vastly increased farm yields while greatly reducing human labor. Improved seeds, irrigation and the mechanization of harvesting and transportation made mock of the 1798 prediction by Thomas Robert Malthus that population growth would soon outstrip food supply.

Cyrus McCormick's achievement spawned competition from some two hundred harvester companies in New England, New York, Ohio, Illinois and Wisconsin. Cyrus Hall McCormick opposed the lawyers Edwin M. Stanton and Abraham Lincoln and others to defend his patent rights. While Cyrus battled his competitors in the courts, William and Leander remained in Chicago running the factory. The chief competition to McCormick came after 1880 with the arrival in Chicago of William Deering from South Paris, Maine. By 1900, the Deering Harvester Company was outselling McCormick. Cyrus McCormick and William Deering dominated the harvester business. After the departure of these pioneers, farm machinery entered the age of Big Business.

In 1902 Cyrus McCormick's sons, Cyrus, Jr., and Harold, together with William Deering's sons Charles and James, oversaw the merger of their family-owned companies with four smaller ones into the International Harvester Company (IHC), the world's largest farm machinery enterprise. Set up by J. Pierpont Morgan & Company and financed by John D. Rockefeller, the Reaper Trust gained 90 percent of the harvester market in the United States and was fast expanding abroad. From 1906 until 1927, IHC thwarted government efforts under the Sherman Antitrust Act to break it up. From its headquarters in Chicago, IHC was a leader in improving workers' conditions through a safer environment, wage hikes,

1

Artwork in the Tomb of Nakht, Egypt, 15th century B.C., XVIII Dynasty, shows plows pulled by animals, but the heavy work of harvesting done by man (Rogers Fund, 1915, Metropolitan Museum of Art, New York).

shorter hours, sickness and death benefits, profit sharing and pensions. Owning forests, coal and iron ore mines, and making its own steel, the International Harvester Company at home and abroad expanded to build all lines of farm equipment, including plows, harrowers, cultivators and fertilizers as well as harvesters. Horses pulled these machines until the development of the all-purpose gasoline-powered tractor. Starting in 1900 with its Auto-Mower and in 1907 with its Auto Buggy, IHC moved into tractors and delivery trucks. International Harvester machines reached into every continent to feed the world. During World Wars I and II, the American company made trucks and tractors for the United States army, while its Canadian, British and Australian subsidiaries supplied the armies of the allied countries.

Living in the shadow of his powerful legend was a challenge to the children of Cyrus McCormick. His obedient firstborn Cyrus, Jr., carried on the dynasty and was followed, less successfully, by the middle son Harold. For Cyrus's youngest son Stanley, the burden of being a McCormick was too great and he sank into permanent madness. With the McCormicks in control, the Deering brothers retired from IHC. In 1914, Charles Deering's daughter Marion married Chauncey Brooks McCormick to again link the two great Chicago reaper families.

"By the sweat of your brow": Harvesters are at work in Hungary, early 20th century. The use of the scythe and the sickle for harvesting grains continued for centuries but was replaced starting in the mid-nineteenth century by mechanical harvesters (author's collection).

After the sons, the McCormick grandsons Cyrus III and Fowler and lastly great-grand-nephew Brooks McCormick took on the responsibility of leading the Harvester Company. Brooks' departure in 1980 ended a century and a half with a McCormick in leadership of the agricultural machinery business. In 1985, the International Harvester Company, suffering heavy losses, sold off its farm machinery enterprises to emerge as the truck company Navistar International. The 154 years between Cyrus H. McCormick's invention of his reaping machine and the demise of International Harvester encompassed the rise of America's industrial might and its decline.

Farm machines gave America an abundant harvest and made the McCormicks and the Deerings very wealthy. Cyrus Hall McCormick and his brother Leander invested in Chicago real estate. Cyrus supported the McCormick Theological Seminary and Leander funded the Observatory at the University of Virginia. William Deering supported the Methodist Garrett Biblical Institute, Wesley Hospital and Northwestern University. Harold McCormick and his wife Edith Rockefeller McCormick supported opera and built the splendid Villa Turicum at Lake Forest.

The McCormicks and the Deerings established foundations and funded the arts, museums, universities, hospitals and historical societies. The Art Institute of Chicago and the Museum of Fine Arts in Boston received many of their finest paintings and objects from the McCormick and Deering families. The John Rockefeller Institute (later Rockefeller University) was founded after the death by scarlet fever of his three-year-old grandson, John Rockefeller McCormick. Charles Deering established an estate at Palmetto Bay and his brother James built Villa Vizcaya at Key Biscayne—two of the grandest homes of Florida's Jazz Age.

Many of the offspring of the reaper families eschewed the family business to seek self-fulfillment as artists, writers, politicians, newspaper owners, art collectors, or philosophers. Robert Sanderson McCormick was American ambassador to Vienna, St. Petersburg and Paris. His oldest son Joseph Medill served as a senator from Illinois and younger son Robert Rutherford McCormick made the *Chicago Tribune* one of the nation's leading newspapers, despite its opposition to the League of Nations, the World Court, and the New Deal. Until the Japanese attack on Pearl Harbor, the isolationist Robert McCormick and his *Tribune* supported the America First Committee (AFC). Members of the reaper families fought in America's wars. Elizabeth Day McCormick assembled a vast collection of embroideries. Robert Hall McCormick and his son (Leander Sanderson McCormick) each formed a distinguished art collection. Leander Hamilton McCormick prided himself on his understanding of human character through the analysis of bodily features. Fowler McCormick's vast cattle ranch spurred the development of Scottsdale, Arizona. Katharine Dexter McCormick funded the research that led to the contraceptive pill. Ruth Hanna McCormick was active in woman's suffrage and politics. The most flamboyant of them was Edith Rockefeller McCormick who lavished her wealth on grand opera and supported many artists and writers, including James Joyce while he wrote *Ulysses*. She was an ardent admirer of the Swiss psychiatrist Carl Gustav Jung. When her brother was building the Rockefeller Center in New York, Edith set out to become Chicago's leading real estate developer, until derailed by illness and the Great Depression. Her ex-husband Harold McCormick squandered much of his wealth in a vain effort to support Ganna Walska, his second wife, in her quest for opera stardom.

Blessed with great wealth but battling physical and mental illness and scandal, the McCormicks were constantly under public scrutiny. The McCormick and Deering harvesters helped feed the world. The McCormicks and Deerings were determined to make Chicago a world-class city. For more than a century and a half they have endured among the leading families of Chicago.

Chapter One

Cyrus Hall McCormick
Comes to Chicago

It looked like "a cross between an Astley chariot, a wheel-barrow and a flying machine," wrote the *Times* of London.[1] It was "an extravagant Yankee contrivance … huge, unwieldy, unsightly and incomprehensible," sneered another newspaper.[2] The object of derision was the McCormick Reaper—known as the Virginia Reaper—one of 588 American exhibitors at the 1851 Great Exhibition of the Works of Industry of All Nations. Better known as the Crystal Palace Exhibition, it was housed in a vast cast-iron and plate glass structure designed by Joseph Paxton at Hyde Park, London. Queen Victoria officially opened the exhibition on May 1. The British were enthusiastic about America's cotton, rice, tobacco and timber but mocked the young country's manufacturing and design skills. Eager to enter the European market, Cyrus Hall McCormick sent from Chicago a special reaper to represent his company at the 1851 World Fair.

Richard Arkwright's cotton jenny and Edmund Cartwright's water-powered loom had long since placed Great Britain at the forefront of the industrial revolution. Manchester became the great center for the manufacture of cotton textiles, while Liverpool received the raw cotton from the American South and exported cotton textiles around the world. By 1851, steam power had replaced water power. Visitors to the Crystal Palace fair saw steam-powered machines that efficiently converted raw cotton into finished cloth. Steam powered engines drove locomotives and ships. But in farming, as in centuries passed, hand-held scythes and sickles were still used to reap wheat, oats and barley.

The United States government paid to ship American exhibits to England but failed to add money to transport the exhibits from the London docks to the exhibition site. George Peabody, an American-born banker and resident of London, advanced £20,000 to bring the exhibits to the fair.[3] Great Britain, as the host and world's leader in the Industrial Revolution, occupied half the exhibition space. France, with 1,740 exhibitors, was the largest of the foreign countries to display its industrial wares. The United States exhibitors were mostly agricultural companies selling grains, cotton, wool and tobacco. New England cotton textile and shoe companies came in force. Several exhibitors displayed artificial teeth. Samuel Colt featured his repeating pistol. A major American attraction of the Great Exhibition was Hiram Power's sensuous statue of a Greek slave.[4]

Cyrus Hall McCormick's main rival in the manufacture of horse-powered reapers was Obed Hussey, whose Baltimore Reaper was featured at Crystal Palace alongside McCormick's Virginia Reaper. The ungainly American reapers attracted larger crowds than even the 186-carat Koh-I–Noor diamond, displayed in the jewelry section of the fair.

A lithograph by Nathaniel Currier of Nassau Street, New York, ca. 1851, shows the Great Exhibition of 1851, American Department. The dapper Yankee Doodle shows John Bull the ships that carried the American products to display at London's Crystal Palace exhibition. At right, a group of English gentlemen examine the American harvesting machine. "Their agricultural implements have taken the prizes," exclaims one. The other responds: "We must be behind the age" (Library of Congress).

On June 24, the Hussey and McCormick machines competed at Tiptree Heath, cutting wheat at the rate of twenty acres a day. The exhibition judges were so impressed by the McCormick Reaper that they awarded it the Grand Council Medal as "the most valuable article contributed within the exhibition, and for its originality and value and its perfect work in the field." The *Times* of London echoed the praise of the judges in describing McCormick's "reaping machine from the United States as the most valuable contribution from abroad that we have yet discovered." Not to be outdone, Hussey himself demonstrated the skills of his reaper in the fields of the Duke of Marlborough at Blenheim, near Woodstock, Oxfordshire.[5] McCormick took his machine on a tour of the provinces, including a visit to the Royal Agricultural College at Cirencester. Another side-by-side challenge of the Hussey and McCormick machines was held September 27 in the wheat and barley fields of Robert Fawcett of Ormesby, near Middleborough-on-Tees. The *Gateshead Observer* reported that it was "curious to see two implements of agriculture lying side by side in rivalry, respectively marked, 'Mr. McCormick, inventor, Chicago, Illinois,' and 'Hussey, inventor, Baltimore, Maryland.' America competing with America, on English soil." Observed by the marquis of Londonderry and a large crowd, both machines "did very good work" but Hussey's had the edge. "The laurels so recently placed upon the brow of Mr. McCormick," reported *The American Farmer*, "have been plucked off—not wholly, but in great part, by his fellow countryman, Mr. Hussey." The English were "determined not to be humbugged" by the reaper machine, which was "the very exemplar of American absurdity." On viewing its performance John Bull's ridicule changed to "the highest applause" with the reaper hailed as a great advance in farming.[6]

By the close of the Crystal Palace exhibition on October 1, 1851, both Hussey and McCormick had gained the publicity they coveted. McCormick contracted with a British company to build his reaper suited to the local market. Despite its success at Crystal Palace the McCormick Reaper failed to find a ready market in Britain mainly because farm wages were so low relative to the cost of buying a machine. At the 1855 International Exposition in Paris, the McCormick Reaper was awarded the Grand Gold Medal of Honor. Horace Greeley informed his readers of the *New York Tribune* that the reaper brought more benefit to the United States "than if fifty thousand of her troops had defeated one hundred thousand choice European soldiers."

For years Obed Hussey and the McCormick family, working independently and without knowledge of the other, invested their energies to create a mechanical reaper. Hussey and McCormick were ready at virtually the same time. Cyrus McCormick was the first to demonstrate his machine but Hussey was the first to receive a patent. The pride of discovery and the quest for sales and profits would dominate their lives for years to come.

Thomas McCormick was Scotch-Irish from Londonderry in Ulster. With his wife Elizabeth Carruth, he settled in rural Pennsylvania in 1730. His fifth son Robert was born in 1738 and married Martha Sanderson. In 1779, Robert and his family left Pennsylvania to settle on a 400-acre farm in the Shenandoah Valley, Virginia. His older children were born in Pennsylvania. His youngest son, Robert, Jr., was born June 8, 1780, in Virginia. Robert, Sr., joined the American cause to fight on March 15, 1781, at the Battle of Guilford Courthouse. Robert and Martha prospered. By 1800, they owned three slaves and eight horses. In 1808, Robert McCormick, Jr., married Mary Ann "Polly" Hall, also of Scotch-Irish descent. Polly brought to the marriage a dowry of horses and cattle worth one thousand dollars. They settled in Rockbridge County to become prosperous, owning 1,800 acres of land worked by nine slaves, two grist mills, two saw mills, a smelting furnace, a carpenter's shop and a small workshop where he spent many a rainy day tinkering on an idea to build a grain reaper, pushed ahead by two horses. Robert owned a distillery,

Robert McCormick was born in 1780 on the family estate of Walnut Grove, situated in Rockbridge County, Virginia, in the Shenandoah Valley. Of Scotch-Irish descent, he was the patriarch of the McCormick family. Robert spent many years trying to build a mechanical reaper. In 1830 he gave the project to his eldest son, Cyrus Hall McCormick (WHS Image ID 8395).

sold spirits at a profit but did not drink alcohol himself. Robert, Jr., and Polly raised eight children—the fourth generation of McCormick family in America—including their eldest, Cyrus Hall McCormick, born February 15, 1809, William Sanderson, born 1815 and Leander James, born 1819. "It was Polly who inspired her children to make a place for themselves in the world." The McCormick family lived in the large two-story Walnut Grove red brick house overlooking the Virginia hills.[7] The children were raised with love combined with a respect for hard work and a strong dose of Calvinist morality. Cyrus attended the Old Field School, but "his best education was gained in his father's workshops and in the harvest field."[8] Both his parents were five feet eight inches in height. The burly Cyrus grew to six feet.

Robert McCormick was an accomplished tinkerer. According to his son Leander, he was a "man of great energy … a remarkable mechanical genius and seldom failed to accomplish what he had undertaken." Robert had success inventing a threshing machine and a plow. Starting early in the nineteenth century, Robert McCormick set his sights on building a harvesting machine. He spent "many years trying in vain to build a reaper." He was not alone in his failure. William Pitt and Joseph Boyce in England, Richard French in New Jersey, Patrick Bell in Scotland and many others had tried but failed to build a serviceable reaper. In 1828, Robert handed the project over to his nineteen-year-old son Cyrus.

Mary Ann (Polly) Hall married Robert McCormick in 1808 and gave birth to four daughters and four sons, including Cyrus, William and Leander. Original photograph taken 1850 (WHS Image ID 8782).

Working in the blacksmith's shop at the Walnut Grove farm, Cyrus set about the project with "a dogged tenacity that defied defeat." Profiting from his father's efforts, Cyrus redesigned the reaper to be pulled by horses, rather than pushed. By 1831, Cyrus was ready to demonstrate his reaper. With Jo Anderson "the Negro slave … who helped build the reaper" on a hot day in July, the 22-year-old Cyrus demonstrated his "new-fangled wheat-cutting machine" before a skeptical crowd of his neighbors. "The reaper marched through the grain…. Jo Anderson walked beside it rake in hand to keep the platform clean of severed grain." And behind strove the young inventor, Cyrus Hall McCormick, tall, square-shouldered and purposeful. The McCormick reaper cut the wheat stalks using multiple iron-tipped fingers working in a scissors-like movement. "The machine which was to give

"WALNUT GROVE." — HOMESTEAD OF THE MᶜCORMICK FAMILY, ROCKBRIDGE CO., VA.

Walnut Grove, the 532-acre McCormick farm, in Rockbridge County, Virginia, contained a manor house, housekeeper's quarters, slave quarters, carriage house, a gristmill and a blacksmith shop. Robert, and later his son Cyrus, designed and built the mechanical reaper in the blacksmith shop. Engraving from *Atlas of Augusta County, Virginia*, 1885 (WHS Image ID 63082).

the prairies the vigor of use was born."[9] An article in the *Lexington Union* of September 14, 1833, was the first published account of the McCormick reaper.

Mankind had long sought a machine to replace the scythe and the sickle and to free people from the bondage of harvesting. In 1825, the Reverend Patrick Bell of Angus, Scotland came close with a horse-pushed device that could harvest an acre of grain in one hour. Bell did not apply for a patent nor did he attempt to make money from his invention. Instead, the advances in reaping came from the United States.

Obed Hussey was born 1792 in Hallowell, Maine to a Quaker family. (Less than fifty miles separate Hallowell from South Paris, Maine, the birthplace of William Deering.) He was "sensitive, modest and unassuming." When still a boy he made his way to the island of Nantucket where his relatives George and Benjamin sailed the whaling ships *Harlequin* and *Mary Ann*. Obed went on a number of whaling expeditions before leaving Nantucket to settle in Baltimore. A tinkerer from his youth, a friend "asked him why he did not make a reaper." "What" exclaimed Hussey "isn't there such a thing?" and immediately turned his mind to build one. In Baltimore he befriended the blacksmith-turned-plow-maker Richard B. Chenoweth who received a patent for his wrought-iron plow with a steel edge, suitable for deep plowing, in 1808. Chenoweth provided the unassuming but determined Hussey with a room for himself and space to work on his reaper. Hussey worked on his own for a

THE TESTING OF THE FIRST REAPING MACHINE NEAR STEELE'S TAVERN, VA. A.D. 1831.

The first public demonstration of the McCormick harvester: In building his mechanical harvester, Cyrus Hall McCormick was assisted by Jo Anderson, his slave. In July 1831, McCormick and Anderson successfully demonstrated the harvester near Steele's Tavern. This 1883 lithograph produced for the McCormick Harvesting Machine Company displays racial stereotypes (WHS Image ID 2497).

decade before he was ready in the winter of 1832–33 to take his machine out into the yard to test it. "The trial was made on a board, drilled with holes, and stuck full of rye straws.... Mr. Hussey, with repressed excitement stood watching, and when he saw the perfect success of his invention, he hastened to his room, too moved and agitated to speak. [He] did not want us to see the tears in his eyes."[10]

Finally satisfied that it would work, Hussey dismantled his reaper and took it to Cincinnati, where he received financial support from Jervis Reynolds to test it in the harvest of 1833. Two horses in line pulled the Hussey machine. The cutting mechanism consisted of triangular steel blades that threw the cut grain onto a platform, from which the man with a rake pushed the grain to the ground. Another man walking behind gathered the grain into bundles. On July 1, a magazine informed its readers, "a large crowd of spectators composed of farmers" of Hamilton County, Ohio, gathered to watch the horse-drawn reaper, traveling at 4–5 miles an hour, efficiently "cutting a swathe five feet three inches" in width. Members of the agricultural society judged Hussey's machine as "a valuable improvement to all large farmers." On December 31, 1833, Obed Hussey received a patent for his harvester. The April 1834 issue of *Mechanics Magazine* carried an illustration of Hussey's Grain Cutter.[11] Obed Hussey and Cyrus McCormick, working entirely independently and unaware of each other, after years of experimentation, had invented the functional mechanical reaper at the same time.

Obed Hussey's grain cutter: Born in 1792, Hussey built a two-man harvesting machine. One man operated the machine and the second guided the two horses pulling the harvester. Hussey patented his machine in 1833, leading to a bitter legal battle against Cyrus McCormick (*Mechanics Magazine and Register of Inventions and Improvements*, vol. 3, no. 4 [April 1834]).

Cyrus Hall McCormick read the article with great interest and concern. "Here was a rival, and without doubt, Mr. McCormick desired to establish the fact of his own priority, and protect his interests…. Cyrus published a warning not to infringe on an already occupied field…. So he applied for and was granted a patent."[12] Writing from Rockbridge on May 20, 1834, Cyrus Hall McCormick sent a stern letter to inform his rival Obed Hussey that the cutting mechanism "is a part of the principle of my machine, and was invented by me, and operated on wheat and oats in July, 1831 [and was] witnessed by many persons…. I would warn all persons against the use of the aforesaid principle, as I regard and treat the use of it, in any way, as an infringement of my right." This was, wrote Professor William T. Hutchinson, "the first shot in the war of the reapers in America."[13] In 1834, Cyrus McCormick and Obed Hussey were the only competitors in the American reaper stakes. Cyrus, younger by seventeen years, was determined to beat down Obed before other reaper inventors tried to compete. McCormick submitted a description of his reaper together with

37

Patrick Bell's machine: While studying divinity at St. Andrews University, Scotland, Patrick Bell (1799–1859) built a mechanical harvesting machine pushed by two horses. Choosing to become a minister of the Church of Scotland, he did not patent or seek to make money from his invention. Drawing by George Heriot Swanson, 1851.

the fee of $30 to the United States Patent Office on June 21, 1834. He claimed he had "invented a new and useful improvement in reaping all kinds of small grains."[14] Based on his improvement of the reaper, McCormick was awarded a patent, allowing him for fourteen years, "the full and exclusive right and liberty of making, constructing, using, and vending to others to be used, the said improvement." Fully aware of Hussey's earlier patent, McCormick, in his 1844 application, did not claim to have invented the reaper, but that he had made "a new and useful improvement." For the rest of his life he claimed to be the inventor and that other manufacturers had copied his design.

The years from 1833 to 1840 were difficult for both men. For McCormick, his "whole soul was wrapped up in his reaper." But he needed money to buy iron, set up a foundry, build his machine and find buyers among in the skeptical and tradition-bound farming community. The first Virginia Reaper advertisement appeared in 1833 in the *Lexington Union*. The early horse-pulled machines were not much more effective in cutting grain than sturdy men wielding scythes. The Panic of 1837 forced McCormick to sell his farm, leaving him in debt. Yet he persisted. With McCormick's first commercial reaper, the operator walked by the side and raked the cut grain off the platform to the ground. McCormick was constantly at work improving his reaper, which he manufactured in the blacksmith shop at the Walnut Grove farm. Cyrus traveled far and wide in search of sales for his $100 reaper. By 1840, McCormick had not sold a single machine. Thereafter, technical improvements steadily advanced the McCormick reaper over work done by hand. In 1844, he sold fifty reapers. In Brockport on the Erie Canal in New York State, McCormick contracted with William Seymour and Dayton Morgan, who operated a small foundry, to manufacture the Virginia Reaper. His first salesman was a cousin J. B. McCormick, who traveled in Ohio, Tennessee and Missouri seeking sales. Cyrus sent his 28-year-old brother Leander to Cincinnati to start a manufactory. In 1845, McCormick sold one hundred and twenty-three machines. In 1845 and 1847, McCormick received patents for improved versions of his reaper, now a "two-horse machine with a wider cut and a seat on the side, whereon the raker sat as he worked." With the improvements after 1845, the McCormick mechanical reaper was clearly superior to hand reaping. His best customers came from the Great Plains, where land was cheap and plentiful but labor scarce, giving McCormick the idea of moving production to the town of Chicago, on Lake Michigan and close to abundant flat and rich farmland. Late in 1844, Cyrus McCormick made his way from Ohio to Michigan and on to Chicago.

"I was astounded when I saw the broad expanse of fertile land here in the west," wrote Cyrus to his family in Virginia. "Prairies as far as the eye can see. There aren't many people out here, but when the west is developed it's going to be the greatest farm country in the world."[15] The death of his father on July 4, 1846, weakened Cyrus's ties to Virginia, and he saw his future and the future of his business in the West. Five hundred McCormick reapers were ordered for the booming harvest of 1847 and Cyrus was able to pay off his debts that had accumulated during the lean years. With their agreement broken, Seymour and Morgan retaliated by building copies of McCormick's machine and selling them under their own label.

Chicago

Jean Baptiste Point du Sable settled on the northern shore of the Chicago River in the spring of 1779. After the Louisiana Purchase, a garrison of sixty Americans built Fort Dearborn on the site of Baptiste's home. The fort was attacked during the War of 1812, and most of the residents fled or were killed. Illinois was admitted to the Union in 1818. By 1829, Chicago had only twenty settlers. The Erie Canal gave access to the Great Lakes, attracting many New Englanders to move into the western wilderness. By 1839, Chicago had 4,600 residents, expanding to 20,000 in 1848 when Cyrus McCormick arrived. Immigrants, especially from Ireland and Germany, came for land and opportunity. In 1848, Chicago was linked by rail to Galena and in quick order railroads connected Chicago to other Midwest cities and beyond. The 96-mile Illinois & Michigan Canal opened in 1848 and linked the Great Lakes to the Mississippi River and the Gulf of Mexico. Chicago received its first telegram in January 1848. Chicago became the great center for grains, cattle, hogs and timber. Steamships, plying the Great Lakes, competed with the railroads to carry these products to markets in New York, Boston, Baltimore and Philadelphia, and across the Atlantic Ocean to Europe. In 1848 two million bushels of wheat were exported from Chicago. Ten years later, ten million bushels were exported out of the booming city.

By 1850, Chicago's population barely reached 30,000. Fifty years later it approached 2,000,000. Chicago's growth seemed unstoppable. The Columbian Exposition would display Chicago to the world. Young Theodore Dreiser arrived in Chicago in 1892 to take a job at the *Chicago Globe.* He was mesmerized by the city "so young, so blithe, so new.... Here was a city that had no traditions but was making them. Chicago was like no other city in the world.... Chicago would outstrip every other American city, New York included, and become the first of all American, if not European or world, cities.... Chicago would be first in wealth, first in beauty, first in achievement."[16]

Charles Gray was the most successful of the early Chicago manufacturers, making grain cradles and scythes. In 1847, the company of McCormick & Gray was set up to build the Virginia Reaper for farmers in Illinois. McCormick & Gray built five hundred machines ready for the 1848 harvest. The machine "gave a good degree of satisfaction and was in considerable demand." Quarrels followed and Gray sold his share of the partnership to William B. Ogden, who put up $50,000. In October 1848, the Virginia farmer and the New Yorker, who served as the first mayor of Chicago (1837–38) and its principal powerbroker, formalized their partnership as McCormick, Ogden & Company. In its first year, 800 reapers were built, and in 1849 over 1500 machines were built. McCormick's forceful ego was too much for Ogden, who sold out after the first year for $65,000. Now in his fortieth year, Cyrus Hall McCormick began the construction of his own reaper factory.

Other prominent Southerners who settled in Chicago were Archibald Clybourn, who arrived in 1823, Richard Jones Hamilton in 1831, Levi D. Boone in 1836 and John B. Rice who arrived in 1847. Clybourn, who was among the first twenty white settlers of Chicago, opened a slaughterhouse and built the first brick residence in the town. Boone served as 17th mayor of Chicago. Rice was an actor who built one of the first theaters in Chicago. During the fall of 1848, Leander James McCormick closed the reaper plant in Cincinnati and moved with his wife and infant son to join Cyrus in Chicago. In 1850, William Sanderson McCormick left Virginia with his wife and infant son to join his brothers in Chicago. Cyrus was determined to keep full control of his factory. His brothers Leander and William came to Chicago as employees, earning wages. Their father Robert McCormick, Jr., died in 1846 and mother Mary Ann died in 1853, making Cyrus, still a bachelor, the titular head of the McCormick family now centered in the city of Chicago.

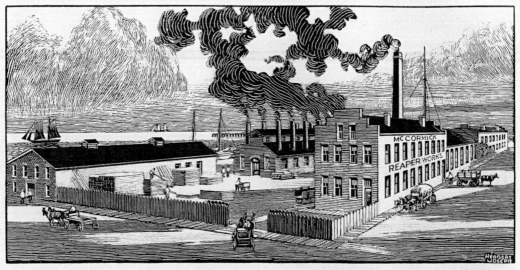

McCormick Works, Chicago, 1847
Looking South towards the Chicago River

The first factory in Chicago: Soon after Cyrus Hall McCormick came to Chicago in 1847, he bought land on the north side of the Chicago River. That fall he commenced the building of a three-story factory. Thirty-three men operated grindstones, forges and saws to build harvesting machines. The factory grew to become one of Chicago's leading industrial enterprises (WHS Image ID 8798).

McCormick's prescient decision to build his factory in Chicago paid off. With the vast Great Plains opening up to farming and workers made scarce by the great flow of men to the California gold rush, the demand for the labor-saving Virginia Reaper increased dramatically. In 1849, Cyrus Hall McCormick built his factory on the lakeshore, north of the Chicago River, at the foot of Rush Street. In the three-story brick building worked 120 men who operated the forges, saws and planes, and the lathes for turning grinding machines, driven by a thirty horse-powered steam engine, and operated the foundry to fashion the Virginia Reaper. Wood, iron ore and coal were delivered to the factory, and completed reapers left the dock to be delivered by rail or by water to customers. By 1849, one hundred and twenty-three workers were at work turning out 1,500 reapers a year. The *Chicago Daily Democrat* hailed it as "the largest factory of its kind in the world."[17] An important part of the enterprise was the sales agents who also trained farmers how to use and maintain the harvesting machinery.

In 1847, the workday for his 123 employees at the McCormick factory began at seven in the morning for ten hours a day, six days a week, with Sundays and occasional holidays off. Blacksmith wages were $1.25, bricklayers $2.50 a day. "A good man," wrote William McCormick in 1856, "could work his way up to fifty dollars a month," working ten hours a day for twenty-six days in the month. Workers bought their own food and found their lodging at $3 a week. By 1856, McCormick was building forty harvesting machines a day, about fourteen thousand a year. In addition to his reaper, he built grass mowers. It was becoming ever harder for Eastern farmers to compete with the wheat and grain farmers of the Great Plains, the breadbasket of the nation. McCormick reapers sold well in the West and his grass mowers sold best in the East.

In 1849, a McCormick reaper sold for $115, increasing by 1856 to $130 with $5 freight charges. McCormick's success came from selling good machines at a fair price, from his closeness to raw materials, closeness the Great Plains, the efficiency of his factory, and to his willingness to extend credit. McCormick's timing was superb. The Scottish agricultural expert and member of Parliament Sir James Caird, touring America in the 1850s, described the Great Plains as "probably the greatest tract of arable land in the entire surface of the globe. In total extent it exceeds England and France together." In 1857, "upwards of 18,000,000 bushels of grain were exported from Chicago." This was only the start, opined James Caird, and a "tenfold increase in production" was soon likely.[18]

A farmer could buy a McCormick reaper for $35 down, with the rest paid after bringing in the harvest. By offering credit, "his friend predicted his certain downfall," but it proved a sound policy winning him many customers.[19] McCormick widely advertised his machine, telling customers to avoid imitations, and buy only the genuine Virginia Reaper. He warranted that the reaper would cut twenty acres in a day; ten times as much as a skilled farmer wielding a scythe. The competitive McCormick advertised the prizes he won, and denigrated the judges of the competitions he lost.

Extension of Patents

Obed Hussey also had difficulties launching his business, and was forced to sell his reaper almost at cost. For several years after he received his patent he was unable to socialize "for want of a decent coat." To save money he prepared his own meals, slept in his shop and survived by borrowing money from a Quaker friend. McCormick and Hussey took their cumbersome machines to agricultural fairs hoping for sales. After 1845, sales and profits increased and the rivalry between McCormick and Hussey heated up. Each man claimed to have invented the mechanical reaper and each claimed his machine the superior. In December 1847, Hussey applied to the United States Patent Office for the renewal of his 1833 reaper patents. The reply came from commissioner Henry Leavitt Ellsworth telling Hussey that his application was denied because it had not been submitted in accordance with patent office rules.[20] It took Hussey a full year to rustle up support from customers and in Congress to get his patent extension approved. On December 10, 1847, Cyrus McCormick submitted his application for a patent extension. Obed Hussey opposed the renewal of McCormick's patent, claiming the McCormick "has not proved a useful invention to the public" while Hussey's was "the best reaping machine which was ever offered to the world." In 1848, the Patent Office hired Charles G. Page to review the original patents of Obed Hussey and Cyrus McCormick. Page concluded, "The knife, fingers: and general arrangement of the cutting apparatus are found in the reaping machine of O. Hussey patented 31 December 1833." McCormick's application for patent renewal was heard March 29, 1848, but was turned down because the operating mechanism of his reaper was similar to Obed Hussey's, who got to the Patent Office first. McCormick's application to extend his patent was officially rejected by the newly appointed commissioner of patents Edmund Burke, backed by James Buchanan, then secretary of state, and, from 1857 to 1861, president of the United States. McCormick sued the United States of America. In 1855, in *McCormick vs. United States*, chief justice Gilchrist threw out the claim as "not founded upon any law of Congress [and] there is in no sense any claim upon the United States."[21] Cyrus McCormick refused to allow his disappointment over the ruling of the patent office to impede his business. "McCormick considered the reaper to be his proprietary invention so he sued newcomers in the industry almost as a matter of routine."[22] To his brother William on April 4, the confident and tenacious Cyrus wrote: "I am now petitioning Congress for the extension.... If I fail to get an extension, I calculate I can hold my own without, but I think I shall succeed."[23]

Both Hussey and McCormick took their case to Congress to begin a ten-year battle for public approval. Cyrus continued to insist that all credit for inventing the mechanical reaper was his, and his alone. The McCormick-Hussey case filed November 10, 1855, was one of the first heard by the newly formed Court of Claims. In his deposition, Cyrus claimed that his father "constructed a machine for cutting grain upon a principle entirely different from mine." His father came to the conclusion that his design "would not answer a valuable purpose.... Very soon after my father had abandoned his machine I first conceived the idea of cutting upon the principle of mine, viz., with a vibrating blade operated by a crank."[24]

Cyrus tried his machine on a neighbor's field. It was a "very successful experiment." From 1848 onward the McCormick business grew by leaps and bounds to become the largest reaper manufacturer in the nation. McCormick expanded west of the Allegheny Mountains, while Hussey focused on the eastern states. Even with his patent extension, Hussey's enterprise floundered, producing less than 500 reapers a year, as new reaper companies opened, especially John H. Manny of Waddam's Grove, Illinois, and Seymour & Morgan of New York. Born in Amsterdam, New York, Manny moved to Illinois in the early

1850s to become a farmer. He learned how to build a reaper, and in 1855 opened a factory in Rockport. From 1854 to 1858, Manny built six thousand reapers and became McCormick's major competitor, and in Illinois to boot. In 1863, the Manny reaper won first prize at the DeKalb County Reaper Competition. At the state fair held in Decatur, Illinois, in 1864, there were "so many excellent machines that it was impossible to say which is best for all purposes."[25]

Cyrus McCormick responded by offering customers better terms and by fighting his competitors in the courts over patent infringements. In 1850, McCormick sued Seymour & Morgan for copying his machine, marketed as the New York Reaper. The battle with Seymour & Morgan continued for four years. McCormick won and was awarded $9,354 in damages and put Seymour and Morgan out of business. In December 1854, McCormick sued John H. Manny for infringement of his patents for the divider, reel supporter and rake supporter of the reaper. McCormick asked for $400,000 in damages—a staggering sum at that time. Manny claimed that his reaper "differed in form and principle from the improvements patented by McCormick, and that the raker's stand or position was an improvement invented and patented by John H. Manny."[26] To plead his case, McCormick hired

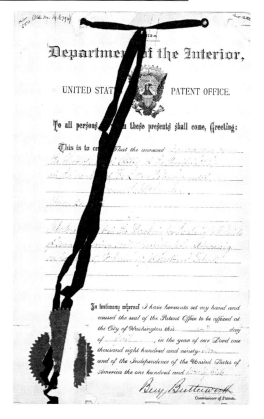

Cyrus Hall McCormick's 1834 patent, from the United States Patent Office. McCormick's patent came a year after Obed Hussey received one for his grain-cutting machine (WHS ID 64380).

Edward N. Dickerson and Reverdy Johnson, leading patent attorneys. Helped financially by other reaper companies, John Manny hired the top-notch legal talent of John Harding and Edwin McMasters Stanton. With the case expected for Springfield, Illinois, Harding and Stanton hired a popular local lawyer, Abraham Lincoln, who was a friend of Judge Drummond. This was the largest case of his career, and Lincoln "prepared himself with the greatest care," learning about reapers and patents. Instead of Springfield, the case of McCormick v. Manny was transferred to Cincinnati, Ohio, with circuit judge John McLean presiding. Looked down on by Stanton as a hick country lawyer, Lincoln was shut out of the proceedings, which began September 20, 1855. Stanton asked Harding: "Where did that long-armed creature come from; and what can he expect to do in this case?" The haughty Stanton went on to lampoon the long-limbed Lincoln as "that giraffe," "the original gorilla" and even as "a low, cunning clown." Lincoln was left to wander about Cincinnati alone before he returned home "greatly depressed … pushed aside, humiliated and mortified."[27] Lincoln was paid $1,000 for his effort, while Stanton received $10,000.

In 1858 Abraham Lincoln said, "A house divided against itself cannot stand. I believe this government cannot endure permanently half-slave half-free." That year saw his masterful debates against Stephen A. Douglas. On December 6, 1860, Lincoln was sworn in as the 16th President of the United States. Six years after *McCormick v. Manny,* President Abraham Lincoln appointed Edwin M. Stanton his secretary of war.

Cyrus Hall McCormick was confident of victory in his case against John Manny, but on January 10, 1856, the trial ended in favor of Manny. Justice McLean found "there was no infringement" by Manny of McCormick's patent and ordered McCormick to pay the costs of the trial. John Manny had only a short time to enjoy the verdict of the court.[28] Three weeks later, Manny died at age thirty of tuberculosis. McCormick took the case the United States Supreme Court, but on May 1, 1858, the Court decided "in favor of Manny on every point. Manny's partners kept their business going into the 20th century."

In 1857, Cyrus McCormick with William Ogden and George Armour opened the Merchants' Savings, Loan and Trust Company. Cyrus expanded his interests into Chicago real estate. He was well on his way to build a fortune.[29] In 1858, Hussey sued McCormick for infringement of his 1833 patent. On September 19, 1859, Hussey won his case. He was declared the first inventor of the mechanical reaper and was awarded damages of $80,000. On August 4, 1860, the victorious Obed Hussey was on his way by train from Boston

In 1855, Edwin McMasters Stanton represented John Henry Manny in his legal battle against Cyrus Hall McCormick. At the time, Stanton was disdainful of Abraham Lincoln, a junior lawyer in the patent dispute. During the Civil War, Stanton served as secretary of war under President Abraham Lincoln (Library of Congress).

to Portland, Maine. The train stopped at a station. A little girl, unknown to him, asked for a drink of water. Hussey got off the train to fetch the water for the girl. On his return the train began to move. Trying to board the moving train, the sixty-eight-year-old Hussey slipped and fell under the wheels and died. His tombstone reads: The Inventor of the Mower.

Twenty years passed between the time Obed Hussey and Cyrus McCormick first demonstrated their mechanical reapers and the time farmers began to buy the machines in large numbers. By the 1850s two or more contiguous farmers would purchase a machine to cut their fields. Even farmers owning a small acreage for grains now gained the economic advantage of a mechanical harvester. Litigious Cyrus McCormick had lost his court battles against his rivals John Manny and Obed Hussey. By 1860, his leading opponents were dead. McCormick put so much pressure on the commissioner of patents, and "Congress stepped in … and wrested the case from his hands." No longer willing to accept McCormick's claims that competitors were stealing his patented inventions, Congress refused to allow McCormick to renew his patents as a means of curbing competition.[30] In 1861, the commissioner of patents D.P. Holloway complimented McCormick whose "genius has done honor to his own country and has been the admiration of foreign nations … but the reaper is of too great value to the public to be controlled by any individual, and the extension of his patent is refused."[31]

The inventor and his reaper were one and the same. From 1831, when he was aged twenty-two years until his death fifty-four years later, Cyrus Hall McCormick claimed that he alone was the inventor of the mechanical reaper, the machine that transformed agriculture. For many years, and at great expense, he litigated against Obed Hussey, John Manny and other reaper builders, accusing them of copying his patented invention. Cyrus said, "Life is a battle." His ruthless championing of his reaper made enemies. His business competitors hated him.

Money and power were not enough; Cyrus McCormick wished to be known as the great inventor of the reaper. Starting at the Crystal Palace Exhibition in 1851, the Universal Exposition in Paris in 1855, and many other exhibitions, the McCormick reaper gathered prizes acknowledging Cyrus H. McCormick as the inventor of the mechanical reaper. Once again the machine was awarded a prize and Cyrus was hailed as the man "who invented and built the first reaper." Accolades came from America as well. In 1856, the National Agricultural Society "decided in an unequivocal manner to show its high appreciation of McCormick's reaping machine."[32] Between 1834

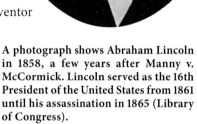

A photograph shows Abraham Lincoln in 1858, a few years after Manny v. McCormick. Lincoln served as the 16th President of the United States from 1861 until his assassination in 1865 (Library of Congress).

and 1854, the U.S. Patent Office granted 138 patents for reaper machinery. It was getting harder and harder for McCormick to claim sole ownership of the machine. McCormick regarded "his competitors as a pack of trespassers." In return, his litigiousness "brought down upon him to a remarkable degree the hostility from his competitors."[33] His real success came not from his inventions but from "his ability to make and sell machines." In 1867 in Paris, McCormick not only received a grand prize, but the emperor nominated him Chevalier of the Imperial Order of the League of Honor. McCormick reapers that cost $37 to make were sold for $120, giving huge profits to Cyrus Hall McCormick.[34] Had he been alive in 1893, he would have been immensely proud to see the McCormick Harvester exhibit at the World's Columbian Exposition in his own city of Chicago.

Cyrus H. McCormick continued to go after his rivals until the close of his life. In 1882, McCormick sued the Minnesota Harvester Works, William Whitley's Champion Machine Company of Ohio, the St. Paul Harvester Company "and others" for infringement of the patents for the knot-tying mechanism for grain binders. From Whitley alone he received compensation of $100,000. In the "Wars of the Reapers," often it was the McCormick who was sued. In 1882, David M. Osborne of Rochester sued McCormick, alleging he did not pay $10 per machine in royalties for using a self-binding device. After McCormick died in 1884, Osborne sued the McCormick estate, demanding $300,000.

Which McCormick Invented the Reaper?

So determined was the authoritarian McCormick to seal his place in history that even his family was fearful of disputing his claim as the inventor of the reaper. For years, his brother Leander nursed his grievances. As far back as 1845 Leander "had offered suggestions for improvements to the Virginia Reaper and he was now convinced that Cyrus had patented these ideas as his own in 1847 and thereby gained large and unmerited profits." In 1866, Cyrus demanded of Leander that he "assign certain mower patents to the firm." After this, hidden resentments began to surface. Cyrus hoped that Leander "may be able to take a more proper view of my cause, and thus make the situation admit of a restoration of good feelings."[35] In 1878, Cyrus and Leander had a bitter argument over the 1831 invention of the harvester. Cyrus insisted that their father's efforts were "an entire failure and was thus wholly abandoned." Cyrus resented any suggestion that his father or his brother deserved credit for the invention. Laying down the gauntlet, Cyrus warned his brother in June 17, 1878, that he would not permit any questioning of "the original principles of operation found in my invention made during the harvest of 1831 and patented in 1834.... What part or parts of my father's machine, referred to by you, resembled any such corresponding part of my invention?" If Leander continued to deny Cyrus his due, Cyrus would defend his just rights, "to publish a full description of my father's machine, that I may not be subject to any slander from misrepresentation of such sacred rights, whether so meant and designed or not."[36] For the next decade there were frequent disputes between the brothers that spread to the rest of the extended McCormick family. Leander "accumulated evidence to prove the truth of his charge" by getting testimonials from Virginia neighbors, and members of the family, including his sister and his wife.[37] Leander was "deeply wounded by Cyrus's pretensions as the inventor." He devoted his later years to secure statements and affidavits to prove that his father was the rightful inventor of the harvesting machine. After the death of Cyrus H. McCormick on May 13, 1884, some members of the family, lead by Leander, began openly to cast doubt on Cyrus's claim of sole originality. Within a year of the death of Cyrus Hall McCormick, his brother Leander published a very different account of the invention and manufacture of the mechanical reaper. Leander had formed "a bitter and relentless animosity" towards Cyrus. His 1885 *Memorial of Robert McCormick* "shows plainly an effort to establish the fact that to Robert McCormick and Leander McCormick of Virginia, belong the credit of inventing the mechanical reaper." The reaper designed by Robert McCormick in 1816 was "very much like" the reaper Cyrus patented. Robert McCormick "continued to be actively engaged in the manufacture and improvement of his reaping machine until his death in 1846." Cyrus's cousin William S. McCormick stated categorically: "Robert McCormick gave the rights to the patent to his son Cyrus, but Robert was the sole inventor of the reaping machine." Leander McCormick claimed that he had a part in designing the reaper, but Cyrus took all the credit and most of the profit. Cyrus failed to keep his promise to his mother to share the benefits with his family. "We do assert," wrote family members, "that C. H. McCormick did not invent said machine [and] was not entitled to any of the honors showered upon him as its inventor."[38] In 1896, Leander McCormick, at age seventy-seven years, published a genealogy of the McCormick family. The book was dedicated to "his beloved father, Robert McCormick, inventor of the reaper." Robert's reaper contained the components (cutting knife, platform, drawing wheel, and the main frame) that Cyrus later claimed that he alone had invented. Robert "neglected the important step of taking out lettered patents." Leander claimed to have "inherited the inventive genius of his father," helped his father to develop the reaper, and "made many improvements of vital importance, without which it could not have been a completed machine, nor have become of world-wide fame." Leander wrote hardly a word about Cyrus's role in inventing and building the McCormick reaper. Leander's book "is in reality an attack on the fame and fortune of Cyrus. It undertakes to show that there was nothing very new after all in the machine patented by Cyrus, that most of the parts were known before, and that Cyrus merely brought together the successful features from the inventions of others."[39]

Robert McCormick began working on the reaper as early as 1809 and systematically continued to modify it until 1830 when the reaper "became a practical success. [This machine] comprised the essential features of all successful grain-cutting machinery to the present day." In 1836, Robert McCormick and his oldest son Cyrus assisted by a Mr. Black started an iron-smelting business called R. & C. H. McCormick. It proved to be "the one great mistake of his life." Mr. Black was a "rascally partner" and the business failed, leaving Robert near bankruptcy. To pay off his debts, Robert sold off much of his farmland and devoted his time to manufacturing reapers. His son William managed the farm, while son Leander assisted Robert in building reapers for sale. Leander took credit for adding the raker's seat to the design of the "greatest labor-saving farm implement that the world had produced." In 1844, Robert and Leander built twenty-five. In 1845, they built fifty, and in 1846, father and son, with the help of slave labor, built seventy-five reapers. Cyrus Hall McCormick was given the task of going on the road to sell the reapers. Cyrus was away for months at a time and was not on hand to deal with problems in production or implement improvements. This arrangement ended in 1846 with the death of Robert McCormick. In the *Memorial* to Robert McCormick, Leander takes away all credit from Cyrus as the inventor of the reaper and reduces him to a salesman.[40]

In 1896, Leander McCormick again took credit for the invention away from his brother Cyrus. Leander's *Family Records and Biography* was dedicated "in memory of his beloved father, Robert McCormick, Inventor of the Reaper." Leander believed that the invention of the reaper was a family affair, and certainly not the work of Cyrus Hall McCormick alone. Leander's life work was "identified with the McCormick Reaper. He inherited the inventive genius of his father, Robert McCormick, and during his lifetime, was associated with him in its development in Virginia." In Chicago, the McCormick brothers, Cyrus, William and Leander "established themselves in a partnership [with Leander] in charge of management and the introduction of the reaper into the broad fields of the West." As the partner in charge of production of the reaper for thirty years, Leander "made many improvements, without which it could not have been a completed machine, nor have become of world-wide fame." Leander credits himself for rebuilding the factory after the Fire of 1871 with "thousands of men thrown out of employment." The factory was "immediately rebuilt, according to our selection of the site and architectural design."

Leander was angry, envious and jealous of the credit of invention and the acceptance of all praise on the part of his older brother. Conceiving of the McCormick reaper as a family affair, Leander was angry to be treated by Cyrus as a salaried employee, getting little recognition as an inventor in his own right. Cyrus fought off competitors with his lawsuits. He traveled the world collecting accolades as the Inventor of the Reaper while his brothers remained in Chicago running the factory and producing the machines. In the 1870s, discord between Cyrus and Leander grew more intense. In 1880, Cyrus effectively fired his younger brother and ensured that his own son, Cyrus Hall McCormick, Jr., would take over the company, while the sons of Leander and William would be pushed aside. Leander was careful not to openly disparage Cyrus's claim to be the inventor of the mechanical reaper. Rather, Leander advanced the claim of their father and Leander's own contributions. In a speech reported in the *Chicago Record-Tribune* of November 21, 1885, Leander eulogized their father as the man who "built the first reaping machine that ever was constructed."

Leander was not alone in accusing Cyrus of stealing other men's ideas in the construction of his reaper. On October 25, 1864, when Cyrus was running for Congress in the First District of Illinois, the *Chicago Tribune* lashed out at Cyrus H. McCormick as a man not to be trusted. Cyrus McCormick had "pirated the most important part of it from Obed Hussey, and picked up, here and there, the results of other men's genius and toil and claimed them as his own, thereby creating a false impression in the public mind that he was himself a great inventor." Cyrus McCormick made "enormous profits from the rich contributions of other men's minds." He used his ill-gotten wealth "as a means of breaking down the small manufacturers of reapers" and was trying to establish a monopoly to demand $500 for a machine that cost him $50 to make. McCormick wished to be in Congress not only to "gratify his vanity," but also to get an act of Congress to extend his patents. Cyrus asserted: "he did not pirate the invention of Mr. Hussey," yet he paid Hussey $1.25 per machine for the use of the Hussey cutter. "Hussey's cutter is a great and valuable invention [and] Mr. McCormick's reel is worthless without Hussey's cutter.... Mr. Hussey's patent is dated one year earlier that Mr. McCormick's earliest patent.... Mr. McCormick seeks to convey the idea that nobody could put together, in complete working harmony, a successful reaping machine, till he did. This is a broad assertion without a particle of evidence to sustain it."

The discord between Cyrus and his brothers was passed down to their children and to generations beyond. In 1910, Leander James McCormick's son, Robert Hall McCormick, together with his cousin James Hall Shields published their 82-page *Life and Works of Robert McCormick, including his Invention of the Reaper*. They assembled affidavits and letters to show that Robert McCormick, but not his son Cyrus, was the rightful inventor of the mechanical reaper. The "proof" came mainly from Mary Caroline McCormick, daughter of Robert and Mary McCormick and mother of James Hall Shields. "My father had been experimenting for several years with his machine to reap wheat," wrote Mary Caroline in 1883. "In the harvest of 1833, I saw the reaper cut wheat again in the field of Mr. John Weirs." Caroline came to realize that her father was "an inventive genius." Cyrus, the first born child of Robert and Mary McCormick was "always very much indulged by my mother... Brother Cyrus never liked to work on the farm [and had] a great desire to be rich.... Ma persuaded Father to give the invention of the reaper to brother Cyrus and it took a lot of persuasion too.... Father said: 'But I owe it equally to the other children.' Ma replied: 'Cyrus has promised me that if the reaper is made a success, all the children shall be intended in it and I know he will keep his word.'" Mary Caroline McCormick Shields testified that Robert McCormick's harvester was a success by 1831. He sent Cyrus out on the road to sell the harvester to make $15 for each sale. The family finances were damaged in 1845 with the failure of the iron furnace project. After Robert McCormick died July 4, 1846, his oldest son, Cyrus Hall McCormick, claimed the reaper as his invention.

Anita McCormick Blaine sprung to her father's defense, saying: "she would forgive no one [who] sought to show my father's life to be a lie." In 1910, Katherine Medill McCormick, daughter-in-law of William McCormick, presented an affidavit disputing Cyrus's claim. Katherine and her son Robert R. McCormick "waged an unsuccessful campaign to keep Cyrus out of the Hall of Fame."[41] This brought an angry retort from Anita, accusing Katherine of seeking "to show my father's life to be a lie." With renewed determination, Anita and her brothers set up "a Historical Association to sift the evidence and prepare a legal brief defending their father's honor."[42] Starting in 1912 in the McCormick mansion at 675 Rush Street, the McCormick Historical Association collected and catalogued the papers of Cyrus Hall McCormick and his reaper company to prove that he was the inventor of the reaper. In 1915 the collection was moved into the two-story, fireproof stone carriage house at the rear of the property.[43] Cyrus McCormick III, in his 1931 book *The Century of the Reaper*, categorically claims his grandfather as the Inventor of the Reaper. Robert McCormick "spent so many years in vain to build a reaper ... but feared that the problem would prove insoluble." His son, Cyrus, "found a better way" to build a reaper.[44]

Money as well as honor was involved in the family arguments. Cyrus McCormick "willed his entire fortune to his immediate family, leaving nothing to his widowed sisters or the orphaned children of his brother William." To establish that father Robert and brothers William and Leander had also contributed to the invention of the reaper could potentially take money out of the estate of Cyrus Hall McCormick. The animosity between the branches of the McCormick family became so strained that in 1911, Anita stated on behalf of herself, her brothers and their mother: "We could not give one cent to any relative on the strength of the proposition that Cyrus McCormick owed them anything, for it would make him out a robber and a thief."[45]

Evaluating the evidence, William T. Hutchinson believes that evidence supplied by Leander was "valueless when compared with the overwhelming volume of proof in Cyrus McCormick's favor. [The] wealth of material on agricultural history [until 1930] makes certain beyond a doubt that Cyrus McCormick invented the reaper which bears his name."

Cyrus Hall McCormick as a person

At his prime, Cyrus Hall McCormick was a dominant figure. He stood nearly six feet in height and weighed 200 lbs. He dressed in black. He was a burly and muscular man, with a full head of dark hair and a bushy beard to match. He was confident and pugnacious. He possessed boundless energy, restless and aloof, a man on the go. He flitted about the nation and abroad, selling his reaper, negotiating deals and always, always challenging anyone who dared to try to take the glory of the invention of the reaper from him. He gave orders and expected them to be followed. He hired managers, accountants and lawyers but mostly trusted his own judgment, reducing them to sycophants. He was the boss, and gave the orders. He treated his own brothers as employees, hired to carry out his orders. Determined to be recognized as the inventor of the reaper, he spared little expense to beat down the opposition through lawsuits. He did not smoke, swear or drink but once owned a distillery. He was a dedicated Presbyterian and yet was a supporter of status quo, including slavery. There were "few busier men" than Cyrus Hall McCormick. He rose at five o'clock in the morning, worked long days and traveled far and wide. He did not attend concerts or go to the theater or court women, claiming he was too busy with his work. Fastidious about his appearance, he visited the leading tailors of London and New York. Even with great success, he still claimed that work was the measure of the man and that life was a constant battle. His relaxation came from going to mineral spas, especially Richfield Springs, in New York. People respected Cyrus H. McCormick, few loved him and many hated him.

"I expect to die in the harness," wrote Cyrus McCormick. "This is the life of work. In the next world we will have the rest." He had little interest in recreation, entertainment or intellectual contemplation. "His energy was the wonder of his friends and the despair of his employees. His brain was not quick. It was not marvelously keen or marvelously intuitive. But it was at work every waking moment, like a great engine that never tires." Cyrus McCormick was a pioneer. He left the details to his brother William and Leander while he focused on the big picture. The reaper was his great interest and he took immense pride in the honors it brought him. "The focus of his endeavor was always the victory to be gained over competitors.... He gloried in a fight, neither asked or gave quarter.... He did not know the meaning of discouragement. A defeat was merely the indication that he must vary his method of attack."[46]

By 1857, the imperious Cyrus Hall McCormick had a thriving business but storm clouds were gathering. His brothers demanded a greater share of the company. William told Cyrus he "calculated upon something considerably more than a salary out of this business." Leander threatened to resign unless he received "a pretty strong interest ... in the business." Cyrus understood that his brothers were invaluable to him and agreed to rename the business C.H. McCormick & Brothers, increase the brothers' income and grant them each one-quarter share of the profits.[47] Both Leander and William were younger than he. They were vigorous men. Leander's son Robert Hall was already ten years old, and Stanley's sons Robert Sanderson, age 8, and William Grigsby, age 6, were also coming into the picture of succession. Cyrus determined that he should soon marry and beget sons to establish his dynasty. Until well into his forties, Cyrus McCormick "had no time for gayeties." There is no record of early romances. He was briefly attracted to the pretty and smart daughters of Mr. Hart "but had other business to attend to."[48]

In the summer of 1857 he was ready to change. Nancy Maria Fowler, known as Nettie, came to Chicago to visit her relative, Mrs. Isaac L. Lyons. Nettie kept busy with household chores, social engagements and singing in the choir of the North Presbyterian Church. Cyrus Hall McCormick and his brother Leander were riding on horseback across the Rush Street Bridge. Cyrus noticed the dark-haired, tall, young and beautiful Nettie Fowler walking by. He asked Leander who she was, to learn that she was an Easterner visiting her relatives in Chicago. Leander and his wife Henrietta arranged a tea party for Cyrus to meet Nettie. At the party the "imperious and forceful, not to say domineering" Cyrus McCormick gave all his attention to Nettie. On July 23, he wrote to tell her: "On my first acquaintance with you I am satisfied that your merits have not been overstated.... The more I have seen and known of you since, the more deeply I have been impressed by your merits and charms until I became a captive at your feet." His letters, Nettie wrote, displayed, "the honest, manly and ardent love for me.... They were love letters." Despite the differences their backgrounds and age, Nettie accepted his offer of marriage. "With tears of pleasure and gratitude for the priceless prize I felt I had won," responded Cyrus, "I felt that the blessing was from God."

They hoped to marry in December, but Cyrus's business concerns and his law case against John Manny caused a delay. The marriage, with only a few witnesses, took place at noon on January 26, 1858, at the Lyons family home on Rush Street with the Reverend Dr. Nathan L. Rice, rector of the North Presbyterian Church, officiating. A grand reception followed that evening at the home of William Sanderson McCormick, with five hundred guests present.[49] With his marriage to the refined and educated twenty-three-year-old Nettie Fowler, the personality of the domineering, single-minded and pugnacious forty-nine-year-old Cyrus McCormick began to soften. Their first child, born in 1859, was a boy. They named him Cyrus Hall McCormick, Jr., and he was groomed to continue the reaper dynasty. "No father was ever more jealous of the future of his eldest son than Cyrus Hall McCormick."[50] In turn, Cyrus, Jr., begat Cyrus III to continue the leadership of a Cyrus McCormick of the McCormick Harvester Company well into the 20th century.

Chapter Two

Cyrus and Nettie McCormick
and Family

Melzar and Clarissa Davis Fowler were of old New England stock. Soon after they married they moved to the wilderness of upper New York to settle in the village of Depauville. They ran a store in the village, supplying the farmers with dry goods brought from New York City, as well as butter, cheeses and other necessities. Their daughter Nancy Maria Fowler was born February 8, 1836. They called her Nettie, the name she kept for the rest of her life. When Nettie was seven months, her father was kicked in the stomach by his horse, and died. Despite her grief, Clarissa kept up the store and her family. Clarissa weakened from tuberculosis and in 1842 she died, leaving Nettie, age nine, an orphan. Nettie moved to live with her paternal grandmother in Clayton, New York, eight miles north of Depauville, on the mighty St. Lawrence River, within sight of the ships sailing the Great Lakes. Under the loving care of grandmother Fowler, Nancy learned to cook, sew, spin and keep house. She was a devout Methodist. She attended school in Clayton until her fifteenth year when she set out for the Troy Female Seminary (now the Emma Willard School, Troy, New York.) Emma Willard offered girls a scholastic curriculum as demanding as in the leading schools for boys. In Troy, Nettie studied English, geography, botany, theology, French and music. "I like school," she wrote from Troy, "but even here one may slip through and get a diploma without deserving it. That is not the way I should do. I would earn it or not take it." Upon graduation, Nettie attended the Genesee Wesleyan Seminary (1844–85) and then returned to the village of Clayton.

A year later, at age twenty-two years, she set out by boat from Clayton to Detroit and on by steam train to Chicago, then a booming city of 90,000 people, arriving in August 1856 to stay with her cousin, Maria Lyon, wife of Isaac L. Lyon on Pine Street (now North Michigan Avenue.) After an absence of two years from Chicago, demonstrating his mechanical reaper abroad and fighting off patent violators, Cyrus McCormick had recently returned to Chicago and was staying at his brother Leander's house. Nettie sang in the North Presbyterian Church choir, where Cyrus first saw her and was captivated by her beauty and her sweet contralto voice. Nettie was planning to return to Clayton in June 1857, the month she met Cyrus Hall McCormick. Cyrus asked his brother Leander to invite Nettie to a tea. Here, the "impetuous, forceful, not to say dominating" Cyrus Hall McCormick "took possession of Miss. Fowler." In a letter he made clear his intentions. "On my first acquaintance with you I was satisfied that your merits had not been overestimated. The more I have seen and known of you since, the more deeply I have been impressed by your merits and charms until I became a captive at your feet." Nettie interpreted this and his other letters as "the

Nancy "Nettie" Fowler McCormick came to Chicago from upstate New York and at age 23, married Cyrus Hall McCormick, 49, more than twice her age (WHS Image ID 8385).

Left: Cyrus Hall McCormick is shown in 1865, at age 56, the year his brother William died. After the Civil War, Cyrus spent time in New York City or traveling abroad, leaving the Chicago factory in the hands of brother Leander (WHS Image ID 4012).

manly and ardent expression of his devoted love for me. They glowed with the fervent fires of manly love.... They were love letters."[1] Six feet in height, weighing two hundred pounds, and more than twice Nettie's age, Cyrus Hall McCormick was now ready for marriage, to start a family and establish a dynasty.

Because of business pressures the date of the marriage was twice postponed. On January 26, 1858, Cyrus H. McCormick and Nancy Fowler were married. Even the honeymoon was cut short. Cyrus took his young bride to Washington to await the decision of the Supreme Court in his suit against John H. Manny, alleging infringement of McCormick's 1845 and 1847 patents. From Washington, the couple journeyed to Saratoga Springs to take the waters. The birth of their son, Cyrus Hall McCormick, Jr., on May 16, 1859, served to anchor Nettie while her husband flitted from city to city in America and abroad. Cyrus was delighted with his heir, whom he called the "Young Reaper." A week later, still in an expansive mood, he set out for Indianapolis to attend the general council of the Presbyterian Church. He offered $100,000 to establish a seminary to train ministers and so spread the Presbyterian doctrine. Returning briefly to Chicago, Cyrus and Nettie purchased their first home at 230 Dearborn Street, a single family dwelling with five bedrooms.

An advertising card shows that McCormick Harvester won the Victoria and Albert Medal at the 1851 Crystal Palace fair, and a gold medal at the 1855 Paris exhibition. Husband to Queen Victoria, Albert, the prince consort, died in 1861 (WHS Imago ID 350121).

The McCormicks and the Civil War

> The reaper is to the North what slavery is to the South. By taking the place of regiments of young men in the Western harvest fields, it released them to do battle for the Union at the front and at the same time kept up the supply of bread for the nation and for the nation's armies. Thus, without McCormick's invention I feel the North could not win and the Union would have been dismembered."
> Edwin M. Stanton, United States secretary of war, 1861.[2]

Even before the Civil War, the McCormicks were dogged by pro-slavery accusations. In 1854 the McCormick brothers left the South Presbyterian Church and established the Fourth Presbyterian Church. With $18,000 of his own money, Cyrus bought land at the corner of Wabash Avenue and Congress Street as the future home for their new church. The following year they chose the Rev. R. W. Henry of Ohio to lead the new church, even though Henry had pronounced abolitionist views. Rumors soon spread that Cyrus H. McCormick was "a rabid pro-slavery man" determined to "promote pro-slavery sentiment" the Chicago. In 1860, the Reverend Henry resigned to take a pulpit in New York.[3] Cyrus was accused of undermining Henry and driving him out to be replaced by the Reverend Nathan Lewis Rice.[4] The alleged pro-slavery manipulations of Cyrus led to a schism in the South Presbyterian Church with many members splitting off to form yet another Presbyterian church. An attitude of "quasi antagonism" now existed amongst the Presbyterian congregations in Chicago. Born in Kentucky, Rice was in his younger days, an outspoken supporter of slave holding, arguing that the practice was not sinful.[5] The Reverend Rice was appointed professor at the Chicago Theological Seminary (funded by Cyrus McCormick) where he remained for three years before taking up the prestigious pulpit of the Fifth Avenue Church in New York City.

The conflict between North and South over slavery caught Cyrus Hall McCormick with distinctly divided loyalties. He was born in the South and still kept "strong ties of blood and of friendship" but had become a proud citizen of Illinois. In Virginia he owned several slaves and, in 1860, they were still his property. He had not freed them but had rented them out after he moved to Chicago. He was a prominent member of the Presbyterian Church, which had adopted a strong abolitionist stance. Cyrus's harvesters sold mainly in the Midwest and he was eager to expand into the Southern market. He strongly supported the Union but believed that a "reasonable" compromise—and even the entrenchment of slavery in the South—was far preferable to an all-out Civil War.

Cyrus McCormick supported the Democratic Party, which was severely fractured when the Southerners withdrew. Cyrus's efforts failed to heal the party. At the Charleston convention of 1860 he sought to find a compromise between Stephen A. Douglas and the Southern delegates. In 1859 he bought the Chicago *Herald* to promote his political agenda and advocating states rights. At first he supported John C. Breckenridge for President.[6] After looking "beneath the surface he saw that Breckenridge could not be elected by the people." Instead, McCormick "made use of the supposed popularity of Stephen Douglas in the northern states to prevent the election of Lincoln by the people." McCormick "placed the name of Douglas at the head of his columns." In 1860, McCormick bought the bankrupt Chicago *Times* and merged his two papers as the *Herald and Times* to support the Democratic Party and Stephen Douglas, architect of the Kansas-Nebraska Act that allowed slavery into the free territory of the North.[7]

Cyrus McCormick advocated a "compromise, but in any event, peace and no war." His brothers wrote: "Cyrus H. McCormick is interested in saving the Union." He wanted to keep the agitation over slavery "out of the [Presbyterian] church as far as possible [as a] means for the preservation of the Union, as well as for the peace of the church." His opponents vilified McCormick as a traitor and a rebel who supported the continuance of slavery. The *Chicago Tribune* claimed that Cyrus McCormick had "not an instinct that was not in sympathy with the rebellion. Like all poor white trash of Virginia he left that State as better friends of slavery than the slaveholders themselves, and the prejudices of his youth, built upon a defective education, a perfect monomania in behalf of man-stealing."[8] Much to the irritation of the McCormick brothers, the Presbyterian Church called for the surrender of the South and the abolition of slavery. With Douglas's defeat, McCormick lost interest in his newspaper and sold it to Wilbur F. Storey for $35,000.[9]

During the Civil War, the sale of McCormick reapers to the South ceased, but increased greatly in the North, allowing many farmers to join the Union Army. The Homestead Act of 1862 drew hundreds of thousands of independent farmers to settle the Great Plains. With sales of harvesters booming and wheat prices high, farmers were quick to pay off their debts to McCormick. Fearing inflation and the fall in the value of the dollar, William McCormick fretted about the rapid accumulation of cash. Writing to Cyrus in England, William considered the most "momentous question" of the time was where to invest the money. "By comparison, I think all other questions are insignificant."[10] The McCormick factory workers demanded more pay and shorter hours, threatening to strike. Cyrus left his brothers William and Leander to deal with the workers and keep the factory running.

The Civil War opened a small divide in the McCormick household. Cyrus opposed both the split in the Union and the declaration of war, while Nettie supported the Northern cause. Cyrus's southern roots and his politics made him unpopular in Chicago and on July 16, 1862, with his wife and young son, he set sail for Liverpool on the S.S. *Scotia*. "I think it would be better if you gave up your trip," pleaded William to his domineering brother. "If not, intimate to me whether you desire me to exercise my judgment on every question…. I prefer I should not have to assume responsibility for you." So began a European stay of over two years. Their daughter Mary Virginia McCormick was born in Europe. The wealthy McCormick family lived in hotels or rented houses. Cyrus conducted his business by letters to his brothers William and Leander. In Europe he busied himself selling and demonstrating his harvesting machine while Nettie enjoyed her new surroundings and, with ample help, took care of her children.

In June 1864, Cyrus returned to Chicago, eager to get into politics and pursue his grandiose plan to mediate a peace between North and South; offering to travel to the South and propose a compromise to the Confederate states. "Stop the war," he urged, "declare an armistice—call a convention and consider terms of peace…. If elected to Congress," Cyrus McCormick announced in October 1864, "I will not vote a man or a dollar to continue the war." Instead he demanded an unconditional peace and an immediate cessation of hostilities. The war was "an utter failure … the rebellion can never be subdued [and] it ought not to be." The Confederacy "can never be put down by force of arms, and ought not to be," said McCormick.[11] He advocated "a peace on a basis honorable alike to the North and the South." He called for a commission from the North to meet with the South "to effect a termination of the war with the restoration of the Union."[12] Such an "honorable peace" would entrench slavery in the South. Cyrus McCormick's pleas for an "honorable peace" fell largely on deaf ears. Paradoxically, his harvesting machines helped defeat the Confederacy. During the Civil War, McCormick sold two hundred and fifty thousand reapers, mainly in the North. Each reaper sale released two or three farm hands to serve in the Union. By 1864, the Union could still replace troops fallen in battle, while the Confederate army was fast running out of replacements.[13] Cyrus McCormick ran as a Democrat the 1864 Congressional election in the First District of Illinois. McCormick lost to "Long John" Wentworth, former mayor of Chicago and editor of the *Chicago Democrat,* by a vote of 14,277 to Wentworth's 18,557. McCormick joined other Illinois Democrats in defeat. In the presidential election that year, Abraham Lincoln, running for a second term as president, won 81 percent of the vote in the First District of Illinois.

The Civil War brought challenges also for William and Mary Ann McCormick. Their sympathies lay with the South and the continuation of slavery. "What a pity," mused Mary, that Illinois "wasn't a slave state."[14] William and his wife faced abuse in the press and accusations that they were "secessionists." Mary Ann's relatives wore the Confederate uniform. Colonels Andrew Jackson Grigsby and John Warren Grigsby featured large on the Confederate side of the Civil War. The South threatened to confiscate William's Virginia property, claiming he was an enemy alien. To prevent confiscation William transferred his Virginia property to his sister-in-law in discharge of debts.[15]

Leander and Henrietta McCormick too were proud of their Southern roots and quietly supported the cause of the Confederacy. Leander's brother-in-law John R. Hamilton served as a major in the Confederate army of general Robert E. Lee. Others of their relatives who remained in Rockbridge Country joined the Confederate cause. Among them were James Zechariah McChesney who served in the 14th Virginia cavalry and Alexander Gallatin McChesney, a captain in the 11th Virginia cavalry. Homer Hill, son of Mary McCormick Hill, fought on the Confederate side. Robert McChesney also fought for the Confederacy and was killed during the early years of the Civil War. Captain Alexander McNutt Hamilton of the 4th Virginian Regiment fought under the command of general Stonewall Jackson. In her *Genealogies and Reminiscences*, Henrietta Hamilton McCormick proudly lists members of her extended family who served in the Confederate Army. Among them were colonel Andrew Jackson Grigsby of the 27th Virginian Regiment, his brother John Warren Grigsby of the 6th Kentucky Regiment, colonel Greenlee Davidson, his son Frederick, Albert Davidson, and brigadier general E. Franklin Paxton of the Rockbridge Rifles who devoted his life "to the cause he held dearest, the defense of his native state and its liberties." Brigadier general Albert Gallatin Jenkins died in the Battle of Cloyd's Mountain on May 9, 1864, at age thirty-three years. Lieutenant Robert McNutt was killed in the Civil War in 1861.

After the Civil War

At the end of the Civil War, one and a half million men from the Union Army returned to their farms and households. By 1865 the superiority of the mechanical harvester over the sickle and scythe was well established and the demand for McCormick's machines increased year by year. Agriculture in the South was slow to recover. The Southern Homestead Act of 1866 offered land to poor whites and to freed blacks. Many of the Southern farmers took advantage of the labor-saving machinery and shifted from traditional cotton and tobacco to planting grains. Overall, the demand for harvesters was so great that the McCormick Company was embarrassed "by its inability to fill all the orders sent in by its agents." The machines were "easy to sell but money hard to collect."[16]

As a wealthy son of Virginia, Cyrus received many requests from the South for financial aid. These came from the now-impoverished planter class as well as the common man; from churches, schools, institutions and universities. Most of these appeals were turned down. The request for help from the former Confederate general Robert E. Lee, now president of Washington University, was an exception. The college was founded in Lexington, Virginia, in 1749, near the McCormick family home in the Valley of Virginia. It began as the Augusta Academy and changed its name fifty years later to honor president George Washington. Cyrus McCormick donated $20,000 to establish the McCormick Professorship of Natural Philosophy. He was one of the college's greatest benefactors and served as a member of its board of trustees. In gratitude, the college (later university) named its library for Cyrus McCormick. In 1931, six thousand people, including members of his family, gathered at Washington and Lee University for the unveiling of a statue of Cyrus Hall McCormick, hailed as the inventor of the reaper that "relieved the world of its food worries."[17]

After the Civil War, Cyrus R. McCormick moved his family to the Fifth Avenue Hotel at the corner of 23rd Street, New York City. After a brief stay in the hotel, he bought a four-story house at 40 Fifth Avenue. Nurses, nursemaids, valets and other domestic help took care of the wealthy McCormick family, now with three children. After two years in New York, the restless Cyrus was eager to return to Europe to demonstrate his reaper at the 1867 Universal Exposition in Paris. With the children dispatched to relatives in upstate New York, Cyrus and Nettie set off for Paris to garner fresh accolades as the inventor of the reaping machine, and receive the Exposition's highest honor. Further accolades came when Emperor Napoleon appointed Cyrus a Chevalier of the Legion of Honor.

In 1868, McCormick Harvester Company replaced its "Reliable" with its "Advance" harvester, selling for $200 per machine. By 1870, McCormick employed 400 workers, making 8,000 reapers a year, with a profit on each machine of $50. The labor unions were still weak and McCormick faced few strikes, giving the company a flowing river of profits.

From 1865 to 1871, Cyrus H. McCormick was largely away from Chicago, living in New York City or traveling abroad. The Great Fire of Chicago began in a barn at 135 DeKoven Street around nine o'clock in the evening of October 8, 1871. With wood as Chicago's principal building material, the fire spread rapidly and consumed much of the residential and business areas of the boom city of 300,000 inhabitants. Chicago's small fire department with only 17 horse-pulled fire engines was no match for the inferno. The Great Fire consumed 17,500 buildings, leaving 100,000 people homeless and 300 dead. The fire destroyed the homes of Leander and William McCormick, the McCormick Building and other properties that had brought Cyrus annual rents of $175,000.

The Great Chicago Fire destroyed the McCormick Works, together with 2,000 completed harvesters ready for delivery, as well as $200,000 of materials. The overall loss to Cyrus came to $1.4 million, of which only a quarter million dollars was covered by insurance. Leander was able to continue some production of reapers at another site while he and Cyrus planned to build a new factory on the South Side at the corner of Western and

Top and above: The Great Fire of October 1871 destroyed much of Chicago, including the McCormick Works. Cyrus built a new and larger works in the southwest manufacturing district of the city (Library of Congress).

Blue Island avenues. Leander claimed the credit for building the new factory. "After the great fire of 1871, whereby the Reaper Works and other properties were destroyed, business suspended, and thousands of men thrown out of employment, by his decision and energy, the works were immediately rebuilt, under his personal supervision and direction, according to his own selection of site and architectural designs."[18] Cyrus claimed the honors for rebuilding the reaper works. "Cyrus was never busier in his life than in 1872."[19] From his apartment in the St. Caroline's Court Hotel, he directed the salvaging of his old works and the construction of his new factory. The new McCormick factory on Blue Hill Avenue, near Western Avenue, "on the north bank of the new South Branch of the Chicago River" was built at a cost of $2 million, to employ 700 workers, to fashion 15,000 reapers a year "to send to every country in the civilized world." The new works comprised four-story buildings, heated by steam and lit by gas, and protected by its own fire-fighting team. Among the buildings were a boarding house and fifty cottages to house single and married workers "at a cheap rate" and close to their work. McCormick was Chicago's biggest financial loser from the fire, but his company was the "most extensively identified with its resolution"[20] The new factory was equipped with up-to-date machinery from suppliers in New England and Ohio. In January 1873, steam was raised and the new factory began production, aided by fine crops on the Great Plains that boosted the demand for harvesters.

With the factory humming, Cyrus Hall McCormick drafted a new agreement granting Leander's 24-year-old son Robert Hall McCormick a small share of the business. With brother William dead, Cyrus and Leander were engaged in a power struggle. For years Leander labored in the factory while Cyrus traveled abroad, collecting awards both as the inventor and manufacturer of the world's leading harvester machine. Leander wanted a share of the glory and a larger role in the company for himself and his son. In May 1873, Leander informed Cyrus: "I cannot continue longer in business with you on such terms as you are disposed to extract." After much haggling the brothers established the firm of C. H. & L. J. McCormick, with Cyrus owning three-quarters, Leander three-sixteenth and young Robert Hall McCormick one-sixteenth of the company. The new arrangement was only a brief truce. "No father was ever more jealous of the future of his eldest son than Cyrus McCormick, and in four or five years, when Cyrus Jr., would be old enough to enter the business, a new crisis was bound to arise."[21]

In 1872, Cyrus attended the State Democratic Convention held in Springfield, Illinois. During 1874 to 1876, he was sporadically mentioned as a possible candidate for governor of Illinois, vice-president of the United States or United States Senator from Illinois.[22] In 1876 he served as chairman of the state Democratic Party.[23] His financial support was eagerly sought. Authoritarian and used to having his own way, he did not have the time or interest in the intrigues of politics. Cyrus managed the Depression of 1873–1879 by lowering the price of its harvesters and drastically reducing wages. When the economy picked up and workers were scarce, McCormick raised wages. The restless Cyrus was frequently away from Illinois, abroad on business, arguing his patent cases or visiting health spas in New York, Arkansas and Wisconsin.

In 1878, Cyrus traveled to Europe where he was again loaded with honors awarded by different societies "where his reaping machines have astounded the natives and added glory to Chicago." Between 1851 and 1872, the Royal Agricultural Society of England conducted a dozen harvester trials. "While great credit is due to Walter Wood, Osborne & Company and C.H. McCormick ... none of them have, as regard the requirements of the English farmers, attained the perfection which would justify the judges in awarding the gold medal of the Society." At the 1878 competition at Bristol "the judges came to the unanimous conclusion that McCormick's sheaf-binder had fulfilled the conditions of the Society and they awarded the gold medal to it accordingly." The 1881 Royal Agricultural Society competition held in Derby was even more gratifying for Cyrus McCormick. Measuring simplicity of construction, security of the binding, ease of performance and freedom from waste, the McCormick harvester was again awarded the coveted gold medal, while its British competitors Johnston harvester and Samuelson harvester received silver medals.[24]

While visiting Paris in 1878, Cyrus developed a large carbuncle on his back. His physicians feared the worst as they lanced the infection. "He seemed shattered, as I have never saw—trembling, high fever—could not collect his mind readily," reported Nettie. "The period of convalescence was very long." Laid up in Paris for months, Cyrus lost his self-confidence and became ever more dependent on his wife.[25] Needing a cane or an arm for support, it was not until the summer of 1879 that Cyrus was able to journey back to America. He was no longer able to engage in politics and was no longer listed among the prominent Democrats of Illinois.[26]

The McCormick mansion at 675 North Rush Street was completed in time to celebrate on May 28, 1880, the twenty-first birthday of Cyrus Hall McCormick, Jr. The pick of Chicago high society was invited, including the governor, mayor Harrison, Joseph Medill, George Pullman and Marshall Field. Cyrus McCormick's brother Leander, already estranged, did not attend. After admiring the grand house perfumed by flowers, the three hundred guests

The 1884 McCormick reaper plus twine binder was "The People's Favorite.... Victorious on over 100 field trials." The new and improved harvesting machine came with a mechanism to bind grain bundles with twine, tie a knot and deposited the bundled grain to the ground (private collection).

Construction began in 1875 on the McCormick Mansion at 675 N. Rush Street, Chicago, and the 35-room mansion was completed four years later. Cyrus enjoyed his grand Second Empire style house for less than five years before he died (WHS Image ID 3839).

were ushered into the concert room where an orchestra under conductor Julius Fuchs played extracts from Haydn's Sixth Symphony, Mendelssohn's Piano Concerto, Beethoven's Eighth Symphony and Mozart's Third Symphony.[27] After a sumptuous dinner, the orchestra played lighter music until 11 o'clock, after which Cyrus, Jr., and his young guests danced "until a late hour."[28]

Until the last years of his life, Cyrus Hall McCormick had enjoyed excellent health. He stood over six feet in height, weighed over 200 pounds, and had a hearty appetite for fine foods. His illness in Paris in 1878 permanently weakened him in body and in spirit. "He never had a secretary," wrote his grandson Cyrus McCormick. "His wife copied his voluminous letters…. His filing cabinet was in his brain or the drawer of his desk." Although steam power already drove railroad engines and ships, the McCormick reaper of his day used horsepower. Cyrus Hall McCormick died "before the tractor was dreamed of or mass production was named." He became an invalid, spending much time in bed or in a wheel-chair, needing a cane or a helping hand to shuffle about. Rheumatism with severe pain in the right hip and knee added to his woes. Using the treatments of his day, Cyrus took the waters at Eureka Springs and Hot Springs, Arkansas and altered his diet to include oatmeal,

Left: **Cyrus and Nettie McCormick, January 1884, four months before his death. Nettie remained a widow for almost 40 years (WHS Image ID 8775).** *Right:* **The 75-year-old Cyrus and his younger sons Harold, age 12 (left), and Stanley, age 10 (WHS Image ID 11079).**

cracked wheat and milk. Physicians subjected him to massages, patent medicines and the latest electrical treatments. In February 1884, he entertained at his home the students and faculty of the Theological Seminary and in April welcomed two hundred and fifty guests to meet the president of Princeton College, James McCosh. That year, his factory employed 1,500 workers who turned out 55,000 reapers, with a worldwide sales force.

By 1884, his legs were so weak that he needed a rolling chair to move about. His mind remained sharp to the end and he was able, with the help of his wife and son, to run his large business. In early May, he weakened. Cyrus Hall McCormick died at 7 o'clock on the morning of May 13, 1884, at age 75 years, with his family at his bedside. His last words were: "It's all right. It's all right. I only want heaven." In his lifetime, Chicago had become the leading granary of the world and a half-million McCormick harvesting machines were at work on five continents. Many "well known businessmen" and 400 McCormick employees attended the funeral. Cyrus Hall McCormick was hailed as "a representative man not only of the Presbyterian Church but of the wider Christianity of which the church is but a part. He was a representative man of the whole country, North and South."[29] He was buried on May 16 at Graceland Cemetery.

Cyrus Hall McCormick at his death left an estate worth $10 million. The bulk of his wealth was in shares of the McCormick Harvesting Machine Company, worth $7.5 million. McCormick owned $2.5 million in real estate in Chicago as well as large tracts of land in Illinois, Wisconsin, Iowa, Nebraska and Minnesota. He left to his wife his grand home on North Rush Street and their summer home at Richfield Hill, New York. Nettie also received one-fifth of the net proceeds of the estate. The remaining four-fifths of his estate was held in trust for five years with his children receiving equal shares of the trust income. After five years the trust was divided equally between his surviving children. Cyrus appointed Nettie and Cyrus, Jr., as executors of the trust.[30]

Nancy "Nettie" Maria Fowler was twenty-three years old when she married forty-nine-year-old Cyrus Hall McCormick. They remained together for twenty-six years until Cyrus died. Nettie gave birth to seven children. Two of Nettie's children—Robert and Alice—died in childhood. At the time of their father's death, Cyrus Hall, Jr., was age 25 years, Mary Virginia age 23, Anita Eugenie age 18, Harold Fowler age 12 and Stanley Robert age 9 years. Many trials awaited Nettie; especially the severe mental illness that afflicted Mary and Stanley in their early adult life, the early death of her son-in-law Emmons Blaine, the death of several grandchildren and the messy divorce of her son Harold.

Nettie was forty-nine years of age when her husband died. She endured widowhood for thirty-nine years before her own death in 1923. She called her husband "Mr. McCormick." With his "intense absorption in the reaper business," his narcissism, need for praise, accustomed to having his own way, he was not "an easy man to live with." Arguments flared so frequently that in 1865, Nettie, a peacemaker by nature, suggested a code of conduct between them. "If either makes an abrupt reply or charge, the other is not to reply in the same strain but to direct the attention calmly to its spirit and effect to the real point involved."[31] In his last years of life, overwhelmed by failing health, Cyrus left the big business and family decisions to Nettie.

With the support of his mother, the 25-year-old Cyrus Hall McCormick, Jr., began the heavy burden of filling his father's giant shoes as president of the McCormick Harvesting Company. When Mary Virginia began her descent into madness, Nettie arranged for her to occupy a camp in the Adirondacks and a home in the west side of New York, close to the Hudson River; complete with a full-time nursing and custodian staff and even a full-time resident physician. A few years later, Nettie had the idea that Montecito, Santa Barbara County, California would make the ideal place for her invalid daughter. On 74-acres facing the ocean she built Riven Rock as a one-patient sanctuary. Mary Virginia spent very little time at Riven Rock. Instead Huntsville, Alabama became her permanent home.

Anita Eugenie McCormick entered the social swirl of Chicago's high society and "the little boys" Harold and Stanley attended the University School in Chicago. Despite the 30-month differences in their ages, Nettie treated her younger boys as if they were a twin-set. Harold was fun-loving while Stanley was serious and bookish. Both boys were good at sports, especially tennis. In 1889, Nettie and her boys moved to an apartment on Madison Avenue, New York, where she enrolled Harold and Stanley in the Browning School, a small college preparatory school for boys, founded by John D. Rockefeller for the education of his son John, Jr. In New York Nettie met John D. Rockefeller and his family. Both families were determined to make their sons serious and responsible and avoid the easy temptation of rich boys to slide into indolence and entitlement. Harold and Stanley became good friends with John D. Rockefeller, Jr., and through him Harold met Edith Rockefeller, soon to be his wife. When Stanley graduated from the Browning School, Nettie returned to Chicago to the huge but empty mansion at 675 Rush Street.

In the fall of 1891, Nettie set out for Egypt for a luxury cruise up the Nile River to Aswan and back. Accompanying her were a physician-companion, a maid, and her youngest child, Stanley. From Egypt, mother and son traveled to Italy and on to Paris. Stanley had a fine voice, and, hoping to be an opera singer, asked for music lessons. After a few months Nettie and Stanley set out for Switzerland. Stanley changed his focus from music to art. His obliging mother took him back to Paris where she engaged an art teacher for him. "There is nothing I should rather do," wrote Stanley to his mother, "than to pursue art here this winter." Nettie would not permit it. Having a brief fling with opera or art was fine but "the clear destiny" of the sons of Cyrus Hall McCormick "was the great business that he had created."[32] Unaware that Stanley was showing early signs of a mental illness, Nettie insisted he leave Paris and return with her to Chicago, before continuing his studies at Princeton.

Nettie delighted in the birth of her first grandchild, Cyrus McCormick III, soon followed by the birth of Anita's son Emmons Blaine, Jr. The joy over the marriage in 1895 of her son Harold to Edith Rockefeller was offset by the sudden death of her son-in-law Emmons Blaine. In 1901, her grandson John Rockefeller McCormick died of scarlet fever. In 1903, Nettie traveled to Geneva, Switzerland to attend the wedding of her son Stanley to Katharine Dexter. That year, her beloved brother Eldridge Fowler died. Two years later, granddaughter Elizabeth died following surgery.

By 1905, Stanley's psychosis had become so severe that he left the harvester company and moved from Chicago to Brookline, Massachusetts, to be admitted to the McLean Psychiatric Hospital. With his condition declared hopeless, Stanley was moved for the rest of his life to Riven Rock in Santa Barbara, originally built for his insane sister, Mary Virginia. "Two ill children drew on Nettie's heart, her thought and her time."[33]

Nettie felt the obligation to "do the work he left me to do," to care for her family and to sustain the great harvester business, of which she was now the principal shareholder. She assisted her son, Cyrus McCormick, Jr., in running the harvester company. She supported the Moody Bible Institute and Princeton University. Nettie funded a wide range of orphanages, schools and hospitals at home and abroad. She supported Pierre University, Jamestown College and other Presbyterian schools in prairie country. Tusculum College in Greeneville, Tennessee was especially attractive to Nettie McCormick. Eager to bind the Northern and Southern Presbyterian churches after the Civil War, Cyrus, late in his life, offered to help Tusculum. Nettie carried out his wish by funding McCormick Hall, a dormitory to house male students, opened in 1892, and Virginia Hall to house female students. (Virginia Hall was named for Mary Virginia McCormick, Nettie's schizophrenic daughter.) McCormick philanthropy paid for four other buildings at Tusculum College.[34] With an interest in domestic science for girls and manual training for boys, Nettie opened her purse to the Jackson Collegiate Institute at Jackson, Kentucky. In 1913, Nettie Fowler McCormick donated $750,000 to the Shantung Christian University and the Nanking University in China, both institutions supported by the American Presbyterian Board of Foreign Missions. The money went to build chapels, a YMCA, dormitories and science rooms at the Chinese universities.[35] She funded Presbyterian missions in Korea, Thailand and India. McCormick Hall, McCormick Library, Stanley McCormick School, Elizabeth McCormick dormitory and other edifices bearing family names popped up in the United States and in Asia.

Nancy "Nettie" Fowler McCormick died on July 5, 1923. Nettie's estate before taxes was valued at $11,775,600, of which federal taxes took $2,653,504 and state inheritance taxes took $1,453,306. The bulk of the estate came from the value of 3,787 shares in the International Harvesting Company.[36] After paying taxes, $1,140,600 went to twenty-four charities. Nettie's principal servants received small amounts ($1,000 to $5,000). The great bulk of her estate went to her sons Cyrus Hall and Harold F. McCormick and to her daughter Mrs. Emmons Blaine. Nettie's will noted that Stanley and Mary Virginia McCormick, both schizophrenic and institutionalized, "were previously provided for."[37]

Chapter Three

The Brothers
William and Leander

Robert and Polly McCormick of Rockbridge County, Virginia, had eight children. Born in 1809, Cyrus was the oldest. Robert and Susan followed and both died young. William, born in 1815, was six years younger than Cyrus. Mary, born in 1817, married the Reverend James Shields and remained in Virginia. Next came Leander, born in 1819, ten years Cyrus's junior. John, born in 1820, lived only 29 years. Lastly, Amanda was born in 1822 and married Hugh Adams. Hugh and Amanda Adams moved to Chicago in 1857, where Hugh formed a successful partnership with Cyrus as McCormick & Adams, grain commission merchants. William and Leander were summoned by Cyrus to leave their Virginia farms for Chicago and take their places in building his great reaper enterprise.

William Sanderson McCormick was born on November 2, 1815, the fourth of the children of Robert and Polly McCormick. Where Cyrus was given the reaper to further develop, William was trained in business. As a boy he studied John Gibson's *A New and Improved System of Practical Bookkeeping* to gain the skills to manage the family farm, gristmill, distillery and blacksmith's shop.

When William was age sixteen he watched with great interest as his brother Cyrus demonstrated the mechanical reaper cutting the wheat in a neighbor's field. William stayed on the family farm and inherited Walnut Grove after his father died in 1846. Two years later, on July 11, 1848, he married Mary Ann Grigsby, daughter of Rueben Grigsby, owner of Hickory Hill.[1] In 1847, Cyrus enticed his youngest brother Leander to leave Virginia and take part in Cyrus's great venture of building reapers first in Cincinnati and then in Chicago. With his ten slaves, William seemed content to remain a Virginia farmer, but yielded to Cyrus's demand that he come to Chicago. With Cyrus constantly on the move selling his reaper and suing his rivals, William was offered an employment contract to run the business side of the expanding venture, with a salary of $3,000 a year. In the summer of 1850, William and Mary Ann and their infant son Robert departed their beloved Virginia for the rough-and-tumble of industrial Chicago.

In Chicago, William supervised seven bookkeepers to run the large reaper factory employing 300 pairs of hands. During the formative years of the reaper company it was William who managed "the sales, collections, and the purchase of supplies."[2] Production in 1851 was 1,000 harvesters, rising to 2,534 in 1855 and over 4,000 in 1856. William was loyal to his brother Cyrus. Called upon in the case of McCormick v. Manny, William testified that Cyrus was the creator of the mechanical reaper. William claimed he witnessed Cyrus "with his own hands made all the particular parts of it … and that my father assisted the complainant in its construction."[3] Settled in Chicago, William became enamored with the fortunes made in real estate. With Leander, he was angry over their positions as employees and believed they deserved higher salaries and shares in the business. Under the day-to-day management of Leander and William, the company thrived and survived the Panic of 1857. After the brothers told Cyrus that they wanted "more than salary" he raised their annual salary to $6,000 each, together with a quarter share of the profits (or losses). In 1859, the factory had a net profit of $300,000, giving Leander and William each $75,000, making them wealthy and eager to speculate in Chicago's booming real estate.[4] Adopting the style of the newly rich, William built a fine house on Rush Street and purchased commercial properties on Clark and Lake Street, owning an entire Clark Street block between Lake and South Water (now Wacker Drive) streets. He bought hotels catering to the new arrivals to the booming city. William purchased 11,000 acres of farmland in Illinois, Iowa, Minnesota, Indiana and Michigan. While accumulating property and wealth in Chicago, William still hankered for the "sacred spot" of his ancestral home in Virginia. "I should love to make my home again at Walnut Grove if pecuniary interest were not in the way of it."[5]

William Sanderson McCormick was born in 1815. He was six years younger than brother Cyrus, who placed him in charge of the business side of the harvester company. Suffering from depression and debilitating anxiety, William, in 1865, entered the State Hospital for the Insane, Jacksonville, Illinois, where he died at age fifty. He was the father of ambassador Robert Sanderson McCormick and grandfather of Senator Joseph Medill McCormick and newspaper tycoon Robert Rutherford McCormick (WHS Image ID 60839).

William and Leander "felt that they had done most of the work and by their ingenuity had kept the McCormick reaper and mower in step with the progress of the art," while Cyrus was mostly away from Chicago.[6] When Cyrus returned to America in 1864 after a long stay in Europe, he found his brothers in open revolt and, with reluctance, he agreed to increase their share of the enterprise. William had a "cheerful disposition, was quick spoken, and, although diffident, was among his friends a most interesting and agreeable man."[7] He was a conciliator who tried to mediate the disagreements among the brothers about money, the invention of the reaper, and the ownership of the factory. Like his brother Cyrus, William "did not know how to relax." He worked long hours and constantly worried about business issues. William came to dislike office work and complained about the dust and noise of the factory. All these pressures played havoc on his nerves and his dyspepsia. William tried various cures, including hydrotherapy, electrical stimulation and spas in Ohio and New York, but to no avail. Becoming depressed, William questioned the value of material success. "We should have enough to satisfy ordinary needs," wrote William to Cyrus on February 18, 1864, "but beyond that why should we be slaves" to greed? "When I think of money-making, I see the folly of it; it is madness." On January 31, 1965, Mary Ann wrote to her sister-in-law Nettie McCormick: "I fear my dear husband is going to have a serious time from nervous headaches, low spirits and general disability, about as he was some years ago." In April William told Cyrus: "I am extremely nervous." By the summer William McCormick was unable to do his work. Fifteen years of hard work under his brother's authoritarian rule had left William a wealthy but depressed and unfulfilled man. Dr. C. A. Spring, Sr., found William "intermittently clear " but consumed with religious and business worries. In August 1865 in desperation, William left his family for the State Hospital for the Insane, Jacksonville, Illinois' first psychiatric hospital. William Sanderson McCormick was a special patient. He was comfortably housed in the residence of the superintendent, Dr. Andrew McFarland, and was free to go on walks and receive visits from his family and friends. Even Cyrus made him a brief visit to discuss business matters.

The vast five-story mental hospital accepted its first patients in 1851, with men and women in separate wings. In 1860, Elizabeth Packard was confined to the asylum, at the request of her husband, the Calvinist minister Theophilus Packard, on grounds that he found her religious beliefs objectionable. At that time, Illinois law allowed a husband to commit his wife merely on his request and without a public hearing. Elizabeth remained three years in the asylum after which her husband kept her a prisoner in their home. Gaining her freedom, Elizabeth Packard established the Anti-Insane Asylum Society and campaigned successfully to rescind the law permitting a husband to commit his wife to an institution without a public hearing, or allow the woman to defend herself.

Elizabeth Packard was under the care of Dr. Andrew McFarland. Born 1817 in Concord, New Hampshire, McFarland attended Dartmouth College in New Hampshire followed by Jefferson Medical College in Philadelphia. The mental illness of his mother took him to a career in psychiatry, to become superintendent of the New Hampshire Asylum in Concord. In 1850, the doctor took a trip to Europe, recording his impressions in letters home that were later compiled in his book *The Escape*. He observed the appalling conditions for the poor in industrial England. He visited mental asylums in England and concluded: "The English lunatic of the lower classes is a happy man. His disease has sheltered him from the grasp of poverty, ceaseless toil and constantly dreaded starvation, and becomes his unquestioned passport to a life of quiet, abundance, and freedom from the treadmill destiny" of the enslaved working people.[8] In 1854, Dr. Andrew McFarland moved west to become superintendent of the Illinois asylum at Jacksonville.

William Sanderson McCormick contemplated returning to his Virginia roots with plans to improve his farm and establish a lumberyard. Instead, he entered in a "religious melancholy" and ruminated constantly about the folly of the pursuit of power and money. Typhoid struck the hospital and afflicted the fifty-year-old William McCormick. He said his goodbyes to his wife and five children, Robert, William, Emma, Anne Rubenia and Lucy, aged from sixteen years to six months. He urged his brothers Cyrus and Leander to "forbear one another with love…. What poor sinners we all are," he uttered, "What good are now the world's goods?" Four months after the Civil War ended, William Sanderson McCormick died in the evening of September 27, 1865, at age 50 years, with his family at his bedside. To Cyrus, the death of William was "an irreparable loss.[9] William's heirs received from Cyrus and Leander $400,000 as his share of C. H. McCormick & Brothers.[10] William Sanderson McCormick was buried at the Graceland Cemetery in Chicago. His position as superintendent of the McCormick Harvester Company was taken by Boston-born Charles A. Spring. Mary Ann McCormick left her sons Robert and William in Chicago, took her share of the harvester business and returned to her Southern roots.

In 1857, Abraham Lincoln assisted in the prosecution of Isaac Wyant, accused of the murder of Aaron Rust. The defense brought in a number of psychiatrists to testify on behalf of Wyant. One of the psychiatrists for the defense was Dr. Andrew McFarland, superintendent of the state asylum at Jacksonville. Wyant was found not guilty by reason of insanity.[11] Dr. Andrew McFarland served as president of the Medical Superintendents of the American Institutions for the Insane (MASAII), the forerunner of the American Psychiatric Association. In 1869, he left the state asylum to open his private Oak Lawn Retreat in Jacksonville. The asylum "was a beautiful spot, laid out with walks and drives and dotted with evergreen trees, commanding an excellent view."[12] Six years later McFarland received a letter from Robert Lincoln, son of the assassinated President Abraham Lincoln, asking him to examine his mother Mary Todd Lincoln, who was committed as insane in the Bellevue Retreat in Batavia, Illinois. On April 14, 1865, Mary sat next to her husband in the President's Box at Ford's Theater on Tenth Street, Washington, when John Wilkes Booth shot Lincoln in the back of the head. After Lincoln died, Mary became increasingly depressed and paranoid. Dr. McFarland examined Mary Todd Lincoln on September 8, 1875, and declared that her "unhappy mental condition [left] her in a helpless and irresponsible state of mind." McFarland had "grave apprehensions" about her condition and suggested that: "the most quietude be observed for the few ensuing months [otherwise] all reasonable hope of restoration must be abandoned." Despite McFarland's "very unfavorable" prognosis, Mary Todd Lincoln was released and moved to her sister's home. For four years she lived in Europe, returning to the United States in 1882, to die.[13]

Born February 8, 1819, Leander James McCormick was the youngest of the sons of Robert and Mary McCormick. Leander describes himself as one "brought up and educated in the Shenandoah Valley, Virginia.... His health and physique are attributable to the climate and outdoor life of his early years. Although he removed to Chicago at age twenty-nine, his love of his native state continued [and he frequently] sought recreation amid its mountains and scenery and health from its restorative waters."[14] As a dutiful son, Leander helped his father and, assisted by their slaves, designed and forged the reaping machine in the blacksmith's shop of the family farm in Virginia. Brother Cyrus was on the road trying to sell the machine. The cumbersome reaping machine was sent from Virginia in sections by wagon and river boat to ports on the east coast, then shipped to New Orleans and sent by steamboat up the Mississippi and Ohio Rivers, to be assembled and sold to famers in Ohio and points further west. The long journey added cost and time, making it difficult to make a profit. Instead, Cyrus hit on the idea of setting up manufacturing franchises closer to his markets. He signed agreements with Seymour, Chappel & Company and Bachus, Fitch & Company of Brockport, New York and with A.C. Brown & Company of Cincinnati, to build the McCormick reaper. Each reaper was warranted to cut 15 acres of wheat per day "when properly attended" and sold for $100.[15]

In 1845, Leander married Henrietta Maria Hamilton. Henrietta was born in 1822 in Rockbridge, Virginia. Like Leander's, hers was a Scots-Irish family. Her great grandfather,

Alexander McNutt, "a planter, slave owner and Presbyterian," fought in the Revolutionary War. Anderson McNutt, born in 1795, was a wealthy sugar planter "who owned one hundred and fifty slaves, whom he freed by will." Her grandfather James Hamilton arrived in the New World in 1771. His son John settled in Rockbridge County, Virginia, married Elizabeth Grigsby, farmed 500-acres, and built their red brick home on Locust Hill. John and Elizabeth Hamilton had seven children, with Henrietta the fourth-born. In her *Genealogies and Reminiscences* (self-published in 1894), Henrietta relates that she was brought up "to ride on horseback. At one time she rode one hundred and fifty miles in ten days, with ladies only as her companions, visiting the Alleghany Mountains." At age fourteen she attended a boarding school in Lexington, Virginia, founded in 1812, that was "one of the earliest promotions of female education in the country." There she studied natural philosophy, chemistry, astronomy, chemistry, logic, botany, ancient and modern histories, music and modern languages. One of her lasting influences was the vision of the crucifixion she experienced during her adolescence. Upon graduation she returned home and, five years later, married Leander. He was "so industrious and energetic he could not spare the time for a bridal tour." Instead he got back to his work with his father "in the development of the Reaper, to which he had already added the reaper's seat and other indispensible features."

Early in 1846, Robert McCormick fell ill and his strength began to ebb. He pushed himself to keep working on the reaper. His death on July 3, 1846, altered the dynamic of the patriarchal McCormick family. Building the reaper at Walnut Grove stopped. Concerned over the quality of the reapers manufactured by A.C. Brown in Cincinnati, Cyrus summoned Leander to supervise the work done there. Leander agreed to move "if the inducements should be sufficient." In 1847, at age 28 years, Leander with his wife Henrietta and their first child Robert Hall McCormick, left Walnut Grove and his beloved Virginia for Cincinnati, Ohio to work for his older brother and earn $15 a week, with a share of the profits. Leander was empowered to hire or discharge workers, maintain quality of workmanship and reject faulty materials.[16] In 1847, Cyrus contracted with Charles Gray and Seth Warner to build the reaper on a larger scale in Chicago, and the following year established McCormick, Ogden & Company, with William B. Ogden, former mayor of Chicago. Soon after Leander had settled in Cincinnati he was summoned by Cyrus to come to Chicago to supervise the manufacture of one thousand McCormick reapers each year.

Leander, Henrietta, and their son, Robert Hall, returned to Virginia to bid farewell to their families. They left November 20, 1848, on horseback in the middle of a heavy snowstorm. The family met the coach at an inn and traveled to Baltimore, then by ship to New York, up the Hudson River to Albany and along the Erie Canal to Buffalo. From Buffalo they traveled on the Great Lakes by steamboat to Detroit, and on to Chicago. Leander, his wife Henrietta and their infant son Robert arrived in Chicago in 1848. To her "dear sister Martha Ann," Henrietta wrote on December 3 of her trip and her first impressions of Chicago. "Leander and myself were both seasick, and I had Hall to nurse. So that I was worn out and tired." From the port of Chicago, Cyrus escorted them to the Sherman Hotel, "the finest hotel in the city." After ten days in the hotel they moved into their own home. "We are very nicely fixed up indeed, and are very much pleased with our new home and friends so far. I would be so glad if you and Ma and my friends could see how well we are fixed for housekeeping." The furniture "is all new and of the best quality, including one dozen cushioned mahogany chairs, a beautiful bureau and a $24 card table…. The stairs are carpeted and the passage floor has oilcloth on it. The dining room has nine chairs and table; my dishes and eatables are kept in the pantry. There are three rooms upstairs; one nicely furnished for Cyrus."

Henrietta and Leander formed a friendship with Mr. and Mrs. Hamilton, who came to Chicago from Kentucky. "She seems to look upon us as kinfolks," reported Henrietta. "A great many Yankees here. Mrs. Hamilton does not like them much. She says we must have a Southern society, and let the Yankees, Germans, Irish, French all alone. The people here seem to be from all quarters of the globe. We will soon have as many acquaintances as we want, and of the best in the city." Leander and Henrietta spruced themselves up to make a good impression. Leander bought "a new suit, overcoat and all." Henrietta showed off her "very fine velvet bonnet bought in New York for $3.50 but would cost $8 in Chicago." The couple had two servants, one in the kitchen and one to clean the house. "The white servants here are greater workers than the blacks in Virginia," Henrietta observed. "They do everything you tell them to do, and do a great deal better than black people.... I have everything here that anyone could wish to make me happy, except my relations." Henrietta delighted in the "excellent markets [that offered] the best of meat of every description for four cents a pound, such as sausages, venison, beef and pork." The apples, peaches and cranberries were all "excellent." In Chicago the "people cook very differently from what they do in Virginia.... They never have a single meal without potatoes."[17]

The Reaper Works was Leander's life work. "After the death of their father," wrote Leander in 1896, "the three brothers, Cyrus, William and Leander permanently established themselves in partnership in the city of Chicago for the manufacture and introduction of the Reaper into the broad fields of the West; Leander assuming the management of the manufacturing department, a position which he held over thirty years. During and previous to this time, he made many improvements of vital importance and without which it could not have been a completed machine, nor have become of world-wide fame."[18] Leander supervised the work of 120 carpenters, 115 iron-workers, 40 blacksmiths and 40 laborers, working ten hours a day, six days a week, with the goal of producing forty reapers a day. Cyrus received dedicated service from his brother Leander who ran the factory and from brother William who took care of the financial side of the growing enterprise. The certainty that his brothers were work-

BORN FEBY 8, 1819.

Leander James McCormick was born in Virginia in 1819. Ten years younger than his brother Cyrus, he was placed in charge of production at the reaper plant. Leander came to resent his older brother and set out to show that their father, not brother Cyrus, was the inventor of the mechanical harvesting machine. Leander sold his share of the company for $3,250,000 and successfully invested in Chicago real estate (WHS Image ID 8389).

ing, year in and year out for his best interests, allowed Cyrus to be absent months on end as he traveled the country and the world in search of new markets and new accolades, and pursued his numerous lawsuits. By 1860, Leander and William developed a mowing machine. In 1870, Leander brought out "The Advance" reaper. With this improved model, production and sales increase to 10,000 machines annually.

Dedication to their older brother was less strong than dedication to their father. Feeling exploited, William and Leander demanded a better deal. Leander claimed that his innovations produced a better machine. He was especially proud of the raker's seat on which a man could sit to rake the grain off the platform and onto the ground. The commissioner of the U.S. Patent Office described the seat as "the crowning glory of the machine." Leander reckoned that his contribution and his inventions entitled him to a larger stake in the company. "As I have said to you," wrote Leander to Cyrus on July 1, 1859, "I have done not a little for the machine and I am resolved not to be satisfied without a pretty strong interest in the business." Though reluctant to yield control, Cyrus eventually agreed to increase their salaries to $5,000 each a year and give William and Leander one-quarter of the net profits. Five years later he increased their salaries to $6,000 each a year, but demanded the right of the company to use, free of charge, any and all the patents they held.

Henrietta's brother James Gilbreath Hamilton trained in the law and moved to Chicago. Their sister Rachel married the Reverend John W. Osborne and also moved to Chicago. In 1883, Leander and Henrietta's daughter Henrietta Laura married Frederick E. Goodhart and settled in England. Leander and Henrietta visited their daughter in England in 1884, 1889 and 1892.[19]

Tensions continued to grow between Cyrus and Leander over the invention and manufacture of the reaper. The passive William McCormick pleaded with his brothers to work amicably together. William's death in 1865 led to a change in the company's structure. Cyrus and Leander established C. H. McCormick and Brother, with Cyrus owning two-thirds, and Leander one-third of the company. They agreed to buy William's share of the business for $400,000 to his heirs.

Leander was the first of the McCormicks to settle on Rush Street. In 1863, Leander and family moved into 78 Rush Street at the northwest corner of Ohio and Rush streets, a yellow brick "handsome double house built of Milwaukee brick with gray stone trimmings.... Several large willow trees brought shade in summer to the grounds." On the night of the Great Fire of 1871, the family fled their home, losing nearly all their possessions. Three days later, Leander and his wife moved to 515 West Adams Street, and in 1875, settled in the Near North Side at 600 N. Rush Street, attached townhouses with a single front entrance shared with their son Robert and his family. The house was designed and built by the German-educated cousins Frederick and Edward Baumann at a cost of $30,000.[20]

The Italianate–style McCormick double house was completed after Chicago's city ordinance of 1874 requiring all construction to be of brick. Leander and Henrietta lived in their house until 1891, when they moved into the Virginia Hotel. The double-house became a single-family house for son Robert Hall McCormick, his wife Susan and their four daughters and son. It was "one of the most dignified and stately residences in Chicago." Robert's splendid private collection of English portraits and landscapes, by such estimable painters as Reynolds, Turner and Gainsborough, covered the walls of the house.[21] Robert lived there until his death in 1917 and Susan until she died in 1922, after which the house was sold to the surgical Publishing Company. In the 1960s, it became the site of Chez Paul's French restaurant.

Leander was determined to place his son Robert Hall McCormick in the harvester company. Leander warned Cyrus: "I cannot continue longer in business with you on such terms as you dispose to extract." Cyrus responded to his brother: "I can not permit you to come to my room to continue and perpetuate your calumnious and bullying abuse of 'an old scoundrel' and 'old scamp' as you have at different times termed me, while I told you that nothing your mouth could utter or fists gesticulate could induce me (at my age!) to foist myself by a personal encounter with you."[22] Much of the discord between Cyrus and Leander had to do with succession to leadership of the company. Cyrus was determined that his son, Cyrus, Jr., still a student, would succeed him. Leander insisted that his son Robert, twelve years older than Cyrus, Jr., should have a position equal to that of Cyrus's young son. The tension between Cyrus and Leander became so heated that they were unable to write to each other, let alone speak face-to-face. Mutual friends such as Henry Day (father-in-law to Robert Hall McCormick) were called upon to mediate. To bring Robert into the business, Leander agreed to sell a quarter of his share to Cyrus. Cyrus now owned ¾; Leander ³⁄₁₆ and Robert Hall ¹⁄₁₆. Leander's salary was raised to $7,000 and Robert Hall was given a salary of $2,000 a year.[23] Robert served under his father as the assistant superintendent of manufacturing. Robert demonstrated the McCormick harvester at the 1876 Centennial Exposition held in Philadelphia.

In July 1878, Cyrus left Chicago for yet another tour of Europe, remaining abroad for "nearly a year. He comes back loaded with honors conferred by different societies abroad where his reapers have astonished the natives and added to the glory of Chicago."[24] His reaper won the first prize in a competition held in Bristol. At the Paris Exposition, the McCormick reaper won the grand prize and a gold medal for "excellence in mechanical construction." In May 1879, The Academy of Sciences of the French Institute elected Cyrus a member for adding to the national prosperity. Cyrus responded that he was more touched than "by any previous honor of my life."[25] In Paris, Cyrus was also honored as a Chevalier of the Cross of the Legion of Honor.

J. CARBUTT.
PHOTOGRAPHER.

24 WASHINGTON ST.
CHICAGO.

Robert Hall McCormick, born in Virginia, was the eldest child of Leander James McCormick. He worked under his father as assistant superintendent of manufacturing. Known as R. Hall McCormick, he left the reaper company to assist his father in real estate transactions. He established a fine art collection of 17th and 18th century British landscapes and portraits (WHS Image ID 43123).

"Few Americans," gloated the *Tribune,* "have received so many honors abroad. Chicago is proud of Mr. McCormick." Cyrus's success inflamed the anger and jealousy of Leander, who felt burdened with the day-by-day responsibilities of running the factory, yet robbed of the glory. Determined to establish his own dynasty, Cyrus was not pleased with the rise of his nephew Robert Hall McCormick. By 1880, Cyrus decided he would be better off without his brother and nephew. Cyrus proposed to the board that: "the position of superintendant of the manufacturing department, occupied by L. J. McCormick, be declared vacant."[26] The company's board of directors censured Leander and Robert for dereliction of their duties and forced them from their management positions. The ailing Cyrus, now the sole authority of the reaper company, had the power to groom his young son, Cyrus Hall McCormick, Jr., to take over the company.[27]

Under Leander's management, the harvester company remained wedded to traditional methods of manufacture, relying on skilled metal workers and carpenters to fashion and assemble the parts. With Leander's ouster, Cyrus hired the New Englander Lewis Wilkinson as factory manager. Wilkinson had worked for the Colt Revolver Company and the Wilson Sewing Machine Company, using mass production methods. At the McCormick factory Wilkinson reduced skilled work and introduced machinery to boost efficiency and raise production to 50,000 reapers annually. The McCormick remained "the standard by which all harvesting machines are to be judged."[28] When Cyrus, Sr., died in 1884, his son Cyrus Hall McCormick took command: production reached 100,000 reapers a year.[29] Leander, still owning a quarter share in the company, threatened his nephew that he would release evidence to prove that Cyrus, Sr., was not the inventor of the mechanical reaper.

Henrietta Maria Hamilton McCormick made a list of the inventions and discoveries that occurred during her lifetime, making life easier and more interesting. Among these was chloroform, daguerreotype images, envelopes, postage stamps, electric lights, gas lighting, horse-pulled street-railroads, rubber shoes, ice-making, Lucifer matches, sewing machines, sleeping railroad cars, telegraphic messages, telephones, natural gas, and canned fruits, meats and vegetables.[30] In her seventies, Henrietta's health began to fail. She died November 26, 1899. The funeral service took place at Chicago's Fourth Presbyterian Church and she was buried at Graceland Cemetery.[31] Leander died February 20, 1900, at age 81 years, of pneumonia, three months after the death of his wife. For thirty years "he had devoted himself almost entirely to the development of the harvester industry.... At the time of his death he had no interest in the McCormick Harvesting Machine Company. Having sold his shares in the company in 1889 for $3,250,000 he became one of the largest owners of downtown real estate."[32] Leander James McCormick left an estate of $6 million; after paying all liabilities and expenses the value was reduced to $3,548,680. The money was left in a trust, expected to earn $300,000 a year. His oldest son, Robert Hall McCormick, was appointed trustee and administrator of the estate to earn a $15,000 a year for twenty years. In addition, each of Leander's children would receive $20,000 a year for twenty years, with any excess going back into the trust. After twenty years the estate would be divided equally between his three living children, Robert Hall McCormick, Henrietta Laura McCormick Goodhart and Leander Hamilton McCormick. Leander James McCormick wanted all his grandchildren "to become American citizens. [He] made his fortune in this country" and wanted it to stay in America.[33] For many years Leander McCormick's Virginia Hotel served as "a center of the fashionable life." With only one bathroom to a suite of four

The Ladies' Entrance on Rush Street, Leander James McCormick's Virginia Hotel, is shown in an 1893 brochure.

or five rooms, the hotel became outmoded. In 1932, the Virginia Hotel was torn down and the space became a parking lot.[34]

After the death of the founding brothers, Cyrus's line took control of the company. None of the descendants of Leander James McCormick entered the farm equipment business. Brooks McCormick, a descendant of William Sanderson McCormick, joined International Harvester in 1940 and served from 1971 to 1980 as its chief executive officer.

Chapter Four

The Rivals
William Deering and Sons

Roger Deering left England in 1663 and settled in Kittery, Maine. Over the generations, the Deerings worked as shipbuilders, fishermen, and farmers. James Deering came to the village of South Paris, Maine, and served as an apprentice to a furniture maker. In 1824, he married Eliza Moore. Their son William was born on April 25, 1826. William was a "very quiet, reserved and industrious boy." At age nineteen years William wrote to a friend: "One ought always to be a learner, a student. Book knowledge brings opportunities."[1] William hoped to study medicine under the tutelage of Dr. Barrows of Fryeburg, Maine. Instead, he went to work as a clerk for his father at the South Paris Manufacturing Company, a woolen textile mill. "No son of South Paris has been more successful in business."[2] In his early 20s, William followed the Yankee migration to the West to buy farmland near Plano, Illinois. After two years he returned to Maine, opened a dry goods store and married Abby Reed Barbour. Their son Charles was born in 1852. Four years later, Abby died and soon after, William married her cousin Clara Hamilton, who bore two children, James and Abby Marion. During the Civil War, William made his first fortune selling woolen uniforms for the use of the Union Army. In 1865, he formed Deering, Milliken & Company with Seth Milliken, also from Maine. For many years (even without William Deering), Deering, Milliken & Company was a successful textile enterprise.

William Deering was one of the hundreds of thousands of New Englanders who left their native soil to settle in the Midwest. Marshall Field opened department stores, William Walter Kimball built a vast piano and organ factory, Gustavus Franklin Swift was one of Chicago's leading butchers, Walter Loomis Newberry funded the Newberry Library, Stephen Arnold Douglas entered politics, George Pullman built railroad cars, Orrington Lunt established Northwestern University and Charles Lawrence Hutchinson envisioned the Art Institute.[3] In 1870, William Deering moved his family to Illinois to invest $40,000 in a partnership with the Methodist preacher-turned-salesman Elijah Gammon, to sell the horse-drawn grain harvester developed by William Marsh and his brother Charles, of Sycamore, Illinois. The Marsh harvester, patented in 1858, had a "cutting apparatus adapted to the rise and fall on passing over the ground." The Marsh machine "cut and elevated the grain to two men who rode on the machine and bound the grain into bundles, which they threw to the ground, where it was piled into shocks." In 1872, the commissioner of patents declared: "The Marsh machine was the first really successful machine put into the field on which the grain was bound on the machine; the difference between the Marsh machine and its predecessors is the difference between failure and success." At the DeKalb County

Reaper Competition of 1863, the Marsh was judged the best reaper and hand binder.[4] The Marsh harvester was first shown abroad at the exposition in Vienna of 1873. William Deering was "neither an inventor nor a mechanic" but his money and business savvy allowed the Marsh brothers to continue to develop their reaper.[5] In 1875, Deering and Gammon bought control of the Marsh Harvester Company, manufacturers of the Warrior harvester. Now labeled the Deering harvester, it cut and bound an acre of grain in fifty-five minutes. In 1875, Gammon and Deering made 6,000 harvesters to McCormick's 5,000.

Around 1880, an automatic twine binder invented by John Appleby of Beloit, Wisconsin, replaced the two-man team of hand binders on the Deering machine. The binder's "strong steel arms could flash a cord around a bundle of grain, tie a knot, cut the cord, and fling off the sheaf."[6] Now, the farmer by himself, leading his horses, could get the job done. Deering procured the strong binder twine from the cordage company of Edwin H. Fitler of Philadelphia. By reducing labor costs, the automatic twine binder greatly increased sales of the Deering harvester.[7]

William Deering at age 76. Deering was born in South Paris, Maine. In 1870 he formed a partnership with Elijah Gammon to sell the horse-drawn harvesting machine invented by the brothers William and Charles Marsh (WHS Image ID 24794).

Adding the Appleby twine binder to his harvester was "a daring stoke that won the greatest success of his business career." Knowing little about farm machinery, Deering had to learn the ins and outs of the business. He had "a genius for business administration." Under the guidance of Deering and Gammon, the Marsh Harvester, built in Plano, Illinois, rose to be a serious competitor of the McCormick Harvester. In 1879, Gammon retired with a fortune of $1 million.

In 1860, one hundred Marsh harvesters were built in the Plano factory. A decade later production reached 1,200 machines. In 1879, the Plano Marsh Harvester Company employed 600 men and made 10,000 machines. Yet the company "has been unable to satisfy the market," and had to move to larger quarters.[8] With his automatic binder, William Deering "swept away competitors like chaff." William Deering, settled in Evanston, Illinois, was now the sole owner of the harvester company. In 1880, "in search of better facilities of manufacture and transportation," he moved his Deering Harvester Company to Chicago to occupy a giant plant on 85 acres at Clybourn and Fullerton avenues, on the north branch of the Chicago River. The plant contained a manufacturing hall, a foundry and a smith shop, holding "the latest and most improved machinery." An 800-horsepower Corliss steam engine gave power to the plant, with 1,000 men making 1,300 harvesters a day. William Deering built a company town next to his factory, with cottages and boarding houses, stores and churches for his workers.[9] At a time when the demand for harvesters was rising fast, the Deering harvester had "attained a reputation for excellence that is unequalled by any

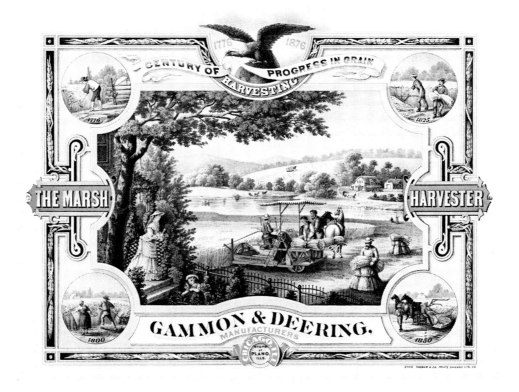

An advertising poster produced in 1876 for Gammon & Deering Manufacturers, makers of the Marsh Harvester, shows progress in agriculture since the American declaration of independence in 1776 (WHS Image ID 4280).

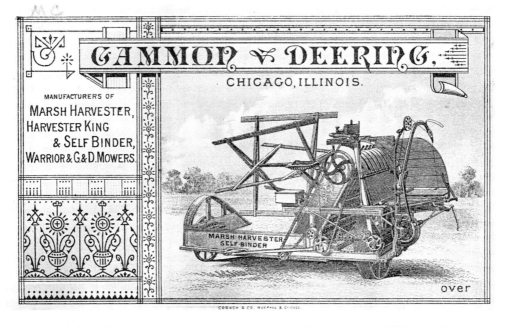

A trade card shows the Gammon & Deering harvesting machine ca. 1876 (WHS Image ID 108221).

In 1880 William Deering, now the sole owner, built his harvester factory at the corner of Fullerton and Clybourn avenues, Chicago. In 1902 William Deering & Company merged into the International Harvester Company (WHS Image ID 6756).

other machine of the same class." McCormick was aware that "the Marsh-Deering machine is fast becoming the most popular machine in the market."[10] The attempt by McCormick and his lawyers to beat down Deering by alleging patent infringement was no longer effective. Deering now had the technological edge over the aging McCormick.

Deering paid his unskilled laborers $1.50, with skilled workers earning $2.50 for a ten-hour day, six days a week. In 1886, his workforce went out on strike, demanding an 8-hour workday and an increase of 20 percent in their pay. Deering offered a 10 percent increase but compromised at 15 percent to avoid the brutal and protracted strikes that plagued the McCormick and Pullman companies.[11]

In the 1890s, William Deering purchased woodlands in Pemiscot County, Missouri, where he established his Wisconsin Lumber Company to process lumber for his harvester factory. The town of Deering, Missouri is named in his honor. In 1893, the Deering harvester was on display in the Hall of Industry at the Chicago World's Columbian Exposition. Deering exhibited his reaper at the 1900 Paris Exposition, winning the grand prize and two gold medals. The French government honored Deering as an Officer of the Legion of Honor.

Like McCormick, William Deering was enmeshed in legal battles over patent rights. Deering Harvester grew to employ 9,000 people with sixty branch offices around the nation and in countries abroad. He had a "passionate love of progress," and encouraged his engi-

An 1895 trade card of the Deering Harvesting Machine Company proudly shows its Chicago-built harvesting machine, with rival companies Buckeye, Plano, Champion, McCormick, Wood, Osborne leaning forward for a closer look (private collection).

This advertising poster shows the arrival at the 1893 World's Columbian Exposition in Chicago of Deering's horse-drawn grain harvester and mower. Across the pond is the Machinery Building, designed by the Boston architectural firm of Peabody & Stearns. Steam engines of various types dominated the exhibits in the Machinery Building (WHS Image ID 41559).

neers to develop a fuel-powered harvester to replace horses, further putting pressure on the McCormick Company. From a modest start in 1871, William Deering had in thirty years built a harvester company larger than McCormick Harvester. It was "one of the great industrial concerns of the nation."[12] In 1901, William fell ill. "My recovery," he said, "was deemed uncertain." Aged 75 years, he placed his business in the hands of his sons Charles and James and his son-in-law Richard F. Howe (married to Abby Marion Deering), while he spent the winters at Coconut Grove, Florida.

In 1902, with its founder aging and ill, Deering Harvester merged with McCormick Harvester Machine Company and three smaller reaper firms to form the International Harvester Company, a virtual monopoly. Orchestrated by the House of J. P. Morgan, the reaper trust gave McCormick 42.6 percent and Deering 34.4 percent of the shares in International Harvester Company. Morgan capitalized the company at $120 million, greatly adding to the wealth of the McCormick and Deering families. In 1905, International Harvester came out with the tractor-powered harvester.[13]

In 1910, James Deering was asked to list the outstanding features of "the character and life" of his father, William Deering. Above all, wrote James, "was his intuitive good judgment.... I once asked him how he succeeded in looking so far into the future, and he replied that often he could not himself tell, and often he had been surprised to see events work out so exactly as he had foreseen them." William's "youth desire was to be a doctor." James was convinced that William could have found "success in any career he might have chose," whether a lawyer, a businessman or a banker "and in all, his success would have been equal." William Deering had a "passionate love of progress. In his business of manufacturing harvesting machinery the very latest was not too new." William's "capacity for work, and for physical and mental concentration ... were always a wonder to me. He loved the activity— the doing." William's "capacity for self-denial was great." If he had work to do, he turned down social invitations and denied himself vacations. William Deering was scrupulously honest and tried to make sure his customers were satisfied with the machines they bought from him. William Deering "was born of a long line of Puritan ancestry." He practiced self-reliance, yet was tender to the sufferings of others. "He expected every man to do his best and judged his employees by their successes." He loved nature and animals. He treated the janitor and the office boy with patience and respect. Despite his great success, William Deering remained modest and caring.[14]

William Deering was president of the board of trustees of Northwestern University, serving with fellow Maine-born Orrington Lunt and the Rev. Elijah Gammon. Deering gave his time and money to various charities, and was a devoted member of the Methodist Episcopal Church in Evanston. He was a major supporter of the Garrett Biblical Institute of Evanston and the Wesley Hospital of Chicago. William Deering died 1913 at age 87 years. He was eulogized for his Yankee qualities of simplicity, kindness, integrity and a single-minded determination to succeed. Chauncey Brooks McCormick sent a telegraph to Charles and James Deering expressing his "deepest sympathy. Your father's life and influence constitute one of the greatest of examples of successful achievement, which our country affords to all."[15] During his lifetime, William Deering gave $1 million to Northwestern University, and ensured his wife was amply provided for. He left an estate of $12,000,000. His sons Charles and James each received $5 million and his son-in-law Richard F. Howe received $150,000, with additional bequests to his grandchildren.[16]

Charles Deering was born in 1852 in South Paris, Maine. The death of his mother, Abby Deering, and the arrival a year later of his stepmother, were emotional blows to the five-year-old boy. "I hope you are a good boy," wrote William Deering to young Charles. "Give your stepmother as little trouble as you can…. Kindness begets kindness, and if you are good and kind, others will be so to you…. I want you to write to me often. It will be good practice for you in writing and composing your letters…. Charlie, I want you to attend school. All the boys have to attend school, and study hard. [Prepare yourself] to take a very high standard among your fellows in the world."[17] "Try very hard Charlie, to control the state of your temper always," pleaded his father. "It will make you very unhappy to get angry with anyone, and because it is wrong. Try all you can to overcome a hasty temper, and always be pleasant."[18]

Charles Deering was eight years old when the Civil War began. He was so thrilled by the actions of the Union Navy that he was determined to have a naval career. "His father did not approve of this plan, but decided it would be unwise to deny his son to carry out his most cherished ambition."[19] At age sixteen, Charles entered the U.S. Naval Academy at Annapolis as a midshipman. There, he learned discipline and developed a deep sense of duty. His best friend at the Academy was William Henry Schuetze. Bright and motivated, Charles and William competed for the top places in their class. In 1873, William Schuetze graduated first, and Charles second, in their class. Charles served on the flagship of the European Fleet, as well as serving in the Far East. In 1875, he married Anna Rogers Case, daughter of Rear Admiral Augustus Ludlow Case, of Newport, Rhode Island. Anna died the following year, age 27 years, of sepsis, soon after giving birth to Charles William Case Deering (1876–1924). From 1877 to 1879, Lieutenant Charles Deering served onboard the USS *Kearsarge*. (Built 1861, in Kittery, Maine, *Kearsarge* defeated the Confederate raider CSS *Alabama* during the Civil War in 1864.) Lieutenant Deering met Ulysses S. Grant in 1878 during the former president's grand tour that took him to Europe, the Middle East and to the Far East. Impressed by the charm and erudition of the 26-year-old Deering, Grant invited him to accompany the presidential party on a tour of China, including a visit with the boy emperor in the Forbidden City.[20]

After resigning his naval commis-

Charles Deering (1852–1927) was a naval officer until 1881 when he joined his father's reaper company. In 1902 he negotiated the merger of the Deering Company into the International Harvester Company. Charles Deering amassed a vast art collection, specializing in Spanish art. Picture ca. 1920 (courtesy Northwestern University Archives).

sion on May 1, 1881, Charles came to Chicago to serve as secretary of the Deering Harvester Company, 1881–1900. In 1883, Charles married Marion Denison Whipple, of Norristown, Pennsylvania, daughter of major general William Denison Whipple, who served as chief of staff, Army of the Cumberland, during the Civil War, when he also served on the staff of generals Sheridan and Sherman. In 1888, John Singer Sargent painted Marion's portrait.[21] In 1893, Charles and his wife went to Paris where he studied painting, but after a few months he had to return to his business duties at the Deering Company. In December 1900 came the announcement: "William Deering has retired from the Deering Harvester Company." William transferred to his sons the ownership of the properties on Clybourn Avenue, Diversey Avenue, Fullerton Avenue and Snow Street. Charles Deering, former naval officer and aspiring artist, was now the senior partner of one of America's largest industrial concerns, making 1,300 completed harvesters a day. Two years later, Charles merged his company into the International Harvester Company, and served as chairman of the board of directors. Charles Deering was "one of the leading men in the farm manufacturing industry."[22] In 1902, Charles's chauffeur was one of seven arrested by the Evanston police for exceeding the speed limit of 12 miles per hour on Forest Avenue. The chauffeur appeared in court with an attorney who paid the $5 fine.[23]

Charles Deering branched out into real estate and banking to become a leading incorporator of the Central Trust Company of Illinois. "No Chicago bank previous to this one has started with so large a capital."[24] Charles Deering served as chairman of the board of International Harvester from 1902 until his retirement in 1910. In 1917, Charles Deering formed a corporation to invest the family's assets. It was named the Miami Corporation in homage to the Deering family's love of Miami. The Deering money was invested in land in Illinois, Oregon, Louisiana and Florida for grazing, timber, oil and gas. Charles Deering died on February 5, 1927, at his Florida home. He was buried in the Graceland Cemetery, Chicago.

His wife, Marion Whipple Deering, gifted the Charles Deering Library to Northwestern University. Three generations of the Deering family were present at the opening ceremony of the library on January 12, 1932: Marion Deering, wife of Charles; her daughter Mrs. Marion Deering McCormick; and 12-year-old grandson Roger Deering who had the honor of laying the corner stone. In all, the Deering family gifted $10,300,000 to Northwestern University. Marion Whipple Deering died age 86 years in Florida on November 30, 1943.[25]

Anna Case Deering (Charles Deering's first wife) died soon after the birth of her son, Charles William Case Deering, in 1876 in Newport, Rhode Island. Charles, Jr., was raised by his father and stepmother in Evanston, Illinois. In 1913, Charles, Jr., received $975,815 from his grandfather's estate. He was a good athlete and noted for his horsemanship and golf skills. It was on the links that his romance with Mary Wentworth Bartlett began. Soon after their marriage, young Charles arranged a hunting party determined "to bag specimens of all the noted game in Colorado." In September 1899, Charles and Mary, accompanied by eight guests, guides, many horses and mules, wagons and equipment set out to hunt (at a cost of $4,000). The party was caught in a snowstorm but managed to make its way to Sullivan's Ranch to find food and shelter. "Otherwise they might have perished."[26] Charles and Mary moved to Honolulu. During World War I Charles served as adjutant of the army in Hawaii.

In 1919, Mary Bartlett Deering's father died, leaving an estate worth $3.5 million, with Mary getting only $1,500 a year. Insulted by so small an inheritance, Mary sued her brothers for a larger share of the estate.[27] After their marriage failed, Charles left Honolulu and moved to San Francisco to lead the high life. In 1923, he briefly married Helen Moyer. That year he was a defendant in a $50,000 breach of promise suit by Margueritte Curl, who was an exceedingly attractive young woman. "Charles has made fools of enough women," Margueritte Curl said grimly, "It's time somebody taught him a lesson." The case was settled out of court for $10,000. A month later, Charles, at age 48 years, was badly injured when his plane "Petral" nosedived to the ground at Crissy Field, near San Francisco. A few months after the accident he was found dead. The police established that he had committed suicide by an overdose of the barbiturate drug Veronal. "Three empty vials containing a Veronal solution were found in Deering's room."[28] Mary Bartlett Deering remained in Honolulu, where she died in November 15, 1926, following an operation on her tonsils.[29]

Charles and Marion Whipple Deering had three children: daughters Marion and Barbara, and son Roger. Around 1910, uncle James Deering took his nieces, "the famous Deering twins" (though they looked and dressed alike, Marion was fifteen months older than sister Barbara) on a tour around the world. In India, one maharaja was so taken with Marion that he asked to marry her. Instead, Marion married Chauncey Brooks McCormick, joining Chicago's two harvester dynasties. Barbara married Richard Ely Danielson. From 1924 to 1928, Danielson, with Christian A. Herter, was the publisher of the *Boston Independent* newspaper. (Later, Herter served as the 59th governor of Massachusetts and was secretary of state under president Dwight Eisenhower). Richard Danielson served later as editor of the *Atlantic Monthly* magazine. He died in 1957. Barbara lived in Groton, Massachusetts and was a trustee of the Boston Museum of Fine Arts and the Perkins School for the Blind. In her younger years she was an enthusiastic member of the Groton Hunt Club. Later she settled in Florida where she died on November 21, 1982, at age 93 years. Barbara Deering Danielson gifted money and works of art to the Art Institute of Chicago. Roger Deering (1884–1934), son of Charles and Marion Deering, grew up in Evanston, close to Northwestern University. He inherited $5 million from his father, and added $6 million with the sale of 212 acres of land in Miami. Disabled from his youth, he did not go to college but spent years living in sanatoria in California and New Mexico, in the hope of improving his health. Roger died on February 2, 1936, in Albuquerque, New Mexico, at age 52 years, probably of tuberculosis. Roger left an estate of $9,490,186, of which $8,757,317 went to Northwestern University.[30] The bequest, worth twice the university's annual income at the time, was opportune. During the Great Depression, Northwestern had severely reduced its faculty and the number of courses offered. Because the Roger Deering bequest was unrestricted, the university used the money to boost its educational offerings, especially in the social sciences.

James Deering, half brother of Charles, was born in South Paris, Maine on November 12, 1859. Seven years younger than Charles, he moved with his parents to Evanston. James attended Northwestern University, then studied at the Massachusetts Institute of Technology. Not graduating from college, at age 21 he responded to his father's wish by going to work at Deering Harvester Company. An avid francophone, James Deering hosted Jules Cambon, the French ambassador to the United States. "So young and yet so great," opined the ambassador of Chicago, after touring Lake Shore Drive, the Chicago Athletic Association and the Board of Trade. James Deering was vice president of the board of the International Harvester Company until 1919. Already wealthy from his stake in International Harvester, in 1913, James inherited a further $5 million from his father's estate. James largely withdrew from the management of the reaper company to indulge his passions in architecture, art and travel. In 1912, James organized a three-week trip in Egypt accompanied by his beloved brother Charles and brother-in-law Richard F. Howe. Taking his watercolors, brushes and paper with him, Charles amused himself by painting scenes of the trip. One painting, set in ancient Egypt, shows Deering introducing the mechanical reaper to the Pharaoh.

James Deering was an immaculate and elegant gentleman. He was "always perfectly groomed and a patron of art and French classics. In fact, he adopted anything and everything French.... His salon was Louis XIV, his bedchamber Louis XVI, his bath and embroidered tent ala Louis XVI and his sleeping couch a copy of Napoleon's from the Petit Trianon," wrote his private secretary. "The greatest talent and genius of the day had been commissioned to bring to reality on the beautiful shores of Biscayne Bay the atmosphere of the Old World, culture and art."[31] In 1914, in collaboration with his partner Paul Chalfin, Deering began the construction of Villa Vizcaya on Key Biscayne, Florida, at a final cost of $10 million. Ill with pernicious anemia, he lived July to October at his home in Paris, and November in his apartment at 9 West 52nd Street, New York. For good measure he kept his Chicago connection with a home at 1436 Lake Shore Drive. From December to May he was in Florida in his sumptuous Italian Renaissance style mansion. Modeled after the 18th century Villa Rezzonico in Italy, the 72-room Villa Vizcaya was "one of the finest residences in America" filled with rare art and furniture brought over from Europe. James Deering was a fluent conversationalist in English, Spanish, French and Italian.

James's day began at 10 o'clock in the morning when his secretary presented the mail, sorted out into five categories: business, social, love, foreign and other. He received many love letters and offers of marriage. Requests for money came as low as $10 and as high as $100,000. Nearly all these letters were answered with a firm "no." James was regularly visited by architects, artists, faded dowagers, aspiring actresses, golf professionals and others eager to take part in his entertainments and get a look at his money. This was the Jazz Age and the fastidious James Deering used his harvester money to live life in its grandest form. His sumptuous parties began on Wednesdays and lasted a week, with fifty guests arriving by private car, plane, rail, or by yacht. Despite Prohibition, the cellars of the villa were stocked with "five hundred thousand dollar shipments of rare brandies, wine, liquors, and cordials, all labeled and stored away in rows upon rows." Formal dinners were followed by "the latest foreign and American films.... Girlfriends, who had been resting since eleven P.M. would reappear and now was the proper time for merrymaking in the swimming pool and billiard room." During the daytime, guests enjoyed

James Deering (1859–1925) was the half-brother of Charles Deering. Picture taken in 1900. After leaving the harvesting business, James Deering built Villa Vizcaya on Biscayne Bay, Florida (WHS Image ID 60636).

Charles Deering was a gifted amateur artist and counted John Singer Sargent among his friends. While on a trip along the Nile River in 1912, Charles amused himself by imagining the coming of the mechanical reaper to ancient Egypt (courtesy Vizcaya Museum and Gardens Archives, Miami, Florida).

fishing and cruising on the yachts. Villa Vizcaya hosted celebrities such as the film stars Lillian Gish and Marion Davies, the inventor Thomas Edison and president Warren G. Harding. "America's foremost tennis and golf professionals were engaged for those enjoying these sports."[32] James Deering kept his yachts *Psyche* and *Nepenthe* handy for the pleasure of his guests. The nearby village housed the staff, including chauffeurs, butlers, a French chef, pastry chef, maids, cleaners, a vegetable and fruit garden and staff to maintain the grounds in pristine condition. The milk came from the village cows, and eggs from the village chickens. For his amusement, James had a collection of monkeys and rare birds.

In September 1925, James Deering was in Paris. As his health failed, the glitter of the high life dimmed and James accepted fewer invitations to dinners and parties. He decided to return to America. Accompanied by two trained nurses, his valet and his secretary, he boarded the train for Havre and took a berth on the S.S. *City of Paris* sailing for America. Attended by the ship's doctor, James Deering died of the complications of pernicious anemia, off the coast of Newfoundland, aged 65 years.[33] James's body was brought to Chicago for burial in the Graceland cemetery.

Chapter Five

The Heir

Cyrus Hall McCormick, Jr.

Born May 16, 1859, in Washington D.C, where his father was attending to business matters, Cyrus Hall McCormick, Jr., was the first child of Cyrus, Sr., and Nettie McCormick. Cyrus, Jr., was bright, attentive and obedient; his delighted father hailed him as the "Young Reaper." Cyrus, Jr., attended Brown grammar school in Chicago followed by Central High School, walking two miles each way between home and school. Cyrus, Jr., received excellent grades in Latin, spelling, scholarship, attendance and deportment.[1] As school valedictorian in a class of 51 boys, his mother wanted him to go on to Princeton College, the nation's leading Presbyterian college. During the summer of 1877, young Cyrus traveled abroad in the company of several Presbyterian ministers. His father took the opportunity to entrust his son with several business errands "which the youngster executed to his parents' great satisfaction." On September 10, two days before the start of college, Cyrus, Sr., "brought up all manner of objections to his going and placed every obstacle in the way" claiming that his son "had enough education to do business"—more than his father ever had, and college would "effeminate" him. Cyrus, Sr., said: "It was not proper that Cyrus Jr. to live the life of ease, while his father did all the work." Nettie argued that four years of college would give her son the "disciplined mind" necessary for business and for life. To break the impasse, the parents consulted the Scottish-born president of Princeton, James W. McCosh, who supported Nettie's position. Eventually Cyrus, Sr., gave in. "Very well, he may go," but insisted that Cyrus, Jr., complete his education as soon as possible. Princeton arranged for Cyrus, Jr., to take a specially designed accelerated course with a heavy study load.[2]

Nettie complained: "The habits of business ... leave little room for any family life." Cyrus Junior's classmates at Princeton included Woodrow Wilson, the future president of the United States, the physicist William F. Magie, a future associate justice of the United States Supreme Court Mahlon Pitney, Charles A. Talcott, U.S. House of Representatives, the editor and writer Robert Bridges, the industrialist Cleveland Hoadley Dodge, as well as those who became ministers, missionaries, doctors, lawyers and politicians.

Cyrus Hall McCormick, Sr., allowed his son only two years of study at Princeton before Cyrus, Jr., entered the company as superintendent of works and his father's "confidential secretary and representative." In 1880, while traveling abroad, Cyrus, Sr., became so ill that "the responsibility for business decisions rested with Mrs. [Nettie] McCormick, aided by a team of lawyers, including Judah P. Benjamin, who was a member of the Confederate cabinet during the Civil War, and now a prominent London lawyer. 'Papa is very dependent now on the will of others,'" wrote Nettie in her diary, "and looks to me to make the decisions and then execute them.... He cannot now be looked to for any independent action."[3] With his brother ill, Leander McCormick pushed for a larger share of the company. Returning to Chicago, Cyrus was "still not able again to carry out the full load of his responsibilities." Yet his ambition remained high and he talked about putting in his name for vice president of the United States. Nettie wanted him to be content with his new home, and warned him that the politicians only "want your money and will give you nothing." During the last years of his life, Cyrus visited mineral spas in Arkansas hoping for relief from his arthritis. "His work was more difficult and he did less of it, entrusting more responsibility to his wife and son."[4]

After his father's death on May 13, 1884, Cyrus H. McCormick, Jr., "a young man of twenty-five ... was chosen president of the McCormick Harvesting Machine Company. [He] found it no easy task to step into the place of one of the nation's leading industrialists."[5] Cyrus was "a serious, dependable young man, already well-trained ... and with a natural interest in the business as his destiny." With competition increasing in the reaper business, concerns over lawsuits, patents and production, and dealing with the ambitions of his uncle Leander, young Cyrus leaned heavily on the guidance and determination of his mother to establish his authority over the McCormick Reaper Company.[6]

Cyrus Hall McCormick, Jr., was 25 years old when he became president of the McCormick Harvester Company. He guided the company through the worker strikes that led to the Haymarket Massacre of 1886. In 1902 he helped arrange the merger of the McCormick Company into the International Harvester Company, and led the Harvester Trust from horsepower to gasoline motor power (Library of Congress).

McCormick and the Haymarket Massacre

The Chicago of the father was very different from the Chicago of the son. When Cyrus, Sr., started his reaper company, the city of Chicago had fewer than 30,000 residents. By 1884 the city's population approached three-quarters of a million people, many of them impoverished immigrants from Europe, desperately seeking employment in Chicago's factories. The German language *Arbeiter Zeitung* denounced Cyrus Hall McCormick, Sr., "for the low wages that he paid his employees, and claimed that the $12,000,000 that he left was the result of the systematic robbery of his workmen, who were mere slaves." These comments evoked a counter response from many McCormick workers who were grateful for their jobs that allowed them to buy homes and save for their retirement years.[7] The mood of the McCormick workers changed when the young Cyrus Hall McCormick introduced power machinery. In December 1884, the nettlesome National Union of Iron Molders went on strike for more money and shorter hours of work. To demonstrate his authority, young McCormick fired the skilled molders and installed the pneumatic molding machines to do the work, using common laborers to guide the machines. With the workers on strike, McCormick hired the Pinkerton detective company to guard the works on Blue Hill Avenue. On April 9, 1895, angry strikers surrounded a bus carrying Chicago policemen and Pinkerton guards armed with Winchester rifles. Someone threw a brick at the bus. The guards responded by firing on the strikers, wounding one of them. The strikers unhitched the horses, causing the Pinkerton guards to flee, leaving their weapons behind. The enraged strikers set fire to the bus.[8]

Elsewhere in Chicago, the Knights of Labor gained strength with demands of "eight for ten"—an eight-hour workday, five days a week, coupled with the pay for ten hours of work. On February 16, 1886, representatives of the Knights, together with the Molders Union and the Metal Workers, came to see young Cyrus McCormick to demand higher pay, shorter hours, the rehiring of the molders, and the firing of non-union workers. They demanded only union men be employed at the works. The unions were determined to remove the machinery that replaced workers.

"Mr. McCormick declared firmly that the company had always and always would decide who were best suited to do its work, and whom and how many men it would employ

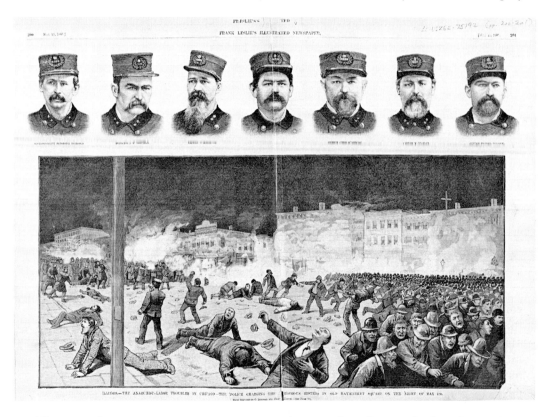

The Haymarket Massacre: On May 4, 1886, seven Chicago police officers and at least four civilians were killed during a labor dispute involving the McCormick Company. Seven men were sentenced to death by hanging. Four were hanged, one committed suicide and the two others were later freed. The Haymarket Massacre was a seminal event in American labor history (Library of Congress).

or discharge…. For thirty years it has been the practice of the McCormick Reaper Works to employ any suitable workmen irrespective of color or nationality," whether or not they belonged to a union. Threatened with a strike, McCormick shut down the factory "for an indefinite period." Young Cyrus continued his father's autocratic policies. He was certain that "the great bulk of the men in the McCormick Company's factory were utterly opposed to the idea of a strike [and that] the agitation was caused by outside malcontents." The new molding machines, even in the hands of "ordinary laborers … turn out daily far more molds and more reliable work than that provided by the old hand method," permitting the company to shed workers and reduce its payroll well below the current $3,000 a day. Cyrus agreed to raise the pay to $1.50 a day, "higher than in any other factory in the country." He announced that the laid-off workers could collect their wages, expecting that his move would bring the men back to work on his terms.[9]

On the morning of February 17, 1886, hundreds of men gathered at the gates of the factory hoping to collect their pay and believing the company "cold not afford to keep closed for very long." But the lockout continued and tempers flared. On February 25, idle workers threatened a factory foreman. Guns were drawn and shots fired into the air. One thousand men signed a petition asking the company to restart production. Others refused to return until all union demands were met. McCormick blamed "outside agitators" for causing the trouble.[10] Negotiations between the unions and management broke down on March 4 when Cyrus H. McCormick announced: "I don't want to see any committees or propositions whatsoever. If any of them want to return to work they can come over, and if their places are not filled, I will give them employment. But you must understand. There are some I wouldn't employ under any circumstances whatsoever."[11] The strikers gathered outside the factory yelling "scabs, scabs, scabs" at the strikebreakers and the replacement workers entering the factory to work. The police arrested a number of demonstrators for carrying weapons. On the way home after work, a number of workers were beaten. By March 5, eight hundred men, old hands and replacement workers, were at work; the rest threatened to "fight to the end."[12] The Knights of Labor raised the stakes by declaring a boycott on the McCormick factory and businesses. "If he owns a building tenanted by a grocer, that grocer will be boycotted unless he moves out at once." The union swore to go after McCormick "for all it is worth and will use every means to down him."[13]

Driven by drink, desperation and hunger, on May 3 "a howling mob" of ten thousand gathered. A union spokesman atop a freight car harangued the vast crowd to "blow up the factory…. Strike for your freedom…. Revolution is the only remedy…. Arm yourselves." Around 2 o' clock in the afternoon, the mob made its way toward the McCormick factory. The demonstrators threw rocks at the police, shouting "Kill the police…. Hang them." "There was a very bitter and virulent spirit manifest on the part of the malcontents towards the police." The police retaliated by firing volleys "to scare but not to kill," followed by charges with "the police striking at heads with clubs or pistols." There was an "incessant discharge of firearms." Police reinforcements were pelted with stones. The First Cavalry regiment left barracks on Michigan Avenue and arrived at the factory. A Gatling gun with ammunition was set up to confront the crowd. In the bitter battle outside the gates of the McCormick Reaper Works, six demonstrators were killed. That evening, handbills were passed around calling for "Revenge…. Your masters have called out their bloodhounds— the police. They have killed six of your brothers because they, like you, had the courage to disobey the extreme will of your bosses." The factory owners seek to enslave you "to satisfy their insatiable greed [and] fill their coffers.... Destruction to the human monsters that call themselves your masters."[14] Incendiary handbills were circulated "calling on working-men to revenge the deaths of their brothers at McCormick's factory."[15] The climax came the following day, Tuesday, May 4, at a mass meeting at the Haymarket on Randolph Street, between Halstead and Deplaines "to denounce the latest atrocious acts of the police, the shooting of our fellow-workmen."

Fifteen hundred people showed up at the Haymarket "but a shower dispersed all but 600." August Spies, a German-born upholsterer and union activist, addressed the crowd on "The Riot at McCormick's." Spies said: "For more than twenty years have the wage earners of this country begged and prayed their masters, the factory lords, to reduce their burdens. Cyrus H. McCormick claimed: Spies was responsible for the massacre committed by the most noble Chicago police. I reply to this that McCormick is an infamous liar. (Cries of 'Hang him.') There will be a time, and we are rapidly approaching it, when men such as McCormick will be hanged."[16] The police arrived and commanded the people to disperse. "Marching abreast the breadth of Deplaines Street," the police approached the angry crowd. Someone threw a bomb and in seconds "the ground was strewn with wounded men." Guns were drawn on both sides and hundreds of bullets fired. The police responded by shooting into the crowd.[17] Seven policemen died and sixty were wounded in what became known as the Haymarket Massacre. At least four demonstrators were killed and many injured. In the following hours and days, the police reaction against the unions and their followers was brutal, with many raids and arrests. Seven men charged with conspiracy were found guilty in a trial that ended August 11. Six were sentenced to be hanged, and one to fifteen years in prison. One of those sentenced to die committed suicide. The death sentence of two men was changed to life imprisonment (later to be pardoned by governor John Peter Altgeld). On November 11, 1887, August Spies and three other men were hanged.

In 1889, Cyrus Hall McCormick, Jr., married Harriet Bradley Hammond. Her ancestors arrived in the New World in 1624 and settled in Salem, Massachusetts. Harriet was born in England and grew up in Haverhill, Massachusetts. At age 12, her father, a ship's captain, died and Harriet moved to Chicago, where she was adopted by her aunt, Elizabeth Hammond Stickney, married to Edward E. Stickney, one of Chicago's leading bankers. Edward Stickney, from an old Yankee family, came to Chicago in 1855 and made his fortune. The Stickney home, close by the McCormick mansion, was a "center of culture" in the rough-and-ready Chicago. Edward accumulated an outstanding collection of works of art (later bequeathed to the Art Institute), as well as first and rare editions of books. Harriet was educated at Miss Kirkland's School for Girls, followed by a two-year tour of Europe.[18] Harriet and her aunt traveled a good deal, spending the winters in Florida and a month in New York during the fall. On March 5, 1889, at age twenty-seven years, Harriet Hammond married Cyrus Hall McCormick, Jr., president of the McCormick Reaper Works. The ceremony was held in the charming St. Mary's-by-the-Sea in Monterey, California. The bride wore the pearl necklace given to her by Cyrus, and a pendant of pearls and diamonds given to her by her aunt, Mrs. Elizabeth Stickney. After the ceremony, the couple journeyed to San Francisco and on to Honolulu for their honeymoon. Returning to Chicago, Cyrus and Harriet lived at 50 E. Huron Street. The house was a wedding gift from Elizabeth Stickney. Cyrus spent $200,000, a fortune at the time, refurbishing the house. As befitting one of

Chicago's wealthiest young couples, Cyrus and Harriet also owned a summerhouse, "Walden" (named for Henry David Thoreau's Walden Pond) on 100 acres at Lake Forest. Marital bliss was followed by motherhood, joy and sadness. The couple had three children: Cyrus III born in 1890; Elizabeth in 1892; and Gordon in 1894.

Cyrus Hall McCormick attended the 1889 Exposition Universelle held in Paris. The distinguishing feature of the fair was the Eiffel Tower, reaching 1,063 feet, the tallest structure in the city. At the exposition, the McCormick harvester competed against five American, three British and four French harvesting machines. Cyrus witnessed the competition of the harvesters, held on a farm in the village of Noisiel, twenty miles northeast of Paris. As it had done at other fairs in America and in Europe, the McCormick harvester showed itself "as the leader in this line of business." Cyrus paid tribute to "American mechanical ingenuity," especially in agricultural machinery that earned "enormous sales" and many prizes.[19]

In 1889, Cyrus, Jr., bought the one-quarter share of the company owned by his uncle Leander to make Nettie and her children the full owners of the McCormick Harvesting Machine Company. Cyrus Hall McCormick heralded the fiftieth anniversary since his father opened the first McCormick harvester plant in Chicago. In 1847, the company produced 500 machines. By 1897, the McCormick Harvester Machine Company had built one and a half million machines. Its factory occupied 60 acres of floor space and was building 200,000 machines a year. McCormick farm machines were "in constant demand in every land where there are grain and grass to be garnered."[20]

Soon after his father's death, Cyrus, Jr., began keeping meticulous records of his many investments and a daily log of cash received and cash dispended. As a leading industrialist,

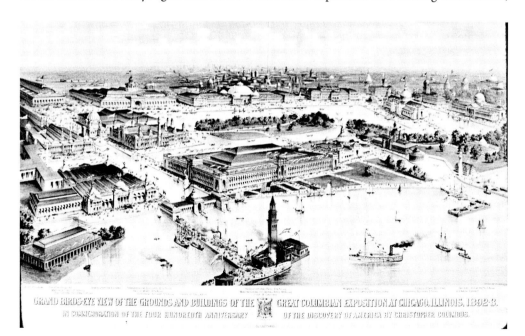

A Currier and Ives bird's-eye view of Chicago's 1893 World's Columbian Exposition, where the competitors McCormick and Deering exhibited their horse-drawn harvesting machines (Library of Congress).

A McCormick exhibit of horse-drawn farm equipment at the 1893 World's Columbian Exposition. The centerpiece shows the vast McCormick factory in Chicago, where the farm tools were made (WHS Image ID 60572).

Cyrus, Jr., was appointed to the board of trustees to stage Chicago's 1893 World's Columbian Exposition. In 1898, Cyrus Hall McCormick arranged for Woodrow Wilson to receive "$2,500 a year for five years" to keep him at Princeton and not yield to tempting offers from the University of Virginia and other schools.[21] Cyrus was a leading supporter of Woodrow Wilson to become president of Princeton College in 1902 and president of the United States in 1912. Cyrus McCormick was among the "few rich men who financed the presidential campaign" of Woodrow Wilson, by personally giving $12,500, with $20,000 more from the Harvester Trust. In gratitude, Wilson "never once denounced the harvester trust in his campaign speeches."[22] Keeping around $10,000 cash in hand, Cyrus regularly donated sums of $100 to $500 to a wide range of causes and charities. In 1904, he spent $1,500 on a trip to Geneva to attend the wedding of his youngest brother Stanley to Katharine Dexter.

Nettie McCormick, widow of Cyrus Hall McCormick, feared continued violence at the reaper plant. "They have bombs." She showed her sympathy toward the McCormick workers by haranguing company officials to do more for them and to meet their grievances.[23] Cyrus Hall McCormick, Jr., served from 1884 to 1902 as president of the McCormick Harvesting Machine Company. In 1902, he negotiated the merger of McCormick with Deering Harvester, serving until 1919 as president of the International Harvester Company, and then chairman of the board.

Cyrus Hall McCormick, Jr., "was the kindest and most friendly of men." His contri-

The McCormick Pavilion at the Paris Exposition of 1900: In front is the auto-mower, McCormick's experimental gasoline-powered, two-cylinder mowing machine (WHS Image ID 9574).

butions to Princeton University included McCormick Hall, to house the School of Architecture and Art Department, the McCormick professorship of jurisprudence, and gifts of rare books to the library. He funded the construction of McCormick Gate at the entrance to University Field, and paid for the dressing rooms for the use of the football and track teams. Cyrus endowed scholarships at Princeton. He funded the Cyrus H. McCormick School for Boys at 138th Street & Eighth Avenue, New York City. In 1919, he served on the endowment committee of Princeton University, raising $14 million.[24] Princeton rewarded him with an honorary degree.

As farms became bigger, larger harvester machines were made. This photograph, taken in 1909, shows thirty-two horses pulling a large harvester. Within ten years, 40hp IHC tractors were rapidly replacing horses on farms around the world (Library of Congress).

It was professor James Howard Gore who involved Cyrus in the outdoors.[25] In 1884, the two men went camping in Wisconsin. In time Cyrus owned a vast territory in the Upper Peninsula of Michigan, now called the McCormick Trust Wilderness Area. The 27 square miles of wilderness has lakes, mountains, and a number of streams that drain into Lake Superior and others into Lake Michigan. A large cabin on White Deer Lake served as the McCormick family retreat. Cyrus willed it to his son Gordon, who, in turn, gave the land to the United States Forest System.

Harriet Hammond McCormick died in 1921.[26] In 1924, Edwin W. Jacobs of New York sued Cyrus McCormick, a widower of three years, for $500,000, alleging alienation of his wife's affections. The case soon ended, but it was not known "whether Jacobs had received anything for consenting to withdraw the action."[27] In 1927, at age 68 years, Cyrus married Alice M. Hoit, his long-time private secretary, and 20 years his junior. Cyrus and Alice sailed for Europe and took an apartment near Hanover Square in London.[28] Cyrus remained chairman of the board of directors of International Harvester until September 1935, when he stepped down, after fifty-six years of service to the reaper company, to make room for his brother Harold. Under his guidance, International Harvester became one of the world's greatest corporations, with assets of $400 million and a workforce of 50,000.[29] On May 29, 1936, Cyrus and Alice McCormick opened their 100-acre "Walden" estate, "one of the most beautiful places on the North Shore," to host the annual Lake Forest Garden Club. On June 4, while examining the glorious array of flowers, Cyrus suffered a heart attack, dying at age

A bird's-eye view of the vast McCormick plant that gave employment to 7,000 workers in Chicago in 1907 (Library of Congress).

77. His father built horse-pulled harvesters. Cyrus Hall McCormick, Jr., led his company, indeed the agricultural industry, into the motorized age in which a single tractor had the power of ten; twenty-five; forty; and later, hundreds of horses pulling together. The funeral service was held at the Fourth Presbyterian Church and he was buried at the Graceland Cemetery, close to his first wife Harriet and his father and mother. Attending the burial were a number of "the most prominent men in American finance and industry," such as John D. Rockefeller, Jr., colonel Robert R. McCormick, Joseph M. Cudahy, and his brother Harold F. McCormick.[30] Cyrus Hall McCormick, Jr., left an estate of $22,359,806 (kept largely in shares of International Harvester Company), of which the federal inheritance taxes were $10,387,942 and Illinois state taxes $1,289,298. To pay the federal inheritance tax, "a substantial block of International Harvester shares were sold at $111 per share."[31] Taxes took 52.2 percent of the estate, leaving the beneficiaries $8,916,662. Alice Holt McCormick received $4 million and his two sons, Cyrus III and Gordon, each received $2 million. Twenty-seven servants and staff received up to $1,000 each, and various charities were left $350,000.[32]

Chapter Six

The Formation
of the International
Harvester Company

"Until 1850, farm work was largely done by human labor. Half a century later, the mechanical harvester and other animal-pulled machines dominated the American farm. In his 1904 report, Hadley Winfield Quaintance detailed the impact of farm machinery on production and labor. Across the nation, the production of oats, wheat, corn, rye and barley had increased six to eightfold between 1850 and 1900, while the population had expanded fourfold. Machinery required fewer hands, took less time and cost less than human labor. Machinery removed much of the drudgery and exhaustion of farm work and offered the farming family "the opportunity for the exercise of a higher order of intellect." With machines to help, farm children could get an education.[1] Early in the twentieth century, with the gasoline tractor replacing the horse, the benefits from farm machines increased even more.

At the start of the Civil War, there were over seventy American companies making harvester equipment. Most were small plants sited in New England, New York, Ohio, and in Illinois. In 1870, the largest harvester plant produced 9,500 machines annually. Starting in 1880, mass production methods using steel to replace iron boosted output with increasingly stiff competition, and concentrated the harvester industry in Illinois. McCormick and Deering emerged as the largest of the reaper manufacturers.[2]

On November 19, 1890, the leaders of the McCormick Harvester, Deering Harvester and eighteen smaller harvester companies met in Chicago to plan their merger into the American Harvester Company—to create a fully integrated company, owning its own steel mill, railroads and lumbar yards. With a capital stock of $35 million, it would be far and away the largest reaper and mowing company in the world, with a planned output of 150,000 machines a year, employing 60,000 workers and 10,000 selling agents. Cyrus Hall McCormick, Jr., was selected as president and William Deering chairman of the board for the proposed Harvester Trust, to be incorporated in Illinois. The objective of the Trust was to reduce costs by sharing information and producing "cheaper and better machines to supply the world."[3] Obstacles to the merger soon emerged. Lawyers advised that such a trust would be construed under the Sherman Antitrust Act of 1890 as a restraint of trade, and would face "grave legal obstacles." Among the farmers of North Dakota, the news "was received with considerable distrust." Fearing a monopoly, they saw it as "nothing more than a grasping trust organized to put up prices."[4] The young Cyrus H. McCormick and the elderly William Deering traveled to New York to seek advice about the merger. "They found the bankers whom they consulted were cold to the new company and were unwilling to provide the necessary financing." Returning to their hotel, McCormick pondered the situation, then knocked on Deering's door. Dressed only in his nightshirt, the old gentleman stood before the fireplace, his hands locked behind his back, and his fine face grave with concern. "McCormick," he said at last, "are these other fellows trying to make the two of us carry water for them?"

"It looks that way to me."

"All right, let's go home and call it off."

"I agree," said the younger man.[5]

McCormick and Deering agreed "to cut prices and make a most interesting war of their old allies…. The American Harvester Company is a thing of the past. It only lived a month or two [and] became practically defunct a few weeks after it was formed."[6] The 1890 failure to merge the twenty harvester companies set off another price war with several companies suing their competitors.[7] "Never was the rivalry among harvester companies, especially the McCormicks and the Deerings, more savage than the years at the turn of the century." The trade rivalry "had become bitter, wasteful and ruinous…. The guerrilla war between the harvester companies brought losses to the dealers and the manufacturers."[8] The 1893 World's Columbian Exposition attracted twenty-six million visitors to Chicago and gave American companies a splendid opportunity to display their rising prowess.[9] Competing on their home turf, Deering and McCormick mounted large displays. McCormick showed three reapers with a self-binding mechanism. Occupying 2,000 square feet, the Deering exhibit was a standout, with "a dazzling display of light-running frictionless roller-and-ball-bearing, twine-binder mowers and reapers, finished in burnished silver and gold plate."[10]

Between 1895 and 1904, thousands of American firms were consumed by mergers, leaving much of the nation's manufacturing in the hands of monopolistic companies controlled by a small number of powerful men. John D. Rockefeller formed the Standard Oil Trust to make him the world's richest man. Almost every commodity was organized into a trust: oil, steel, sugar, tobacco, copper, and many more.[11] Pressures grew to establish a harvester trust. "In 1897, they very nearly solved by themselves the problem of their rivalry. It was proposed that the McCormicks should buy out the Deerings, who were willing to retire. A purchase price for the whole business was agreed on [but neither company] was able to get the necessary money together."[12] The rivalry between Deering and McCormick reached new heights at the Paris Exposition of 1900. Deering displayed 43 models of its harvesters while McCormick set up its own pavilion and displayed, for the first time, its experimental gas-powered two-cylinder Auto-Mower. This was the last time the two giant harvester companies competed head-to-head.[13]

Elbert H. Gary served as lawyer to William Deering. In 1901, Gary, with the help of J. P. Morgan, set up the Steel Corporation of America. Gary learned that Deering Harvester had purchased a mine and was about to build its own steel plant, thus shutting out his steel company. In February 1902, Gary had "a long talk" with Cyrus Hall McCormick to propose a merger of Deering and McCormick to end the brutal competition and cost-cutting in the harvester business, and to ensure that U.S. Steel was the supplier. Working with George W. Perkins of J. P. Morgan & Company, Gary brought McCormick and Deering together to set up the Harvester Trust. Next, McCormick and Deering approached Plano Manufacturing

Company, Warner, Bushnell & Glessner, Milwaukee Harvester Company, Minneapolis Harvester, as well as George Easterly & Company and ten other smaller harvester companies, from Massachusetts to Minnesota, to form a single company; the International Harvester Company, based in Chicago, with Cyrus H. McCormick as president and Charles Deering chairman of the board.[14] The negotiations were difficult. "The more they talked the further they were apart."[15]

The McCormick Harvesting Machine Company was "the world's largest reaper works." Occupying 150 acres, the plant employed several thousand men, and each year used 200 million pounds of pig iron and steel and 35 million feet of lumber. Each working day, one hundred railroad cars of freight were shipped to markets at home and abroad. While known as a harvester company, McCormick also made binders, mowers, huskers, rakes and other farm implements. McCormick Harvester had a network of 15,000 selling agents in the United States and 1,500 in countries abroad. McCormick's publicity department churned out two million catalogs a year, "translated into every modern tongue."[16] In 1902, McCormick's output was 300,000 machines, Deering 250,000, Champion 75,000, Plano 50,000 and Milwaukee Harvester 40,000.[17] Showing great patience, Gary and Perkins's merger plan gradually took shape. McCormick and the slightly smaller Deering dominated the Trust; the other companies were bought out for cash or shares in International Harvester. By 1904, International Harvester was "Chicago's Greatest Industrial Organization," with three factories in Chicago (McCormick, Deering and the Plano Works), the Champion Works in Springfield, Ohio, the Milwaukee Works and a factory in Hamilton, Ontario, Canada.[18] The total employment of International Harvester in 1904 reached 15,000.

The documents of incorporation called for the International Harvester Company not only to "manufacture, sell and deal in harvesting machines" but also to make "agricultural machinery of all kinds," including binders, mowers and shredders. The company was valued at $120 million, of which the McCormick share was $53 million and Deering $40 million. John D. Rockefeller (father-in-law of Harold Fowler McCormick) invested $9.3 million and J. Pierpont Morgan & Company was awarded a $5 million stake in lieu of services to establish the company. There was evidence of "secret negotiations between the McCormicks and J. P. Morgan prior to the general negotiations [to ensure that the] Rockefellers and McCormicks own the majority of the capital stock."[19] With over 50 percent of the stock, Rockefeller and

Herbert W. Perkins was the top aide of J. Pierpont Morgan. He negotiated the formation of U.S. Steel and General Electric. He was brought in to negotiate the merger of Deering and McCormick, and several smaller harvester companies, to form in 1902 the International Harvester Company. (Library of Congress).

International Harvester workers take their lunch at the McCormick plant in Chicago, 1905 (WHS Image ID 9610).

International Harvester employed many women in its twine mills. The McCormick plant in 1912 has balls of twine stacked near the machines. The twine was used to bind the sheaves of grain (WHS Image ID 9108).

the McCormick family gained "control of the harvester combination."[20] "The McCormicks were determined to control the new trust.... This struggle for control was to go on for ten years after the formal merger.... Rockefeller's primary motive ... stemmed from his daughter Edith's marriage to Harold McCormick."[21] Cyrus Hall McCormick was appointed president of the Harvester Trust, and Charles Deering was elected chairman of the executive council. Harold Fowler McCormick and James Deering were elected vice presidents of International Harvester.[22] Stanley, the youngest of the McCormick brothers, attended Northwestern Law School after graduating from Princeton. In 1903, Stanley was appointed comptroller of Harvester. The formation of International Harvester shifted the control of the agricultural business from rough-hewn men and placed it in the hands of their gentlemanly, college-educated sons. Workers feared that the merger would lead to increased mechanization, layoffs and reduction in pay. In April 1903, thirty-five hundred workers from the McCormick and Deering plants in Chicago went out on strike. The strikers picketed the plants and kept "watch on the works and the non-union workers employed there.... Hundreds of girls struck with the men."[23]

McCormick, Deering and the smaller companies that formed International Harvester were primarily harvester makers. "Immediately after the amalgamation, Harvester ... turned its attention to the intensive development of new lines," including tilling machines, manure

Workers in 1916 at the Milwaukee plant of International Harvester are machining engine blocks for the Titan and Mogul lines of tractors (WHS Image ID 12128).

spreaders, corn planters, corn huskers, shredders, seeding machines, mowers, rakes, wagons, tractors and trucks. In 1903, Harvester "secretly bought D.M. Osborne & Company of Auburn, New York, its largest remaining competitor."[24] Next, Harvester bought the Keystone Company of Rock Falls, Illinois, Minneapolis Harvester Company and the Weber-Wagon Company of Chicago. In 1906, Senator Henry C. Hansbrough of North Dakota demanded the harvester company be investigated by the federal Commission of Corporations to determine whether "healthy competition" existed in the farm implement business. "Not only does Harvester control output and prices," stated Hansbrough, "but it was putting out inferior machines…. We cannot permit such a gigantic trust as International Harvester to continue to grind the farmers."[25]

"The harvester trust controls over nine-tenths of the farm-implement trade [and] so dominates the market as to compel what opposition is struggling against it to do business at a loss," wrote the muck-raking writer Alfred Henry Lewis in 1906. Unless it was broken up, the Harvester Trust would extend its monopoly to steamships and railroads. Lewis regarded the harvester, beef, sugar, steel and tobacco trusts as menaces to American enterprise bent on destroying "the last lean vestige of rivalry or opposition."[26] Not so, responded Cyrus Hall McCormick. International Harvester was "the farmers' friend" determined to produce better machines and to hold down the cost to the farmers. Harvester was also a good employer, offering its workers "profit sharing plans, pensions, hospitals and safety in working conditions." Harvester's return on its capital was a skinny 7 percent.[27]

The 1907 two-seater International Auto Buggy's two-cylinder engine was placed beneath the car body. A chain system connected the engine to the back wheels to move the car (WHS Image ID 12222).

A 1909 four-seater Auto Buggy image appeared in an International Harvester advertising brochure.

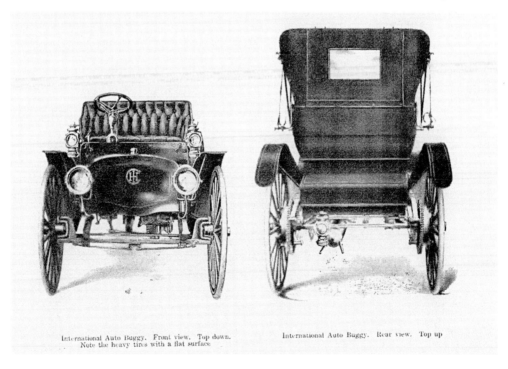

A 1909 International Auto Buggy is shown in front and rear views. In 1912, International Harvester stopped the production of cars to concentrate on delivery vans and trucks. Image from an International Harvester brochure.

In 1907, the "fair cash value of the stock" in the International Harvester Company exceeded $84 million. Members of the McCormick family (including the mentally ill Mary and Stanley) each had shares worth $11,250,000, while William, Charles and James Deering each had shares valued at $5,636,000.[28] The company grew rapidly, especially from foreign sales, with a net profit in 1907 of over $9 million. Its success in France and Germany spurred these countries to impose heavy import duties on Harvester products and to subsidize their domestic farm machinery manufacturers.[29] Still hoping "to climb back into the management," in 1910 Charles and James Deering made a determined final effort to gain control of International Harvester. They were thwarted by a further loan of $10 million from John D. Rockefeller to support the McCormick family.[30]

To keep the loyalty of their customers, International Harvester, for its first twenty years, kept separate its McCormick and Deering sales agencies. Many farming communities housed both McCormick and Deering agencies in open competition. In 1894, the 18-year-old mechanical genius Edward A. Johnson joined the McCormick Harvesting Machine Company. He designed the Auto-Mower that won a prize at the Paris Fair of 1900. He designed and built Harvester's Auto Buggy and set about to build a gasoline engine for use in agriculture. In 1906, Harvester launched its first gasoline-powered tractor. This cumbersome machine was built in Chicago. In 1907, one hundred and fifty-three tractors were built, rising to 629 the following year. With its early success, Harvester constructed a special tractor plant in Chicago. The tractors were sold by McCormick dealers under the Mogul label, and by Deering dealers under the Titan name. (After 1921 the duplication of dealer

20 & 25 H.P. MOGUL   I-6148

A 1912 Type C Mogul tractor, 20–25 horsepower, built by the International Harvester Company, heralded the beginning of motor power to replace horsepower. The Mogul tractor was sold by McCormick dealerships (WHS Image ID 63601).

networks was abolished.) After 1909, these rugged and dependable 20–30 horsepower tractors, with their huge rear wheels, were scaled down to 5,000–8,000 pounds. "In 1916, the
new line volume for the first time exceeded the old."[31] Tractor sales rose sharply during
World War I. By 1919, production of the Mogul and Titan tractors, selling for $700 each,
exceeded 9,000 units. The gasoline-powered tractor and truck replaced the harvester as
the company's leading sales items. The International Harvester tractors faced stiff competition from the tractor divisions of car companies General Motors and Ford. General Motors
gave up on tractors in 1922 and Ford discontinued its Fordson tractor in 1928, leaving International Harvester, with its nimble Farmall tractor, the leader with two-thirds of the American tractor business.[32]

Cyrus Hall McCormick took Harvester into the motorized age with its Auto-Mower
and Auto Buggy. Displayed at the 1900 Paris Exposition, the experimental Auto-Mower
was a gasoline-powered, two-cylinder mowing machine. The 1907 Auto Buggy was a wagon
with a motor, capable of producing 14 horsepower and designed for the rutted roads of the
rural market. The sturdy Auto Buggies came either as a two or four-seater. Manufacture
of the first one hundred Auto Buggy was at the McCormick plant in Chicago but was soon
moved to Akron, Ohio. The following year, International Harvester introduced its Auto
Wagon, with a load capacity of 800 pounds. Each Auto Buggy and Auto Wagon was equipped
with three oil lamps, two gas headlights and a horn. International Harvester dropped the

**A 1916 photograph shows a group of farmers examining the Titan tractor. The Titan tractor was
sold by Deering dealerships (WHS Image ID 72968).**

Auto Buggy in 1912 to focus on tractors and trucks that became ever-larger parts of the company's business. By 1915, the trucks were equipped with pneumatic tires.[33] By 1908, Harvester had become an integrated company. Not only did Harvester sell ninety percent of all American harvesting machines, it also sold "a good part of everything else the farmer uses in planting, tilling and gathering his crops. It takes ore from its own iron mines, wood from its own forests, makes its own pig iron and steel and owns its own coal mines."[34] In 1910, International Harvester grossed $190 million in sales and had a force of 25,000 workers. With competition virtually eliminated, Harvester net profits increased during 1909–1911 by 12½ percent. International Harvester was the fourth largest company in the United States, trailing only U.S. Steel, Standard Oil and U.S. Tobacco.

In 1908, the United States Department of Justice sent deputy attorney general Burdette T. Townsend to investigate International Harvester. The Townsend Report of 1911 was damning. Townsend claimed the McCormicks had engaged in "secret negotiations" with J. Pierpont Morgan. He said Harvester charged the domestic market more for its products than it charged foreign buyers. To gain dominance, Harvester had formed sweetheart deals with U.S. Steel, Standard Oil and the railroads for discount prices that were "murderous to the competitors." The company expanded from harvesters to plows and tractors and other farming tools. To sell and service its machines, International Harvester set up a vast network of agencies that dominated the world market. The company bribed legislatures and avoided paying taxes. International Harvester has "maintained a persistent campaign to destroy competition [for the] obvious purpose to monopolize the trade in everything that a farmer buys." The Townsend Report accused Harvester as being "a trust of the most vicious character [and] in violation of the antitrust act of 1890."[35] Edgar Addison Bancroft, general counsel for International Harvester and president of the Illinois state bar association, responded with the claim that the "Townsend report is false [and] nearly every important statement is either grossly inaccurate or entirely untrue."[36]

J. P. Morgan & Company, George Perkins and International Harvester were among the largest financial supporters of Theodore Roosevelt. In 1907, Perkins persuaded president Roosevelt not to file an antitrust suit against International Harvester. The Townsend Report was suppressed. "There is every indication that Mr. Roosevelt personally decreed the death of the report."[37] In September 1911, the United States government offered not to prosecute the Harvester Trust on the condition "that the company agrees to reorganize" and split into four independent companies; the McCormick, Deering, Milwaukee and Plano harvesting companies.[38] In November, the Supreme Court of Missouri found Harvester guilty of violation of antitrust laws, imposed a fine of $50,000 and ousted the Company from the state. International Harvester offices in Missouri, according to Justice Graves, were "part and parcel of the gigantic and nefarious scheme" to monopolize the farming implement business.[39] Despite mounting criticism, International Harvester expanded at home and abroad and reduced prices to beat out the few remaining rivals.[40] Cyrus and Harold McCormick, backed by John D. Rockefeller, "controlled sufficient shares to enable them to swing the election" of the board of International Harvester their way."[41] After William Deering died in 1913, his sons Charles and James let the McCormick family run the business while they indulged their passions as art patrons, world travelers and purveyors of the leisured life.

Under president William Howard Taft, the United States government broke up the monopolies of Standard Oil and the American Tobacco Company. In 1912, the government filed suit against International Harvester under the Sherman anti-trust act, alleging the company was "attempting to monopolize the manufacture and sales of harvesting machinery." The merger of McCormick Harvesting Machine Co., Deering Harvesting Co., Plano Manufacturing Co, Warder, Bushnell & Glessner Co. and Milwaukee Harvesting Co. joined together the largest harvesting companies in America. The International Harvester Company represented "a substantially monopolistic—85 percent of the total output—in the harvesting–machine business." The great resources of J. Pierpont Morgan and John D. Rockefeller backed Harvester. "An important feature of the operation of the International Harvester Company," noted a government report in 1913, "is found in the extensive loans by John D. Rockefeller to the company. Mr. Rockefeller is father-in-law to Harold F. McCormick."[42]

International Harvester extended its power by buying smaller companies such as D. M. Osborne & Co., of Auburn, New York, the Keystone Company and the Aultman-Miller Company. International Harvester was accused of establishing a near monopoly in the harvester business and raising prices.[43] Unless the harvester trust was broken up, insisted the United States Government, the company would have "complete unchallenged domination of every branch of the trade in agricultural implements."[44] Among those called by the government to testify were members of the staff of J. P. Morgan & Company, Elbert H. Gary of United States Steel, Cyrus and Harold McCormick, Charles and James Deering and their brother-in-law Richard F. Howe. Cyrus H. McCormick labeled the report of the Commission of Corporations "manifestly unfair." Rather than increasing the price, "the harvesting machine is the cheapest thing a farmer can buy."[45] To weaken the government's case, International Harvester raised the weekly wage of its female workers from $5 to $8 a day. A parade of witnesses stated: "the merger was a good thing alike for the dealer and the consumer."[46]

Responding to government pressure, in 1913 Cyrus H. McCormick announced that the Harvester Trust would divide into two companies, one domestic, the other foreign. The new corporation, with his brother Harold Fowler McCormick in charge, would "take over the business and properties of the International Harvester Company in foreign lands, including the manufacturing plants in Canada, France, Sweden, Germany and Russia." This decision was made to "protect the company's foreign trade and credit [from the government's charge of] a monopoly of domestic commerce in the harvesting business."[47]

By 1913, International Harvester Company operated several farm machinery plants in the United States with a workforce of 30,000, together with its own steel and lumber plants and a railroad network. Abroad, Harvester operated plants in Hamilton in Canada, Sweden, Croix in France, Neuss in Germany, and Lubertzy, near Moscow in Russia, with 6,000 workers.[48] In 1915, International Harvester introduced a new range of delivery trucks equipped with pneumatic tires.

On August 12, 1914, the United States District Court, sitting in St. Paul, Minnesota ruled that the Harvester Trust was a monopoly and was in violation of the Sherman anti-trust act of 1890, and should be broken into three parts.[49] The company appealed this decision to the Supreme Court, where International Harvester promised "to restore competitive conditions in the harvester trade." While battling in the courts, International Harvester was faced with union unrest. In 1916, Chicago experienced a "spring fever strike epidemic" that idled 7,500 workers at the McCormick plant and 4,000 more at the Deering plant.[50]

Cyrus Hall McCormick claimed that the strike was unwarranted as International Harvester had raised wages between 1902 and 1916 by two-thirds and had also instituted "10 hours pay for 9 hours work." McCormick appealed to the strikers to return to the "good, steady jobs that await them." Early in May, news spread that police reservists would escort strike-breakers into the factories. "Excitement among the strikers was at white heat" over rumors that the company was bringing in replacement workers from Mexico.[51]

The effort to break up monopolies such as International Harvester was delayed when the United States entered World War I, to ensure that these large companies produced tanks, planes and trucks. International Harvester divested itself of the Milwaukee, Champion and Osborne lines of harvesters. In August of 1918, Cyrus H. McCormick announced plans to reunite the domestic and international divisions of International Harvester into one company. "The war has played havoc with the assets and business in Russia and the central empires [Germany and Austria-Hungary]." Harvester suffered "immense war losses" but anticipated success with its "new lines such as tractors and auto trucks."[52] With the World War nearing its end, Cyrus McCormick unveiled grand plans to build enough harvester machines to feed both America and war-ravaged Europe, and rebuild the factory in Lille, France that had been stripped of its raw materials and machinery by the retreating German army, and reopen its Russian plant.[53]

After World War I, Harvester returned to the courts on several occasions to deny government accusations of monopolistic and antitrust activities. In 1923, the United States government again claimed that International Harvester was engaged in restraint of trade and should be split into three separate companies. There should be two harvester companies "of substantially equal size; one of which would feature the McCormick harvester machines, the other would handle the Deering line." The third company to be split off would control the "steel and coal subsidiaries."[54] The St. Paul District Court, in 1925, found that Harvester's share of the market had declined, prices were low and trade was free. Still largely intact, in 1926 International Harvester appeared before the United States Supreme Court to answer the government's charge that it still controlled two-thirds of the nation's farm machinery business. The heavy burden of opposing the government's anti-trust suit fell upon Alexander Legge, the recently appointed president of Harvester. Using a team of high-priced lawyers and accountants, Harvester claimed that it controlled only a fifth of the market and that "active competition existed."[55] In the case of *United States v. International Harvester Company 274 U.S. 693 (1927)*, the Supreme Court determined "that not only has the International Company complied with the specific requirements of the consent decree but that competitive conditions have been established in the interstate trade in harvesting machinery to bring about a situation of harmony with the law." The company won the argument, and "at last, after so many years of doubt, the International Harvester Company was free." After fourteen years of litigation, Alexander Legge claimed that the decision of the Supreme Court "definitively determined that the company has the right to live."[56] Cyrus McCormick III recalled the anxiety and then the whoops of triumph in the Harvester offices as the news of the Supreme Court decision came across the long-distance telephone call from Washington to Chicago.[57]

In 1918, engineer Bert R. Benjamin was given the green light to design a compact tractor with three forward speeds and one speed in reverse. Several years of design and experimentation went into the machine to compete with the Ford Company's Fordson tractor. In 1924, International Harvester introduced its all-purpose, red-painted Farmall tractor. Smaller, lighter, with its front wheels close together, more versatile and powerful, with a small turning range and high ground clearance, and cheaper than the Titan and Mogul brands, the Farmall tractor heralded the great advance of farming into the machine age. It sold for a little under $1,000. In 1930, Farmall sales exceeded 47,000. "This little tractor revolutionized both the farm equipment industry and farming itself.... Harvester engineers designed an extensive series of implements specifically for the Farmall, including cultivators, [and] plows."[58] The Farmall was the world's first row crop tractor. International Harvester expanded into plows, tractors and trucks, competing with John Deere and Henry Ford.[59] International Harvester net profits for 1925 were $19,171,240. Total assets of International Harvester that year were $287,266,864. By 1931, over million all-purpose gasoline-powered tractors were in use on farms on all continents to pull plows, harvesters, mowers and other farm implements, while the number of horses and people working in agriculture declined rapidly.

Corporate Welfare

The Panic of 1893 depressed business across the nation, leading to plant closings and massive unemployment. The recession hit the farm economy and reduced the profits of archrivals McCormick and Deering. The Civic Federation of Chicago grew out of the Panic of 1893 as an effort to prevent labor unrest and a second Haymarket incident, and harmoniously bring together the bosses of industry and the workers to resolve amicably their economic and social differences. Ralph M. Easely led the organization with Gertrude Breckenridge Beeks (his future wife) as his secretary. Born in 1867 in Greenville, Tennessee, Gertrude was educated in Chicago and gravitated to progressive causes. In 1901, Mrs. Harriet McCormick, wife of the president of McCormick Harvester, attended a meeting of the Chicago Business Women's Club and heard Gertrude Beeks speak on the actions companies should take for the betterment of their workers "over and above the payment of wages."

Some years earlier, Harriet Hammond McCormick had visited her husband's reaper works. "As I passed through those vast rooms," she wrote in her diary, "I felt thrilled and over-

Cyrus H. McCormick hired Gertrude Beeks in 1901 in an effort to bind the workers to the harvester company and keep out of the trade unions. A protégée of Jane Addams, her arrival signified the beginning of welfare capitalism (Library of Congress).

whelmed with the immensity of the place, but mingled with those thoughts was solicitude for our grave responsibility for the place." Harriet took note of the poor working conditions and the "weary faces" of the workers. "It seemed to me as if something would have to be done for the vast army in our employ." Harriet saw "how little was really being done for our employees."[60] On hearing Gertrude Beeks speak, Harriet at last found a way to help the bedraggled workers of the McCormick Harvesting Machine Company. Harriet persuaded her husband to hire Gertrude as Harvester's first social worker.[61] McCormick Harvester was among the first American companies to show concern for the wellbeing of its workers. From 1901 to 1903, Gertrude Beeks directed the newly established welfare department of McCormick Harvester. "See what you can do," McCormick instructed Beeks, "to make the three hundred girls and the five hundred men who work for us like to work for us." Look to their welfare, "their comfort during the work hours, their care in sickness, and their pleasures." Focusing first on the immigrant female workers, Beeks recommended larger mirrors and more toilets in the rest rooms, better meals, a trained nurse, a reading room and club house, a summer camp for workers' children and a faster response to workers' demands.

After the merger, the improvements made at the McCormick plant riled the workers at the Deering plant. The workers at Deering organized the "largest labor fight that has been waged in the history of industrial Chicago." They formed a union and issued demands for a shorter workweek, a healthy work environment, clean toilets, the right to sit down when ill, and the right to take time off to eat their meals. In 1903, McCormick workers, who toiled ten hours a day, six days a week, demanded a reduction to 54 hours. Management responded by shutting down the factory. Unable to face a week without pay, the workers were quickly defeated and returned to work. Earning on average $1 a day (pretty fair in

Three McCormick harvester machines pulled by a Mogul 25-hp tractor in 1912; a boy is leaning against a stack of grain in the foreground (WHS Image ID 44843).

comparison with the pay in other factories), the Deering workers demanded the same improvements as in the McCormick plant. "If William Deering had kept the business," wrote Beeks, "the troubles would not have come but the people say the company has gone into a Trust; why should we not combine?" Cyrus H. McCormick sent "Miss Gertrude Beeks to better the conditions and surroundings of the girl workers" at the Deering plant.[62] She believed that fair wages were the foundation for company peace.[63] For her two years' effort at McCormick and Deering, Beeks was known as the "Florence Nightingale of factory womanhood."

The presence of social workers angered the managers and foremen who saw their authority undermined. Union leaders viewed social workers as management tools to divert the workers from militancy and strike action. Two years of friction wore Gertrude down and she left the company. From Chicago, Ralph and Gertrude carried their message nationwide to form the National Civic Federation, based in New York City. During the early 20th century, Gertrude Beeks Easely was involved in such lofty issues as workmen's compensation, social insurance, profit-sharing and minimum wages.[64]

The McCormick family wanted International Harvester be a corporation with a soul. At the suggestion of Stanley McCormick in 1904, Harvester budgeted $75,000 to build a clubhouse on Blue Hill Avenue to show its "good fellowship" towards its workers. The red-brick clubhouse came with a reading room, gymnasium, baths and a recreation room."[65] There was a billiards table and poolroom, a bowling alley and classrooms to teach English and mechanical drawing. It was "the only place of gathering in the neighborhood which was not connected with a saloon." The clubhouse showed "the sympathy that exists between the company and its employees." Stanley McCormick lauded the clubhouse as a "place to drop into at leisure moments to smoke a cigar and become acquainted with your fellow workmen."[66] By 1906, Stanley's psychosis was so severe that he would never again play an active role in the company. On September 1, 1908, Harvester launched its Employees' Benefit Association plan to compensate its workers "for death or injury.... In every case of accident, with the exception of those caused by intoxication or the willful disregard of safety appliances ... the company will assume liability." Death benefits would be at least $1,000 (equal to three years of wages) but no more than $4,000. Injury to an arm or leg would be compensated by at least $500 but no more than $2,000. The benefit fund would be supported annually by $25,000 of company money and by worker payments of 2 percent of their wages, amounting to 6 to 10 cents each a month. Each Harvester plant housed a physician to assess illness and impairment. The Harvester liability plan for shop injuries was judged more liberal than worker plans in England or Germany.[67] With participation voluntary, three-quarters of the workers joined the Harvester Employees' Benefit Association. The major causes of disability were tuberculosis, pneumonia and heart disease.[68] The Employees' Benefit Association elicited much interest from other businesses across the nation who copied Harvester's ideas of corporate welfare.[69] In December 1916, Harvester gave the workers a 10 percent wage rise. Next came the pension plan and the Industrial Council Plan. In 1919, Cyrus Hall McCormick made the case for "humanizing industry" through employee participation, improved pay, shorter workdays, sick leave, disability insurance and pensions for the workers. McCormick compared his vision of American capitalism with a heart with the chaos in war-torn Europe. Bolshevism demanded "the entire management" of industry and the confiscation of private property. American free enterprise, he said, will triumph

Fred Rodenbeck's International Model M truck in 1913 makes a delivery of Dolly Varden chocolates (WHS Image ID 71661).

Dolton Bakery's 1909 International Auto Wagon is out on deliveries (WHS Image ID 27318).

over Soviet dictatorship.[70] Drawing from the vast pool of immigrant labor in Chicago, Harvester secretly recruited "the cheapest labor available…. Slavs, Italians and blacks" to build a workforce drawn from various ethnic communities to allow the company to weaken the unions and keep "a businesslike distance from the diverse cultures of its workers."[71]

Under the guidance of Cyrus Hall McCormick, International Harvester became a leader by promoting the wellbeing of its workforce. The company increased wages, introduced the eight-hour workday, provided sick days, workmen's compensation and offered a pension fund for its workers. "The day has gone when an employee was merely a machine with legs and arms," wrote Cyrus McCormick III in 1931. Each leader has the responsibility to "add something" to the enterprise." His father displayed "a willingness to compromise [to successfully lead Harvester] through the precarious but glowing years of its youth."[72]

Cyrus Hall McCormick grew International Harvester into a $400 million company, employing 50,000 workers in plants the world over.[73] Harvester emerged as a major producer of vans and trucks. After thirty-six years at the helm of McCormick Harvester and then International Harvester, Cyrus resigned as president and was replaced by his brother Harold.

"The Harvester Company and its employees have already learned from our own experience some of the values of genuine cooperation," announced Harold Fowler McCormick.

Two 1917 International 1½ ton trucks belonging to John D. Rockefeller's Standard Oil Company, advertising Polarine motor oil and Red Crown gasoline (WHS Image ID 7122).

A group of soldiers pose on a 1917 International Harvester Model F truck (WHS Image ID 46296).

The success of the company and the wellbeing of the workers were intertwined. In 1919, Harvester instituted a policy to prohibit discrimination on the basis "of race, sex, political or religious affiliation." Many African Americans moving from the South found steady work in Harvester's factories. In 1920, Harold outlined the "Extra Compensation and Stock Ownership Plan, together with the forthcoming Savings and Investment Plan [which] will be of lasting benefit to all of those interested in this Company's welfare."[74] Harold's father-in-law, John D. Rockefeller, considered the plan an utter waste of precious dollars. Harvester's welfare programs and workers councils were set up to keep the trade unions out of the factories. These methods "proved to be the perfect union repellent. They gave the company an unprecedented twenty-one years—1920–1941, free of strikes."

On January 1, 1937, the federal Social Security Program came into effect, giving workers pensions after age sixty-five and protection to families in case of early death. In 1940, International Harvester modified its long-established pension fund to "provide additional retirement income above social security benefits." All full-time salaried employees with at least five years of continuous service were eligible to join the new Savings and Extra Compensation Plan, in return for 5 percent of their wages. Men would receive their company annuity at age sixty-five and women at age sixty years. Until 1941, Harvester was "one of the few large companies still holding outside unionism at bay."[75]

Chapter Seven

International Harvester Expands Abroad

Soon after Cyrus Hall McCormick, Sr., established his factory in Chicago in 1847, he set out to expand abroad. He was much encouraged by his successes at the 1851 Crystal Palace Exhibition in London, and at the 1855 Universal Exhibition in Paris. In 1867, the McCormick Reaper won the grand prize of the Universal Exhibition and, in 1878, he was made an officer of the Legion d'honneur. These awards opened overseas markets to McCormick machines.[1] While the United States led the world in the production of corn, Europe and Russia were ahead in oats, wheat, barley and rye. Starting in 1875, McCormick sent his harvesters to Canada, the Argentine, Mexico and Chile. McCormick Harvester was among the 223 American companies on display at the 1880 International Exposition held in Sydney, Australia.[2] Cyrus, Jr., shared his father's enthusiasm to grow the company abroad. When he took over the company in 1884, he made sure that "the sun never set upon McCormick machines." By 1898, "McCormick's foreign sales exceeded 23,000 machines ... and represented a seventh of total sales."[3] The McCormick harvesters, mowers and other farm machines made in the United States found ready markets the world over. At the Bohemian Fair in Prague in 1902, "nearly all the crowds gathered around the display of the McCormick Harvesting Machine Company." The success of McCormick so angered their European competitors that the police were called to prevent a riot.[4] The McCormick success in oversees markets continued with the merger into the International Harvester Company.

By 1907, Harvester boasted plants in Illinois (Deering, McCormick, Plano, Weber and Keystone Works), Ohio (Akron and Champion Works), Wisconsin (Milwaukee Works), Minnesota (St. Paul Works) and New York (Osborne and Newark Valley Works). Harvester's first international subsidiary was the Hamilton Works in Hamilton, Ontario, Canada. Harvester opened a motor truck factory in Chatham, Ontario. Harvester's farm tools, tractors and trucks were beating their European competitors. In response, Germany, France, Russia and other European countries imposed high tariffs on imported goods.[5] By 1908, despite high transportation costs and stiff tariffs, Harvester enjoyed "a tremendously profitable trade throughout Europe."[6] In 1908, Cyrus Hall McCormick allocated $3 million to establish assembly plants in Croix in France, Neuss in Germany, and Lubertzy, near Moscow in Russia. International Harvester offices opened in Hamburg and Paris to handle sales throughout Europe and Asia.[7] Sydney G. McAllister was in charge of International Harvester's manufacturing throughout Europe.[8] Dedicated company men like J. F. Boeyer were sent from the United States to Europe to run Harvester's subsidiaries. Boeyer went to Holland in 1900, and moved to Germany, Russia and Prussia. He returned to the United States during the

World War but was back in Germany from 1919 to 1921, and then returned to a senior position with Harvester in Indiana.[9]

From the start, McCormick harvesters competed against British companies, including the Britannia Iron Works. Edward Hamilton McCormick, born in 1889, was one of a few descendants of Leander James McCormick who continued in the farm machinery business, albeit in England. After graduating Trinity College, Cambridge, in July 1913, he married Phyllis Mary Samuelson, granddaughter of Sir Bernhard Samuelson, owner of the Britannia Iron Works in Banbury, Oxfordshire. Starting in 1848, Samuelson manufactured farming equipment, including self-raking harvesters. At the Great Exhibition at Crystal Palace in 1851, Cyrus Hall McCormick "first explored the possibilities of a European market ... and hoped to find several manufacturers in each of the principal grain-growing countries" who would make the McCormick harvester.[10] Samuelson was one of the British manufacturers who entered into such an agreement with Cyrus Hall McCormick. In the process, Samuelson transformed the quiet market town of Banbury into a leading industrial center specializing in farming machinery. He was a strong advocate of technical education.[11] Bernhard Samuelson was "one of the few Anglo-Jewish entrepreneurs in heavy industry [and] was Liberal Member of Parliament for Banbury."[12] The Samuelson "Omnium" and "Eclipse" reapers were judged to have "only one opponent in the field, Mr. McCormick."[13]

The International Harvester Company of Great Britain was incorporated on December 31, 1906, with its offices at 115 Southwark Street, London. Several years later the company moved to Harvester House, 259 City Road, London, EC1. The British company imported complete machines from the United States or Canada. In 1923, an assembly plant was

Horses were not the only draught animals used to pull heavy loads. This 1910 photograph shows a Russian farmer using camels to pull an International Harvester mower (WHS Image ID 9441).

erected close to the Liverpool docks. Full-scale manufacturing began at the Doncaster works in 1939. At the start of World War II, the British government requisitioned the Doncaster plant to produce military trucks and tractors. Doncaster returned to International Harvester in 1946, with Brooks McCormick in charge of production of tractors and farm machinery. By 1970, International Harvester gained one-tenth of the British market in harvesters and tractors.

The McCormick harvester first reached Russia in 1858. With serfdom still in place, the mechanical harvester had few sales in the vast breadbasket of Europe. The emancipation of the serfs in 1861 offered fresh opportunities for McCormick. In 1880, the McCormick Harvesting Machine Company appointed George A. Freudenreich of Odessa as its Russian sales agent. Freudenreich established dozens of independent sub-agencies throughout Russia. Sales picked up in the last years of the nineteenth century and by 1901, eleven thousand McCormick machines, made in the United States, were at work on Russian farms. Imperial Russia accounted for thirty percent of all of McCormick's overseas sales.[14]

The American ambassador to Imperial Russia from 1903 to 1905 was Robert Sanderson McCormick (son of William Sanderson McCormick). He brought the McCormick name to popular attention. International Harvester dominated the Russian market in reapers and binders.[15] In 1904, Harvester formed a partnership with James Street of the Street Steamship

International Harvester of Russia opened its Lubertzy Works in 1910 to make harvesters and mowers. The factory closed during World War I and was later taken over by the Soviet government, resulting in heavy losses to the International Harvester Company (WHS Image ID 24469).

Company to carry upwards of 250,000 tons of American-made farm implements to markets in Europe, where the company was experiencing "tremendous growth."[16] In 1907, Harvester set up sales offices from Kharkov to Vladivostok. In July 1909, Cyrus, Jr., courted government officials in St. Petersburg. The Russian government offered to cut tariffs on the condition International Harvester built a manufacturing plant on its soil. In 1910, International Harvester established a separate Russian company, incorporated in the State of Maine. Soon after, Cyrus Hall McCormick, Jr., announced from his Chicago office that since Russia had "a great future as an agricultural nation," the Harvester Company was building a factory at Labertzy, close to Moscow, with 2,000 workers to build 22,500 reapers and mowers annually. In December 1910, both Cyrus and Harold McCormick were at Lubertzy for the opening of Harvester's Russian plant, built on 64 acres, with warehouses, a hospital and a workers' club-

house. International Harvester machines replaced the traditional scythes and sickles to bring in the harvest from the Ukraine to Siberia. Harvester adapted its machines to local conditions. Before the coming of the gasoline tractor, the reapers in Asian Russia were pulled by camels. By 1913, International Harvester had 3,558 agencies, mainly outside the big cities, to gain the leading share of the Russian agricultural equipment market.[17]

Cyrus Hall McCormick, president of International Harvester, reported optimistically on his 1911 tour of the company's European subsidiaries. The Russian workers at Lubertzy were slowly grasping the methods of modern manufacture. McCormick had "great confidence in Russia's industrial future [which was] on the threshold of a marvelous development."[18] The twine mill in France was among the best in the world. The factory in Norrkoping, Sweden had "reached a state of excellent practice" equal to the best work done in the American plants. Manufacturing of tractors and harvesters had started in the new plant near Budapest. Soon, barges on the Danube River would carry Harvester products to the farms of Romania, Bulgaria, Serbia, Macedonia and Albania. "The greatest future for expansion," announced McCormick, "is in the foreign business."[19]

International Harvester became one of the largest industrial enterprises in

President Woodrow Wilson appointed his Princeton classmate Cyrus H. McCormick as a member of the Root Commission. In 1917 Elihu Root and his fellow commissioners traveled to Petrograd to offer loans on the condition that the Russians remained in the war against Germany. The trip gave Cyrus the opportunity to visit IHC's Lubertzy factory, outside Moscow (WHS Image ID 74356).

Imperial Russia. Factory output fell after 1914 when Russia entered the First World War allied to Great Britain and France. In 1915, the Lubertzy factory received an order from the Russian government to make 150,000 grenades and percussion caps. The war against Germany went badly for Russia. Soldiers joined striking workers in St. Petersburg, forcing the abdication of Czar Nicholas II on March 15, 1917, ending 300 years' rule of the House of Romanov.

On April 6, 1917, the United States entered the war against Germany. The Russian provisional government under Alexander Kerensky desperately needed loans from its allies. President Woodrow Wilson sent a mission headed by Elihu Root, a distinguished elder statesman and former secretary of state, "to consult with the Russian government as to the best means of cooperation and convey a message of goodwill from the United States."[20] The real motive was to offer aid but only on the condition that the Russian army stayed in the field of battle. Wilson appointed his Princeton classmate Cyrus Hall McCormick as a member of the Root Commission. The commission arrived in Vladivostok late in June and traveled on the Trans-Siberia Railroad in the deposed czar's carriages to Petrograd for meetings with the provisional government.

Root was blunt. "No fighting, no loans." Desperate to withdraw from the war, but facing bankruptcy, the provisional government agreed to continue to fight in return for $325 million in United States loans. But the American money was too little and too late. The Kerensky government lost favor, and in November was ousted by Vladimir Lenin and his Bolsheviks. Cyrus Hall McCormick used his visit to assess Harvester's Russian assets. "The war has played havoc [and caused] immense losses" to Harvester's business in Russia. International Harvester had invested 100 million rubles in the Lubertzy plant and would sell harvesters and tractors only in return for U.S. dollars.[21]

McCormick's 1917 visit to Russia brought him into contact with Russian classical music. At the Winter Palace he met the brilliant 26-year-old pianist and composer Sergei Sergeyevich Prokofiev. The composer recognized the McCormick name from the harvesters his agronomist father used on the farm. Born in a remote part of eastern Ukraine, Prokofiev displayed his musical genius at an early age. He composed many symphonies, concertos, music for operas and, for Sergei Diaghilev, he wrote delightful music for Ballets Russes. Cyrus McCormick, a trustee of the Chicago Symphony Orchestra, asked Prokofiev for copies of his music and suggested the composer move to America to make his fame and fortune. Cyrus arranged for Prokofiev to come to Chicago, arriving in August 1918. Prokofiev was overwhelmed by Chicago's energy and mobility. In December, Sergei Prokofiev received thunderous applause as the soloist with the Chicago Symphony Orchestra for the premier of his First Piano Concerto. He appeared with the Chicago Symphony Orchestra as soloist or conductor on many more occasions before he returned to Russia in 1936.

Several years after the Soviet government gained power, Harvester closed its failing Lubertzy factory. In 1924, the Soviet government nationalized the factory without paying compensation. Harvester kept an office in Moscow with the expectation that the Soviet government would need assistance to maintain its existing machinery and make new orders. In the 1920s, Soviet Russia, using $40 million in borrowed money, imported thousands of tractors from the United States, many of them from International Harvester.[22] The foundation of Leninism, wrote Joseph Stalin, is the combination of "Russian revolutionary sweep and American efficiency."

In the summer of 1917 in Petrograd, Cyrus Hall McCormick, Jr., met the 26-year-old Russian composer Sergei Sergeyevich Prokofiev. As a member of the governing board of the Chicago Symphony Orchestra, McCormick arranged for Prokofiev to come to America and perform his music. In December 1918, Prokofiev gave the U.S. premier of his first piano concerto with the Chicago Symphony Orchestra (Library of Congress).

American industrial prestige was high after World War I. Alexander Legge, president of International Harvester, accepted the reality of the Soviet power over Russia. He saw opportunities for the company from the Soviet Five Year Plan, with Harvester providing technical expertise to build new factories and train Russian engineers to design and build tractors. In the mid–1920s, a group of Soviet engineers came to America to visit International Harvester factories. Based on their report, Harvester was invited to assist in the first Five-Year Plan to modernize Soviet Russia's agriculture. A key part of this plan was to build huge tractor factories in Stalingrad and Kharkov. Three hundred and eighty American engineers, on one-year contracts, set up the Stalingrad and the Kharkov Tractor Works to build tractors modeled on Harvester's Farmall.[23] The Soviets were determined to build tractors at any cost. "Russia spends $36,000 to build a single tractor; and then sells it for a mere $6,000," ran the newspaper headline in 1931.[24] With a capacity of 100,000 tractors a year these

factories, at great expense, met the needs of Soviet agriculture. The Stalingrad Tractor Factory, with 11,000 workers, was hailed as "one of the Soviet Union's greatest industrial achievements."[25] Sixteen more International Harvester technicians were recruited to go to Russian collective farms (kolkhovs) to repair their existing tractors. One such man was Jacob Reimer, who was sent to Petochovo, "a typical Siberian railway stop," to repair 100 tractors (half of them Soviet-built copies of McCormick and Deering tractors and the others imported from the United States) and plows. Working around the clock under primitive conditions and hindered by the lack of spare parts, Reimer trained the Russians to repair

At their start, both the Stalingrad and Kharkov Tractor Works built copies of International Harvester Company's 15–30 tractor, introduced in the United States in 1915. This 1931 picture shows tractors from the Kharkov assembly line (*Projector*, issue 11, April 28, 1931).

and care for the valuable tractors.[26] After the German invasion of the Soviet Union in 1942, production at the Stalingrad plant was switched to tanks and rocket-launching trucks. The factory was destroyed during the fierce Battle of Stalingrad. After the war, the Volgograd Tractor Factory was rebuilt.

International Harvester of Germany was established in 1908. Two years later a factory was built at Neuss am Rhein, near Dusseldorf, permitting river transport of raw materials and shipping of manufactured goods. Beginning in 1911, the Neuss factory began the manufacture of mowers, reapers, hay rakes and fertilizers, carrying the brand names of Deering and McCormick. A twine mill was completed in 1914. The Neuss plant suffered heavy losses during World War I, with shortages of men and raw materials. After the War, American loans helped the Neuss Works to retool and resume production. Work came to a sudden halt in the 1920s when French troops occupied the Ruhr and took over the coal and iron ore riches as part of French reparations claims. In the 1930s, the Neuss plant shifted from

This 1912 photograph shows Mr. M. M. Black sitting in his Auto Buggy with a trailer filled with farm implements, outside the offices of the International Harvester Company of New Zealand, Christchurch, New Zealand (WHS Image ID 24872).

Farmall tractors line up outside Harvester House of the International Harvester Company of Australia, 1941 (courtesy Museums Victoria, Melbourne, Australia).

A branch office of International Harvester Company of Australia, was located in Adelaide, South Australia, 1940 (courtesy Museums Victoria, Melbourne, Australia).

An International Farmall tractor seen in Australia 1941 (courtesy Museums Victoria, Melbourne, Australia).

Delivery of McCormick-Deering tractors on International trucks, from a branch office of International Harvester Company of Australia, in 1941 (courtesy Museums Victoria, Melbourne, Australia).

agricultural implements to produce tractors. With Nazi control, the plant was nationalized and turned to armaments. During World War II, the Neuss plant was largely destroyed by Allied airstrikes. American troops liberated Neuss in March 1945.[27] At war's end, International Harvester returned to Neuss to build tractors after the Farmall design, with the hallmark bright-red color, and carrying the name McCormick-Deering. Starting in 1950, the German factory built new lines of powerful diesel tractors.[28]

In 1888, Cyrus McCormick, Jr., entered an arrangement with H. J. Mott to sell McCormick harvesters, mowers and rakers in France. In 1908, International Harvester set up Compagnie Internationale des Machines Agricoles (CIMA) to sell machinery carrying the Deering and McCormick labels. To combat French tariffs, Harvester erected a large agricultural equipment factory at Croix, near Lille, run by 25 American managers with 1,600 French workers. The factory closed in August of 1914, with most of the Americans evacuated to Paris and the Frenchmen joining their national army to fight the approaching Germans. The plant manager, Frank A. Ericson, and superintendent Parke Randall remained behind to watch over the abandoned factory. German troops occupied Lille in October 1914, and soon bands of German troops entered the Harvester factory to loot, especially wood and copper wiring. After Ericson and Randall were ordered to leave in December 1917, the factory was stripped and all the machinery taken to Germany, leaving only the empty buildings.[29] The Croix factory reopened in 1920 but was shut down during World War II. International Harvester returned to Croix in 1948 and built a tractor plant at Saint Dizier in the eastern part of the country. By 1951, Harvester supplied one-fifth of the tractors and farm equipment sold in France.[30]

SPAIN—In this land of romance and song, Modern Agricultural Machines are making farming a profitable business.

In 1910, the Chicago headquarters of International Harvester issued a series of postcards advertising the use of the harvester in various countries. Here, an ox-pulled harvester is at work in Spain, the "land of romance and song" (author's collection).

ENGLAND—American Harvesting Machines play an important part in harvesting the crops of England.

A horse-pulled International reaper brings in the harvest in England (private collection).

MEXICO—MODERN AMERICAN BINDERS NEAR THE PYRAMIDS OF CHOLULA. MOUNT POPOCATEPETL IN THE DISTANCE.

American-built harvesters are at work near Mexico's pyramid of Cholula with Mount Popocatepetl in the distance (private collection).

The first McCormick reaper reached Australia in 1852. By 1858 there were thirty-five McCormick harvester machines at work in Australia and New Zealand. The International Harvester Company of Australia was incorporated in 1904, with headquarters in Melbourne. Kits for harvesters and other farm machines were sent from the United States for assembly at Spotswood. After the Australian government levied high taxes on imported farm machinery, Harvester established a manufacturing plant at Geelong. Completed in 1939, it built farm machinery for only a year before the Royal Australian Air Force took over the plant to produce guns, shells, trucks, tractors and the Fairey Firefly fighter airplane for its armed forces serving in Africa and Europe. Seventeen hundred Fairey planes were built at the Geelong plant. Limited production of farm machinery and tractors continued to ensure adequate food supplies at home. At the end of the war, the Geelong plant was enlarged and returned to building farm machinery. In 1952, the Geelong plant sent out its 10,000th tractor carrying the Farmall name.[31] International Harvester in Australia expanded to build trucks and earth-moving equipment. In the 1970s, International Harvester's Australian subsidiary faced stiff competition from the Sunshine Harvester Works and Massey-Ferguson of Canada.

By 1914 International Harvester was the world's leading agricultural machinery company. Its reapers, plows, cultivators, tractors and trucks operated on the great plains of the United States, the vast fields of Canada, on the pampas of the Argentine, in sight of the Aztec pyramids of Mexico, on the steppes of Russia, and on the grain fields of Algeria, Chile, South Africa, Australia and New Zealand. International Harvester's overseas subsidiaries suffered during the Great Depression but picked up in 1937 with a "good volume

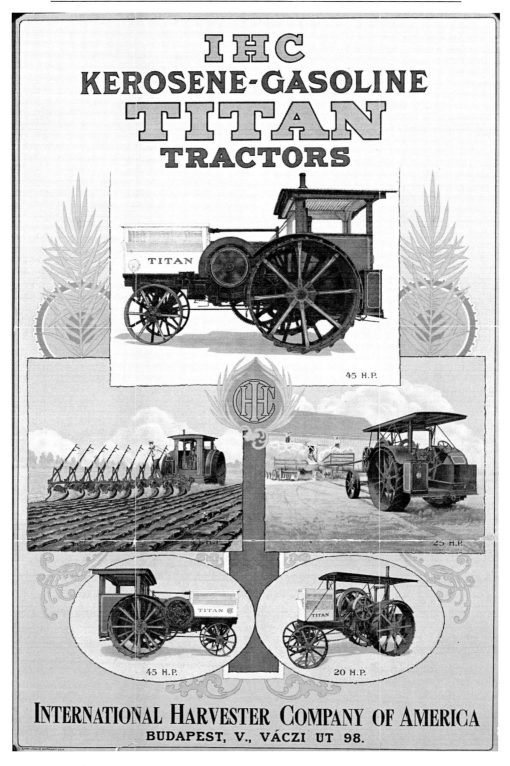

A poster advertises the 20 and 40 hp kerosene-gasoline Titan tractors for sale by the International Harvester's offices in Budapest, Hungary (WHS Image ID 3580).

People emerge in 1933 from two large buildings advertising McCormick and Deering in Paris (WHS Image ID 8921).

In September 1937, 12 McCormick Farmall tractors are ready for shipment from the International Harvester Company Neuss works in Germany in 1937. Civil war was already raging in Spain, and in May 1938 Nazi Germany occupied Austria in the *Anschluss.* World War II was soon to follow (WHS Image ID 23129).

of business" in France, Germany and South America. On March 11, 1941, President Franklin Roosevelt signed the Lend-Lease program into law. At a cost of over $50 billion ($600 billion in 2018 dollars), the United States supplied its allies, mainly Great Britain but also the Soviet Union and China, with desperately needed military supplies and foodstuffs. International Harvester supplied thousands of tracks and tractors. During World War II the Harvester's American, British and Australian plants turned to military equipment for the Allies, while the German plant, until it was bombed, produced tanks for the Nazis. After the war, Communist China sought help from the Soviet Union. The Russians helped China to build its first automobile plant. Both Communist powers produced copies of International Harvester's KR-11 truck, called in China the Jiefang ("Liberation").[32] Starting in the 1970s, International Harvester in France, England and Australia experienced the same pattern of decline as in the United States. Harvester sought support from the French government to keep operating its money-losing plants at Croix and Saint-Dizier.[33] With International Harvester's sale in 1985 of its agricultural unit, these overseas subsidiaries were sold to Tenneco, Inc., which merged them with its subsidiary J. I. Case to form Case IH.

Chapter Eight

The Middle Son
Harold Fowler McCormick, Sr.

Harold Fowler McCormick, born May 2, 1872, was the sixth child and second surviving son of Cyrus and Nettie McCormick. He was twelve years old when his father died. Harold attended the University School of Chicago. Moving with his mother to New York, Harold, with his younger brother Stanley, were among the first pupils of John A. Browning's preparatory school for boys, attending 1889–1891. In the fall of 1891, Harold entered the freshman class at Princeton College. In December 1894, Harold visited his friend from their Browning School days, John D. Rockefeller, Jr., son of John D. Rockefeller, the world's richest man. In the grand Rockefeller home on West 54th Street, he noticed a young woman scurrying about and preparing to send hundreds of Christmas "packages of all shapes and sizes." The busy lady was Edith Rockefeller, youngest daughter of John D. Rockefeller. Born in Cleveland, Ohio and raised in New York, Edith had spent weeks buying gifts for her "one thousand protégés." Harold was "anxious to meet the girl who thought so generously of her less fortunate fellow-beings. [He] fell in love with her at first sight…. Miss Rockefeller had about made up her mind to go to Japan as a missionary of the Baptist Church, but Mr. McCormick convinced her that he needed her more than the Mikado's subjects did."[1]

The June 1895 announcement of the engagement of Edith and Harold "caused great interest throughout the country," spurred by the knowledge that she was "one of the richest heiresses in America" with a prospective inheritance of $35 million. Edith Rockefeller stood a little over five feet in height with a plumb figure. Raised in the strict Baptist faith, Edith did not dance, drink alcohol or "indulge in ultra-fashionable dressing."[2] She was not beautiful but was "clever and highly cultivated." She was "well-educated in languages and music." In addition to English, she spoke "Spanish, French, German and Italian and has recently been studying Japanese." She was an enthusiastic sportswoman, a good skater, excellent swimmer and "very fond of the bicycle and horse riding."[3]

From her childhood, Edith Rockefeller was emotionally labile, with a fixation on diet and weight. "Reading has always been more important to me than eating. Except in the case of dire starvation, if a bottle of milk and a book were placed on the table, I would reach for the book, because I must feed my mind more than my body." At age twenty-one years she was admitted under the care of the neurologist Dr. S. Weir Mitchell to the Philadelphia Orthopedic Hospital and Infirmary for Nervous Diseases. The treatment comprised of rest, good food, massages and electrical stimulation of the muscles. In preparation for her marriage, Edith went on a strict diet and by November was skinny with a small waist.

By the close of the nineteenth century, Chicago was "the most commanding social, financial, literary and financial eminence in the west." In 1890, John D. Rockefeller donated $600,000 towards the establishment of the Baptist-supported University of Chicago.[4] Now his twenty-three-year-old daughter Edith was to marry Harold Fowler McCormick, from one of the leading families of Chicago. One thousand guests were invited to the wedding on November 26, 1895. The Rockefeller house was "a mass of flowers." Every room was "festooned with roses, including a solid bank of Jacqueminot roses nearly fifteen feet high." White daisies, lilies of the valley, and chrysanthemums reached to the ceilings. Twenty police officers were stationed outside the home to direct the traffic. The wedding of Harold and Edith united two of America's wealthiest families. A few days before the wedding, Harold fell sick with pneumonia and pleurisy and was ordered to bed, "swathed in cotton and carefully nursed." All arrangements for the large ceremony were abruptly cancelled. On the morning of the wedding, Harold was pronounced well enough to take part in a brief wedding ceremony, after which he was "ordered back to bed." Fifty guests assembled for the elegant celebrations at the Buckingham Hotel. They included Mr. and Mrs. John D. Rockefeller, and Harold's mother, brothers and sister. In keeping with John Rockefeller's temperance beliefs, no wine or spirits were served. "Mr. Rockefeller settled a number of millions outright on the bride," as well as giving Edith a pearl necklace valued at $20,000. Harold gave Edith a diamond tiara; Nettie McCormick gave a full silver table service. Edith's jewelry collection included a Cartier necklace with ten large emeralds and 1,617 tiny diamonds, worth $2 million.[5] The Rockefeller-McCormick marriage was likened to the Vanderbilt-Marlborough and the Whitney-Paget marriages to make "the season famous."

As vice president of the McCormick Harvesting Machine Company and an heir to his father's fortune, Harold received an income of $100,000 a year, (equivalent to $2.7 million in 2018 dollars). Edith's income was larger. So began the opulent married life of Harold and Edith Rockefeller McCormick. Soon after the honeymoon, the couple departed for Council Bluffs, where Harold served as manager of the McCormick harvester agency. After one year in Iowa he came to Chicago and, in 1898, and at age 26 years, was vice president of McCormick Harvester. Four years later, he was appointed vice president of the newly formed International Harvester Company, led by his brother Cyrus and largely financed by loans amounting to $10 million from his father-in-law, John D. Rockefeller. Rockefeller money greatly boosted Harold's standing in the company.[6] In 1903, Harold took part in discussions about shortening the workweek from 60 hours to 54. International Harvester bought peace with the unions by reducing hours of work and improving conditions of work. In 1908, Harold became treasurer of the reaper company.

The grand mansion at 1000 Lake Shore Drive was built in 1883 for Nathaniel Jones, a member of the Chicago Board of Trade. Designed by Solon S. Berman, architect of the Mines and Mining Building of the World's Columbian Exposition, the Romanesque Revival granite mansion was imposing. The rumor spread that John D. Rockefeller gave his daughter the house as a wedding present. In 1896, Harold and Edith McCormick moved into the forty-one-room house and spent millions on furnishings. Using royalty as her guide, Edith laid down 600-year-old Persian carpet once owned by Russia's Peter the Great, gilded chairs used by Napoleon Bonaparte, and the gold dinner service that the French emperor gave to princess Pauline Borghese. Mrs. Potter Palmer, the reigning queen of Chicago society, lived in a three-story rock-fronted mansion at 1350 Lake Shore Drive. Edith quickly established herself as competitor to Mrs. Palmer. Harold found his outlets at the University Club and the Chicago Athletic Association.

Tragedy came early to Edith and Harold when their first child, John Rockefeller McCormick, died January 2, 1901, at age three years of scarlet fever. In his memory, in 1902, Edith and Harold established the John Rockefeller McCormick Memorial Institute of Infectious Diseases, housed at Rush University.[7] The following year, Edith and Harold gave $5,000 a year to establish the Journal of Infectious Diseases, edited by professors at the University of Chicago.[8] In New York, John D. Rockefeller, Sr., had long considered funding an institute for medical research. After the death of his much loved grandson, the idea saw action when Rockefeller gathered together a group of leading scientists to establish the John Rockefeller Institute for Infectious Diseases.[9] With an initial donation of $200,000, John Rockefeller established his Institute and hired such eminent scientists as Simon Flexner to work fulltime at medical research. He bought the land between 64th and 67th streets on the East River to build his Institute and erect a hospital. By 1907, John D. Rockefeller had contributed $93 million to fund his New York Institute and to support smaller institutes

Harold Fowler McCormick Sr. (1872–1947) and his wife Edith Rockefeller McCormick (1872–1932), are shown in c. 1899, with their two oldest children, John Rockefeller McCormick (born 1896) and Harold Fowler McCormick, Jr., (born 1898). Their firstborn, John Rockefeller McCormick, died of scarlet fever in 1901, leaving the parents emotionally brittle (WHC Image ID 3631).

Edith Rockefeller McCormick in 1904, dressed for a night at the opera, wearing her diamond tiara and pearl necklace (Library of Congress).

in Chicago affiliated with the University of Chicago and Rush University.[10] In 1963, the Institute was renamed Rockefeller University.[11]

In 1906, the *Chicago Tribune* published a flattering account of "the millionaire" Harold Fowler McCormick, then in his mid 30s:

Harold Fowler McCormick is the second best racquets player in the United States and one of the best all-round sportsmen. He is well built and has a most genteel manner of speaking to anyone. He is a hard worker, getting to the office at an early hour and never putting anything off till the next day because he wants to go and play a game of racquets. When he is finished his work he goes over to the Athletic Club and plays hard for an hour or so. He is fond of riding and in the early morning on his own one can see him going through Lincoln Park on a fine chestnut horse. In the last year he has taken up auto-motoring and is now one of the most expert drivers in the city.... His habits are exemplary. He never drinks and does not allow any liquor in his home. The ill health of his wife and children has been a source of a great deal of anxiety to him, as he is devoted to his family.[12]

John D. Rockefeller was the father of Edith Rockefeller McCormick and financial supporter of the McCormick family in the International Harvester merger (Library of Congress).

Harold and his brother Stanley were the Midwest doubles tennis champions in 1903. Harold represented the University Club of Chicago in racquets (royal tennis). In 1909 and 1913, playing at the plush Tuxedo Tennis and Racquets Club, Tuxedo Park, New York, Harold won the national racquets championship and was runner-up of several other occasions.[13]

Harold and Edith McCormick lost another child Editha, who died in 1904 at nine months of age. Their surviving children were Harold Fowler, Jr., born in 1898, Muriel in 1902 and Mathilda in 1905. Edith and Harold regularly took their children eastward to visit with their Rockefeller grandparents. "The McCormick children are the favorite grandchildren of John D. Rockefeller." He took them on automobile rides to the seashore and "enjoyed many romps with them."[14] Motherhood suited Edith Rockefeller McCormick. "In the capacity of mother," Edith wrote in 1909, "woman finds her greatest glory. [Motherhood] makes us more rounded in our development, increases our chances of usefulness, and deepens our prowess of enjoyment. [It is] a great, overwhelming joy."[15]

In her concern for wayward children, Edith funded the probation officers of Chicago's Juvenile Court system and sent money to Hull House to uplift immigrant children. But her principal goal was to dazzle Chicago and make it a great city of high culture. Edith and Harold in 1910 established and funded the Grand Opera Company, Chicago's first residential opera company, opening on November 5, selling out the vast Auditorium Theater with a production of Aida. The production set a standard "that has never been known here before." The company folded soon after Edith and Harold departed for Switzerland. In 1915, Harold formed the Chicago Opera Association, serving as its president. Even though Edith and Harold spent most of their time in Switzerland, each year they made up the Association's deficit. The Opera Association went out of business in 1921 "in a blaze of glory" with Harold making up the deficit of $1 million.[16]

Harold and Edith McCormick paid $2 million to purchase 300 acres at Lake Forest, abutting Lake Michigan. In 1907, Harold commissioned Frank Lloyd Wright to design a grand house on the site. Wright designed a fabulous Prairie style house built over a ravine. Preferring something European and classical, Edith refused Wright's offering and in 1909, hired the architect Charles A. Platt to design and build a two-story Italianate mansion of solid brick covered with stucco, containing forty-four rooms. Completed in 1912, Villa Turicum was one of the grandest summer homes built in America. The house featured a marble-walled ballroom, a dining room large enough for sixty guests, and thirteen bedrooms, each with its own bathroom and fireplace. There were thirteen staff bedrooms and an equal number of rooms for the servants of visiting guests. Facing the house was a landscaped mall 500 feet long by 100 feet wide. Family and visitors parked their cars in the twenty-one garages. Close to the lake were a swimming pool and a bowling green. The estate had its own polo field with stables for twenty-one horses. Most of the land was left in its natural state with oak, maple and ash trees. The house, furnishings and landscaped acres cost an additional $5 million, small change for the daughter of America's richest man, who gave her a dowry of $40 million. The grand estate offered all of life's pleasures except peace of mind. By 1913, Edith was emotionally crippled by depression and phobias and took off for eight years to Switzerland to become a disciple of Dr. Carl Jung. In her absence, Villa Turicum was hardly used.[17]

In 1910, Harold became interested in air travel as the means to getting from his summer home and his office in downtown Chicago. He provided funding to a company for the development of an airplane called "The Merry Widow" invented by William S. Romme of New York. In April 1911, the plane caught a gust of wind and crashed to the ground."[18] Harold tried again. On July 30, 1913, Harold and his pilot "made a successful flight from his summer residence in Lake Forest over the waters of Lake Michigan to Grant Park, Chicago, a distance of thirty miles." Christened "Edith" for his wife, his plane flew sixty feet above the lake surface, greeted by crowds lining the shore. The "engine never missed a stroke" and after twenty-eight minutes aloft, the plane landed smoothly at Grant Park. The delighted Harold McCormick announced that he would regularly fly to his Chicago meetings "unless storms prevent."[19] Ever the enthusiast, Harold started a daily water taxi from the North Shore to Chicago, $28 round trip. The winds and waves of Lake Michigan proved too much for the little plane "Edith" and twice Harold and his co-pilot were dumped into the lake. The watchman in the McCormick motorboat reached the plane before it sank. After the second dunking the plans for an air taxi service were abandoned.[20]

After the early deaths of two of her children, Edith's emotional vulnerability returned. She had mood swings, became reclusive, rigid and phobic, and obsessively immersed in the study of literature and philosophy. In April 1908, the announcement came that Edith was receiving many anonymous letters demanding money and issuing threats. She felt unsafe in her own home and the couple planned to leave for Europe. This explanation allowed overwrought McCormicks to leave town and seek psychiatric care. For a cure, the intellectual Edith much preferred the new science of psychoanalysis to the McCormicks' preference for cures by visiting mineral spas. Himself suffering from depression, Harold

Harold F. McCormick (right) with F. J. Bersbach pose in a Curtis Hydro-Aeroplane, June 1913, to fly between his Lake Forest mansion and downtown Chicago (Library of Congress).

Fowler McCormick, accompanied by Edith, traveled to Switzerland in 1908 where he was admitted to the Burgholzli Psychiatric Clinic under the care of Dr. Carl Gustav Jung. The following year, Harold's cousin Joseph Medill McCormick (known as Medill), grandson of William Sanderson McCormick, troubled by depression and alcoholism, was briefly hospitalized under Jung's care.

In 1909, Carl Gustav Jung accompanied Sigmund Freud on their famous visit to the United States to take part in a psychoanalytical conference sponsored by Clark University in Worcester, Massachusetts. That conference legitimized psychoanalysis in the United States. Born in 1875, the son of a pastor in the Swiss Reform Church, Jung went on to medical school to become a psychiatrist. In 1906 he met Sigmund Freud who came to regard Jung as his potential heir. Their theories began to diverge with Jung claiming that humans shared a collective unconscious as well as each having an individual unconscious process focused on early experiences. Freud and Jung went their separate ways in 1912, with Jungian psychoanalysis developing its own field of knowledge.

In 1912, Jung was again in America to attend a psychiatric conference. Medill McCormick recommended that Edith seek Jung's help. Eager to be treated by him, Edith offered to pay Carl Jung and his family to settle in Chicago and support him until he was well established in a medical

Carl Gustav Jung, Swiss psychiatrist who analyzed Harold and Edith Rockefeller McCormick and their children, ca. 1908 (Wikimedia Commons).

practice. To display her wealth and authority, Edith took Jung to meet her father at the Rockefeller country home, Kykuit, set on 3,000 acres near Tarrytown in the Hudson River Valley. But Jung's wife Emma refused to move to America. In February 1913, Edith left Chicago for New York where she met Jung for daily therapy over fourteen days. Edith agreed to move to Zurich to continue psychoanalytical treatment under Jung. From New York, Edith with her children Muriel, Mathilde and Harold Fowler, Jr., accompanied by Jung, and a retinue of servants ferrying large amounts of luggage, left America for a prolonged stay in Zurich, where she, her husband and their children, underwent long-term psychoanalysis by Carl Jung himself. The family settled in the luxury Hotel Baur au Lac. For eight years, Harold Fowler McCormick traveled back and forth to spend time with his family in Zurich and to fulfill his responsibility in Chicago as vice president and treasurer of the International Harvester Company. All this occurred while the terrible World War I was raging around neutral Switzerland's borders. The sinking of the *Lusitania* on May 7, 1915, with the loss of 1,198 lives, revealed the risks of trans-Atlantic travel in wartime, yet Harold and his son Fowler made several trips between the United States and Europe. Due to her phobias and fear of travel, Edith did not return to America to attend the funeral of her mother, Laura Spelman Rockefeller.

Edith in Zurich

During her first year in Zurich, Edith had daily therapy sessions with Carl Jung. Edith was one of the coterie of women admirers of Carl Jung, known as *Jungfrauen.* Dr. Jung determined that Edith was very much on the edge and diagnosed her as a latent schizophrenic.[21] In contrast to his introverted wife, Harold McCormick was an extravert, "a man's man" who relished company and activity. Jung judged Harold McCormick as having "a first-class temperament and a second-class intellect. [Harold was] a peacemaker, a placater and a surface skimmer." Harold and Carl Jung became good friends who socialized together, shared hearty meals and motor trips, and enjoyed long walking jaunts in the Swiss Alps. Harold considered Jung "as nearly perfect to my mind as a man can be." Now a convert, Harold addressed Jung as "Dear Father." In a 28-page letter to his skeptical mother Nettie Fowler McCormick, Harold concluded that Jungian "analytical psychology is wonderful for Edith and me." Back in America, the stern Presbyterian McCormicks and the Baptist Rockefellers feared that Harold and Edith had become entrapped in an un–Christian cult with Carl Jung as the high priest.[22] The ardent disciples, Edith and Harold, were determined to convert to Jungism their children, members of their families and their friends. They gave Jung $70,000 and, in 1916, founded and financed, with borrowed $120,000, the Psychological Club, on the fashionable Gemeindestrasse in Zurich "as a meeting place for the dissemination of ideas and information about analytical psychology, and especially ... the ideas of C. G. Jung."[23] Edith's largesse paid the bills for the Psychological Club, including all the membership dues. Edith's investment in the Psychological Club was undermined when the bookkeeper Irene Oczeret diverted some of the money to her therapist husband, intent on setting up a number of his female patients as his mistresses.[24]

By funding the translation of *Psychology of the Unconscious* and *Collected Papers on Analytical Psychology,* Edith made Jung's work available to the English-speaking world. Edith appealed to her father for money to support Jung's enterprises. "I on my own path have my psychology and my religion which guide me," she wrote. "As a woman of forty-three I should like to have more money to help with," she wrote to her father. "I am worthy of more confidence on your part." John D. Rockefeller increased Edith's monthly allowance to $5,000 and pleaded with her to devote less attention to Jung and more to her children who "sadly need your presence.... You could have been a great comfort and help to your mother and me." Edith's daughters Muriel and Mathilde were away at boarding school in Lausanne, with a focus of drama, literature, languages and music. Edith's son Fowler became a lifelong devotee of Carl Jung.

During World War I, while Edith Rockefeller McCormick was living in great luxury in a suite of rooms at Hotel Baur au Lac, Zurich attracted many impoverished artists, writers, academics, philosophers and oddballs from all over Europe. Among them were the Dadaist Tristan Tzara, the writers Romain Rolland, James Joyce and Stefan Zweig, and the middle-aged Russian exile Vladimir Ilyich Lenin. Researching in Zurich libraries, Lenin was putting the finishing touches to his book *Imperialism as the Highest Stage of Capitalism.* On August 8, 1917, Lenin set out from the Zurich train station on one of the most momentous journeys of the 20th century. He traveled through Germany in a sealed railway car. His journey ended eight days later when he arrived at the Finland Station in Petrograd. Taking charge, Lenin mounted the roof of an armored car to announce that he would take

Russia out of the devastating World War, destroy the Tsarist rule and launch the Bolshevik Revolution.

In Zurich, the phobic Edith rarely left her hotel and started her own analytical practice, seeing patients in her luxury suite. "New patients are coming to me all the time and I have some fifty cases now," she wrote enthusiastically to her father. "I hear in a year twelve thousand dreams. The work is very concentrated and very different, but so intensely interesting. It is so beautiful to see life and joy into the eyes of those who come to me so hopeless and seemingly lost."

One of Edith's patients was 16-year-old Lily von Charasoff, a schoolmate of Muriel McCormick. Lily was much interested in dance and theater and received money from Edith to pursue her studies. She was the daughter of Georg von Charasoff, an Armenian-born economist who in 1909 wrote a book on Karl Marx and in 1910 completed *Das System des Marximus* (The System of Marxism). The reason for Edith's popularity as a therapist was her habit of giving money to patients who pleaded a need.[25]

Edith supported promising artists, writers and musicians then living in Zurich, among them Otto Leuning, Ermanno Wolf-Ferrari, Philipp Jarnach and James Joyce. A composer of chamber music and comic operas, Wolf-Ferrari lost his creativity. Jung concluded that Edith's money was to blame and advised cutting off the support. When Wolf-Ferrari began again to compose, Jung took the credit. "I looked into my mailbox and found a letter from the familiar Eidgenossische Bank," wrote Otto Luening, a young musician from Milwaukee, studying in Zurich. The letter notified him that Edith would provide financial support while he advanced his career as a flutist, composer and conductor.[26]

The best known of Edith's Zurich protégés was the Irish writer James Joyce, who had already finished *Dubliners* and *A Portrait of the Artist as a Young Man*. Since June 1915, he was living in poverty in Zurich and writing his epic *Ulysses*. Early in 1918, Joyce received a letter from the Eidgenossische Bank saying that an anonymous benefactor had awarded him 1,000 Swiss franc a month for twelve months to continue his creative work. On the first of each month, Joyce went to the bank to collect his money. Joyce was "dazzled and perplexed by the gift" that made up two-thirds of his monthly income. Joyce used part of the largesse to entertain his friends with fine food and drinking at the Zimmerleuten restaurant on the right bank of the river. After a few months he met his benefactor, Edith Rockefeller McCormick, who "had patronized a great many writers

James Joyce in Zurich 1915, around the time he was writing *Ulysses*. Edith Rockefeller McCormick regarded him as her secret protégé worthy of her financial support (Library of Congress).

and musicians." Joyce thanked Edith for her generosity. She replied: "I know you are a great artist," and told Joyce that his work would be improved through Jungian analysis and that she would pay for his therapy under Carl Jung himself.[27] Joyce "had no great opinion of psychologists" and refused her offer. On October 1, when he went to the bank, he was stunned to learn that Edith had cut off his credit. In a desperate effort to win her over, Joyce sent her part of the manuscript of *Ulysses*. She responded in writing on October 13:

> Dear Mr. Joyce,
>
> Thank you for the fine manuscript.... As the bank told you, I am not able to help you any longer financially, but now that the difficult years of the war are past, you will find publishers and will come forward yourself.

Edith returned the *Ulysses* manuscript unread. Years later, Carl Jung wrote to a friend: "While James Joyce lived in Zurich he became acquainted with Mrs. McCormick, whom I knew very well. She absorbed a great amount of psychological knowledge and Joyce was one of her protégés." Edith lectured Joyce on Jung's theories. "I don't suppose," continued Jung, "that the points in *Ulysses* apparently referring to my psychology have anything to do with what he heard from Mrs. McCormick."[28] Edith's pique had an affect on Joyce's writing of his masterwork, published in 1922. He based the sadistic The Honourable Mrs. Mervyn Talboys on Edith. "I'll scourge the pigeonlivered cur as long as I can stand over him," says Mrs. Talboys in a "sudden paroxysm of sudden fury.... I'll flay you alive.... I'll make it hot for you. I'll make you dance Jack Latten for that."[29] In *Finnegan's Wake*, Joyce lampoons Jung. A character in the book is admonished for having homosexual tendencies and is told: "Get yourself psychoanalised." He responds indignantly: "I can psoakoonaloose myself any time I want."

Edith wished to be taken seriously by her father. She resented that her brother John was given so prominent a role in running the family businesses and its philanthropies. In 1915, she wrote to her father. "I would like to help in your philanthropies." Speaking also on behalf of her sister Alta, Edith added: "I am sure that as women we are serious minded and earnest and deeply interested in mankind and that we would only be too glad to shoulder our inherited responsibilities if we were permitted to." Edith returned to this theme in a letter to her father dated January 24, 1918. "I sometimes wish you would forget that I am a woman, so that you might give me some of the advantages which John has in administrating. I am very capable and everyone finds me very resembling you."[30]

In 1915, while in Zurich, Harold McCormick had a creative burst of his own and wrote *Via Pacis,* on how to end World War I. His ideas were published in book form two years later.[31] Wars continue until one side wins and the other loses. At that stage the winning side dictates the terms of the peace to its advantage. "The better side of human nature wants peace" but the violent side of human nature demands continued conflict until absolute victory. Harold McCormick suggested that statesmen on both sides in the heat of the battle, with the outcome still uncertain, prepare their peace terms "containing mingled elements of both victory and defeat." These peace terms should be set aside until the outcome of the battle becomes obvious. Then "one side or the other stops and accepts the conditions of peace as named by the other." McCormick believed that his plan would permit "the better side of human nature" to win, thus shortening the war and saving lives and resources. He sent copies of his book to the American ambassador to Switzerland, President Woodrow

Wilson and to high government officials. Harold contacted his friend general Charles G. Dawes, head of the purchasing board of the American Expeditionary Force. A Chicago banker, Dawes served as controller of the currency under President William McKinley. During the war, Harold served under Dawes as head of the bureau of coordination of purchases.

Harold's book came to the attention of Dr. von Haniel of the German foreign office. In September 1917, Harold met with German officials in Zurich to discuss peace plans. President Woodrow Wilson, a close friend of Harold's older brother, gave his encouragement. The Germans offered to hold off an offensive and withdraw from Belgium as the basis for further negations for an eventual peace agreement. In May 1918, Harold left his wife in Zurich. "He gave me no reason at all," claimed Edith, "and there was no reason." Harold made his way through France to board an American battleship that carried him to America to show the peace initiative to President Wilson. But Wilson deemed the initiative as "too late. I couldn't trust the Germans."[32]

From the nation's capitol, Harold Fowler McCormick, in June of 1918, returned to Chicago after three years in Switzerland. This would be "only a short stay" to visit his mother and family.[33] While undergoing psychoanalysis, writing a book on how to end the war, and assisting the American Expeditionary Force, Harold had sorely neglected his responsibilities as vice president and treasurer of Harvester. In Chicago, his mother Nettie and brother Cyrus sternly reminded him of his obligations to the family business. On December 26, Cyrus Hall McCormick retired as president of International Harvester to become chairman of the board of directors. Cyrus had served 18 years as president of the McCormick Company and then 16 years as president of Harvester, "making 34 years of continuous service." With government efforts to break up the company suspended, it was now time "to pass on to my brother the obligations and opportunities of the presidency."[34] In 1918, Cyrus, Jr.'s son, Cyrus III, was not ready to assume the leadership. Instead, the task went to his brother Harold.

Harold Fowler McCormick (right), president of the International Harvester Company, with Alexander Legge (center) in 1919 watch a test of an experimental motor cultivator (*Alexander Legge, 1866–1933***, Chicago: 1936, p. 130).**

"H. F. McCormick Takes New Job," announced the *Chicago Tribune* on December 28, 1918. Harold had served sixteen years as vice president of International Harvester and as its treasurer. Without ceremony he moved into his brother's old office on the fourteenth floor of the Harvester Building on Michigan Avenue. "Like my brother, I have given all my working life to Harvester business," said Harold. "The change was made at my brother's urgent request…. It has always been a matter of close teamwork between my brother and me." Harold envisaged no change in policy, merely one McCormick replacing another.

As president, Harold Fowler McCormick extended Harvester's policy of reaching out to its workers by setting up the International Harvester Industrial Council. The impetus came from his brother-in-law John D. Rockefeller, Jr., who believed that industrial strife was harmful and could be lessened by company-sponsored joint councils of workers and management. With his 1915 *Via Pacis* book, Harold used his knowledge of Jungian psychoanalysis to suggest a way to end World War I. In 1919, he was ready to by-pass the unions to apply Jungian principles to end labor conflict at Harvester. The International Harvester Industrial Council, with equal representation of management and workers, aimed to consider "all questions of policy relating to working conditions, health, safety, hours of labor, wages, recreation and other similar matters of mutual interest." In 1919, Harold announced that Harvester had established a Department of Public Relations to explain company policies "from the viewpoint of their effect upon public opinion and the public welfare." In 1920, Harold F. McCormick announced that while Harvester had not yet found "the right solution of the industrial relations problem, we are at least on the right track."[35] During his tenure as president, Harold helped Harvester "with the fruits of the most winning of all personalities," encouraging subordinates to express themselves fearlessly about organization policies.[36] The plan instituted by Harvester gave workers the right to a pension after thirty years of service. Though undermined by the Great Depression, the company pension plan remained in effect until 1935 when it was folded into the federal social security plan that required continued working until age 65.

In September 1919, Harold received a letter from the 32-year-old Polish-born Ganna Walska (born Hanna Puacz), an aspiring opera singer. That year, Ganna sang at the Havana Opera House in the leading role in Umberto Giordano's "Fedora." Her performance was a failure and she was hooted off the stage.[37] From Havana she traveled to America looking for an opportunity to sing. The 46-year-old Harold was intrigued and arranged to meet the gorgeous but tempestuous singer. Convinced that she had great talent, Harold invited Walska to come to Chicago to perform with the opera company he financed. In 1920, she was scheduled for the title role of Zaza, in the opera by Ruggero Leoncavallo. Among opera devotees it was said that while Mme. Walska "possessed a well-trained soprano voice it has been found unequal to the role of Zara for which she has been warmly sponsored by Harold McCormick who personally escorted her to Chicago for the rehearsals." Opening night was sold out but Walska argued with the director, and, struck by stage fright, she refused to perform. Instead, her understudy took the role. Walska fled Chicago by train to New York to go to her apartment at 101 E. 94th Street. For Harold McCormick, the sexual appeal of Ganna proved stronger than years of Jungian analysis. Throwing caution to the wind he was head over heels in love, and resolved to divorce Edith.

Learning of Harold's affair with Ganna, Edith left Zurich and returned to America after an absence of eight years. Accompanying her on the *George Washington* were her children Fowler and Muriel, and the 26-year-old Swiss self-proclaimed architect Edwin Krenn—once her private client and now her protégé. Short and stout with a ruddy face, Krenn's job was "to sit on deck with Mrs. McCormick and read to her." Also on board ship were her private nurse, and the Swiss psychoanalyst Dr. Heinz Hartmann, who it is rumored was paid $50,000 to get Edith safely to Chicago, after which he returned to New York to board the same ship back to Europe. Edith Rockefeller McCormick brought with her 25 trunks of clothing and jewelry. Despite her phobias and mood swings, Edith presented herself as a liberated woman. "I am a psychologist," she claimed. If her husband "finds entertainment in anybody's company it is all right."[38]

On October 3, 1921, Edith and Harold separated. Edith stayed in her grand home at 1000 Lake Shore Drive, Chicago, while Harold moved to their country home at Lake Forest. Edith's profligate spending alarmed her father. "Edith seems not to get on well in managing her finances," wrote John D. Rockefeller, Sr. Her annual income was "$800,000 to $1 million," yet she had "large indebtedness" and was asking for more money. John D. Rockefeller hoped she had learned from her past errors and become more frugal. He was willing "to chip in [but] I do not contemplate further gifts." If John, Jr. "should find Edith at any time, now or later, in straightened circumstances you [should] be on the alert to render some assistance to prevent dear Edith becoming utterly stranded financially."[39]

A portrait of Ganna Walska, Polish opera singer in 1921, when she was married to Alexander Smith Cochran: Later divorced, on August 11, 1922, she married Harold Fowler McCormick (WHS Image ID 8787).

Disappointed in marriage and motherhood, Edith formed great plans to beautify and civilize the city of Chicago, especially funding grand opera. She also planned to "develop her doctrine of synthetic psychology, treating neurotics in her home." Using the psychobabble she acquired in Zurich, she likened the neurotic mind to a dilapidated house filled with broken furniture. It is first necessary to get rid of repressed notions that clutter the mind and replace them with fresh new ideas. "Of course the furniture we throw out are the old worries, understood in psychoanalytical terms as repressions," explained Edith. "The more difficult work is the introduction of new ideals. The extent to which the patient suffers depends entirely on how much of the furniture cluttering up the brain is ugly and broken down."[40] Addressing the Chicago Institute of Commerce, Edith Rockefeller McCormick laid out her grand vision to make Chicago "the great cultural center of America." During her years abroad she had "heard all the great operas of Europe." Opera was the essence of culture. "It is only in cities which have reached a certain cultural height which have opera.... Grand opera is a biological necessity for human development.... Where there is no culture there is no actual development." Her plan was to gather together five hundred people, each to donate $1,000 a year and make Chicago a world center for grand opera.[41] Responding the Edith's appeal, the women's section of the Chicago Civic Opera, in 1922, raised over $200,000 in pledges of $1,000 a year for five years.[42]

"After many years of study," Edith said "I have concluded that the whole happiness of life, and what brings poise and serenity to the soul, consists in understanding one's self." The woman has "a negative force, man a positive." So long as women "play the game according to men's rules they are apt to fail."[43] No longer Mrs. Harold Fowler McCormick, Edith was now Miss Edith Rockefeller McCormick. Marriage was a form of enslavement. "Motherhood is important, but it is not everything," insisted the recently divorced Edith, at odds with her children. "All the modern woman wants is to be let alone, to develop, to demonstrate and to expand."[44]

In December 1921, after twenty-six years of marriage, Edith Rockefeller McCormick and Harold F. McCormick were divorced on grounds of his desertion. The divorce proceedings were smoothly orchestrated by their lawyers and lasted less than an hour. Harold was represented in court by John P. Wilson and Clarence S. Darrow. In 1888, Clarence Darrow opened his law office in Chicago, defending high-profile clients and workers alike. In 1924, Darrow represented Nathan Leopold and Richard Loeb, charged in the killing of 14-year-old Bobby Franks. In 1925, Darrow achieved great fame defending John T. Scopes of Tennessee in the Scopes Monkey Trial.

So ended the marriage joining the Rockefellers and the McCormicks, two of America's richest families. The properties were divided. Edith took 1000 Lake Shore Drive and Harold the estate at Lake Forest. No money changed hands. Edith kept her annual allowance of $800,000 given by her father, and Harold kept full control of his shares in the Harvester Company, then worth $20 million–$25 million.[45] During the first quarter of the 20th century, Edith and Harold subsidized Chicago's Grand Opera. Their donations came regularly even during the eight years Edith was in Switzerland. Without their support, grand opera in Chicago could not exist. Even in divorce, Edith and Harold agreed to continue funding the Chicago Grand Opera Company, a project on which they had already spent $5 million. Harold underwrote Prokofiev's comic opera *The Love of Three Oranges*, premiered by the Chicago Opera Association on December 30, 1921, at the Auditorium Theater. After that performance, Harold ended his support of the Opera Association.

Harold announced that "because he could not afford to retain it" he hoped to sell Villa Turicum, the Lake Forest villa and grounds, to Edith for $3 million, half its original cost.[46] Edith paid $1,954,000 to Harold to buy Villa Turicum.[47] Ever grandiose, she planned to make it a second Psychological Club, "a Mecca for the devotees of psychoanalysis," in particular "synthetic psychology which Mrs. McCormick studies under Dr. Carl Jung."[48] Edith regularly visited her beloved Villa Turicum for an hour or two to enjoy the view, but she never stayed overnight. For ten years more until the year of her death she kept a staff of seventeen to take care of the house and grounds.[49] After Edith McCormick Rockefeller died in 1932, the abandoned house went into a steep decline. In 1942, one hundred acres were sold to pay $340,000 in accumulated taxes and fines. In 1947, the remaining 200 acres were sold at auction for a pitiable $77,000.[50] In 1966, the house was torn down and the land divided into one to five-acre lots and sold off at $3,750 an acre. "This is the finest residential riparian property in the entire Midwest," said the developer.[51]

Harold moved back to the ancestral home at 675 Rush Street. The McCormick children were given the "choice as to which parent they wished to take up residence. All chose to live with their father." Since Mathilde was still a minor, the judge appointed Harold her guardian.[52] At age 16, Mathilde McCormick fell in love with a Swiss book illustrator turned riding instructor, 43-year-old Guillaume Max Oser. (Oser was nearly as old as Mathilde's father. His relatives in Switzerland claimed that he was aged 57 years.) Her engagement to a man "nearly three times her age attracted international attention."[53] In February 1922, Harold formally announced the engagement of Mathilde to Max Oser.[54] John D. Rockefeller was not pleased and appealed to his Swiss-educated granddaughters Muriel and Mathilde to be "true Americans and to love your own country and not be enamored with the allurements that come especially to our American girls sometimes by the fortune hunters of the world." He was reacting to the highly publicized marriages of daughters of America's newly rich to the sons of British noblemen. For a hefty price the American family gained prestige while the land-rich but cash-poor British blue bloods gained the money to keep up their stately homes and live in luxury. Best known of these marriages was Consuela Vanderbilt to Charles Spencer Churchill, the future ninth Duke of Marlborough: and the marriage of Jennie Jerome of Brooklyn to Lord Randolph Churchill. Mary Leiter, daughter of Levi Ziegler Leiter, who established a department store in Chicago with Marshall Field, grew up close to the home of Cyrus Hall McCormick. She married the British politician George Curzon, who, as Lord Curzon, served as Viceroy of India.

Convinced that Max Oser was a fortune hunter, Edith tried to prevent the match. She told Mathilde that the age gap between her and Oser would yield children at risk of mental illness, citing the marriage of Cyrus and Nettie that produced two schizophrenic offspring. Edith asked her father to cease sending money to Mathilde. Harold McCormick, who had sole custody over the girl, and with the reluctant consent of the aged John D. Rockefeller, permitted Mathilde to marry Max Oser when she reached age 18 years. Educated in Switzerland, Mathilde was more fluent in German and French than in English. The "tall, dark-haired, straight-limbed, with large black eyes and pleasant, though not regular features" girl told reporters that she wished to remain in Switzerland "where she rides, tramps, knits, plays the piano and reads" and to be close to her Max.[55] Tongues were wagging over Harold's affair with Ganna Walska, coupled with Mathilde's "unshakeable determination" to marry Max Oser. Reporters were scurrying about in Chicago and New York, and on the Continent to report on the McCormick family. "Friends today were discussing," wrote the gossipmongers, "the possibility of a double wedding for Mathilde and her father."[56]

Edith Rockefeller McCormick made one last effort to prevent Mathilde's marriage to Max Oser. In her brief to the court, Edith insisted that Oser was too old a man for Mathilde and that he was "without a regular and certain income or means of livelihood." His true motivation, she claimed, was "to secure large sums of money and financial gain." If married, the innocent Mathilde would be "subject of machinations and intrigues of designing persons." Edith appealed to her father to cut off her children's allowances "to make it less possible for them to be taken in by swindlers and by evil-minded people." Unhappy with the public airing of his family's dirty linens, John D. Rockefeller pointed out that Mathilde would soon reach age eighteen and would be "of legal age to select her husband without any parental consent, if she desired." With her father's intervention, Edith stopped her efforts to prevent the marriage, but she still seethed in anger toward her daughter. Max Oser categorically denied that he was a fortune hunter, and insisted he was marrying for love. He sold his riding school to raise enough money to live a simple life with Mathilde without seeking financial support from her family.[57] Max claimed that they would have enough money "if they lived simply as they proposed to do."[58]

In 1920, Harold substantially sweetened Harvester's profit-sharing plan by giving "extra compensation ... to all workers, even those who would not subscribe for it voluntarily."[59] John D. Rockefeller did not approve. Referring to Harvester's Extra Compensation and Stock Ownership Plan, John, Sr., believed that Harold "recently threw away on the employees ... a vast sum of money under the guidance of some impulse. [He] threw away a million dollars of precious gold.... And such is life."[60]

The recession of 1920–21 saw a sharp fall in the stock market, a drop in agricultural production and a steep rise in unemployment. Harvester net profits tumbled from nearly $17 million in 1920 to $4 million in 1921 and $5.5 million in 1922.[61] On June 2, 1922, after three and a half years of day-to-day responsibility at Harvester, Harold F. McCormick, at age 50, quit. Replacing him as president was Alexander Legge. Born in 1866, he quit school at age seventeen to work as a cowboy in Wyoming. In 1891, the self-educated country boy with only a few years of grammar schooling went to work as a debt collector for the McCormick branch office at Council Bluffs, where he first met Harold McCormick. The two became close friends. When Harold returned to Chicago as company vice president, he brought Alexander Legge with him. With the formation of International Harvester, Legge served as head of worldwide claims collections. At the start of World War I, Cyrus Hall McCormick, Jr., recommended Legge to president Woodrow Wilson to serve under Bernard Baruch as vice-chairman of the War Industries Board, to ensure adequate supplies for the army and navy. Bernard Baruch entrusted Legge with "complete authority" to run the Board. At the close of the War, Legge helped draft the section of the Treaty of Versailles, dealing with reparations and economic adjustments between European countries. The Treaty called for the establishment of the League of the Nations, set the boundaries of Germany and the cost of reparations, and required the entry of goods into Germany without tariffs or duties. For his service, President Woodrow Wilson awarded Legge the Distinguished Service Medal.

"We have been working together since 1896," said Harold of Alexander Legge, "and I have for him a deep personal friendship." The Harvester board had created a new position for Harold, as chairman of the executive board of directors. This position would give him the time to consider "the policies of the company.... I do not contemplate any diminution in my interest or service to the company."[62] Cyrus III was placed in charge of International Harvester manufacturing plants worldwide.[63] Under Alexander Legge's leadership, the Harvester Company enjoyed eight profitable years with little open worker discontent. Legge extended the range of Harvester products, especially trucks and the Farmall tractor. By 1930, harvesting machines constituted less than one-tenth of total Harvester sales. Output and profits fell precipitously in 1931 when the Great Depression hit agriculture. In 1932, Harvester lost $7.5 million dollars, leading to layoffs and wage cuts.[64]

Instead of serving the 40,000 workers, shareholders and the customers of Harvester,

Harold McCormick focused on his personal and family issues. "If Mathilde loves Oser," Harold said, "and wants to marry him, I am in favor of it. I am in favor of anything which promises to bring happiness into this family." Mathilde McCormick, approaching her 18th birthday, did her shopping in Paris in preparation for her marriage to Max Oser.[65] Mathilde married Max Oser on April 13, 1923, at the Lewisham Registry Office in London. The couple set out to Scotland for their honeymoon, after which they settled in Switzerland. Mathilde had an income of $10,000 a year. She bore two children, Anita and Peter. Anita was the first great-grandchild of John D. Rockefeller. In 1932, Mathilde inherited $2 million from her mother's estate. In 1938, Mathilde was injured when her car struck a pole near Geneva, Switzerland. Max Oser died in Switzerland at age 65. Mathilde and her children moved to the United States to settle in a home on 35 acres at Redondo Beach, California. Mathilde died from complications after surgery on May 18, 1947, at age 42 at the Good Samaritan Hospital in Los Angeles.[66] Mathilde left $3,500,000 to her two children.[67] Her daughter, Anita Oser, married Linus Pauling, Jr., son of twice Nobel prize-winner Linus Pauling; the Chemistry prize in 1952, and the Peace Prize in 1962. Mathilde's son Peter Max Oser attended Pomona College, and settled in Switzerland.

Harold Fowler McCormick, at age fifty-one, took pride in his youthful appearance. He was a member of several sports clubs and took part in regular exercise and gymnastics. In preparation for his marriage to Ganna Walska, the "tempestuous Polish opera singer," Harold consulted several physicians. One doctor told Harold that "vigorous exercise was too strenuous for a man more than forty, and advised him to consider gland transplantation; grafting the glands from a younger man, or from a goat or a monkey" that could extend his life by ten to fifteen years, and increase his sexual virility. On June 13, 1922, Harold F. McCormick, chairman of the board of directors of the International Harvester Company, entered the Wesley Memorial Hospital in Chicago, under the care of the urologist Dr. Victor Darwin Lespinasse, to insert donor testicular tissue into his scrotum to ensure "perpetual youth."[68]

The newspapers had a field day. At the same time Harold entered the hospital, "a virile youth of formidable stature and highly developed athletic proportions, carefully selected for his physical attainments" was also admitted. Sleuthing reporters determined that the unknown youth had "acquired some of Mr. McCormick's wealth in return for a sacrifice" of one or both of his testicles, to be used in the transplant operation. The operation seemed to be successful, with Harold McCormick quickly recovering and cheerfully smoking and talking with his visitors.[69] Dr. Lespinasse claimed a man is as old as his glands, but other physicians were skeptical that such a procedure could work. Lespinasse insisted "no glands of a monkey, goat or human being were used in the operation."[70] Harold was discharged from hospital on June 22, "in the best of spirits [with evidence of] rejuvenation already noted," and the following day he set out for New York with plans to depart with Mathilde for Europe July 20 aboard the steamship *Olympia*.[71] Dr. Lespinasse reportedly collected $50,000 for Harold's operation. Some years later, Harold underwent an operation in Paris by the charlatan surgeon Serge Voronoff, who claimed success in rejuvenating men of any age by grafting sections of monkey testicle onto the testicles of men. The monkey-gland procedure did not help Harold.[72]

The ambitious and tempestuous Ganna Walska was on her third marriage when she met Harold F. McCormick in December 1920. Her first husband, Baron Aracadia d'Eingorn, was a Russian nobleman and army officer killed during the First World War. In New York, she consulted Dr. Joseph Fraenkel about a throat condition. Ten days later she married the besotted ear, nose and throat physician. Fraenkel was twice her age and soon died, leaving Ganna his apartment and half his estate. In 1918, Ganna married Alexander Smith Cochran, Yale class of 1896, owner of the Alexander Smith Carpet Company in Yonkers, and worth $20 million. Cochran was a yachtsman who owned a townhouse at 820 Fifth Avenue and a winter home in Aiken, South Carolina.

On December 29, 1920, Ganna and her husband, Alexander S. Cochran, left New York for France, where Ganna planned to launch her operatic career. Cochran objected to her all-consuming focus on opera. In a huff, Cochran left her and Ganna sued for divorce. "If he wants to get rid of me, he must pay until it hurts," said Ganna, demanding half his worth. "He must realize that a woman is not a toy to gratify a whim, and then cast aside like a house, a yacht or a racehorse."[73] From Paris in July 1922, Ganna Walska announced that she had no intention of marrying Harold McCormick as she "would not abandon her artistic career in favor of matrimony with him."[74] To win her over, Harold promised Ganna he would devote his resources to help her achieve her heart's wish to become a prima donna. His sexual prowess reinforced by the gland transplantation, on August 11, Harold married the newly divorced Mrs. Alexander Smith Cochran in a Parisian city hall.[75] Her first concert in Europe was a success. Pleased with her reception, Ganna exclaimed: "I am happy to be known here only by my work.... I hope Chicago will take my singing seriously." Ganna was scheduled to sing at the Paris Opera in Rigoletto with the great Italian baritone Bastiasini, but he cancelled because his wife had died. "Bastiasini is the only good baritone left in Europe," claimed Ganna. "All the good baritones have been carried off to America, principally to Chicago, except him, and I do not wish to make my debut at the Paris Opera with a second-class baritone."[76]

In Paris, Harold created a new opera company "to star his bride." In September 1922, his daughter Muriel sailed for France to join her stepmother in the company, taking the operatic career name of Nawanne Micor.[77] On December 2, at the 2,000-seat Champs Elysees Theater, Ganna sang the solo part in Beethoven's 9th Symphony. "Harold McCormick was delighted with the success of his wife and was enthusiastic as to her future career."[78] On January 3, 1923, Ganna, "accompanied by her husband," set sail for a two-month concert tour of America. "It will be a chance for my American friends to see what a splendid wife I have," beamed Harold. Ganna was studying English. "I am intensely interested in all things in America, the country of my adoption."[79] Visiting Chicago, Harold and Ganna married again, to meet the requirements of Illinois divorce law.[80]

Harold Fowler McCormick gave much of his time and money to furthering the operatic ambitions of his new wife. She embarked on a tour of smaller American cities, appearing "gorgeously attired and in addition to other jewelry a rope of pearls, a gift of Mr. McCormick." The Detroit critic observed that "nature has endowed her neither with the vocal gift nor the keen intellect to ease her path" to a brilliant singing career.[81] Highly sensitive to criticism, Ganna cancelled her March 23 appearance at Chicago's Orchestra Hall and on March 29 set sail to establish her career in Paris. On June 27, she appeared in Verdi's Rigoletto at the Paris Opera in a concert she financed with Harold's money. Her performance was met with "audible titters and at least one high-pitched whistle clearly heard around the auditorium." Singing a famous aria, her voice "scarcely carried across the footlights ... faltered, stammered and produced a series of squeaks," answered by peels of laughter from the packed audience. Her much-anticipated Paris debut was "a complete fiasco."[82]

By 1924, rumors circulated that "Mr. McCormick finds his wife's operatic ambitions too costly." In Paris she opened a perfume shop, and, using Harold's money, bought the Champs Elysees Theatre, the largest and finest playhouse in Paris, with the intent to "make it the home of the finest expression in dramatic art."[83] Determined to conquer her nervousness, Ganna sang in smaller towns under the name of Anna Navarre. With Harold's financial backing, Ganna appeared in January 1925, as Cio Cio San in Puccini's Madame Butterfly at the Nice Opera House. This was a "do-or-die test of her prowess." But, again, she was overwhelmed by stage fright. Her voice "lacked strength and clarity and her mannerisms provoked the unfeeling audience to laughter [followed by] an ominous silence and then hisses."[84] In May of 1925, Harold left New York on the steamship *Majestic* for Europe. Asked whether he would see his wife there, he responded, "I would rather not talk of that."[85]

In January 1926, Ganna announced that she would sing the title roles of operas in various European opera houses. She assured her American admirers that she would be back in New York by the fall to sing in Madame Butterfly. Ganna's great ambition, handicapped by a weak voice and brittle nerves, was affecting her marriage. On January 16, 1926, Harold and Ganna, accompanied by two maids and fifteen large pieces of luggage, boarded the French liner *Paris*. When asked why she had received poor press in America, Ganna responded that she expected greater success in Europe. An argument ensued between Harold and Ganna, and ten minutes before the time to sail, an agitated Harold bounded off the vessel, took a taxi into the city and boarded the *Twentieth Century Limited* for Chicago.[86] Rumors of divorce reached the newspapers. Living abroad as husband to an untalented but hugely ambitious singer was demeaning to Harold Fowler McCormick. Asserting his McCormick lineage and position in Chicago, Harold "demanded that Ganna give up her career as a singer and take her place as his wife in Chicago." He had spent "millions of dollars in a vain attempt to satisfy her heart's desire—a brilliant opera career." The effort left him "terribly disillusioned with the marriage and feeling bitterly the ridiculous position I had been forced to occupy. I can feel the pity in my friends' hearts for me.... Chicago is my home. I was born and raised here."[87] Ganna demanded a settlement of $4 million in addition to the shares in International Harvester that Harold had given her at the time of their marriage.[88]

In 1928, Ganna moved to California, taking her jewelry and heaps of cash to establish "a legal residence separate from that of her husband."[89] Despite her humiliation at Paris and Nice, Ganna Walska went on to find success at the Volksoper in Vienna and had offers of a career in film. In February of 1929, Ganna Walska and her husband Harold arrived in New York and were "hurried out to a sparkling new Rolls Royce to motor up to Ganna Walska's Park Avenue apartment."[90] She gained mild applause at Symphony Hall in Chicago and Carnegie Hall in New York singing Bach's Coffee Cantata and Schubert songs. Her voice, noted one critic, was "better adapted to lullabies and ballads than to operatic arias."[91] "The birdlike notes of Mozart's glorious music," commented another critic, "shrunk into nasal squeaks."[92]

After her tepid reception in America, Ganna Walska returned to Paris. On October 10, 1931, Harold F. McCormick, chairman of the executive committee of the International Harvester Company, finally "received a divorce from his wife, Ganna Walska, the famed

Polish beauty and opera singer" on grounds of her refusal to live in Chicago, and deserting the marriage. "Our lives were essentially along separate paths," said Harold. No alimony was paid. Ganna had received $3 million from the estate of her former husband Alexander Smith Cochran and was satisfied with the "large settlement from Mr. McCormick at the time of their marriage," together with a house in Paris and a chateau near Versailles.[93] Her opera career had ended. "Critics and her audience generally found her wanting, but Mr. McCormick was still convinced she had a career before her."[94] The German film *The Blue Angel* by Josef von Sternberg came out in 1930. It portrays the middle-aged high school teacher Immanual Rath who is reduced to the role of a cabaret clown through his unrequited infatuation with the young and beautiful singer, played by Marlene Dietrich. Harold F. McCormick allowed himself to be similarly humiliated by Ganna Walska. Orson Welles based his film *Citizen Kane* on Harold Fowler McCormick's folly.

Alexander Legge (1866–1933) began work with the McCormick Harvesting Company in 1891 as a debt collector. During World War I he served as vice president of the War Industries Board. In 1922, he replaced Harold F. McCormick as president of International Harvester. From 1929 to 1931 he served president Herbert Hoover as chairman of the Federal Farm Board. He returned to International Harvester and served as president of the company until his death in 1933 (WHS Image ID 11042).

Alexander F. Legge served as president of International Harvester from 1922 to 1929. President Herbert Hoover offered him the position of commerce secretary, but Legge declined. At the insistence of President Hoover, Legge served from 1929 to 1931 as chairman of the Federal Farm Board aimed to solve the nation's "farm surplus problem." In this position, the patriotic Legge took a salary drop from $100,000 a year at Harvester to only $12,000 a year with the government. Despite the death of his wife and his poor health, in 1931 Legge returned to Harvester and remained president until his death in 1933. The 41-year-old Cyrus McCormick III, once considered heir apparent, resigned in 1931 as vice president of International Harvester, but remained a member of the board. Addis E. McKinstry followed Legge as president but soon retired due to failing health. On April 24, 1935, Sydney G. McAllister took the top job and held it for the next six years. Born in a humble Ohio home, McAllister attended public schools until age sixteen, when he went to work in 1897 for McCormick, quickly rising through the ranks. During McAllister's tenure, International Harvester became "one of the biggest industrial concerns in the United States," with 18 manufacturing plants, six twine mills, and 15,000 independent dealers throughout the world. Harvester was the nation's largest manufacturer of trucks, accounting for one-fifth of all the trucks on the road. The half-ton truck sold for $360 while the two-ton truck sold for $995, before tax.[95]

Harold McCormick served as director First National Bank of Chicago, and trustee of the University of Chicago, McCormick Theological Seminary, and the Chicago Civic Opera. From 1927 to 1929, he was engaged in legal battles against his sister-in-law Katharine Dexter

Meehan Grocery Company's International delivery truck, 1929 (WHS Image ID 26158).

The 1924 IHC 10–20 hp tractor replaced the heavyweight Titan and Mogul models. For safety, all parts of the engine were enclosed (WHS Image ID 35037).

McCormick over the custody of the insane Stanley McCormick. Harold McCormick served on the executive committee of the International Harvester Company board of directors from 1922 to 1935.

Until 1935, Cyrus Hall McCormick, the oldest son of the founder, still exercised his authority as chairman of the executive board and the largest single stockholder. In September 1935, Cyrus left the company with the intention to spend more time traveling and in recreation. He was succeeded by his brother Harold, recently divorced from Ganna Walska.

Harold's son Fowler was appointed vice president, in charge of foreign sales.[96] At the time of his death in 1937, Cyrus Hall McCormick owned 258,000 of the 5 million shares in International Harvester, worth over $23 million. Inheritance and other taxes reduced Cyrus's estate to less than $12 million. Harold owned 100,000 shares, with other members of the McCormick family owning far fewer shares. From 1922 to 1941, no McCormick was in day-to-day command of International Harvester. By the early 1930s, the influence of the McCormick family had greatly diminished, owning together fewer than ten percent of International Harvester's common stock. The McCormick family had lost control of the company, and "the part the family has played in the active management has shrunk."[97]

Edith Rockefeller McCormick Realty Trust

Edith Rockefeller McCormick returned from Switzerland in 1921. In Chicago, Edwin Krenn was her constant companion. The two of them met daily for lunch and dinner and often for afternoon tea. Edith and Edwin were chauffeured in her Rolls Royce to afternoon movie shows and in the evening to the opera, where the bejeweled Edith occupied her box. Edith set Edwin up in the real estate business, where he formed a partnership with Russian-born Edward Dato.

Edith's interest in real estate began early in her marriage when her father gave her a large tract of land facing the Desplaines River in Riverside Village, west of Chicago. In 1910, she developed Maplewood Road by dividing the land into forty lots to form "a most beautiful residential section."[98] Nine years later she donated the rest of her land to the Chicago Zoological Society to establish Brookfield Zoo.[99] In the 1920s, her brother John D. Rockefeller, Jr., embarked on the construction of the vast Rockefeller Center that would stretch from 48th to 51st streets, facing Fifth Avenue, in New York City. It was the largest project in New York during the Great Depression. Edith determined that in Chicago she could show her talents as a large-scale property developer. In 1923, she formed the Edith Rockefeller McCormick Realty Trust to raise millions of dollars to buy land and build upper-class towns replete with shopping centers, schools, playgrounds, churches and golf courses. She planned vast "civic projects to do great things for the community." She worked with the real estate firm of Krenn & Dato at 928 North Michigan Avenue. "Here is $5,000,000 to start with," she announced to Edwin D. Krenn and Edward A. Dato, and then added $4 million more. With Rockefeller money, the two men bought a golf course at Niles Center that became part of the town of Skokie, and spent $5 million to lay down roads and bring in electricity, sewerage, and water systems. Before the Great Depression, "hundreds of lots were sold at good prices." After the Crash, land sales dropped and there was "practically no building on the tract." Krenn & Dato developed hundreds of acres of land in Skokie between Dempster and Church streets, sixty-two acres in Chicago near Crawford and Devon avenues, as well as land in Highland Park, Riverside and Berwyn. The project dearest to Edith was Edithton Beach, to display "the good name and prestige of its founder." Situated fifty miles north of downtown Chicago, the 1,500-acre project (bought for $1.5 million), just north of the Illinois-Wisconsin state line, had four miles of frontage on Lake Michigan. It promised a sandy beach, golf course, polo grounds and tennis courts. With Edith's money and her expansive schemes, the firm of Krenn & Dato became one of the nation's largest real estate companies, with a staff of 1,500 designers, architects, brokers, office workers, construction workers and executives. In the 1920s, Krenn & Dato sold 16,000 house lots worth $27.5 million.[100] The plans of Krenn & Dato were "some of the most ambitious subdivision developments that ever were started in the vicinity of Chicago."[101] John D. Rockefeller, Sr., was alarmed by his daughter's ambitions and her reliance on Krenn and Dato. "It is my duty to warn you of the pitfalls and vagaries of life [and urge you] to select an honest, courageous and capable man to advise you in these affairs."

After her divorce in December 1921, Edith Rockefeller McCormick gained control over her great personal wealth. In addition to the millions her father gave her on her wedding day, he set up a trust for her consisting of 12,000 shares of stock in the Standard Oil Company. By 1925, the trust had accumulated dividends worth $7,500,000. Edith planned to use this money to fund her vast real estate schemes. Her ex-husband, backed by six legal firms, claimed that the trust fund was established not for Edith but for her children. Each year Harold received $30,000 from the trust.[102] After a long and costly legal fight, Edith was granted full control of the trust and its dividends.

In 1926, Edith's brother, John D. Rockefeller, Jr., took his family on a trip to the West. "We started the homeward trek in July and made the final stop in Chicago to see aunt Edith Rockefeller McCormick ... in her palatial home," wrote her nephew David Rockefeller. "Aunt Edith was a devoted patron of the Chicago opera.... She obviously relished her position as one of the grande dames of Chicago society; she entertained us at a formal luncheon complete with liveried footmen in tights behind each chair."[103] During her last years, Edith Rockefeller McCormick led a highly regimented life. Divorced and alienated from her children, she lived in isolated splendor in her forty-four-room mansion at 1000 N. Lake Shore Drive. Assisting her were a secretary, a personal maid, a butler, three footmen, three cooks, three chauffeurs, one horseman, one gardener and a staff to clean and maintain the house. She never spoke to the servants and they never spoke to her. All instructions were conveyed to her secretary to pass on to the staff. "Everything was just so. Everything had its proper time." Edith had her breakfast in her room. At a set time she took her daily walk along the lakeshore with detective Edward McNamara "a few steps behind her." Edwin Krenn came to lunch every day. Four members of staff "were needed to serve the simplest luncheon." Menus were typed daily in French. The cooks prepared whole turkey, duck or cuts of meat. Edith would eat a slice "but would not have it the next day." In the afternoon, one of her chauffeurs would drive Edith and docile Krenn in the Rolls Royce to a movie house to take in as many as three movies a day. She was always home by eleven o' clock at night, except for opera nights when the bejeweled Edith occupied her box, as the dowager queen of Chicago society. When she returned home there were always two footmen to welcome her; one to open the front door and the second to greet her in the reception room.

In June 1929, near the height of the stock market, Edith took out a half-page advertisement in the *Chicago Tribune* seeking to raise $11,000,000 to pay off bank loans "and for the operation, and development of real estate properties." The five-year notes would pay six percent interest and were guaranteed by her trust fund shares in the Standard Oil Company and other shares with a combined value of $17,840,000.[104] Paying top dollar for the land, Edith had to dig ever deeper into her fortune, borrow from banks, and mortgaged her properties at 1000 Lake Shore Drive and Villa Turicum in Lake Forest. Plans for her new towns were developed, but after the stock market crash on October 29, 1929, little got built. The land at Edithton Beach sold for $150,000, one-tenth of the purchase price.[105] With the Great Depression came the "end of the real estate boom … causing the shrinkage of her fortune of perhaps $40,000,000 to a mere fraction of that figure." Krenn & Dato Realty Company folded on March 31, 1932.[106] At her death in 1932, Edith Rockefeller McCormick, once one of the richest women on earth, was in debt.[107] The Edith Rockefeller McCormick Trust "had reached a financial crisis…. The lands it owned are no longer worth what they cost." The mortgages were overdue, the trust was no longer able to borrow money and there were no buyers for the assets."[108]

Early in 1932, riddled with cancer, Edith moved out of her lavish home to take a suite of rooms at the Drake Hotel. At her bedside during her last hours were Edwin Krenn, ex-husband Harold F. McCormick, her son Fowler and her daughter Muriel. Her youngest daughter Mathilde, Mrs. Max Oser, "raced to Chicago from her home in Switzerland to be with her mother…. Mrs. McCormick was unconscious when her daughter arrived" but briefly recovered "to give her daughter an affectionate greeting."[109] The fractured family was briefly united for Edith's last hours. Edith Rockefeller McCormick died of cancer on August 25, 1932. John D. Rockefeller, at age 93, was unable to make the trip to Chicago to attend the funeral.[110] Edith's brother, John D. Rockefeller, Jr., and his son Nelson arrived from New York to represent the Rockefeller family. The McCormick family attended in force. The service was held at the Fourth Presbyterian Church, where a string quartet played her favorite pieces that included a Bach aria, Tchaikovsky's Andante Cantabile and Bizet's Andante. Seven trucks were needed to carry the thousands of bouquets of flowers to Graceland Cemetery where Edith was buried next to her son, John Rockefeller McCormick, who died a half-century earlier of scarlet fever. Twenty thousand people thronged the cemetery to witness her burial, "taxing the efforts of the police to the utmost."[111]

Edith Rockefeller McCormick died of breast cancer a sad and lonely woman, ten days short of her sixtieth year. Her mansion at 1000 Lake Shore Drive, built at a cost of $4 million, was worth only $525,000 in 1932. Edith had spent millions to furnish her homes at Lake Forest and Chicago. At her death, her personal property was valued at $1,032,348, far less than the purchase price. Her jewelry, purchased in the swinging twenties for $5 million, had a value of only $777,567. Her famous necklace (bought in 1924 from Cartier for $1,500,000) contained 23 pearls and 1,657 diamonds. The tiara Harold gave her as a wedding present had 600 diamonds. Edith had purchased emeralds previously owned by Catharine The Great of Russia. She owned the gold dinner service once used by Emperor Napoleon, bearing his imperial crest and the letter "N."[112] The American Art Association sold her tapestries, French and English silver, lace, carpets, period furniture, jewelry and old books at auction in New York. A total of 918 lots yielded a measly $330, 615, of which daughter Muriel McCormick Hubbard bought $60,000 worth. The sales in Chicago at Edith's home yielded only "ridiculously low" prices.[113] Although her estate (property and jewelry) was heavily mortgaged, Edith was "far from being poverty-stricken at her death."[114] What money Edith had left, she bequeathed one-third to her daughter Muriel. Mathilde was left one-sixth and Fowler only one-twelve, with the remaining five-twelfths bequeathed to the dapper Edwin Krenn. In 1935, a court ruled that the $10 million in the Rockefeller Trust be equally shared by her three children, with Edwin Krenn cut out of any share. Her mansion was a jumble of expensive objects. "She never had the flair for putting two things together. The house was big, ugly, heavy and overwhelming."[115]

After Edith's death, the house at 1000 Lake Shore Drive was quiet. The temperature in Chicago on March 31, 1933, reached a balmy 57 degrees. "In the yard of the late Mrs. Edith Rockefeller McCormick … now unoccupied except for a caretaker, the bed of tulips, which during her lifetime, was as inevitable as spring itself, thrust its green spikes through the soil." The grand house remained unoccupied for twenty years until it was demolished in 1955 and replaced by an apartment building. Edith Rockefeller McCormick claimed immortality, stating that she was the reincarnation of Queen Ankhesenamun and was devoted to the occult and astrology and that at age sixteen she married King Tutankhamun. The Great Depression, she said, was the advent of a new astrological era, an event that occurs once every two thousand years.[116] After her death, her faithful protégé Edwin D. Krenn was at last free to find his own path. In November 1932, he resigned as trustee of the Edith Rockefeller McCormick Trust, and two years later, he married Mae Clayton, an art student in Chicago.

John D. Rockefeller outlived his daughter by five years, dying at age 98 at his home near Tarrytown, New York. He started as a poor office boy and became the world's richest man, worth $1,500,000,000. During his lifetime, he gave $500,000,000 to various charities, including his own Rockefeller Institute. His Chicago relatives "sent several hundred pounds of flowers to New York on a United Airlines plane for the funeral service…. Among the offerings was a spray of 100 orchids and 2,500 lavender violas" sent by his grandson, Fowler McCormick.[117]

In November 1932, Harold Fowler McCormick, chairman of the International Harvester Company, "was admitted to Johns Hopkins Hospital, Baltimore under the care of the eminent urologist Dr. High Hampton Young. Dr. Young specialized in the treatment of prostate enlargement and prostate cancer."[118] A few weeks later, Harold was well enough to whistle Mozart's Wiegenlied on the Chicago radio. "Ordinarily Mr. McCormick whistles only for his intimate friends. Tonight he whistled in behalf of a campaign to build a temple of music at the Century of Progress," at Chicago's 1933 World's Fair.[119]

Despite two divorces, Harold had a roving eye. In Paris, Harold met Rhoda Tanner Doubleday, divorced from the son of New York publisher Frank Nelson Doubleday. Harold found her "the most charming woman I have ever known. She is very fascinating." Harold and Rhoda were frequently seen together. Rumors of a marriage began to swirl, but in October 1933, Rhoda sued Harold for $1,500,000, alleging breach of promise of marriage and that his affections for her had noticeably cooled after his discharge from Johns Hopkins Hospital.[120] "This was no mild flirtation or platonic affair," alleged Rhoda's lawyers. In his letters to her, Harold "declared his devotion in the most affectionate terms and their approaching marriage was mentioned in them several times." In the end, Rhoda accepted a settlement of $65,000. In 1935, Harold received a note written in block letters on cheap paper demanding $30,000. "If you don't pay you will be in trouble plenty." The Chicago police, cooperating with federal agents, traced threatening phone calls to Chicago's Far West Side.[121]

Due to heavy smoking and vascular disease, Harold's health was failing and he spent most of his last years in California "to get the benefit of the climate." There he met Adah Wilson from Shoshone, Idaho, who served in 1936 as nurse to Jean Harlow, MGM's leading lady, known as the "Blond Bombshell." Harlow, at age twenty-six, died in 1937 of kidney failure. The next year, the thirty-one-year-old Adah Wilson was hired to take care of the ailing and aging 66-year-old Harold F. McCormick. Their relationship turned romantic and he gave her a "big diamond ring" as an engagement present. Tired of pursuing aspiring opera singers and socialites, Harold married nurse Adah on May 31, 1938, in the Pasadena house that had served as a one-patient locked psychiatric facility, first for his sister Mary and then for his brother Stanley.[122] But Harold's problems were not over. At the close of 1938, Mrs. Howard A. Colby of Kansas City claimed $2 million for breach of promise of marriage. Mrs. Colby claimed that in 1933 Harold had twice proposed marriage but then notified her that "he would not marry her."[123] The case was settled out of court with Mrs. Colby collecting $12,500.[124]

In 1940, Harold retired as director of the First National Bank of Chicago, but retained the title of chairman of the board of the International Harvester Company. "Throughout his career the white lights of publicity beat strongly on Mr. McCormick." He died at age 69 at his home in Beverly Hills on October 16, 1941, of a cerebral hemorrhage. A decade later, the remains of Harold Fowler McCormick were sent to Chicago for burial in the McCormick lot at the Graceland Cemetery. Harold Fowler McCormick's estate was "not quite so large" as his brother Cyrus's $22 million.[125] Harold left an estate worth $9,412,765. After federal inheritance and state income taxes, the net was reduced to $5,192,127 and placed in trust. Married for three years, Adah had an annuity of $40,000 for three years, after which time she received half of the trust. Harold's children Fowler, Muriel and Mathilde divided equally the remaining half of the funds.[126] Thirteen months after Harold McCormick died, Adah Wilson McCormick, age 38, married a thirty-year-old aircraft engineer, George Tait 2nd in Phoenix, Arizona. That marriage soon ended in divorce. On July 22, 1970, while on a visit to the Grand Canyon, Adah fell to her death near the Navajo Bridge.

Ganna Walska long survived Harold, Edith and Adah. After her divorce from Harold, Ganna remained in Europe, continued her efforts at an operatic career and lived a life of great luxury until the onset of the Second World War. Boarding the last liner to leave France, she made her way to New York, and from the East Coast to the West Coast. There she met Theos Casimir Bernard, the self proclaimed "White Lama." American born, Theos turned to Tibetan Buddhism and developed a small following in Los Angeles. In 1942, 54-year-old Ganna Walska married Theos, twenty years her junior.[127] She purchased a 37-acre home and property, which she named Lotusland, and set about to develop a beautiful garden. In 1943, she wrote her autobiography, *Always Room at the Top,* claiming that Edith Rockefeller McCormick had bribed officials in an attempt to prevent Ganna from singing in Chicago.[128] In 1946, Ganna divorced Theos Bernard to devote herself to her home and garden. She was the "Enemy of the Average," determined to remain remarkable for her beauty, her singing, her marriages and her wondrous garden. Towards the close of her life she sold her jewelry at auction and used the money to further develop Lotusland. Ganna Walska died in 1984, aged 97 years.

Chapter Nine

The Grandsons
Cyrus McCormick III
and Harold Fowler McCormick, Jr.

Cyrus Hall McCormick, Jr., and Harriet Hammond McCormick had two sons, Cyrus III and Gordon. Born September 22, 1890, Cyrus McCormick III graduated from Princeton University in 1912 and studied at Oxford University from 1912 to 1914. Cyrus III was judged "rather more studious than the majority of the wealthy young men of today."[1] In 1914, the 24-year-old Cyrus spent time near Smyrna in Asia Minor as one of twelve Americans supervising 800 local workers in an unsuccessful archeological dig for the key to the Lydian language, an Indo-European dialect.[2] On February 13, 1915, Cyrus III married Dorothy Caroline Linn, daughter of a Chicago grain operator, and a graduate of Miss Potter's School in Farmington, Connecticut. Dorothy trained for the stage at the Stuart Walker dramatic school in Cincinnati. The wedding was held in Chicago at the Fourth Presbyterian Church. It was one of the leading events of the Chicago social calendar for the year. "The wedding presents comprise jewelry which made Mrs. McCormick owner of one of the most costly assortments in Chicago." Her gifts included "a large string of pearls" given by her parents-in-law. After the wedding, the couple set out on honeymoon to Monterey, California, traveling via the Panama Canal.[3]

Cyrus III served during World War I as a lieutenant in the aviation division of the signal corps. In 1921 he was employed as a salesman for International Harvester in Madison, Wisconsin, then moved to branch manager of the tractor plant in Chicago. At age 32, as heir apparent to the vast McCormick dynasty, he was appointed vice president of the International Harvester Company. Mr. and Mrs. Cyrus McCormick III lived in grand style at 50 E. Huron Street, Chicago. Despite his position in the company, Cyrus III remained interested in history, archeology and the arts, in particular about Italy.

Newspapers had a field day on June 25, 1926, when they descended on the Grand Opera House in Cincinnati to review the play "Crime." Their interest focused on a thirty-second scene depicting an actress named Mary Butler, dressed as an old woman who "walked across the stage while a hold-up scene was in progress, and was jostled by two gangsters." The aspiring actress was none other than Dorothy McCormick, wife of Cyrus McCormick III, the grandson of the founder of the harvester company.[4] On June 29, Dorothy spent $7,000 to travel back to Chicago "on a special Pennsylvania railroad train with herself as the only passenger." On reaching Chicago, she tried to dodge reporters before entering the Drake Hotel, refusing to tell why she returned alone and in such haste.[5]

On April 12, 1930, Cyrus McCormick III (grandson of Cyrus Hall McCormick) drove the 100,000th Farmall tractor off the assembly line. In front is the factory superintendent E. H. Sohner. Usually in red, this tractor was painted silver for the occasion (WHS Image ID 12105).

Cyrus III and Dorothy separated in 1929 and divorced in 1931 on grounds of cruelty. Dorothy claimed that on one occasion Cyrus "seized her by the wrist" after she asked him where he had been all night long. On another occasion, he "roughly seized her by the arm and struck her on the shoulder, knocking her over a chair." Witnesses testified that she had been "a perfect wife to Mr. McCormick." Cyrus and Dorothy had no children. He was not present in court and did not contest the divorce.[6]

Soon after his divorce, Cyrus married the sculptress Florence Sittenham Davey in a "quiet wedding" at the Union Church in Havana, Cuba. She was the ex-wife of Randon Davey, a New York artist. Cyrus moved with Florence to Santa Fe, New Mexico.[7] In 1941 he was appointed "price executive of the automobile and truck section of the federal Office of Price Administration and Civilian Support," giving him nationwide authority to set the price of cars and trucks.[8] Cyrus III died of a cerebral hemorrhage in Hartford, Connecticut, on March 31, 1970, at age 79.[9] His younger brother Gordon McCormick graduated from Princeton in 1917 and fought with the 86th Division during World War I, attaining the rank of captain and aide-de-camp to the commanding officer. A quiet philanthropist who lived off his trust fund, Gordon showed little interest in the harvester company. In 1939 the brothers Gordon and Cyrus donated $1,109,767 to Princeton University for its new library. The money was given in memory of their father, Princeton class of 1879.[10] Neither Cyrus III nor Gordon had children. Instead, the McCormick legacy passed to their uncle Harold Fowler McCormick, Sr., and his son, Harold Fowler McCormick, Jr.

Harold Fowler McCormick, Jr., known as Fowler McCormick, was born in 1898. He was the son of Harold Fowler McCormick, Sr., and Edith Rockefeller McCormick. From an early age he knew that he was special. At age nine years he was sent to visit his maternal grandparents in New York. From the day of his arrival, "the guards at the Rockefeller home were doubled … to prevent the kidnapping of the McCormick child. The boy plays about the grounds near the house but never for one instant is he left alone by his French maid. Within calling distance two stalwart guards walk about."[11] Fowler McCormick was fourteen years old when he accompanied his mother to Zurich. He learned French and German and received his early education in Switzerland. While still in his teens, Fowler McCormick was psychoanalyzed by Carl Jung. For the rest of his life he remained devoted to Jung and to his psychology. Fowler returned to the United States to attend Groton School in preparation for admission to Princeton College. In 1916, Fowler was accepted to Princeton, but took a year off to join the Gentlemen Volunteers as an ambulance driver in France. At Princeton, nineteen-year-old Fowler McCormick became friendly with his classmate, James "Bud" Stillman. Fowler was besotted by Bud's mother, Anne Urquhart Potter "Fifi" Stillman, the mother of three other children, and nineteen years his senior. Fifi was "a striking red-head with a flirtatious manner and volatile temper." Anne's marriage to James A. Stillman, president of the National City Bank, came unstuck in 1919 with accusations on both sides of infidelity. She accused her husband of "infidelity with Florence Leeds, a former chorus girl." In turn, James accused Fifi of having an affair with an Indian guide named Fred Beauvais and claimed that Fred was the father of Fifi's youngest child, Guy Stillman. The salacious publicity around the protracted divorce trial forced James Stillman to resign as president of the bank.

Anne and Fowler made their relationship public on June 19, 1921, when Anne "attended the Princeton University commencement exercises as the guest of Harold Fowler McCormick Jr., a member of the graduating class."[12] After graduating from college, Fowler debated joining his grandfather's Standard Oil or his father's International Harvester. Instead he dabbled in music composition, psychology, and accountancy, and even started a brokerage firm. Close to thirty years of age, duty required that he enter the harvester business. Fowler went to work in the International Harvester plant in Milwaukee, starting at the bottom earning $15 a week "as a day laborer wresting 200-pound ingots of pig iron for nine hours a day." For this effort, Fowler received a handwritten letter from his grandfather, John D. Rockefeller. "My dear grandson, I am very pleased by the manner in which you have chosen to learn the harvester business starting at the bottom. By doing this you will glean first hand the knowledge that will greatly benefit your later life."

In March 1925, Fifi Stillman met Fowler "at the gate as he came out in his grimy cap and overalls and carried him away in her automobile."

> "Fowler," said Fifi, "I couldn't—just couldn't, go on west to the Grand Canyon without stopping over and saying hello…. I knew that Fowler would be lonesome up here at the plant. I thought it was my duty to come here and see the boy…. I am a friend of his best friend, my son Bud…. Fowler is getting a lot of experience. But the poor boy was so tired that his lids were drooping as we talked. His hands are all calloused now."[13]

The handsome and wealthy Fowler McCormick was inundated with perfumed letters "from girls and hero hunters," which he threw unread into the wastepaper basket.[14] Fowler took time off his work to visit Anne "Fifi" Stillman and her children at their hunting lodge, Grand Ans, in Canada. There he ostensibly visited his Princeton classmate "Bud" Stillman, but his real interest was Fifi herself.[15] His parents Harold and Edith McCormick were strongly against the relationship and wrote in desperation to Dr. Carl G. Jung in Zurich asking him to come to America to talk Fowler out of his embarrassing infatuation. Rearranging his schedule in Zurich, Jung sailed on December 13, 1924, officially to study the unconscious mind of the city-building Taos Pueblos of New Mexico, with Fowler as his guide. For weeks Carl and Fowler toured Chicago, Santa Fe, Taos and the Grand Canyon. At Taos, New Mexico, Jung had his famous meeting with the Hopi elder, Mountain Lake. " I was able to talk to him as I have rarely been able to talk to a European," wrote Jung. Jung and Mountain Lake, with Fowler listening, conversed for several hours. Mountain Lake expressed his distrust of the white race.

"See how cruel the whites look," said Mountain Lake. "Their lips are thin, their noses sharp, their faces furrowed by folds. Their eyes have a strange expression. They are always seeking something. The whites always want something; they are always uneasy and restless.... We do not understand them. We think they are mad."

Jung asked Mountain Lake why he thought the whites were all mad.

"They say that they think with their heads," he replied.

"We think here," he said, indicating his heart.[16]

The following year, Fowler accompanied Jung on a trip to "darkest" Africa to study the collective unconscious "and the psychology of the savage peoples." On his return to International Harvester, Fowler McCormick headed to the accounting department on his rapid way up the corporate ladder. Neither therapy with Jung nor exotic travel dissuaded Fowler from pursuing his Fifi.[17]

Probably at the suggestion of Fowler McCormick, Fifi and James Stillman made one last attempt to save their marriage by sailing to Europe to consult Fowler's guru Dr. Carl Jung. Society women such as Mrs. Stillman "must be taught to study their own minds," said Jung. Mrs. Stillman had become the latest and "most sensational convert to his the-

Fowler McCormick (1898–1973) was the son of Harold Fowler McCormick, Sr., and Edith Rockefeller McCormick. His grandfathers were Cyrus Hall McCormick, Sr., and John D. Rockefeller, Sr., two of America's most successful entrepreneurs. Fowler served as president of International Harvester from 1941 to 1946, and chairman of the board from 1946 to 1951. Picture taken in 1945 (WHS Image ID 34872).

ories." She was making good progress in therapy, reported Jung, and "there is every possibility of a full reconciliation of the Stillmans."[18] This was not to be, and the divorce between Fifi and James Stillman was finalized in 1931, with Anne receiving their New York house but no cash settlement. James Stillman set aside $3 million in trust to be shared equally by his four children. In addition, the Stillman children were heirs to a $6 million trust fund set up by their grandfather. These trusts would provide each of Anne's children an annual income of $125,000 to $150,000 (approximately $2 million in 2019 dollars). Hours after her divorce was finalized, Anne, at age 51 years, married 32-year-old Harold Fowler McCormick, Jr.[19]

The Great Depression reduced sales of farm equipment. "By the mid–1930s, Deere had captured huge pieces of Harvester's market."[20] International Harvester was acutely aware of the competition from John Deere and Allis-Chalmers. These companies were selling rubber-wheeled tractors for $475 each, while a similar International Harvester Farmall tractor was listed at $835. Harvester spent $3 million to modernize its Chicago plant to build a $515 farm tractor to better compete against its rivals.[21] Fowler McCormick served as an International Harvester salesman in Omaha, Nebraska and then as branch manager. Fowler served under the leadership of Addis E. McKinstry. Born in Eaton, Ohio, McKinstry went to work at age sixteen as a Deering machinery repairman. With the formation of International Harvester, he was placed in charge of Canadian sales. In 1913 McKinstry came to Chicago in charge of farm equipment design. In 1919 he was promoted to vice president and in 1933, at age 63, he was appointed president of International Harvester.[22] In 1934, Addis E. McKinstry showed his gratitude to the founding family by promoting Fowler McCormick vice president in charge of foreign sales. McKinstry resigned April 1935 "because of poor health." That month, Cyrus Hall McCormick, chairman of the board, announced the appointment of his nephew Fowler McCormick to the board of directors, and the selection of Sydney G. McAllister as chief executive officer, with a yearly salary of $83,419. McAllister joined the McCormick Company in 1897 as an office boy and rose quickly through the ranks. From 1914 to 1931 he served as director of the company's European subsidiaries.

The Decatur Cartage Company of Chicago used International trucks. Decatur was the core of Walter F. Mullady's transport company, with 80 trucks and 2,000 employees. A graduate of Loyola University, he served as president of the American Trucking Association. Picture taken in 1937 (WHS image ID 59323).

The early years of the Great Depression were rough going for Harvester, with large layoffs and heavy losses. In 1933, International Harvester had a deficit of $7,683,000. The year 1934 saw improved sales of tractors and trucks with a profit of $3,349,000.[23] Harvester's employment dropped in 1932 to 18,900 workers, but rose to 43,700 three years later. The year 1936 was even better, with employment reaching 53,000 workers. In 1937, the company reported big sales gains, surpassing pre–Depression levels. Harvester invested $3 million on a factory in Indiana and hired 3,000 workers to build engines for its trucks.[24] The year 1935 also saw the resignation of Cyrus Hall McCormick, son of the founder, as chairman of the board. Succeeding as chairman was his brother Harold F. McCormick, Sr. Harold's authority rested on his owning 101,390 shares in International Harvester, a much larger share of the pie than McAllister's 1,080 shares and McKinstry's 6,931 shares.

On December 4, 1937, Carl Gustav Jung and the wealthy Fowler McCormick set out together on yet another exotic voyage. They traveled by ship from Marseilles on a 20-day journey to India. Teacher and disciple visited Delhi, Benares, Mysore, Madras and other cities. For Jung, the India trip came at "a decisive point in my life." He was interested to study the Indian take on good and evil in contrast to his views gained "through the prism of Christianity." Jung found Indian imagery suffused with sexual themes, especially at the Temple of Konark. Fowler had a different impression of India. "Everywhere there was evi-

An International school bus drives in 1936 along a dirt road in a rural area (WHS Image ID 65121).

This 1942 photograph shows two women driving Farmall tractors with attached cultivators at work on the farm (WHS Image ID 50961).

dence of animal sacrifice, everything filthy, dried blood, betel nuts."[25] In 1938, Fowler was put in charge of the company's manufacturing in the United States.[26] As vice president, Fowler defended International Harvester against the accusation that machinery was causing severe unemployment among farm workers. Farm machinery "shortened the farmer's working hours and lightened his job [while] releasing millions of farm workers for urban jobs." Gasoline-powered tractors, harvesters and other machines used in agriculture had assured the nation's food supply and offered freedom from famine. The machines took the grunt work and the drudgery out of farming and offered farmers more time for leisure activities. The small tractors recently introduced by the company would help "preserve the family-operated farm as an American institution."[27] Fowler became president in 1941 and in 1946 chairman of the board of International Harvester Company, positions previously held by his father and his uncle.

    The Second World War began in September of 1939 after Germany invaded Poland, bringing Great Britain and France into the fight. The United States officially entered the War on December 7, 1941, after the Japanese attacked the American fleet at Pearl Harbor, Hawaii. During 1940 and 1941, the United States embarked on a $160,000,000 armament spree for home needs as well as supporting Great Britain. The International Harvester Company alone received orders of $60,000,000, leading it to convert its factories to the production of army trucks and tractors, artillery, gun carriers as well as specialized guns

A 1956 photograph shows workers loading logs onto an International Harvester PF-230 truck (WHS Image ID 26160).

for aircraft use. Military contracts provided one-fifth of the work for International Harvester. The American automobile makers, steel companies and other farm implement companies received huge government military contracts. The awarding of these contracts unleashed a wave of union-led strikes from the East Coast to the Midwest demanding better working conditions and more pay.

In January 1941, workers in the Chicago plants of International Harvester downed tools to form picket lines. "A few hundred workers went into the foundry to urge non-union workers to quit." Each side attacked the other using shovels and bricks. After four workers were seriously injured, the company, on January 29, 1941, closed the factory to its 6,400 workers. "We don't want people killing each other."[28] International Harvester accused the unions of "preventing the company from fulfilling defense contracts and from manufacturing equipment needed at once by farms."[29] To prevent further violence, a force of 1,386 police officers was assigned to keep the peace outside the McCormick plants. It was "the largest concentration of force ever assigned to a strike in the city's history." Union members paraded outside carrying banners that said "Solidarity Forever." Union leaders charged that International Harvester had bribed "high police officers to provoke violence."[30] Union boss Grant Oakes claimed: "Thousands of Harvester workers have sweated and toiled for many years in these plants to pile up profits for the McCormick family." If violence occurred during the strike, the responsibility "shall lie solely and heavily on the heads of this greedy family which will do anything to gain its enormous profits. The unions demanded a 20 percent increase in wages, and financial compensation for conscripted workers with the guarantee that jobs would be waiting for them on their return from military duty."[31]

The United States secretary of labor warned that the strikes were "holding up hundreds of millions of dollars worth of defense and Allied-aid production." If the strikes were not quickly settled, the government threatened to take over of the defense factories. Management and labor, he warned, "Should not mistake Uncle Sam's patience for weakness."[32] With tempers still high, the men returned to work. On May 12, 1941, 43-year-old Fowler McCormick was elected president of International Harvester, replacing Sydney G. McAllister, who became chairman of the executive committee.[33] As head of the harvester company, Fowler followed in the footsteps his grandfather, uncle and his father. Fowler announced that in 1941, defense contracts provided 20 percent of the work of the vast company.

During the years of the Second World War, Fowler McCormick oversaw International Harvester's massive production of military trucks, tanks, diesel engines, torpedoes and

A 1942 International K-7 truck produced for the United States Army: During World War II, International Harvester received large government contracts to manufacture war equipment (WHS Image ID 26157).

This 1943 photograph shows an International Harvester plant converted for war production with women workers (caps and uniforms embroidered with the IHC logo) assembling torpedoes (WHS Image ID 63773).

other war materials, amounting to over $500 million dollars (in 1944 currency). Harvester continued to build farm machinery. In 1942, Fowler McCormick introduced International Harvester's cotton-picking machine. The cotton picker took forty years of experimentation before it was ready for sale. Attached to a gasoline-powered tractor, the machine did the work of fifty to eighty hand cotton pickers. Fowler appealed to the government, even in wartime, to allocate the raw materials to build more of these machines since cotton "requires more human labor than any other agricultural crop."[34] It was in the interest of the nation, claimed Fowler, for the government to provide materials to manufacture farm machinery, both to ensure the food supply and to free men to join the army.[35] In 1942, International Harvester issued a film to show how ready the company was to fight on several fronts at the same time: to produce enough food at home and to feed the troops fighting abroad; and to make the military equipment to win the war. Harvester modified its Milwaukee plant to produce 75mm shells. It built M-5 military trucks at its Fort Wayne plant and modified its tractor plant to produce high-speed tractors to pull or push cannons.[36] With thousands of men enlisting to fight, Harvester employed increasing numbers of women for factory work.

In 1944, Fowler announced that the company was setting up a separate truck division with factories in Fort Wayne and Indianapolis, Indiana and Springfield, Ohio.[37] Production was booming. That year International Harvester was one of fourteen companies across the nation to "receive the joint Army-Navy production award in recognition of outstanding performance in war work."[38] War products accounted for a whopping 71 percent of total sales. As the war wound down, government military orders to International Harvester declined sharply.[39] In 1945, International Harvester reporting a 70 percent decline in military orders.[40] Fowler McCormick prepared his company for peacetime production. With fewer American farmers, there would be a need for better and cheaper farm equipment. The International Harvester Company moved into refrigeration and other household equipment "to make the life more attractive to wives."[41]

Towards the end of World War II, International Harvester rolled out ambitious plans to spend $100 million to build new factories and increase its workforce to 70,000 in a bold effort to return to a peacetime economy of tractors, trucks, harvesters, and machinery to pick cotton, potatoes, peanuts, sugar beets and corn.[42] New plants were opened in Indiana, Kentucky and Tennessee. The farming revolution based on gasoline or electric-powered machines took the heavy physical labor out of farming, yielding bumper crops with fewer and fewer workers.[43]

At the end of World War II, thousands of men returned to their jobs at International Harvester, displacing the women workers. The end of the World War brought a burst of trade union activity with demands for higher wages. In October 1945, Harvester offered a 10 percent raise to all workers. This offer was rejected and a strike began. In January 1946, the "production of farm equipment machinery and tractors was paralyzed." Since International Harvester "makes 95 percent of the farm machinery made in the United States" the stoppage had serious consequences for farm output.[44] On January 21, production halted at other International Harvester plants as thousands of members of the United Farm Equipment Union walked off the job to demand a 30 percent increase in wages. The strike ended after a loss of 80 days of work, significantly weakening the company.

On May 16, 1946, Fowler McCormick was elected president, chief executive and policy-making officer, the man in charge of the business of the International Harvester Company. The position of chairman of the board of directors (once held by his father, Harold) was eliminated.[45] Fowler announced the company was expanding abroad, to Canada, Mexico and England. Sales during the fiscal year 1946 came to $632 million. The company experienced labor strife in ten plants, involving 24,000 workers on strike for 45 days or longer.[46] In 1947, Fowler McCormick commemorated the one hundredth anniversary of the founding in Chicago of the McCormick Harvester Company. From a single plant in Chicago, a century later the harvester company had grown to eleven factories in America, ten abroad, and possessing its own steel mill. His grandfather's harvester "extended the American frontier westwards at the rate of thirty to fifty miles a year," said the proud Fowler McCormick. Before the McCormick harvester, it took a farmer 64 hours to hand reap one acre of wheat. The modern harvester and tractor could cut 20 bushels in two hours; sixty times as fast as cut by hand.[47]

Fowler McCormick applied his training in Jungian analysis to the world of business. He "held a deep conviction that people should be dealt with as individuals, not as groups." He insisted on "fair employment policies in all Harvester plants throughout the country."

Establishing one of the nation's first policies of equal employment, Harvester had long applied this principle to its northern plants. Starting in the 1940s, the company extended its non-discrimination policies to its plants in the south. Fowler treaded softly to integrate black workers into the Southern plants. "It is our belief," Fowler McCormick announced, "that all of us have a responsibility to hire colored people…. We must give them an opportunity to earn a living." Black workers would receive "the same wages for the same work" as the white workers.[48] He instituted "one of the most progressive racial policies in American industry," and intensified Harvester's longstanding commitment for the wellbeing of its workers. "Non-discrimination as the guiding principle of employment in our plants has been the policy of the International Harvester Company for many years," announced Fowler McCormick in 1943. "It is our policy now and will continue to be our policy in the years to come."[49] Under Fowler's leadership, black employment in Harvester's southern plants "rose sharply" and the policy had "strong top-management support." Blacks and whites in Harvester plants across America were "working shoulder to shoulder."[50] Fowler was active in the Committee on Race Relations and the United Negro College Fund.

Speaking before the American Management Association in 1947, Fowler said, "The very existence of American industry depends on the success of its human relations…. In this country we have everything we need. But if the people do not believe in American industry, American industry will not last…. More than any other group," declared Fowler McCormick, "management has the opportunity to improve the economic status of all people." Under Fowler's watch, International Harvester grew to employ nearly 100,000 workers, scattered among twenty-three plants at home and abroad. It was "the world's biggest manufacturer of farm machinery," as well as a major producer of trucks.[51] Big business "had become impersonal and human relations were neglected." At Harvester, Fowler McCormick sought a balance of the needs "of the tripod of stockholders, customers and employees." The golden rule, considered Fowler, was to treat others as you wish them to treat you. Sixty years after the Haymarket Massacre, Fowler, who had benefited mightily from family nepotism, still believed that the bosses knew best and that "individual enterprise" rather than government control or union interference was the best means to preserve workers' "essential freedom."

Grappling with the rapid growth of his company, yet trying to maintain respectful relations with the workers, Fowler McCormick instituted a training program. Harvester's college recruitment program selected prospective managers who went through rigorous training. In 1946, Fowler set up Harvester's Central Training School at 70 West Maple Street in Chicago, where foremen and managers from its plants and offices at home and abroad underwent two weeks of training in human relations and company policy. Faculty of the University of Chicago, under contract with Harvester, conducted much of the training. In 1950, a five-story training facility was built at 186–194 East Delaware Place, housing ten classrooms and a library, with a staff of thirty-five.[52] Harvester boasted: "our home is still Chicago. Here are our general offices, our largest group of employees, six of our manufacturing plants, our biggest payrolls."[53] To colonel Robert R. McCormick, the great and lasting success of International Harvester was a shining example of the American free-enterprise system and the power of "capitalism harnessed to the welfare of civilization."[54] In 1950, company sales reached $942,602,000, with a net profit for the year of $61 million. International Harvester introduced a stock-buying plan for its employees.[55] In addition to its plant in Chicago, International Harvester had established plants in Memphis, Fort Wayne, Indianapolis, Louisville, East Springfield, Ohio and Evansville, Indiana. Despite Harvester's benevolence, in 1950 the employees affiliated with the United Auto Workers' Union went on strike for higher wages, more benefits and longer vacation time.[56]

After World War II, Harvester greatly expanded from its core business of harvesters, tractors, wagons and trucks. Harvester made planters, broadcast seeders, cotton pickers, corn pickers, crop dusters, cultivators, fertilizer spreaders, and even refrigeration equipment. Fowler, in 1947, defended Harvester against the accusation that it was making too much money. Harvester, responded Fowler, "is operating equally in the interests of the shareholders, the employees and the customers."[57] In 1947, Harvester introduced its 180-horsepower crawler tractor, called "The Big Red Machine." In 1948, the federal government again accused International Harvester of antitrust actions, filing suit against Harvester, J. I. Case and John Deere, "the three big names in farm machinery." The government alleged that these companies colluded "to suppress competition by agreements with retail dealers which prevent rival manufactures using these market outlets.... The chief purpose of the suits is to open up the market on a competitive basis for the benefit of the farmers, competing manufacturers and dealers alike." Harvester fought back against these charges. "I do not believe," stated the company president, "that any company in the country made a greater effort [than Harvester] to observe both the spirit and the letter of the antitrust laws."[58]

Fowler McCormick, a heavy smoker, suffered from pneumonia and was frequently absent from his office. Conflicts flared between Fowler McCormick and John L. McCaffrey. On May 18, 1951, the executive committee "voted to make John. L. McCaffrey the chief executive officer" of the International Harvester Company, leaving Fowler McCormick "without power or authority." Possessing the McCormick name and being the largest individual shareholder with shares worth over $10 million, the action of the board came as a shock to Fowler. "I do not believe," said the aggrieved 52-year-old Fowler McCormick, "that my record justified the demotion that the directors decided upon."[59] Kicked upstairs to the board of directors, Fowler joined his cousin Cyrus III, but neither had an "active part in the everyday management of the business." Fowler "was not much of a fellow to stand aside and watch others do the work."[60] Fowler resigned from the board of International Harvester in 1951. Citing poor health, Cyrus McCormick III also resigned from the board.[61] During the long history of McCormick and International Harvester, the McCormick clan was always in a top executive position. The McCormick role in International Harvester (temporarily) ended in 1951.

John Lawrence McCaffrey was born in Fayetteville, Ohio, in 1892. His father was a blacksmith who repaired Harvester farm equipment. John entered the company in 1909 as a $40 a month warehouse clerk. At age twenty McCaffrey joined the newly formed International truck division, selling the Auto-Wagon, with "high wheels to permit travel on muddy, deeply rutted roads." During those early years, the Auto Wagon was a hard sell, yet the 6-foot 3-inch McCaffrey got the sales. With his success in Ohio he steadily worked his way up the company ladder. In 1940, he moved to Chicago as head of the company's truck sales in the United States and Canada.[62] After he replaced Fowler McCormick as chief operating officer, McCaffrey expanded International Harvester to make every type of agricultural machinery, as well as trucks, tractors and refrigerators, with a 90,000-person workforce and 9,000 retail dealers in the United States and abroad.[63] In 1952, McCaffrey opened the state-of-the-art motor engineering laboratory at Fort Wayne, Indiana. America's vast highway projects of the late 1950s were a boon to Harvester's truck division. McCaffrey saw the continued rise of the motor trucks and tractors with a steady decline in sales of farm machinery.[64] McCaffrey advocated better products for less money and was a severe critic of the trade unions, which were "continually seeking increased wages" and imperiling the company's competitive edge.[65] Taking advantage of America's post-war move to the suburbs, McCaffrey introduced a range of home appliances, including refrigerators, and its Cub Cadet motorized lawnmower.

Muriel McCormick

"I want to win on my ability, if I have it; certainly not on my name," exclaimed Muriel McCormick. "The newspapers published two lines on my work and almost a whole page on who my grandfather is, and who my parents are."[66] Born in Chicago in 1903, educated in Lausanne, Switzerland, Muriel studied drama, literature and music. Returning to Chicago, Muriel objecting to the presence of Edwin Krenn, became estranged from her mother and moved to her father's home. Muriel believed that her talents lay in the theater. She studied voice at the Chicago musical college, the Eastman school in Rochester, New York and at a junior college in Millbrook, New York, studying under the playwright and poet Charles Kennedy. In 1922, Muriel appeared with the French Modern Theatre of Chicago in the lead role of "Le Passant," a one-act play in French verse by Francois Coppee. Edith Rockefeller McCormick arrived and was seated in the front row of the theater. Harold and Mathilde arrived a little later, and seeing Edith, they chose seats toward the rear. Muriel performed "deftly as the boy hero." As she came forward for a curtain call "a mammoth basket of pink roses from Edith was handed over the footlights." As Harold embraced his actress daughter, he exclaimed, "Splendid, darling, just fine. You are a good sport." Of Muriel's career on the stage, the exuberant Harold declared: "She loves it, and I can think of nothing better if she really loves it…. I knew she was good, but I didn't know she was that good." The only embarrassing moment amidst the triumph came when Edith shook hands with Mathilde. "How are you today?" asked Edith. "Very nicely, thank you," was the reply as mother and daughter parted.[67]

Muriel acted in several plays using the stage name of Nawanna Micor. Under the spell of her stepmother Ganna Walska, Muriel hoped for a career in opera. With her father marrying a Polish lady, her sister marrying a Swiss man and her mother rumored to marry an Austrian, young Muriel McCormick made clear her disapproval, and believed that "Americans should marry Americans."

In 1929, Muriel moved to Palm Beach, Florida to become a member of the smart set of the winter colony, where she met Elisha Dyer Hubbard. On September 10, 1931, Muriel McCormick, aged 28 years, married Elisha Dyer Hubbard, 24 years her senior. Hubbard hailed from Middletown, Connecticut, where his family, one of the town's oldest and wealthiest, owned a manufacturing business. A graduate of Yale, he fought in World War I "in the home-front trenches." Muriel's marriage "came as a surprise" to her family. "This is news," proclaimed her brother Fowler. "I never heard of Hubbard." Muriel and Elisha enjoyed a few years together. In Middletown they lived in the grand mansion on the 82-acre Lone Tree Farm. During the winter season they departed the frigid north for their villa in Palm Beach, where Muriel opened the Palm Beach Playhouse. Muriel inherited several million dollars from her mother's estate and lived lavishly with homes in Connecticut, Reno, Nevada, Palm Beach, Florida, Bar Harbor, Maine and St. Regis Lake, New York. Elisha Hubbard, who had been ill for a number of years, died in December of 1935. With no children of her own, Muriel adopted five orphans, whom she named John Rockefeller McCormick Hubbard, Harold Fowler McCormick Hubbard, Anna Jones Dyer Hubbard, Jr., Edith Rockefeller McCormick Hubbard and Elisha Dyer Hubbard, Jr.

In March of 1943, Muriel enlisted in the Women's Army Corps (WAC) to be trained in truck repair. Serving 39 months, she rose to the rank of sergeant, employed mostly in recruiting and public relations. Away from home, Muriel left her two youngest adopted children, Edith and Elisha, in the care of her housekeeper. In March of 1943, Fowler, president of the International Harvester Company, alleged that his sister was "addicted to the excessive use of alcohol," was an abusive mother and unfit to have control and custody of the children. She spanked her children with a hairbrush, forced them to hop a thousand times on each foot, and filled their mouths with wooden blocks. Assuming the moral authority of the family, Fowler McCormick started legal proceedings to remove two of the children, Edith, age 14, and Elisha, age, 10, from their adoptive mother's care.[68] Daughter Edith told the judge that Muriel had given Elisha "a good thrashing until he bled.... She struck him thirty times on the bare skin." The two children told the judge they did not like their adoptive mother and did not want to live with her.[69] Guardianship went to Fowler McCormick, who placed the children with a family on Ridge Avenue in Evanston, Illinois.[70]

A wealthy if unstable widow, Muriel McCormick Hubbard moved between her estate in Middletown and her other homes. She gave money to strangers, especially to servicemen, preferring to hand out $10 bills rather than the dimes given out by her grandfather, John D. Rockefeller. When Muriel died on March 18, 1959, at age fifty-six years, she left several million to charities as well as a personal estate largely of International Harvester shares worth $4,563,577.[71] After state and federal taxes were paid, her adopted children shared the remaining $2,255,152. Muriel inherited $7.5 million from a trust fund established by her father, Harold Fowler McCormick. In 1958, her brother Fowler, together with the children of her deceased sister Mathilde, contended that the adopted children were not "her issue" and were not entitled to any money from Muriel's trust fund. The case was settled out of court with the adopted children receiving 30 percent of the $7.5 million.[72] In addition, Muriel was heir to a $2.5 million trust fund set up in 1917 by her maternal grandfather, John D. Rockefeller. By the time of Muriel's death, her share of this trust had grown to $9 million. Her cousin, John D. Rockefeller III, claimed that the adopted children were not "legal issue" and were not entitled to any share in the Rockefeller trust. Instead, he proposed giving the money to the Lincoln Center to build the Juilliard School of Music. The battle over the Rockefeller Trust involved leading New York lawyers on both sides of the dispute. During the five years of legal wrangling, the trust grew to $12.7 million. The court allotted $9 million to the Lincoln Center, leaving "most of the remaining money to be shared by the four adopted children." Legal fees in the case exceeded $800,000.[73]

Labor conflicts continued to bedevil International Harvester. On October 3, 1952, fifty-two year-old William Foster, a longtime employee, was killed after crossing the picket line.[74]

In 1961 came the startling news that the vast McCormick Works, built by Cyrus Hall McCormick after the Great Fire of 1871, would be razed and the manufacture of farm implements moved from Chicago to factories in Moline and Canton, Illinois and to Wisconsin and Tennessee. After a century and more of manufacturing, the International Harvester Company was moving manufacturing out of the Chicago for good.[75]

In retirement, Fowler McCormick and his wife Anne spent several months each winter at their 4,236-acre ranch in Scottsdale, Arizona. Anne raised Angus cattle and Arabian horses, and built the Paradise Park equestrian center at the edge of their vast property. The annual Scottsdale Arabian horse show was held on the McCormick ranch. The couple also had homes at 1500 Lake Shore Drive, Chicago, in Palm Beach, in California and in Zurich, Switzerland. Fowler sold the ranch for $10 million. Fowler became Jung's "boon companion in the last several decades of life."[76] In 1956, Fowler spent time with the aged Carl Jung. No longer able to drive, Jung delighted in taking trips with Fowler in his Oldsmobile and touring the Swiss countryside, stopping for delicious meals at elegant restaurants. Jung dedicated the 1958 English translation of his book *The Undiscovered Self* to "My friend Fowler McCormick." Despite Carl Jung's pre-war identification with Nazi ideas, Fowler remained dedicated to him until Jung's death in 1961.

Anne McCormick died in Arizona in 1969, aged ninety years, and Fowler died December 31, 1972, of emphysema, aged seventy-four years. Fowler McCormick's funeral service was held at the Fourth Presbyterian Church in Chicago.[77] He was buried in the Graceland cemetery. Fowler McCormick was not the last of his clan to occupy the top seat in the harvester company. Two months after Fowler resigned, John L. McCaffrey appointed 34-year-old Brooks McCormick (a grandson of William Sanderson McCormick) as managing director of Harvester's plant in Doncaster, England. In 1968, Brooks became chief executive officer of the entire company.

Chapter Ten

Brooks McCormick
The Last McCormick as Chief Executive Officer

William Grigsby McCormick, the younger son of William and Mary McCormick, was the first McCormick born in Chicago. As a student at the University of Virginia, soon after the Civil War he became aware of the lack of social clubs at the school. William Grigsby, together with his friends Frank Courtney Nicodemus, John Covert Boyd, George Miles Arnold and Edmund Law Rogers, founded on December 1, 1869, the Kappa Sigma Fraternity, which grew into one of the world's largest college fraternities. Its first honorary member was Jefferson Davis, former president of the Confederate States. Jefferson Davis was "much pleased at being made a member of the Kappa Sigma Society." William Grigsby McCormick fathered seven children. His daughter Anne Reubenia (Ruby) married Edward Tyler Blair. Their son established William Blair & Company, investment bankers. Their grandson, William McCormick Blair, Jr., was the law partner of Adlai Stevenson, future governor of Illinois and twice unsuccessful Democratic candidate for President of the United States. William served as Stevenson's "invaluable aide-de-camp" and showed a "talent for organization, liaison and general trouble shooting."

Chauncey Brooks McCormick (1884–1954) was the sixth child of William Grigsby and Eleanor Brooks McCormick. He was named for Chauncey Brooks, a banker and president of the Baltimore & Ohio Railroad. When he was 12 years old, Chauncey's parents gave him a booklet written in 1896 by the department store mogul Marshall Field titled *Elements of Success*. To be successful, wrote Field, a person needs energy and common sense; to be thorough in work; choose good friends; to be honest and devoted to duty; exercise self-control; save nickels and avoid habits of indulgence; maintain high principles; and strive to advance further. Character is more valuable than money. Chauncey McCormick kept the booklet as his guide throughout his life. Even though his parents were not wealthy, they sent Chauncey to Groton School, where he was a student at the same time as his cousin Robert Rutherford McCormick and Franklin Delano Roosevelt. At Yale University, Chauncey studied Latin, History, English and French. The knowledge of the French language and the French people served him well during the coming World War.

Members of the McCormick family had a deep regard for young Chauncey. Mrs. Harriet H. McCormick wrote to him when Chauncey was a senior at Yale. "All your college mates must be so happy to be with you—how dear are the friendships made when life is at its springtime. Chauncey, I feel desirous that you should have all the opportunities. They help a young man to know his own bearings." Harriet offered to pay his expenses so Chauncey could attend a Yale camp where he would meet the right kinds of people. When a man has responsibilities, surmised Harriet, "he is no longer his own. Now you are free to choose your course, your affiliations and the stand you mean to take…. How many lives one sees that have reached middle age and are yet without a compass. They have drifted rather than sailed for port."[1]

In 1906, while a senior at Yale, Chauncey, in the company of his Evanston friend and fellow Yale student Fleming H. Revell,[2] were enjoying a walk in the grounds of Marvelwood, an estate owned by Peter Griest. A vicious elk charged Chauncey, tossing him in the air. Chauncey managed to get near a tree but the elk attacked again, opening a deep gash on his side and severely bruising his legs and neck. To escape the buck, Chauncey climbed up the tree and fainted. Hearing the commotion, farmers rushed to the scene and drove off the elk.[3]

"I saw by the papers yesterday," wrote the serious but practical Cyrus Hall McCormick, Jr., "that you had a serious accident from the most extraordinary cause, being hurt by the antlers of a buck in the park…. If there is anything that I can do in helping to see that you get proper medical attention, do let me know. I hope, as is frequent in most cases, the matter has been exaggerated by the press reports."[4] Cyrus's younger brother, the jocular Harold Fowler McCormick wrote: "You certainly had a close call, but now that it is over, I suspect you have a remarkable story to relate. I have no doubt you could rather have taken the charge of bucking the line in any football game than try to get by that elk."[5] Chauncey replied he was on the road to recovery. "I am relieved to get your good letter," responded Cyrus, "and am thankful you have escaped serious injury."[6]

To prove his worth, in 1906, Chauncey donned overalls to work as a day laborer at the family reaper company. Boarding at Hull House, each morning he caught the Blue Island Avenue streetcar to reach the reaper works by 6 o'clock in the morning. Chauncey said he had gained "a deep interest in the working conditions of the plant."[7] After his graduation from Yale in 1907, Chauncey tried to branch out on his own. "I am pleased that you have progressed so well with your work," wrote his father. "When you have had sufficient experience, and the opportunity arises, I am going to provide you with the necessary capital, at a substantial sacrifice, to give you a good start in business life."[8] Family funds were not forthcoming, and Chauncey joined International Harvester. His ascent up the corporate ladder was rapid and he was sent to the Paris branch of the company.

Chauncey began a romance with Marion Deering, daughter of Mr. and Mrs. Charles Deering of Evanston, Illinois. Her parents objected to the match saying, "the young McCormick did not take life seriously enough." To separate the young couple, Charles Deering spirited his daughter away on the Cunard ship *Lusitania* for an extended trip abroad.[9] Chauncey followed in hot pursuit to Egypt and through Europe, determined "to snatch his bride from under the noses of her unwilling parents." From the Park Hotel in Lugano, Marion wrote to her "dear Chauncey" that she was getting tired of the "usual European idleness [and was] thinking of going home…. I hope all goes well with you and your affairs."[10] During their furtive meetings, Marion finally agreed to follow her heart, even if it meant angering her parents.[11] In Monday, July 6, 1914, a week after Archduke of Austria Franz Ferdinand and his wife Sophia were assassinated in Sarajevo, Marion, with the belated approval of her parents, married Chauncey at the home of her uncle James Deering at 32 rue Spontini in the swanky 16th Arrondissement of Paris.[12] World War I officially began on July 28, 1914.

The marriage of Marion and Chauncey merged the Deerings and McCormicks for the second time. The happy couple returned to America in August of 1914, when they "took their first ride in Evanston, which was halted unfinished, when they were arrested for speeding."[13] Marion and Chauncey moved into 1519 North State Parkway, Chicago: a 3,600 square-foot, three-story townhouse with three bedrooms and three bathrooms. In 1915, after the birth of their first child, they restored and furnished 713 North Rush Street, in McCormickville, the home once owned by Chauncey's parents.

In 1917, with World War I raging, Chauncey McCormick felt it was his duty to serve. Leaving Marion and their little children in Chicago, he volunteered for the ambulance corps of the American Expeditionary Force and set out for France. The McCormick and Deering influence machine immediately got to work to assist Chauncey. James Deering furnished Chauncey with letters of introduction to important Frenchmen, and he wrote to Robert W. Bliss at the American Embassy in Paris: "I would like to introduce to you the husband of my niece, Mr. Chauncey McCormick who goes to Paris to serve with the American Red Cross." Bliss directed Chauncey to the American Field Ambulance Service that had sent ambulances from America to the war front. Cyrus Hall McCormick wrote to major general Hugh L. Scott, chief of staff of the United States Army: "My cousin, lieutenant Chauncey McCormick might be of some service to you…. He was a most successful man of business [and has] industry, fidelity, loyalty and common sense." Major general Scott met with Chauncey and reported back to Cyrus: "He seems to be a very bright young fellow, who speaks good French and is well acquainted with French methods. I spoke to the officers surrounding general Pershing's headquarters about trying to get him a commission."[14]

In an act of patriotism, James Deering gave permission to Chauncey to billet Red Cross personnel in his Paris home. "I should rather the house be used for officers rather than privates," wrote James Deering. "Yet I have no right and no real desire to make this distinction."[15] "To me it is important and exceedingly interesting event that you are going to France to serve your nation. [It will] remain one of the largest episodes of your life. [While Chauncey was abroad] I will do my best to keep Marion cheered up…. I do not like the idea of you fighting rather than to look out for the Red Cross work, but you know best, and I trust that you will come out right."[16]

James Deering arranged for International Harvester to donate $300,000 to support the Red Cross work in France, including sending fully equipped ambulances. He regularly sent money to enhance Chauncey's work in France. With this money, Chauncey set up "a canteen at the front. It will supply the troops with pens, ink, paper etc. There are cups of coffee and electric light. There is a large stove where they can warm up and get the only comfort they had." Much to the delight of his benefactor, Chauncey put up a sign: "James Deering of Chicago Canteen." Chauncey asked James's permission to grant 1,000 francs to a French captain's widow who was left penniless with four children to feed.

"Did you ever think I would be running an orphan asylum?" wrote Chauncey proudly to his wife, Marion. Stationed in Moselle, he described the "trenches running" through the town, "and the children living in cellars, and gas attacks sweeping the villages. The conditions are indescribable. [I have] seen conditions that wring your heart…. I have about 300 refugee children that we got out of the towns. They have awful skin diseases, and fleas and lice." Chauncey was put in charge of a staff of twelve, including three doctors, to look after the displaced children. "The great thing after cleaning up the refugees is to keep them busy; school, games and some work for the children, and sewing etc. for the mothers.... We can do nothing more important for the soldiers than to make them think their children are being cared for."[17]

"You can now write me as Lieutenant Chauncey McCormick.... I am so happy in my work."[18] "General Rockenback of the Tank Corps has formally asked for me to join his staff. This is the third general to do so. [But I have been] refused transfers on the grounds that my services being too valuable.... I am now in charge officially of the Manufacturing and Metal Department. Meanwhile, jackasses arrive from America with all kinds of high rank who know nothing—c'est le guerre."[19]

The Army recognized Chauncey's activities with the refugee children, helping the troops on the frontline, and setting up the James Deering canteen. "He is a young man of high standing, character and ability," and was promoted to lieutenant. Later, general John J. Pershing approved Chauncey's promotion to lieutenant colonel. Chauncey was awarded the Purple Heart, and the French government awarded him the Legion of Honor and Croix de Guerre.

Chauncey journeyed to Zurich to visit Edith Rockefeller McCormick in her rooms at the luxury Hotel Baur au Lac. Edith wrote to thank him for the visit. Forever proselytizing, she added: "I should like to tell you about Synthetic Psychology—the Service, Philosophy, the Religion to which my life is dedicated."[20] Cocooned in neutral Switzerland from the brutal War, Edith believed that Synthetic Psychology could prevent both domestic strife and wars.

In addition to Chauncey, at least five other members of the McCormick family fought in World War I. Robert Rutherford McCormick served in France and fought in the Battle of Cantigny with the rank of colonel. Fowler McCormick joined the Gentlemen Volunteers to serve in the American Field Ambulance Service. Captain Leander McCormick fought in France. Alister McCormick was an aviator and Cyrus III was a lieutenant in the signal corps. Harold McCormick wrote *Via Pacis*, a plan to end the war. International Harvester was a major supplier of war equipment. (At age eighteen years, Ernest Hemingway from Oak Park, Illinois joined the Red Cross to drive ambulances during The War to End All Wars. After two months he was seriously wounded. He tells of his wartime experiences in his book *A Farewell to Arms*.)

In 1918, Chauncey was sent by future president Herbert Hoover to administer food aid through the American Relief Administration to alleviate the famine gripping Poland. In 1920, he organized the food relief to the city of Lemberg (Lwow) in southeastern Poland to keep the city from falling to the Bolsheviks. For his able work, the Polish government awarded Chauncey the Order of the White Eagle of Lwow. Chauncey became a life-long advocate for the Polish people. In 1933, Chauncey McCormick organized the art exhibition at A Century of Progress World Fair held at Soldiers' Field, Chicago. "There were no available funds, the times [during the Great Depression] were hard. There was no money to build a fireproof gallery." Despite all these obstacles, Chauncey toured the country to interest famed collectors like the Whitneys and the Rockefellers as well as Chicago collectors like Max Epstein. He also drew freely from the Deering collections, owned by his wife Marion Deering McCormick and her sister, Barbara. In addition to their own Goyas, Velasquez, and El Grecos, Chauncey assembled for the exhibition "a room full of Cézannes," another filled with Gauguins, several paintings by Seurat, Toulouse-Lautrec, Renoir, John Singer Sargent, and James Abbott McNeill Whistler's famous Portrait of his Mother.[21]

In September 1939, the Polish government in exile issued an urgent call for food aid. Herbert Hoover again asked Chauncey McCormick to organize and deliver $6 million worth of food to the Polish people.[22] During World War II, Chauncey served as chairman of the Commission for Poland Relief. Chauncey arranged for American food (in the form of evaporated milk, rye flour, sugar) to be sent to Sweden and on to Poland. With the brutal Nazi occupation of Poland, these food shipments became ever more difficult. In Chicago, Chauncey served as vice president of the Art Institute for 11 years and as president from 1944 to his death in 1954. He never sought political office but freely gave his time to charities, including Chicago's Foundling Home, Chicago's Council of Social Services, the Illinois Child Welfare Commission, and the American Foundation for the Blind.[23]

Chauncey and Marion enjoyed horseback riding. In the 1920s they bought a 260-acre farm in Warrenville, Illinois. Named St. James Farm, it held a house for the family and stables for their horses. Chauncey and Marion added a herd of Guernsey cows and built a state-of-the-art dairy. In July 1929, Marion and Chauncey hosted 500 members of the Illinois Guernsey Breeders Association. The guests were able to view "Mrs. Chauncey McCormick's famous cow, Rose, which had produced 91 pounds of milk in one day and averaged 86 pounds daily for thirty days—both world records." Rose also held the record for annual production—19,888 pounds of milk, containing 902 pounds of butterfat.[24] The family lived in an elegant condominium building at 2450 Lake View Avenue, Chicago, enjoyed their weekends at St. James Farm, and spent their summers at their estate at Seal Harbor, Maine.

Chauncey Brooks McCormick served as a member of the board of International Harvester Company from 1926 to 1954, to safeguard the interests of both the Deering and McCormick families. He served also as president of the Miami Company.

Chauncey McCormick died September 8, 1954, at age 69 years, of a rupture of an aortic artery aneurysm, at the Mount Desert Hospital, Bar Harbor, Maine, close to his summer home at Seal Harbor. His body was brought to Chicago for burial at the Graceland cemetery. With his death, "Chicago lost one of its most distinguished and useful citizens."[25] In 1958, Marion established the Chauncey and Marion Deering Foundation to fund their favorite causes, especially higher education, hospitals, art museums and child welfare.

Marion Deering McCormick was one of the richest women in America, worth over $120 million. She was a cultural leader in Chicago. Marion shared her husband's passions for Northwestern University, donating $10 million. She was director of the Illinois Children's Home and funded the Chauncey and Marion Deering McCormick Home for adolescent homeless boys at 5415 Greenwood Avenue, Hyde Park. With her sister Barbara, she donated many splendid paintings to the Art Institute of Chicago, including works by Paul Gauguin, Winslow Homer, El Greco and Vincent van Gogh. After her husband died, Marion spent the summers at Seal Harbor, Maine and the winters in Villa Vizcaya, which she and Barbara inherited from their uncle James Deering. Marion Deering McCormick died in 1965, at age 78.[26] Chauncey and Marion McCormick owned a splendid art collection. The collection included Picasso's 1902 "Woman with Crossed Arms" that sold at auction in 2000 for $55 million.[27]

Chauncey and Marion Deering McCormick had three sons—Charles, Brooks and Roger.

Like his father, Charles Deering McCormick attended the Groton School and graduated from Yale University in 1938. For two years he worked at the Guarantee Trust Corporation of New York. In 1940, he joined the navy to become a radar watch officer on the
20,000-ton aircraft carrier USS *Hornet*. During the battle of the Santa Cruz Islands, the
Hornet was sunk on October 26, 1942, after being hit by Japanese bombs, torpedoes and
dive bombers. Charles spent 45 minutes in the waters of the South Pacific before he was
rescued. In 1947 he married Nancy Hoskinson, a former model and daughter of the vice
president of the Riggs Bank of Washington. Although he lived in Miami, he followed family
tradition and served from 1955 to 1980 on the board of Northwestern University. He funded
the Charles Deering McCormick Library for Special Collections. Charles Deering McCormick
died in 1994 at age 79 years.[28] Nancy McCormick outlived her husband by 23 years. She too
was active in supporting Northwestern University and the Art Institute of Chicago. After
moving to Florida, she took up the cause of the Vizcaya Museum and Gardens. She died
in 2017 and was buried alongside other McCormicks and Deerings at Graceland Cemetery
in Chicago.[29]

Roger S. McCormick was the third son of Marion and Chauncey McCormick. He was
born in Neuilly-sur-Seine, France and attended Yale University. He served as a lieutenant
during World War II. He was a director of the Miami Company and president of Universal
Mutual Casualty of Chicago. He served as a trustee of the Chicago Opera Company. Roger
McCormick died in his sleep age 48 on November 13, 1968.[30]

Brooks McCormick was the middle son of Marion and Chauncey McCormick. He
was born in 1917 in Chicago. Brooks attended Groton School in Massachusetts, followed

Chicago children in 1966 board International buses after a tour of the Lincoln Park Zoo (WHS Image ID 6621).

by Yale University, and earned a degree in Victorian English history. One of his classmates at Yale was Henry Ford II. In 1940, Brooks married Hope Baldwin of Bedford Hill, New York.

Fowler McCormick selected his cousin Brooks to enter the International Harvester training program. Brooks steadily worked his way up the corporate ladder. He sold Harvester equipment in Indiana, supervised the tractor works, was in charge at Melrose Park, and in the late 1940s went to Kansas City to sell trucks. Described as "highly capable" and getting along well with people, Brooks was selected as managing director of International Harvester of Great Britain with its manufacturing plant in Doncaster. "He is the only member of the McCormick family to hold an executive position since the resignation of Fowler McCormick, a cousin, as chairman of the board." Under Brooks's guidance, the British subsidiary showed sustained growth, with increased employment and rising sales.[31] He returned to Chicago to take the position of executive vice president, and was appointed a member of the board of directors of International Harvester. Brooks developed plans to establish truck and harvester plants in twenty countries.[32]

In the 1950s, Brooks inherited St. James's Farm, where he opened the Riding School for the Handicapped and developed steeple chasing. St. James Farm is close to Cantigny, the 500-acre estate owned by his cousin, Colonel Robert Rutherford McCormick of the *Chicago Tribune*. The St. James property, expanded to 600 acres, was later sold to the Forest Preserve District of DuPage County.

The International Harvester Company emerged from World War II as one of America's largest industrial concerns, with a workforce of 70,000—making trucks, tractors, engines and farm equipment. Industrial turmoil followed, with American companies buffeted by foreign competition, demands for higher wages and benefits, and by strikes. International Harvester's dominance in farm equipment was steadily eroded by competition from Caterpillar and Deere & Company. Harvester's factories were old, its products stale and its costs high.

In May 1958, John Lawrence McCaffrey, at age 66, resigned as president and chief executive officer of International Harvester. McCaffrey had advanced Harvester to become a major truck and tractor maker. Replacing McCaffrey as president was another company veteran, Frank W. Jenks, born in Richmond, Virginia, the son of a conductor on the Chesapeake and Toledo Railway. Straight out of high school, Jenks started out as a clerk in the International Harvester office in Richmond. Showing skills in finance, he moved to the Chicago head office in 1930 and worked his way up the corporate ladder. In 1958, Harvester's motor truck division accounted for 47 percent of revenues, farm equipment 34 percent, construction equipment 12 percent, and Wisconsin Steel the remaining 7 percent of company revenues. Total sales exceeded $1.7 billion with a profit of $43 million. The company entered the aircraft business. "We have growth potential in every division," reported Jenks. In 1957, Harvester established a research center in Hinsdale in the belief "the company's very existence depended on the development of products that are needed by its customers." International Harvester ventured into household appliances, refrigerators and freezers. By 1960, motor trucks accounted for half the company's revenue, with farm equipment falling to one third of revenues. During Jenks's four-year tenure as chief executive officer, company sales were booming. Sales and profits "will be the largest we have ever had."

By 1979, International Harvester had grown into an international behemoth with 95,000 workers spread over fifty manufacturing facilities and nine joint ventures. Based

Display of 1973 International 464, 574 and 674 Farmall tractors; 40 to 99 hp (WHS Image ID 25257).

largely in the United States, Harvester had subsidiaries in fifteen other countries. The company had grown so large it was divided into six groups. Its agricultural group made every type of farm equipment: its construction and industrial group built digging, excavating, loading machines and crawler tractors; its turbine group entered the aerospace business; its truck group built school buses, delivery trucks, and heavy-duty trucks; its components group controlled the foundries and built gas and diesel engines; and Harvester's support facilities coordinated its worldwide activities. Reaching age 65, Jenks retired in September 1962 and was replaced as president and chief executive office by yet another company veteran, Harry Oldham Bercher, who began his career at Wisconsin Steel Company.

Like McCaffrey, Harry Bercher's identity was molded by his long career with the company. He was solid, responsible, predictable, loyal and free of scandal. Bercher devoted large sums to product development and moved into the suburbs with lawn and garden equipment, including a seven-horsepower yard tractor that promised to get the job done quickly and easily. Harvester opened a truck factory in Europe to supplement its existing farm machinery plants in England, France and Germany, and to take advantage of lower wages than in the United States. In 1971, Harry Bercher reached the company's mandatory retirement age.

By 1971 the company was facing strong headwinds, with employee unrest and declining sales. International Harvester Company was in serious trouble. In January, 40,000 workers struck International Harvester plants in twelve states. The United Automobile Workers Union had successfully negotiated with General Motors, Ford and Caterpillar and wanted an agreement with International Harvester "within the framework of these settlements." The Union demanded a thirty percent rise in hourly income from the current level of $4.12 an hour, together with cost of living increases and early retirement. With its labor problems, "Harvester reported sharply lower profits."

Harry Bercher groomed Brooks McCormick to become International Harvester Company's next chief executive officer. Brooks McCormick was a great grandnephew of Cyrus Hall McCormick and grandson of William Sanderson McCormick. After a quarter of a century, a McCormick was again in charge of the reaper company. Brooks McCormick saw a bright future for the company, especially in truck sales. Harvester expanded into Japan, Turkey, Venezuela, El Salvador, Tunisia and India, "and we have plans to open new plants in 12 other countries," announced the ebullient Brooks McCormick. In the Nixon era the United States was beset with raising wages, price increases, a weakening dollar and the call for tariffs to keep out foreign competition. America was fast losing its place as the world's largest exporting nation. International Harvester "has always been for free trade.... No nation can build walls around its borders and expect to survive.... Barriers beget barriers." With the advice of Booz, Allen & Hamilton, Brooks McCormick began the reorganization of International Harvester. He sold off the unprofitable Wisconsin Steel Company and the money-losing pickup truck division. He attempted to renegotiate the company's agreement with the unions and thereby reduce the steep pension fund obligations.[33] In 1975, Brooks McCormick traveled to Iran and the Soviet Union to boost overseas sales, which accounted for 30 percent of International Harvester's output. After meeting with the Shah, Brooks announced: "Iran has an appetite for equipment that is insatiable." In Moscow, Brooks met with the Soviet premier Alexei Kosygin who was "eager to rekindle U.S-Soviet trade in the new era of détente." Brooks McCormick reminded the Soviet leader that McCormick harvesters were first introduced to Russia a century earlier. Before the Russian Revolution, International Harvester had an assembly plant outside Moscow that was later nationalized. Brooks McCormick was a free trader who "abhors tariffs and other trade restrictions."[34]

In 1909, International Harvester was the fourth largest corporation in the United States. By 1971, it had fallen below 100 other companies on the Fortune 500 list. Once "one of America's industrial giants [it had become] lethargic, debt-laden and awesomely inefficient." Harvester's return on sales in 1977 was an anemic 3.4 percent, much lower than Deere & Company's 7.1 percent and Caterpillar's 7.5 percent return.[35] International Harvester was the Old Lady of North Michigan Avenue.

Brooks McCormick handpicked and hired 51-year-old Archie R. McCardell for a signing bonus of $1.5 million, an annual salary of $460,000 and incentive pay, as "a second pair of eyes." Before coming to International Harvester, the tough, cost-cutting McCardell had moved from the Ford Motor Company to second in command of the Xerox Company. McCardell was the first outsider to serve as chief executive officer of Harvester. His arrival was "a culture shock" to the tradition-bound International Harvester. He cut the workforce by 11,000 to reduce spending by $460 million in two years. One in seven of the corporate staff was retired. The company sold Wisconsin Steel in 1977, and its foundry at Waukesha, Wisconsin, and sold off its construction equipment business to Dresser Industries.

International Harvester was weighed down by heavy retirement and health costs, little

Brooks McCormick (right front) is shown on a visit to drum up business in the Soviet Union. In this October 2, 1975, photograph, he is negotiating with Alexei Kosygin (left front), premier of the Soviet Union. A picture of Karl Marx is on the wall. Brooks (1917–2006) joined International Harvester in 1940. In 1968 he was appointed president and from 1971 to 1978 served as CEO. He was the last McCormick to lead the harvester, tractor and truck company (WHS Image ID 120329).

innovation, outmoded plants, rising oil costs, and low productivity. McCardell was no messiah. His blunt speaking and abrupt actions proved too much for a company "that had lost its sense of purpose and fallen prey to the myth of its own historical greatness."[36] McCardell closed a number of factories and consolidated manufacturing into fewer work sites.[37] McCardell's slash and burn methods angered the workers, leading to a company-wide strike involving 35,000 members of the United Auto Workers Union in seventeen plants across eight states. The punishing strike lasted six months, from November 1979 to May 1980. Strikers received only $55 to $65 a week from their union, forcing many to exhaust their savings. The company lost $479 million during the strike. This was "the longest and most continuous strike in the firm's one-hundred-and-forty-nine-year history and significantly weakened International Harvester's financial position."[38] The strike allowed Deere and Caterpillar to penetrate deeper into Harvester's territory. In 1979, McCardell added another layer of bureaucracy to the beleaguered company by bringing in another outsider, William J. Hayford, as chief executive officer. McCardell became president of the board and Brooks McCormick chairman of the executive committee of the board.

On October 32, 1980, 63-year-old Brooks McCormick announced his retirement from International Harvester, thus ending "150 years of the McCormick family's active management in the company." He did not want any of his children in the company "because he did not like nepotism, considering it not viable in today's economic setting."[39] Forty years after joining International Harvester, October 31, 1980, was Brooks' last day of work as president. The prolonged workers' strike caused "the worst year ever [and was] the greatest disappointment" for Brooks McCormick and for the company, with its debts downgraded by the rating agencies. Still erect and tall, but showing a "bit of grey at the temples," Brooks McCormick remained optimistic about the company's future under the guidance of his successor, Archie McCardell. "The company seems to be going on without me," announced Brooks McCormick, then chairman of International Harvester's Advisory Council. "It's time to clear us old guys out" and give the new leadership "a clear track." He was not in the least distressed that no McCormick would lead the harvester company forward. "There is no room in this world for emotionalism and sentimentality."[40]

Interest rates in the early 1980s reached twenty percent, increasing farmer's debts and reducing their spending on tractors and farm implements. "This is a very difficult period," McCardell announced in 1982. International Harvester suffered losses of $383.8 million in 1980, $393.1 million in 1981 and a $518 million loss in 1982, mostly from its agricultural implements division. In 1981, McCardell sold Harvester's Solar Turbine International Group to raise a much-needed $505 million. Deere and Company won an infringement suit against International Harvester. Severe losses were experienced at Harvester's overseas plants. The French subsidiary lost 81 million francs in 1981 (about $10 million) and 415 million francs ($54 million) in 1982, leaving it in a critical condition. In 1982, the Australian subsidiary

A 1984 International heavy-duty truck is loaded with logs (WHS #84213).

declared bankruptcy. Between 1980 and 1984, Harvester lost $3 billion and the company was on the brink of bankruptcy. Shares in International Harvester began to slide, forcing McCardell to borrow from banks. By 1982, International Harvester was deeply in the red with bank borrowings of $4.2 billion. "The damage to Harvester's financial capacity was irreversible [and] panic seized the top management."[41] The board decided that Archie McCardell had lost the respect of the unions and was "not up to the job of completing the company's turnabout." In his place, the board hired Louis W. Menk, a former railroad executive, "to guide Harvester through the turbulent months ahead." In France, Germany and England, International Harvester was falling behind local tractor makers. In 1983, Harvester appealed to the French government for financing to keep its money-losing French unit afloat. Menk shut down the plant in Hamilton, Ontario, and sold plants in Mississippi, Indiana, Australia and Japan. "We are walking a tightrope," said Menk. "The real challenge is to be able to afford to remain small."[42]

Efforts to conserve cash did not help. In early 1984, Menk departed and Donald D. Lennox was named chief executive officer. Formerly with the Xerox Corporation, Lennox joined International Harvester in 1979 as assistant to Archie McCardell. International Harvester had suffered four years of losses. Harvester cut its farm tractor line from 47 models to 10. With factory closings and staff cuts of fifty percent, Lennox was hopeful that International Harvester was on the path to recovery. In June, Lennox reached the mandatory retirement age but agreed to remain with the company three more years to try to save it from tumbling into bankruptcy. Lennox sought desperately to find a buyer for Harvester's Agricultural Equipment Group. On November 26, 1984, after many hours of negotiations, Lennox announced the startling news that International Harvester "would abandon its farm equipment business by selling the money-losing division to Tenneco Inc. for $430 million." Tenneco, a Houston-based oil-producing conglomeration, folded the remains of Harvester's agricultural group into its J. I. Case agricultural subsidiary to form the nation's second-largest farm equipment company, with 35 percent of the market. "You can only pay so much for tradition and history," announced the chief executive. "You have to let emotions stand aside and let good business judgment take over." The farm equipment business had become a "cash drain." The agricultural machinery company founded one hundred and thirty years earlier by Cyrus Hall McCormick and led by him and his descendants had come to an end.[43] The new board, without a McCormick at the helm, took the Harvester out of International Harvester. All branches of International Harvester's Farm Equipment Group, including its factories in Germany, France, Great Britain and Australia, were sold to Tenneco. What remained of the company was renamed Navistar International, to signal "the rebirth of International Harvester" as the maker of engines, trucks, tractors and defense vehicles. At its peak, International Harvester had a worldwide workforce of 120,000. By 1992, Navistar employed 15,000 workers.

Brooks McCormick was a noted conservationist. In typical Deering and McCormick fashion, Brooks owned an outstanding collection of works of art, later given to the Art Institute of Chicago. Brooks McCormick assembled a magnificent collection of books on ornithology, including the paintings of John James Audubon and Mark Catesby. Sotheby's sold his ornithology collection in 2007 for the benefit of the International Crane Foundation. Brooks McCormick, the last McCormick to lead the harvester company, died on August 15, 2006, and was buried at Graceland Cemetery.

Chapter Eleven

The Collectors

In 1879, a group of prominent citizens assembled with the aim of establishing an art institute fitting the high aspirations of the booming city of Chicago. Under the leadership of banker Charles L. Hutchinson, the necessary money was gathered to buy land on Michigan Avenue and hire the Boston architectural firm of Sheply, Rutan and Coolidge. The Art Institute of Chicago was completed in time for the 1893 World's Columbian Exposition. In January of the following year, the Art Institute hosted an exhibition of 391 works of art, loaned mainly by wealthy Chicago collectors. "The display of English works (chiefly in the R. Hall McCormick collection) is especially worthy of attention," noted the catalog of the show. R. Hall McCormick, son of Leander James McCormick, had thirty-seven works on display, largely by the leading British artists of the seventeenth and eighteenth centuries.

Robert Hall McCormick was born in 1847 at Locust Hill, Rockbridge, Virginia. Known as R. Hall McCormick, he was named after his grandfather, who died the year before. "On leaving college," he wrote, "I connected myself with the firm of C. H. McCormick & Brother, on salary." In 1871, at age 24, he married Sarah Lord Day in New York City. In 1874, his uncle Cyrus Hall McCormick reluctantly gave him a one-sixteenth share of the McCormick harvester company, with the position of assistant superintendent of manufacturing, under his father, Leander. In 1875, with his parents, Robert built a 3½ story palatial double home at 660 N. Rush Street. In 1880, together with his father, he stopped working for the harvester company. Nine years later, Leander and son R. Hall McCormick sold their stock in the company and invested the money in Chicago real estate. After 1890, when his parents moved into a suite of rooms at the Virginia Hotel, Hall remodeled the grand house to suit the needs of his family. Shut out of the harvester business, Hall devoted his working life to the management of his father's Chicago properties, and trying to prove that his grandfather Robert, not his uncle, was the true inventor of the mechanical reaper. Hall was a keen yachtsman but is best remembered as a serious collector mainly of British portraits and landscapes, including works by John Constable, George Romney, William Hogarth and Thomas Gainsborough, Joshua Reynolds, Anthony Van Dyck and Hans Holbein. In addition, R. Hall McCormick had "an interesting collection of American historical portraits" that included portraits of George Washington painted by Gilbert Stuart and Rembrandt Peale.[1] His splendid collection of paintings was shown at the World's Columbian Exposition in 1893, in Boston in 1900 and again at the Art Institute in Chicago in 1905. In addition to his grand house and art collection, R. Hall McCormick enjoyed other Gilded Age perquisites of great wealth that included a summer place at Bar Harbor, Maine, where he kept a yacht. R. Hall was the first of a succession of Robert Hall McCormicks who managed the portfolio of properties assembled by Leander James McCormick after he left the McCormick Reaper Company.

Mr. and Ms. R. Hall McCormick regularly entertained with great pomp and circumstance. In 1915, the grand home at 660 North Rush was opened to auction fine examples of Belgian lace. The money from the sale went to support "the women lace workers of Belgium" who were being replaced by electric Jacquard looms. The charitable act gave the McCormicks the opportunity to show off their home with its "most exquisite old English stairway and its library."[2]

R. Hall McCormick left the bulk of his estate to his youngest child, his only son and namesake. "Not to show any favoritism above my daughters, all of whom I love as dearly as my son, Robert," he wrote disingenuously in his will, "but for the reason he is my only male heir and the only child through whom my family name may be perpetuated."[3] The decision did not sit well with his daughters Henrietta, Elizabeth, Mildred and Phoebe, who sued to have their brother removed as sole trustee, alleging that he had taken $191,285 from the trust for his own use, and thus "endangered the security of the plaintiffs' shares of the trust."[4] Robert Hall McCormick III "was one of the best known yachtsmen of the world and kept his boat moored in the Mediterranean." A graduate of Yale, he completed his law degree at Columbia. In 1903, Robert married Eleanor Russell Morris, only daughter of Henry Lewis Morris.

In the depths of the Great Depression, Mr. and Mrs. Robert Hall McCormick III traveled in their private railroad car to Bar Harbor, Maine to open their Eden Street "cottage," Burnmouth, for the summer season. Accompanying them were their daughters Eleanor and Patty. At Bar Harbor they were joined by Mr. and Mrs. F. Hamilton McCormick-Goodhart, Miss Mildred McCormick and by others of their wealthy set, that included the Rockefellers, Vanderbilts, Astors and Morgans, to enjoy dinners and dances at the Bar Harbor club, sailing their yachts out of the Bar Harbor yacht club, and attending the art-deco Criterion Theater that specialized in plays by Noel Coward, A. A. Milne, Oscar Wilde and other British playwrights.[5]

Elizabeth Day McCormick was the second child of R. Hall and Sarah Day McCormick. Born in 1873 and known as Elsie, she was educated at Miss Kirkland's School in Chicago, where one of her teachers was Ellen Gates Starr, who with Jane Addams established the Hull House in 1889. Next, Elizabeth attended Miss Peeble's School in New York City. Returning to Chicago, Elsie, like many other young daughters of the wealthy classes, devoted her time to good deeds. At Hull House, Elsie McCormick set up a fund to teach the elements of good nutrition to poor children. She also supervised an embroidery class for immigrant girls. This experience led Elsie to find her "profound purpose in life" by collecting embroidered textiles, European needlework, costumes and accessories, especially of the 16th to 19th centuries. These objects became her "precious treasures." Her passion for embroidered textiles took her to Europe, the Greek islands, and into the convents and monasteries of Asia Minor, everywhere adding to her collection. She collected dresses worn by Queen Elizabeth I and other royal ladies, the ceremonial garments of bishops and cardinals, and even a pair of silk gloves once owned by Robespierre. In 1938 she returned to Chicago, explaining: "With Hitler on the rampage, I grasped the idea that I had better get out."

Elsie used her inheritance from her grandfather, Leander James McCormick, to assemble a splendid collection of 6,000 objects, including 2,056 costumes, 1,189 textiles and hundreds of prints, glass, and miniatures. She was "far and away Chicago's most distinguished collector of textiles."[6] As early as 1920, Elsie formed a connection with Gertrude Townsend, curator of textiles at the Museum and Fine Arts, Boston. Wanting to place her beloved collection into "interested, scholarly hands," Elsie donated it to that museum. On October 21, 1943, the trustees of the Museum of Fine Arts "accepted from Miss Elizabeth Day her extraordinary collection of embroideries, costumes and costume accessories."[7] Between 1943 and 1957, Elsie sent to Boston the bulk of her costume collection together with some paintings she inherited from her father.[8] It was her hope "to provide new ideas and inspiration for all of our composite populations of this great land of ours."[9] Chicago too, benefited from her generosity. The Goodspeed Manuscript Collection at the University of Chicago holds the Elizabeth Day McCormick Apocalypse, a rare 17th century Greek work with 69 miniature illustrations. Elizabeth Day McCormick died August 14, 1957, at age 84, in her apartment at 40 E. Oak Street, Chicago. She was buried with other McCormicks at Graceland Cemetery.[10]

The youngest of Leander James McCormick's children was Leander Hamilton McCormick, born in 1859 in Chicago. To distinguish him from his father, he was known as L. Hamilton McCormick. He attended Phillip's Academy. At age 17, he traveled with his father to Philadelphia to the 1876 Centennial Exhibition, where the McCormick Company displayed its harvesters. The Agricultural Building, wrote Hamilton, "had a very fine display of farming instruments such as reapers, binders, plows, threshing machines, etc."[11] Touring the exhibition, he witnessed a "large variety of races [that included] Asiatics, Italians, Chinamen, Japanese, Brazilians and Africans." This experience evoked his interest in human appearance and behavior that he later developed into the so-called science of Characterology. L. Hamilton McCormick attended Amherst College, Class of 1881, where he showed a great interest in spirituality and the destiny of the soul. At Columbia University he studied law and architecture. In New York he worked briefly for the law firm of Lord, Day & Lord, owned by relatives.

Writing at the time of the workers' strike at the McCormick Reaper Factory, L. Hamilton McCormick supported the bosses against the workers. "The laborers of the United States are massing their strength and growing constantly more and more powerful. They are dictating to their employers in regard to what wages they shall pay, whom and how many they shall employ," he wrote in 1887. "This should be put down before it grows even more unmanageable than it is today.... Take the McCormick strike, after receiving a pay raise the unions demanded that non-union men, good, faithful workers, should be discharged from the firm simply because they did not believe in labor unions." L. Hamilton McCormick suggested the capitalists take the initiative and form their own union "for self-protection." A manufacturers' union "could afford to pay a large part of the cost of a lock-out or a strike." A manufacturers' union would tell striking workers that if they do not immediately return to work they will be fired and will not be able to find a job anywhere in Chicago.[12]

In 1887, Hamilton married Constance Plummer of Canterbury, England. Their three sons, Leander James, Edward Hamilton and Alister Hamilton were all born in England, attended Eton and went on to Trinity College, Cambridge. In addition to his enlarging art collection, Hamilton patented 100 inventions, including a motorcycle and a watch. Hamilton devoted his time to writing, inventing, and collecting furniture, rugs, silverware and coats of armor. At the start of World War I, Hamilton and Constance left England for Chicago to live at 631 Rush Street, the grand mansion vacant after the death of his older brother Robert. With Hamilton and Constance in residence, the grand house once again became "the scene of innumerable receptions for visiting nobility and celebrities." He joined the family real estate company to keep track of the investments made by his father and grandfather. Hamilton was an exacting employer, requiring his staff at home and in the office to follow precise rules and carefully document all revenues and expenses.

Living off his large trust fund, L. Hamilton McCormick, in competition to his older brother Robert, "devoted most of his time to the forming of a large and important collection of works of art, largely of the seventeenth and eighteenth centuries, of the Dutch and English schools."[13] L. Hamilton inherited and expanded the collection built by his father that included paintings by Joshua Reynolds, Thomas Gainsborough, Aelbert Cuyp, Rubens and Botticelli.[14]

Hamilton's first passion was the human body and its relation to behavior. He called it Characterology. Hamilton "spent many years studying and testing his theories," and claimed he had perfected Charaterology into a precise science, akin to "mathematics, economics, chemistry, medicine and the law.... Character is indicated by facial and cranial outline, by size, contour and refinement of features: by the proportions of the head, body and limbs; by complexion; by expressions of countenance; by speech, deportment, and by all the products of the mind."[15] Successful people are in command of their character while unsuccessful people do not "understand themselves or their associates." Hamilton's books were widely advertised as guides to high achievement in life. Going beyond the quackery of phrenology, L. Hamilton McCormick claimed that the close study of the head, ears, nose, eyes, lips, hair and posture reveal telltale clues to a person's character. "The McCormick system," he alleged, "combines all branches of character into one comprehensive science." Large teeth indicate power. Delicately formed ears indicate a love of music, coarse hair "is a sign of strength" and a florid complexion indicates "an excitable temperament." L. Hamilton McCormick displayed the racial stereotypical prejudices of his age. Blond hair, blue eyes and a Roman nose indicates firmness, forcefulness and assertiveness. Black skin "implies affection, lethargy, a love of music and a lack of motivation." The Semitic nose signifies a "willful, assertive disposition and strong money-making proclivities," while an "American nose presupposes energy and the executive capacity to command." Criminals have small brains, low foreheads, large, staring eyes, shaggy eyebrows, crooked noses, a heavy lower jaw and a slouched posture.[16]

At his death in 1934, Hamilton left money "for the dissemination of his theories," based on forty years of misspent study. Hamilton established trust funds of $800,000 for his wife and for each of his three sons, Leander, Edward and Alister.[17] The "tall, dark-haired and very handsome" Leander McCormick married Alice Cudahy, youngest daughter of Mr. and Mrs. Edward A. Cudahy, of the meatpacking firm. As befits a daughter of a Chicago millionaire, Alice was sent to Paris for her education. She returned to Chicago an "intellectual, if not highbrow."[18] A stunning beauty, Alice had "hair of a vibrant copper red, her eyes dark brown, her skin milk white and her expression charmingly thoughtful and serious." She was "a perfect vision of grace and real liveliness." To add to her virtues, young Alice gave several days "each week to charity in the children's hospitals or doing visitor's work in poor neighborhoods."[19] Leander and Alice were excellent dancers. "They'll make an unusually good-looking couple," gushed one writer. "She with her Titian red hair and he with his dark-coloring, good figure and air of distinction." The military wedding held in the evening during October 1917 was brief, with no honeymoon to follow. Captain Leander McCormick "only had enough time" from his military training to attend the wedding ceremony before taking his new wife back to her parents. In 1918, captain Leander James McCormick left for France with the Illinois Division. On his return to Chicago the young couple moved to 1356 Astor Place, but the bloom of the marriage was already off the rose. In 1929, Alice Cudahy McCormick announced: "she will never live with her husband again."[20] Alice got a divorce in Reno on grounds of cruelty and lack of affection. Soon afterwards she married John Noble Stearns, Jr., of Brookville, Long Island, New York.[21] John Stearns, a silk manufacturer, was a descendant of Isaac Stearns, who arrived in the New World in 1630, a passenger on governor John Winthrop's flagship, *Arabella*.

Leander McCormick, a prominent architect with the firm of Rebori, Dewey & McCormick, designed several Chicago buildings, including 2430 Lakeview Avenue and the Racquet Club of Chicago. Leander was an expert on game fish and wrote *Fishing Around the World* and *Game Fish of the World*.[22] Leander's passion for fishing took him from the shores of Lake Michigan to the ultimate angling of the giant fish of the rivers and oceans. He described the trairao of the rivers of South America as "a vicious sulking brute, lying motionless in still and shallow water, waiting to pounce murderously on any small fish.... They will even attack a man if he ventures too near."

In 1933, at age 44, Leander married 33-year-old Renee de Fleurieu Fontrace, the countess de Fleurieu, and adopted her two children. Renee was the author of several novels set in her native France, including *Dangerous Apple*. Using the money from his trust fund, Leander and Renee settled on an estate in Hampshire, England. In December 1933, their house burned to the ground. Leander and Renee escaped but two of their guests died in the flames. In 1939, Leander and Renee came to live in Chicago at 179 Lake Shore Drive. Accompanying them was Marie-Blanche, Leander's 17-year-old adopted daughter, "an attractive addition to the debutante group."[23] In 1947, Leander moved to France to live in St. Tropez as an abstract artist, even holding a one-man show in Paris in 1959. The adopted children, Thierry Leander McCormick and Marie-Blanche McCormick Fergus, moved to the United States to reside in Lake Forest. Leander attempted to make his adopted children heirs to his trust fund established by his father. He claimed that his father unfairly "demonstrated greater love and affection" for his brother Alister and family "probably because they resided in the United States of America" while he lived in France. He also claimed to be sterile and not able to have natural children of his own. In 1960, the court denied the adoptive children any share of the trust fund, ruling that only Leander's direct "issue" was entitled to inherit his trust fund. Leander was ordered to pay the full cost of the trial, amounting to $21,430.[24] Leander James McCormick died in 1964 at his home on Le Buisson Road, St. Tropez, and was buried in France.[25]

Alister Hamilton, born in England in 1891, was a graduate of Trinity College and Cambridge College, an accomplished tennis player and an aviator during World War I. After the war, Alister settled in Chicago. "Being engaged to Alister, for me, meant my family let me stay out longer in the evenings, so long as I was with him," said Mary Landon Baker. "While hundreds of society people sat hushed in the Fourth Presbyterian Church, Chicago … waiting for the appearance of Miss Mary Landon Baker, daughter of Mr. and Mrs. Alfred

Baker, and Alister McCormick, son of Mr. and Mrs. L. Hamilton McCormick, the wedding was called off. Miss Baker failed to appear…. Due to the sudden indisposition of Miss Baker, the wedding was called off."[26] "There will be no wedding today," announced the Rev. Dr. John Timothy Stone. While putting on her bridal dress, Mary "looked in the mirror, went into her mother's room, and said: 'I can't go through with this.'" Mrs. Baker replied: "You must do what you feel is best." Mr. Baker added: "My daughter has a very nervous temperament…. This is only a postponement." The McCormick and Baker families and other befuddled guests left the church and went home. Dressed in his navy uniform, and left standing alone at the altar, Alister rushed to see Mary but "she was too ill to see him." The news of the bride who did not come to her own wedding spread across the world. English papers dubbed Mary the "shy bride." Gifts worth $100,000 were returned, including a dozen traveling clocks and seven waste paper baskets. "Getting engaged, you weren't necessarily going to be married," explained Mary Baker.

A week after the abandoned wedding, Alister sailed to Liverpool on the White Star liner *Baltic*. Before "a squad of photographers," he announced that Mary had suffered a nervous breakdown, but after a brief period of recovery, would follow him to London for a quiet wedding. At least four other wedding days were set only to be broken. At the start of 1923, the jilted bridegroom announced that he no longer wished to marry Mary Baker. In the 1920s, a person who failed to turn up at a party was described as "Mary Bakered." Mary's story continued to fascinate for decades to come. In 1927, her father died and her mother sold their big house in Lake Forest and set out with Mary for Europe. They moved from London to Paris, Rome and Venice. During her lifetime, the lively but marriage-phobic Mary Baker received sixty-seven other proposals of marriage. "Mary didn't say yes to any of them." Mary Baker died in London, unmarried, alone and poor.[27]

On vacation at Le Touquet, France, Alister met Joan Tyndale Stevens on the tennis court. On October 6, 32-year-old Alister married 18-year-old Joan at the British Embassy in Paris. She came from a titled family "dating back many centuries," and was the niece of the Earl of Hastings.[28] Alister and Joan McCormick moved to Chicago, where their children Michael and Constance were born. Despite Alister's trust fund, it was not smooth sailing. In 1928, Joan McCormick took "a position in the fashion department of the Marshall Field Store," because, she said, "I need the money."[29] In the 1930s, Alister and Joan, with their children, moved to Santa Barbara, California. Joan Tyndale McCormick modeled for Pond's creams to "maintain her delicate English beauty…. It was in Chicago where the winters are stinging and the summers burning that I realized how absolutely necessary Pond's Two Creams are if one's skin is to keep its young-girl freshness." Moving to California, "I spend most of my time working in my garden. Here again Pond's Two Creams have proved themselves invaluable."[30] Their son Michael studied at the Sorbonne in Paris and daughter Constance married George Richmond Fearing, Jr., of Boston. Constance McCormick Fearing gathered a vast collection of pre–Columbian objects, which she donated to the Los Angeles County Museum of Art.

Charles Deering first met the painter John Singer Sargent in Newport, Rhode Island at the time of his marriage to Anna Case. Deering loved to paint and was passionate about art. Sargent was impressed and told Charles "he might have a great career as a portrait painter and encouraged him to enter upon such a life." Instead, Charles was summoned by his father and did his duty to come to Chicago to expand the Deering Harvester Company.

Rather than becoming an artist, Charles would use his great wealth to be a benefactor of the arts and patron of talented artists. Charles Deering also formed close friendships with the Swedish artist Anders Zorn, the Catalan artist Ramon Casas and the sculptor Augustus St. Gaudens.

Charles Deering loved Spain and Spanish art. He built a grand home at Sitges, south of Barcelona. In his Sitges mansion, Deering displayed his superb collection of Spanish paintings by El Greco, Francesco Goya, and Diego Velasquez. Charles funded the Maricel Art Museum at Sitges.[31] In 1920, Charles Deering moved his art collection to Florida where, at a cost of $4 million, he established his 450-acre estate at Palmetto Bay, Dade County, Florida. He restored the Richmond Cottage and in 1922 built the Stone House. Charles Deering was a compulsive collector, amassing over 4,000 pieces of art, valued in 1922 at $60,000,000. In 1924, Charles gifted his art collection to his daughters, Marion and Barbara. His brother James, who lived close by at Villa Vizcaya, also bequeathed his art collection to Marion and Barbara, who in turn donated major works to the Art Institute of Chicago, including paintings by El Greco, John Singer Sargent and Mary Cassatt. The Deering family was among the most generous benefactors of the Art Institute.[32]

In 1917, the artist John Singer Sargent visited Villa Vizcaya and kept busy painting pictures of the house and grounds. Sargent described Villa Vizcaya as "a combination of Venice and Frascati and Aranjuez, and all that one is likely never to see again." Sargent "used the muscular laborers who were constructing Vizcaya's gardens as his models … combining his sensuous delight in rendering the male nude figure with his favorite watercolor themes of sunlight and water."[33]

James Deering "was delighted when the eminent one [Singer Sargent] expressed the wish to do a likeness of his classic profile.… The easel was placed close to the gorgeous macaws, those glorious birds who perched day after day, uncaged, on standards of gold. [The portrait] was intended to be cherished through the generations."

"Well, how do you like it?" Deering asked about the portrait. "Huh, it's no good. Guess I'll give it to my brother to place among his Zorns, Whistlers, Childe Hassams and others. Sargent painted brother, too, and he don't like his, so we'll make a fair exchange and be satisfied."[34]

James Deering willed important works of art to the Art Institute of Chicago, including works by Giovanni Battista Tiepolo and Edouard Manet. With no children of his own, James left Villa Vizcaya to his brother Charles who, in turn, willed it to his daughters Marion Deering McCormick (wife of Chauncey McCormick) and Mrs. Barbara Danielson. In 1952, the daughters sold Vizcaya and its grounds to Dade County for $1.5 million, a fraction of its original cost. Renamed the Dade County Art Museum, Vizcaya opened to the public in 1953, as Biscayne Bay's greatest showplace. "The indescribable place was filled with a large assemblage of European architectural backgrounds and fragments and filled with a gigantic assortment of furniture and decorative objects, all dating from the fifteenth to the nineteenth century." The grounds, fountains and sculptures had all been restored to the splendor when occupied by James Deering himself.[35]

Chauncey Brooks McCormick illustrated how William Deering set the example for his family. He "wanted to be a doctor, but was unable to carry out his plans." Instead, he used his wealth to build a church in South Paris, support a hospital in Portland, Maine and fund Wesley Hospital in Chicago. His deep respect for education led him to support Northwestern University. His sons wanted to be artists. Instead, they became great patrons of the arts. Charles's daughters, Marion and Barbara, were also outstanding supporters of the arts and universities, in particular, Northwestern University.[36]

Abby Marion Deering Howe (only daughter of William Deering) married Richard Flint Howe in 1898. Howe was born in Green Bay, Wisconsin, graduated Harvard College and returned west to serve as treasurer for the Deering Company, and then International Harvester. In 1906, Abby went on vacation to the Adirondacks. On her return to Chicago she fell ill and underwent an operation "which was not regarded as of a serious nature." She died November 17, aged 39 years, leaving an estate worth $5 million.[37] Several years after Abby's death, Richard Howe moved to New York where he built Linden Hill, a grand home on Long Island. Their only child, William Deering Howe, was born in 1900. He graduated Harvard College in 1922 and married Polly Brooks of Baltimore. Trained as an attorney, he worked for the National City Bank. William Deering Howe settled in the village of Brookville on Long Island, New York where he served as its first mayor and used his Deering inheritance to build a grand estate.[38] The Howe estate was leased to the Duke and Duchess of Windsor.[39]

Chapter Twelve

Madness

"Mary is talking everything," wrote the delighted Nettie, when her daughter was two years old, "and is a great strong girl, running everywhere, climbing up on all the chairs, and trying to do everything anybody else does—a great mimic, obedient too, with one of the clearest perceptions of right and wrong."[1] Mary Virginia, born in 1861, was the second of the surviving children of Cyrus Hall and Nettie Fowler McCormick. For a while, she attended public school in Chicago, but was later sent to private school. She grew into a "gifted, charming, high spirited girl, with an independent mind" and with a talent for piano playing. At age 17, she accompanied her parents on a trip to Europe. Accompanying her mother, she walked vigorously and joyfully up and down the Swiss mountainsides.

Several eligible men courted the beautiful and talented Mary Virginia but the suitors were "discouraged after anguished family counsels." By age eighteen, Mary Virginia McCormick's anxiety and weakness of body were evolving into a severe mental illness, with agitation, wandering about at night, climbing out of windows, and bouts of weeping and praying. She expressed delusional ideas and hallucinated. Two periods of mental hospital treatment did not help.[2] After the death of Cyrus in 1884, Nettie devoted "endless time and effort to the choice of places for her daughter's residence … and to the trial of every scientific aid."[3] Mary was set up in a house in the Adirondacks and moved to the northwest side of New York City, near the Hudson River. She was again moved to Toronto, which proved too cold for her. In 1897, she was moved to Santa Barbara, California. Nettie sent her son Stanley to California to supervise the building of Riven Rock, a grand house overlooking the Pacific Ocean. With a retinue of nurses and attendants, the insane Mary was watched day and night.

Until the late nineteenth century, the care of the mentally ill involved such brutal methods as physical restraint, isolation, bloodletting, purging, and submerging the patient into a tank of cold water until air bubbles no longer came up. These methods were meant to break the will of the mentally ill. Such management for Mary Virginia was unacceptable to Cyrus and Nettie McCormick, who sought a more humane approach. They found this in Dr. Alice Bennett, chief physician of the women's section of the State Hospital for the Insane, Norristown, Pennsylvania. Born in 1851 in Wrentham, Massachusetts, the daughter of a blacksmith, Alice Bennett graduated from the Women's Medical College in Philadelphia and went on to become the first woman to receive a Doctor of Philosophy from the University of Pennsylvania. In her day, Dr. Bennett was the leading female psychiatrist in America. At the State Hospital, Dr. Bennett removed physical restraints, which, she wrote, "increase the violence they are intended to prevent. Freedom of action is a wonderful tranquilizer." In their place, she introduced occupational and educational therapies as part of a more humane approach to the care of the mentally ill. In 1896, Dr. Bennett resigned her position at the State Hospital to become the full-time leader of the therapy team caring for Mary Virginia McCormick. She negotiated a three-year contract with Mary's brother, Cyrus Hall McCormick, and moved with her patient to California. Dr. Bennett left after the second year of her contract to open a medical practice in her hometown of Wrentham.

Around 1905, Mary Virginia was moved to a mental asylum in Huntsville, Alabama. When it closed, Nettie bought the grand "Kildare" estate in the town. While living in Huntsville, Mary, through her managers, made several philanthropic contributions, including funding the local YMCA and building a hospital for black residents of the town, complete with a nurses' residence and a doctor's office.[4] In 1926, Mary Virginia McCormick was moved back to California to occupy a three-story Mediterranean-style home overlooking the ocean at Huntington Palisades, near Santa Monica. Built on fourteen acres, the home had twenty rooms to house Mary and her staff of over thirty servants, including a resident physician, nurses and three musicians. For forty years Grace T. Walker served as head of Mary Virginia's household. On several occasions during the seventeen years Mary lived there, a complete symphony orchestra was hired to play for her. After Nettie died in 1923, other members of the McCormick family supervised, at a distance, the care Mary Virginia received. Despite every luxury and comfort and every available medical aid, the reclusive Mary Virginia McCormick remained psychotic for over sixty years, to die at age eighty years on May 25, 1941.[5]

In her childhood, Mary Virginia McCormick (1861–1941) was lively and gifted. She descended into madness while still in her teens. Mary lived most of her long life in Huntsville, Alabama, closely supervised and secluded from the outside world. Photograph taken in 1883 when she was already ill with schizophrenia (WHS Image ID 42488).

Despite the great expense in providing her care, Mary Virginia McCormick left an estate valued at $19,751,770, of which three-quarters were in International Harvester shares. Federal inheritance taxes took nearly $12 million and Illinois inheritance taxes another $1 million, leaving $6,350,802 for distribution.[6] Her sister, Anita McCormick Blaine, received one-fourth, as did the estates of her brothers Harold and Stanley. Cyrus III and Gordon, sons of her deceased brother Cyrus, Jr., each received a one-eighth share of Mary Virginia's funds.[7]

Stanley Robert McCormick was the youngest of the children of Cyrus and Nettie McCormick. He was born in 1875, in the sixty-sixth year of his father's life. Stanley was thirty months younger than his brother

Harold. Stanley was reserved and quiet and loved books, while Harold was more sociable and outgoing. "The boys," as Nettie called them, hung out together and played competitive doubles tennis at Newport and Bar Harbor. Stanley attended the University School in Chicago, followed by Princeton University (graduated 1895), where he excelled in tennis and football. After his graduation from Princeton, Nettie and Stanley set out for a tour of Egypt and Europe. Accompanied by a "physician-companion and a nurse," they sailed on the luxury boat *Sesostis* up the Nile River and explored the pyramids. Nettie purchased antiquities to send back for the Art Institute. Mother and son climbed the mountains of Switzerland and spent several weeks in Paris, where Stanley had singing lessons. It was time to return home and Stanley's wish for an artistic career began to fade. Stanley was slender and stood over six feet in height and "had his mother's delicate beauty."[8] He studied law at Northwestern University (1896–1897). At age twenty-five, Stanley took possession of properties worth $1 million left to him by his father. After graduating law school he was entrusted to manage the vast McCormick family real estate. Stanley bought a range at Cimarron, New Mexico, in the false hope of soothing his nerves.[9] In 1900, Stanley represented the McCormick Harvesting Machine Company at the World's Fair in Paris. Stanley financed at the cost of "many thousands of dollars" an archeological dig in New Mexico and Arizona that yielded 3,000 pieces of prehistoric Pueblo pottery, later given to the Field Museum in Chicago. During 1901–02, he assisted his brothers Cyrus and Harold in the integration of the McCormick Company into the International Harvesting Company, the world's largest farm equipment manufacturing company. In 1904, Stanley became the comptroller and director of International Harvester.[10] His mother expected Stanley to wave the family flag as a prominent philanthropist supporting worthy causes. Stanley was appointed to the board of the Art Institute of Chicago. In 1904, Stanley served as a member of the National Child Labor Committee, joining such luminaries as Jane Addams, Florence Kelley, Lillian Ward and his aunt, Mrs. Emmons Blaine. Other prominent members of the Child Labor Committee were Felix Adler, the bankers Isaac N. Seligman and Paul Warburg, and newspaper publisher Adolph S. Ochs.

The public view of young Stanley's accomplishments was at odds with his inner turmoil. His wish was to study art and voice but the urge to be an artist conflicted with his responsibilities to the family business, causing the mental turmoil his physicians believed contributed to his mental illness. Stanley's "inborn trait of thoroughness [was] exhausting to him." The desperate Stanley McCormick remembered Katharine Dexter from her Chicago days and in 1903, he traveled to Massachusetts to find her. Her ancestor, Samuel Dexter, served as secretary of the treasury under Presidents John Adams and Thomas Jefferson. Katharine was born in 1875 in the town of Dexter, Michigan, founded by her grandfather. The Dexter family moved to Chicago, where her father established himself as a prominent lawyer, moving in the same circles as the McCormick family. Katharine was a serious and focused girl. At age fifteen, her life took a serious turn with the death of her father. Josephine Dexter moved her children, Katharine and Samuel, to Massachusetts. Further tragedy struck in 1894 when Samuel died of spinal meningitis. In 1896, Katharine Dexter was one of the first women accepted to study at the Massachusetts Institute of Technology. Describing her qualifications to enter college, Katharine noted that she had attended the Lowell lectures on evolution, mastered the French language, "studied thoroughly the German language, at the same time pursuing courses in the ancient languages such as

Greek, Hebrew and Sanskrit, in order to be better prepared for the study of English at the Institute." She graduated in 1904 and hoped to go on to medical school.[11] Courted by Stanley McCormick, Katharine agreed to marry him and give up her plans to become a physician. The wedding ceremony was held in September 1904 at Chateau de Prangins, fifteen miles northeast of Geneva, Switzerland. Built in 1724, the chateau, sitting on fifteen acres of pristine land, was once owned by Joseph Bonaparte, brother of Napoleon, who served as emperor of Spain and Naples. Later, the chateau was sold to Katharine's mother.[12] On the day of the wedding, Stanley was highly agitated, saying he was bedeviled. While on their honeymoon, Stanley spoke of his guilt due to incessant masturbation. He stayed up all hours scribbling in notebooks. He expressed fears of returning to work at the harvester business. Stanley had irrational concerns about the weight, texture and the material of his underpants. On their return to Chicago, he became even more agitated and bizarre in his thoughts. Due to Stanley's sexual delusions, their marriage was not consummated. Katharine became so afraid of him that she moved to her own bedroom and locked the door.[13]

By the summer of 1906, "his physicians forbade nearly all work in the business." Stanley and his wife moved from Chicago to Brookline, Massachusetts, to distance him from the stresses of his hometown. He was admitted to McLean Psychiatric Hospital, Belmont, Massachusetts. By November, "his nervous system gave way and he, like his older sister, lived thereafter in shadow.... Nettie McCormick was not to see her adored youngest child again except at a distance."[14] Speaking of his mother in a saner moment, Stanley said: "Mama urged me too strongly to carry on Papa's work. It was too much."[15] During his long stay at McLean, Stanley had periods of catatonic withdrawal and outbursts of violent behavior interspersed with periods of lucidity. The leading psychiatrist of the day, Adolf Meyer, diagnosed Stanley as schizophrenic with prospect of improvement rated as "extremely dim." The McCormick family decided to move Stanley to Riven Rock, the caged mansion on an 87-acre estate originally built to house his sister Mary Virginia McCormick, but vacant after she was moved to Huntsville, Alabama. On April 8, 1909, Stanley Robert McCormick was legally declared "incompetent by reason of disease to manage his estate." His illness was characterized by "a state of apathy and indifference to current events pertaining to every day life [with] episodes of intense nervous excitement when brought into contact with strangers or unexpected situations."[16] Since he was especially sensitive to the presence of his wife and mother, the attendant psychiatrists ordered an all-male treatment team for Stanley. Nettie and Katharine could view Stanley from afar but were forbidden for many years to come close to him. Katharine Dexter McCormick, together with Stanley's brother Harold and sister Mrs. Emmons Blaine, were appointed conservators of his estate with the right to guide his treatment and care.

A succession of leading psychiatrists, including Adolf Meyer, Edward Kempf, William White, and Charles McFie Campbell, evaluated and treated Stanley McCormick. In 1912, Dr. Carl Gustav Jung was invited to travel to California to evaluate Stanley, but he turned down the offer. At great expense the McCormick family in 1908 hired Emil Kraepelin, one of Europe's leading psychiatrists, to travel to California and examine Stanley McCormick. It was Kraepelin who divided severe mental illness into two categories: disorders of mood and disorders of thought. The mood disorders were characterized by deep depression or by alternating periods of mania and depression, manic-depressive psychosis. Disorders of thought comprised hallucinations and delusions; which Kraepelin labeled dementia prae-

Stanley Robert McCormick (1874–1947) and Katharine Dexter McCormick (1874–1967) in October 1904, a month after their wedding: The picture was taken at the Chateau de Prangins, outside Geneva, Switzerland. An excellent student at Princeton and a star tennis player, Stanley was already showing signs of the schizophrenia that would severely impair him for the rest of his life (WHS Image ID 11073).

cox. After examining Stanley, Kraepelin concluded that he suffered from dementia praecox of the catatonic type, characterized by disturbances in thoughts, mood and movement, with sexual preoccupations. His condition was caused by "years of internal family conflict." As therapy he recommended cold baths and sedatives to quell Stanley's violent outbursts.

Desperate to find a way to calm Stanley, his treatment team introduced an orangutan called Julius to Riven Rock. Much to the amusement of locals, Stanley would take Julius along on his daily automobile rides, and the pair was often seen arm in arm.[17] In the 1920s, Dr. William A. White, head of St. Elizabeth's Hospital in Washington, D.C., was hired to supervise Stanley's care. In return for $11,000 a year, Dr. White reviewed the medical and nursing notes concerning Stanley's care and, each year, spent two weeks in Santa Barbara evaluating Stanley in person. Dr. White combined these trips with his annual vacation. For $150,000 a year (worth over $1 million in 2018 dollars), Dr. Edward J. Kempf, in 1927, gave up his New York private psychiatric practice to move to Santa Barbara to become the leader of Stanley McCormick's therapy team. A graduate of Indiana University, Dr. Kempf had trained in psychiatry at St. Elizabeth's Hospital. Kempf concluded that Stanley's peculiar behaviors (putting his hands into the toilet bowl, then washing his hands excessively; his foot fetish) stemmed from repressed psychic traumas. By November 1927, Kempf contended that Stanley was "improving emotionally." Stanley questioned whether he and Katharine were sexually and mentally compatible. "While he wishes you were here for the summer," wrote Kempf to Katharine, Stanley still had "to be very careful about his feelings," especially in contact with females.

While still a student at the Massachusetts Institute of Technology, Katharine Dexter joined the College Equal Rights League (CERL), founded by two Radcliffe College graduates. With her marriage to Stanley McCormick, she briefly filled the traditional role of wife and homemaker to a man of business. After Stanley was declared incompetent by reason of insanity and sent to Riven Rock in California, Katharine returned to 393 Commonwealth Avenue, Boston. Without a husband or children, the 34-year-old Katharine rejoined the suffrage struggle as a member of the National American Woman Suffrage Association (NAWSA). She was part of the audience of 2,500 at Tremont Temple in Boston on October 22, 1909, to listen to Emmeline Pankhurst, leader of the Women's Social and Political Union of England. In 1912, Katharine was elected treasurer of NAWSA. Katharine's efforts culminated on August 26, 1920, with the passage of the 19th Amendment of the Constitution. That year, Katharine Dexter McCormick was one of the founders of the League of Women Voters.

Katharine believed that Stanley suffered from hormonal imbalance. In 1927, she funded the Stanley R. McCormick Foundation for Neuro-Endocrine Research at Harvard Medical School, (later called the Neuro-Endocrine Research Foundation.) Chronic schizophrenic patients at Worcester State Hospital became the research subjects to determine whether they showed abnormalities in endocrine function that could be corrected. Katharine openly voiced her displeasure with the psychoanalytical treatment her husband was receiving in his prison-like estate, with the windows barred and the doors secured by heavy iron bolts. There were no women among the attendants at Riven Rock. He was "always kept under watch by seven nurses" supervised by Joseph Barnard, a retired army officer, earning $30,000 a year. Often, Stanley became violent and struck out at his nurses. "He used to make a rush at us for a rough-and-tumble to impress the visitors ... sometimes striking with both his fists and elbows." Dr. Edward Kempf was Stanley's resident psychiatrist. Each day, Dr. Kempf

After her husband was placed in seclusion, Katharine Dexter McCormick (at left) became active in the National Woman Suffrage Association. Believing that mental illness was inherited, she later donated the money that led to the development of the oral birth control pill (Library of Congress).

would meet with Stanley for a two and one-half hour session of Freudian psychoanalysis aimed to free the patient from his early sexual traumas.[18]

Katharine wanted to fire Dr. Kempf, alleging that Stanley was showing no improvement. She was especially vexed by his order that she "absent herself" and not see her husband for years on end. Treatment under Dr. Kempf "excludes all approaches of a physiological sort and insists upon relying solely upon psychoanalytical treatment." Katharine sought full guardianship over Stanley and the right to change the treatment by using hormones in place of psychoanalysis. She wanted Dr. Roy G. Hoskins, director of the Neuro-Endocrine Research Foundation, to take over Stanley's care. Stanley's brother Harold (a disciple of Carl Jung) and sister Anita opposed Katharine and wanted Dr. Kempt's psychoanalytical approach to continue.[19] During 1928–1929, the custody case of Stanley Robert McCormick was aired in court with leading lawyers and leading physicians on both sides of the conflict. The judges waded through 64,000 pages of medical reports dated over the previous twenty-three years.[20] Katharine's efforts for sole guardianship of her husband failed.[21]

During the forty years of his illness, Stanley Robert McCormick had occasional periods of clarity of thought and the capacity to function in a purposeful manner. But these episodes did not last. He was a solitary patient in his own asylum. By 1932, his trust had accrued $2,844,201 in interest: of this sum, $1,817,000 went in legal fees to Chicago law firms to fight for control of the estate. Other expenditures included medical fees of $150,000 annually, $4,710 for three special concerts "held in hopes of improving his condition," $5,000 to cultivate roses, $2,500 to purchase a piano and $200,000 in repairs on property. Katharine received money from Stanley's trust fund. In 1933 she was awarded $250,000 a year, much of it going to charity.[22] In 1940, Stanley's trust fund was worth $38 million, yielding an income for the year of $1.4 million.[23] By the 1940s, the total cost of keeping Stanley McCormick locked out of sight at Riven Rock exceeded $800,000 annually, an amount easily covered by the yearly income from his trust fund, which had grown to over $2.5 million.[24] Stanley Robert McCormick, who suffered over forty years from schizophrenia, died January 19, 1947.

The severe depression that took William Sanderson McCormick in 1865 into the State Hospital for the Insane, Jacksonville, Illinois, afflicted his grandson, Joseph Medill McCormick, known as Medill. Born in Chicago on May 16, 1877, Medill was two years younger than his cousin Stanley Robert McCormick. The cousins lapsed into mental illness at the start of the 20th century. Named for his maternal grandfather, Medill was the son of Ambassador Robert Sanderson McCormick and Katherine Medill McCormick. Medill and his younger brother Robert Rutherford McCormick began their schooling at the University School for Boys in Chicago. In 1889, the family moved to London, where Robert took up the posting as second secretary of the American Legation. Medill was a handsome and precocious youngster. Much was expected of him, especially by his doting and emotionally brittle mother. Medill took the examination for Harrow School that required a keen knowledge of Latin and mathematics. Founded in 1571, Harrow School, 12 miles north of London, educated such illustrious Englishmen as Lord Byron, Lord Shaftesbury and Sir Robert Peel. Winston Churchill entered Harrow the same year as the American boy Medill McCormick. Coming mainly from England's wealthiest families, the Harrow boys wore high collars, light-colored waistcoats, short black jackets, and straw hats. On formal occasions the boys put on black top hats.

Medill returned to the United States to enroll in the fall of 1892 at Groton School in Massachusetts. He studied Latin, Greek, English literature, algebra and French history. The 15-year-old boy wrote short stories and a play and submitted articles to the monthly *Grotonian*. He wrote gleefully to his grandfather and namesake that he was "urged on to greater efforts." From Groton, Medill entered Yale University (Class of 1900). While at Yale, "he had no intention of becoming a newspaper man and his own definite ambition was to go into politics [with the aim to become] the governor of his state."[25] His ambition notwithstanding, straight out of college he followed his mother's wishes by joining the *Tribune*, serving under his uncle Robert W. Patterson. "He took his assignments on police details and other routine jobs, read 'copy' and studied the work of the various departments."[26] His first major assignment was covering the Philippine-American War, where he was attached to the staff of general Jacob "Hell Roaring Jack" Smith. Returning to the United States, Medill served as telegraph copyreader and then assistant in the newspaper's Washington bureau. Medill McCormick rapidly climbed up the corporate ladder and by age twenty-nine years was the publisher of the largest and most prosperous newspaper in the Midwest, and by its own account "the greatest newspaper in the country."

"Possibly not in the history of the country did such a distinguished gathering attend a wedding." So wrote the *New York World* on June 10, 1903. The guests at the wedding on June 9, 1903, of Ruth Hanna and Joseph Medill McCormick included members of the United States cabinet, many senators, "the top crust of American society" and an assortment of diplomats. Most came out of respect for Ruth's father, Marcus Alonzo Hanna; United States senator from Ohio, chairman of the Republican national committee and the kingmaker who brought William McKinley to power. It was the assassination of McKinley in 1901 that elevated 42-year-old Theodore Roosevelt to become the 26th president of the United States. Marcus Hanna and Theodore Roosevelt were politician rivals and had long circled one the other. When Roosevelt asked to be invited to the wedding, Hanna immediately sent an invitation. President Roosevelt, accompanied by his daughter Alice, arrived in Cleveland on a special train. From that day on, Alice Roosevelt and Ruth Hanna McCormick "become life long friends."[27] The wedding ceremony was held at St. Paul's Episcopal Church at the corner of Caser Street and Euclid Avenue. After all the guests had left, Hanna and Roosevelt made their peace. "Delighted, I assure you again," said Roosevelt, flashing his famous smile. According to George E. Condon, "The marital union of the Hanna and McCormick families was, without question, the most exciting social event that Cleveland—possibly the state of Ohio—ever had known. It was the kind of special event that they talk about a hundred years later."[28]

Born 1880 in Cleveland, Ohio, Ruth Hanna attended Miss Porter's School in Farmington, Connecticut. Medill first met Ruth as a teenager when he accompanied his grandfather on a visit to the Hanna home in Thomasville, Georgia. "Nine years passed before the two were married, in a ceremony postponed by the disapproval of Medill's mother."[29] Exasperated by his mother's sharp tongue, Medill wrote that both he and his mother were "nervous persons and she continually interferes." He could no longer tolerate his mother's "bitterness." "Mother must not only be civil to her but she must bridle her tongue when she discusses Ruth in the family, or out of it."[30] Joseph Medill McCormick was supported at the wedding by his parents, ambassador to Russia Robert S. McCormick and his mother Katherine, his great aunt Mrs. Nettie McCormick, his brother Robert, as well as uncles

William Grigsby, Stanley, Cyrus, and Harold McCormick. Mrs. William McKinley, the widow of the slain president, also attended the wedding.[31] She presented the couple with a rare Italian vase. Medill's parents gave them a team of horses imported from Russia.

Soon after the marriage, it became clear that Medill's difficulties were more than eccentricities. "He was moody and subject to depression, with alternate periods of energy and euphoria," made all the more serious by heavy drinking.[32] Ruth had to change her role from wife to "a relationship of protection and mother." Medill suffered a major breakdown in 1906. Katherine Medill McCormick had warned her son: "You are nervous, unstable, strung up, over-tired. Don't forget the horrid possibility—which unfortunately all the McCormicks have to face—Hereditary tendencies are *hereditary tendencies*." In an equally blunt letter to his wife Ruth, Kate wrote: "Medill drinks all the time. He never stops the whole day. His nervous system is completely degenerated by alcoholic poison. You, my dear, are now face to face with one or two certainties. Either a crazy husband or a dead husband."[33]

Joseph Medill McCormick suffered from bipolar disorder and alcoholism. He was the older brother of Robert Rutherford McCormick. He left the *Chicago Tribune* for politics to become a U.S. representative and later a senator. In 1925 he committed suicide (Library of Congress).

In 1908, Medill entered a manic phase with grandiose thinking and pressure of speech. His family was alarmed by "All his talk about enormous things [and his] love to talk about Napoleon."[34] On November 18, 1908, the directors of the *Tribune* approved Medill's request for a leave of absence. Officially on a business trip to Germany, Medill, accompanied by Ruth, went to Zurich to consult Dr. Carl Gustav Jung, the eminent Swiss psychiatrist who would figure large in the McCormick saga. Medill spent two weeks as a patient at Burgholzli clinic. Jung "diagnosed McCormick's illness as stemming from a disabling dependence on his powerful mother. [She was] a power devil of the very first rate." Medill needed to get away from her influence. Mixing treatment and pleasure, Medill accompanied Jung on a bicycle trip near Zurich. Jung sent a letter to the directors of the *Tribune* declaring that Medill was bent on self-destruction and was "a hopeless alcoholic and permanently incapable of performing his duties."[35] Jung told Medill that his "infantile relations with his mother" drove him to a "wild and immoral life."[36] Still in a state of mania, Medill proposed a trip to Albania, Turkey and Greece. While in Europe, Medill relapsed several times into heavy drinking. Jung warned Ruth: "The struggle will last for a long time." Medill's trip to Zurich brought Jung a steady stream of wealthy American patients that included Harold Fowler McCormick, his wife Edith Rockefeller McCormick and their children.

Returning to the United States, Medill McCormick left the newspaper made famous by his grandfather. He kept his financial interests in the *Tribune, Cleveland Leader* and the *Cleveland News*. His mother Kate had planned for Medill to become the heir to the *Tribune* empire. With that path blocked, she told him: "You've now a splendid chance to be a politician." Politics "offered Medill a degree of freedom from her grasp that he had never before known."[37] Aided by his wife Ruth, politics became Medill's passion. He was active in the progressive Republican movement. Theodore Roosevelt hailed McCormick as the man "striven to make the conditions of life better and more favorable for the wage earner of the right kind, and for the farmers." Medill McCormick was a fine mix of "some radicalism [and] common sense."

On August 8, 1913, Medill McCormick got drunk while traveling from Chicago to New York on the Twentieth Century Limited. Becoming belligerent, he hit a Pullman conductor and was removed from the train at Syracuse, New York at 3:21 in the morning. Arrested at the station, he was rudely yanked into court still in his pajamas and charged with public intoxication.[38]

In 1913, Medill was elected to the Illinois House of Representatives. A member of the Republican Party, he served 1917–1919 in the United States House of Representatives, and from 1919 to 1925 served as Senator from Illinois in the United States Senate. Medill and his brother Robert were leading isolationists who believed that America should keep out of the affairs of other countries. Like his brother, Medill opposed America's entry into the League of Nations and the World Court and was against American aid to Europe in the aftermath of the First World War. As a member of the Senate's Foreign Relations Committee, he claimed: "Europe is sick with various ills … none of them curable by anything which the American people or its government might do." Europe must heal itself starting with "effective economic remedies." Advocating a passionate "America First" policy, Medill called for reforms at home, getting rid of waste and cutting back on government spending.

Although staunchly in the Republican camp, Medill and Ruth kept some progressive values. In 1912, "Medill McCormick made it possible for the Negro to enter a place in national politics that had never been granted before."[39] In 1922, Senator Medill McCormick proposed Resolution 232: "That Congress shall have power to limit or prevent the labor of persons under eighteen years of age."[40] Medill took pride that "the McCormicks have given more money to Negro institutions than any family in the west." In Medill McCormick's words, his amendment would ensure that American children were properly educated "to discharge their duty as citizens of the state."[41] Medill and Ruth developed the 2,200-acre Rock River Farm, near Byron, Illinois, where they raised prize-winning Holstein cattle and dairy herds. He was largely able to stay away from alcohol but took various drugs in a vain attempt to control his manic-depressive disorder. His mood shifts placed an enormous strain on the marriage and at times Ruth separated from Medill. He suffered from gastric bleeding that required several periods in the hospital. Through all his mental and physical anguish, Medill was sustained by his political ambitions and the hope of "one day inhabiting the White House." Against all expectations, Medill McCormick was beaten by a narrow margin by Charles S. Deneen. Medill blamed the loss on the *Tribune's* "strident opposition to Prohibition."[42]

After losing his bid for re-election, the 47-year-old Medill gave his young children a tender farewell, telling them he needed to go to Washington to wind down his affairs before the official end of his Senate term on March 4. The rumor mill had him appointed the American ambassador to Germany. Joseph Medill McCormick spent time on the floor of the Senate and in his office. He rented a room at the Hotel Hamilton and was last seen entering the hotel at 11:00 P.M. on the night of February 23, 1925.[43] Getting into his night-clothes, he took the contents of several vials of barbiturates. He was found dead the following morning. The official cause of death was gastric hemorrhage and myocarditis. His wife Ruth "kept his suicide a well-guarded secret for years."[44] Joseph Medill McCormick left an estate worth $2 million.

Joseph Medill McCormick married Ruth Hanna in 1903 and Stanley McCormick married Katharine Dexter the following year. Both women had to deal with their husband's severe mental illness. They found their purpose in the Woman Suffrage movement and in progressive politics. Katharine funded the research that yielded the contraceptive pill. Ruth Hanna McCormick was the chairperson of the congressional committee of the National American Woman Suffrage Association (NAWSA) from 1913 until 1920 when the Nineteenth Amendment of the Constitution was ratified, granting votes to women. She was 44 years old when Medill died, leaving her to care for their three children, Katrina Augusta, age 12, John Medill, age 9, and Ruth Elizabeth, age 4. Medill's death "devastated Ruth and their three children … [Ruth's] "thought was to give up politics," but her close friend Alice Roo-

Daughter of the kingmaker Marcus Alonzo Hanna, Ruth married Joseph Medill McCormick in 1903. This equestrian picture shows Ruth with her daughter Katrina and her son John in 1923. After her husband's death, Ruth Hanna McCormick served in the U.S. House of Representatives, but later lost her bid to become the first woman to sit in the Senate (Library of Congress).

sevelt Longworth told her she "must not get out of politics even temporarily, not even for a day. She was quite right about it."[45] Ruth served as a member of the Republican National Committee. She served as a Republican in the Seventy-First Congress, and in 1930, was the first woman to run (unsuccessfully) for a seat in the United States Senate. She married Albert Gallatin Simms, a member from New Mexico in the 71st Congress, and settled on their ranch Los Poblamos, near Albuquerque.

Tragedy followed Ruth to New Mexico. Her son John Medill was passionate about mountain climbing. On June 22, 1938, Johnny, at age twenty-one, fell to his death off a peak of Mt. Sandia. At the urgent appeal of his mother, skilled mountain climbers arrived from New Mexico and Colorado to search for Johnny, "the heir to the McCormick printing fortune." A party of Sandia Indians found the body. It was "one of the most intense mountain searches ever conducted in this part of the country." Johnny was planning to follow his uncle Robert Rutherford McCormick, with a career as a journalist for the *Chicago Tribune*.[46] Ruth Hanna McCormick Simms died December 31, 1944, from pancreatitis. Her daughter Ruth Elizabeth, known as Bazy, was a journalist. At age 26, her uncle, Robert R. McCormick, appointed her editor of his *Washington Times-Herald*. After she married Galvin Tankersley she had a falling out with her uncle and left Washington to breed Arabian horses in Tucson and Flagstaff in Arizona.

Chapter Thirteen

Ambassadors and Politicians

Robert Sanderson McCormick was sixteen years old and his brother William Grigsby McCormick was fourteen when their father William died in 1865. Both boys remained in Chicago to finish high school before setting out to complete their education at the University of Virginia. Founded in 1819 by Thomas Jefferson, the University of Virginia became a leading college in the American South. With the coming of the Civil War, most of its students supported secession and joined the Confederate Army. The university continued during the war years but with few students and faculty. Its famed Rotunda served as a hospital. At the end of the war many of its students were "men of years" who had fought for the Confederacy.[1] In the decade after the Civil war, Robert Sanderson (class of 1868) and William Grigsby McCormick (class of 1870) were among only a small number of northerners who chose the University of Virginia.

In 1870, the brothers Robert, age 20, and William, age 18, set out to tour Europe. In Paris they "awoke to find that Napoleon III had abdicated and a republic had been declared." They made their way to the American embassy to meet Elihu B. Washburne, the American minister to France and a friend of the McCormick family. Washburne "advised them to leave France at once, advise which was promptly taken."[2] Robert Sanderson McCormick affected the demeanor of a Southern aristocrat. He was a skilled equestrian, well-spoken, well-read and somewhat of an authority on the life of Napoleon. Soon after graduation, Robert returned to the Midwest to form a business partnership with his cousin Hugh Leander Adams. In 1872, the young men built a grain elevator near the depot of the Chicago & Alton Railroad Company, St. Louis.[3] The enterprise fell upon hard times and went into bankruptcy, losing much of his family's money. Robert's prospects improved greatly in 1876 when he married 23-year-old Katherine "Kate" Van Etta Medill, oldest daughter of Joseph Medill, editor and publisher from 1855 to 1899 of the *Chicago Tribune*. She attended boarding school in Indiana followed by music and voice training in Munich.

Joseph Medill was born in 1823 on a farm near St. John in the Canadian Province of New Brunswick. A half-century earlier, New Brunswick was established as the Loyalist Province to settle exiled Americans still loyal to the British king. When Joseph was nine, his family moved to Ohio, where he later began his career as a newspaperman. The *Chicago Tribune* began in 1847 in a one-room office in a building at the corner of Lake and LaSalle streets. In 1855, the 32-year-old Joseph Medill left Cleveland and bought an interest in the *Tribune* to make it Chicago's leading Republican newspaper on a platform of resistance to slavery and no more slave states or slave territory. Medill was an early supporter of Abraham Lincoln, who was a frequent guest in the Medill home. Medill used the columns of the *Tribune* to promote Abraham Lincoln, described as: "Stands six foot four inches in his stockings. In dress by no means precise. Always clean, he is never fashionable; he is careless but not slovenly." Lincoln "never drinks intoxicating liquors of any sort, not addicted to tobacco ... never gambles.... A scrupulous teller of the truth." The *Tribune* "advocated the aggressive persecution of the Civil War."[4] This stand made Medill and his newspaper opponents of Cyrus, William and Leander McCormick. The *Chicago Tribune* vilified Cyrus McCormick as a pilferer of other men's ideas, power-hungry and a rebel sympathizer—a man not to be trusted to hold public office. During the Civil War, the *Tribune* attacked Cyrus Hall McCormick as a supporter of the Southern rebellion. "Like all poor white trash while back in Virginia he left the state as better friends of slavery than the slave owners themselves." Joseph Medill served as mayor of Chicago from 1871 to 1873, in the aftermath of the Great Fire, and guided the rebuilding of the city.

Joseph Medill opposed the marriage of his daughter to a McCormick, but the strong-willed and ambitious Kate persisted. "In marrying Robert Sanderson McCormick, Kate had linked the Medills to another of Chicago's eminent names, but not to one of its fortunes."[5] On June 8, 1876, Robert Sanderson McCormick married Katherine Medill at the Second Presbyterian Church of Chicago. Robert began as the literary critic of the *Tribune*. In May 1877, at their home at 156 East Ontario Street, Kate gave birth to Joseph Medill McCormick, the first of the Medill grandchildren. In 1879, their daughter Katarina was born but died in infancy. The death of her daughter rendered Kate apprehensive and depressive. A year later Kate delivered a second son, Robert Rutherford McCormick.

Robert Todd Lincoln, son of the slain president Abraham Lincoln, moved to Chicago, where he established a highly lucrative corporate law practice. He served 1881–1885 as United States secretary of war under presidents James Garfield and Chester A. Arthur. In 1889, Lincoln was appointed American ambassador to the Court of St. James. In his turn, Robert Lincoln appointed as second secretary to the legation Robert Sanderson McCormick, the son-in-law of his friend and neighbor, Joseph Medill. On May 15, ambassador Lincoln and his staff, including Robert McCormick, departed New York for London on the steamship *City of Paris*. "My parents were splendid diplomats because they had no inferiority complex," claimed their son Robert Rutherford McCormick in his memoirs. "My father, one of the last of the pre–Civil War school, looked upon himself as of the Virginia aristocracy, the equal of any aristocrat in Europe. My mother reached her viewpoint by another route. Her father had been an intimate ... of President Lincoln, and a supporter and intimate friend of General Grant."[6]

Reaching London, Robert McCormick and his family rented a house on Brook Street in posh Mayfair, close to Grosvenor Square. Medill was placed at Harrow School to become a classmate of the young Winston Churchill. Younger brother Robert "Bertie" was sent to Ludgrove School, some thirty miles west of London. Supported by Joseph Medill's money, the family enjoyed frequent trips to the Continent. But Robert McCormick was not content to be the second secretary of the legation. He demanded a promotion to first secretary. In June 1890, after ambassador Lincoln refused his request, McCormick promptly resigned.[7] Permitting McCormick to remain in London, President Benjamin Harrison appointed him resident commissioner to promote the World's Columbian Exposition to be held in Chicago in 1893. It was hard going for McCormick to excite British interest in the Chicago fair. Despite high American tariffs on imported goods, Robert McCormick persuaded hundreds of British firms, including Coleman's Mustard, Royal Dalton, and Crosse & Blackwell, to display their goods at the Chicago fair. British colonies from the Cape Colony, New South Wales, India and Canada also brought their wares to Chicago to tempt the American customer.[8] At the close of the 19th century, Robert and Kate returned to Chicago where he served on the library board.

On March 7, 1901, Robert Sanderson McCormick was appointed envoy extraordinary and minister plenipotentiary to the court of Austria-Hungary. The next year he was promoted to the rank of ambassador. On June 26, 1902, "heavily gilded court carriages conveyed" ambassador McCormick and his staff from the American embassy in Vienna to the royal palace where he was received by emperor Franz Josef.[9] While in Vienna, McCormick dealt with the complex issue of "the cruel tariff laws of the United States" that impeded Austrian exports. He protested Austrian discrimination against its ethnic minorities, and hailed the United States as offering "asylum to the oppressed of all lands."[10] After fifteen months in Vienna, Robert S. McCormick was sent to St. Petersburg as the American ambassador to Imperial Russia. McCormick presented his credentials to the Tsar on January 13, 1903. He believed that Tsar Nicholas II was "a very remarkable man, and a wise and humane rule."[11]

Three months after ambassador McCormick arrived in Russia, the Bessarabian city of Kishinev was rocked by anti–Semitic riots. "There was a well laid-out plan for the general massacre of Jews on the day following the Russian Easter," reported the *New York Times.* "The mob was led by priests, and the general cry, 'Kill the Jews,' was taken up all over the city. The Jews were slaughtered ... like sheep. The dead numbered 120 and the injured about 500. The scenes of horror attending this massacre are beyond description. Babes were literally torn to pieces by the frenzied and bloodthirsty mob. The local police made no attempt to check the reign of terror. At sunset, the streets were piled with corpses and the wounded. Those who could make their escape fled in terror, and the city is now practically deserted of Jews."[12]

News of the Kishinev massacre spread rapidly around the world. The State Department requested further information from ambassador Robert McCormick. Quoting the Russian government statement, McCormick stated that it was "officially denied that there is any want or suffering among Jews in southwest Russia and aid of any kind is unnecessary."[13] McCormick sent the state department a copy of a report on the Kishinev massacre that appeared in the *London Standard* of May 1, 1903. There had been "a savage and merciless attack on the Jews." In the Jewish quarter of the city "not a house or shop was spared."[14] When ambassador McCormick returned to the United States in June for consultations he acknowledged that a massacre of Jews in Kishinev had taken place.

Q. Do you think the Russian government is in any way responsible for the massacre?
A. No. I have no idea that the government in any way fathered the incident.
Q. Do you think the authorities condone it?
A. I do not.[15]

Ambassador McCormick was in St. Petersburg when the Japanese navy attacked the eastern Russian fleet at Port Arthur, China. Russia and Japan were at war over their competing claims on Manchuria and Korea. The victory established Japan as a major Asian power but the loss was a deep humiliation to the Russians. While the United States declared its neutrality, the Japanese government entrusted its affairs in Russia to the American embassy.

Ambassador McCormick negotiated the release of 900 Japanese subjects stranded in Russia. He sought to protect American interests in Korea and the safety of American shipping in Asian waters.[16] McCormick took part in the negotiations that lead to the Treaty of Portsmouth, signed in September 1905, to end the Russo-Japanese War. President Theodore Roosevelt received the 1906 Nobel Peace Prize for settling the dispute between Russia and Japan.

Ambassador McCormick was an eyewitness of Bloody Sunday, the January 22, 1905, uprising in St. Petersburg. Angry workers led by the priest Georgy Gapon marched toward the Winter Palace to hand their petition to the Tsar. Imperial troops opened fire on the crowd, killing and wounding many. Bloody Sunday was one of the key events that led to the Russian Revolution. On January 31, ambassador McCormick wrote the secretary of state, John Hay, that the instigators were "a group of socialists with Father Gapon … a sort of Second Savior at its head. [This] renegade priest" had violated "a young girl of 12 years of age, and was a thorough-paced revolutionist [who] had utterly deceived the working men into the belief that his sole purpose was to aid them and better their condition…. His real intention was to get to the person of the Emperor and hold him as a hostage." The protesters included "some of the scum of the capital … rough-looking workmen and sneering, overbearing students." Many came "armed with knives, pieces of piping, sticks, and some even with revolvers." McCormick claimed that the troops and officers "moved along the front of the crowd, begging the people to disperse," but as the crowd "grew larger and bolder … the troops resorted to charges with drawn swords, striking the crowd with the flat of their swords." As a result of Bloody Sunday, concluded McCormick, Tsar Nicholas II "has lost absolutely the affection of the Russian people [and] will never again be safe in the midst of his people."[17] Soon after Bloody Sunday, president Theodore Roosevelt notified McCormick that he should "proceed to Paris without delay" to become the American ambassador to France. McCormick was "loath to sever his many pleasant relations with the Russians." On March 27, McCormick bade farewell to the Russian emperor at Tsarskoe-Sela. As parting gifts the Tsar, his wife and the dowager empress gave McCormick their autographed portraits. On March 29 the ambassador and his family left St. Petersburg on the Northern Express for Paris. "Practically the entire diplomatic corps was present" to bid the Americans adieu.[18]

On May 2, 1905, ambassador McCormick and his staff entered the Elysees Palace to be received by Emile Loubet, president of the French republic. As the military band played the American national anthem, the "French tricolor was dipped in salute." McCormick spoke of the "century of friendship between the United States and France." In response, Loubet said: "France had no prouder heritage than her participation in the work which brought the powerful American nation into being." The ills of the world, McCormick believed, stem from uncontrolled wealth and power. Competition between nations for possession and trade drives the world towards war. It is necessary to "crush out racial prejudice." Japan's success in its war against Russia showed that the East was the equal of the "civilized world."[19] McCormick appealed for a world court to negotiate the political and economic stresses between France and Germany, and between Russia and Japan; otherwise there would be a world war.

Robert Sanderson McCormick remained two years in France as the American ambassador before ill health forced his early retirement. He returned to the United States on

March 18, 1907, on the Hamburg-American liner *Amerika*. His wife Kate remained in Europe to "take the waters of Carlsbad ... and will not come home until there is milder weather here." McCormick proudly carried home the honors he received. The Japanese government awarded him the First Class Order of the Rising Sun for handling Japanese interests in St. Petersburg during the Russian-Japanese War. Tsar Nicholas awarded McCormick the Order of St. Alexander Nevsky, and the French government honored him with its Grand Order of the Legion of Honor—France's highest honor to a foreigner. (In 1879, his uncle Cyrus Hall McCormick had received a lesser French award.) As a good diplomat, Robert S. McCormick credited his government for these honors. "All the nations of the world seem friendly to the United States. They all respect her and president [Theodore] Roosevelt is considered a great president.... My stay of two years [in France] was most enjoyable."[20]

Robert Sanderson McCormick served as American ambassador to Austria-Hungary (1901–02), Russia (1902–05) and France (1905–07). Born in Virginia in 1849, he was the son of William Sanderson and Mary Ann Grigsby McCormick, and father of U.S. Senator Joseph Medill McCormick and newspaperman Robert Rutherford McCormick (from *Family Record and Biography,* Leander James McCormick, 1896).

On the death of her father in 1899, Katherine inherited $1 million, and Robert received a large share of stock in the *Tribune*. Using their inheritance, Kate and Robert lived in grand style. To remain part of the power set even after retirement, Robert and Katherine McCormick built a splendid home at 3000 Massachusetts Avenue Northwest in Washington, D.C., and kept a home in Hinsdale, Illinois. His health declined due to "softening of the brain caused by syphilis" and alcohol excess.[21] Robert Sanderson McCormick died on April 16, 1919. The aristocratic European world he loved died with him. Austria-Hungary collapsed, Germany was defeated, France was exhausted in the First World War, and Tsar Nicholas II, his wife Alexandra and their children were assassinated. The 300-year rule of the House of Romanov ended with the Russian Revolution.

After the splendor of the courts of Austria-Hungary, Russia and France, Katherine Van Etta Medill McCormick did not adjust well to life in America. She preferred her suite at the Ritz Hotel in Paris and her home at Versailles. The embittered Kate outlived her husband by thirteen years.[22] The McCormick home in Washington became the Brazilian Embassy. Kate was fond of relating anecdotes about presidents Abraham Lincoln and Ulysses S. Grant, who were friends of her father. She spoke fluent French and German. She died in Versailles on July 4, 1932, aged 79 years. Her body was brought on the liner *Leviathan* to New York, where her son Robert met it and escorted it to Chicago for burial.[23] Katherine Medill McCormick left an estate worth $100,000; half to her son Robert Rutherford

McCormick, and the other $50,000 to be divided in equal shares by Katarina, John Medill and Ruth, the children of her deceased son, Joseph Medill McCormick.[24]

William McCormick Blair, Jr., born in 1916, was the grandson of William Grigsby McCormick and grandnephew of ambassador Robert Sanderson McCormick. He attended Groton School but, in a departure from other McCormicks who attended eastern Ivy League colleges, William went to Stanford University. After graduation from the University of Virginia law school, he settled into a law partnership in Chicago with Adlai Stevenson. Unlike his deeply conservative first cousin Robert Rutherford McCormick, William was a liberal. Showing a talent for organization and behind-the-scenes-negotiating, he served as chief aide to Adlai Stevenson in his bids for President of the United States. William McCormick Blair, Jr., raised the funds to build the John F. Kennedy Center in Washington, D.C. He served as ambassador to Denmark (1961–64) and to the Philippines (1964–67).[25] Yet another distinguished member of the family was Robert McCormick Adams (1926–2018), born in Chicago, who earned his doctorate at the University of Chicago and served as director of the Oriental Institute. His scholarly work focused largely on the agricultural history of the Middle East. From 1984 to 1994 he served in Washington as secretary of the Smithsonian Institution.

Chapter Fourteen

Robert Rutherford McCormick and His *Chicago Tribune*

Robert Rutherford McCormick, known in his youth as Bertie, was born in 1880. He was the grandson of William Sanderson McCormick, and the son of Robert Sanderson McCormick and Katherine Van Etta Medill McCormick. He grew up in McCormickville, "among McCormicks and McCormick ideas."[1] Robert attended the Church of England-affiliated Ludgrove School, Wokingham, England, and then Groton School, run by New England Episcopalians. At Groton he was one form ahead of Franklin Delano Roosevelt. Bertie was unhappy at Groton, and resented the airs of the Boston and New York boys who looked down on Midwesterners.

Groton to Yale was the path for several of the McCormick boys. Bertie enrolled at Yale in September 1899 and took up residence in Pierson Hall on Chapel Street. "Bertie Rubberfoot" McCormick was a member of the Yale graduating class of 1903. His brother Joseph Medill was of class of 1900; his cousins R. Hall McCormick, Jr., class of 1900, J. M. Patterson, class of 1901, McCormick Blair, class of 1906 and Chauncey McCormick, class of 1906. (The sons of Cyrus Hall McCormick went to Princeton.) After Yale, Bertie returned to Chicago to begin law school at Northwestern University. Robert Rutherford McCormick entered politics at age twenty-four as alderman representing Ward 21, the Near North Side of Chicago. "It is good to see young men from our well known families entering public life." To meet the voters, McCormick "felt obliged to spend ninety percent of my time in saloons and the remaining ten percent in barrooms."[2] McCormick, candidate for the Republican Party, beat Mr. Wenter, a Democrat, by 87,443 votes to 79,670. He served as president of the Sanitary District of Chicago, responsible for a $60 million sewage-disposal project. In 1907 Bertie McCormick was admitted to the Illinois bar.

In the summer of 1910 he traveled through Europe to study "the management of city government with particular reference to harbors." On his return to America he published a monograph on European harbors. "The sanitary district offers one of the richest opportunities for plunder and political corruption." McCormick presented himself as a man of "integrity and wakeful zeal," determined to protect the peoples' property.[3] Robert McCormick supervised the construction of Chicago's drainage channel that carried the sewage water of two million people along a 35-mile canal to be cleaned and purified for re-use. The $60 million sewerage scheme created "the greatest artificial waterway the world has ever seen."[4] He was a member of the Republican Committee of 100 "to take control of the party out of the hands of Senator William Lorimer." Ten years after graduation, the Yale Class of 1903 was well on the way to success as lawyers, physicians, bankers, teachers, businessmen and ministers, with occasional farmers, writers and artists. Robert Rutherford McCormick listed his occupation as the president of the Tribune Company of Chicago. Not yet thirty years old, McCormick was already a forceful political persona. As publisher of the *Chicago Tribune*, he presented himself as the champion of fiscal restraint and the enemy of plunder and corruption. Robert was a delegate to the Republican National Convention and was a part of the reform movement to purge the Republican Party "of its criminal members and once more become the governing party in the country."[5] His switch from the rough and tumble of Chicago politics to the life of a newspaperman began with the self-destruction of his mood-driven and alcoholic brother Medill. Robert persuaded the board of the *Chicago Tribune* not to sell the paper but to give him the chance to run it. In 1910 the brothers swapped roles. Medill went into politics, while Robert became president of the Tribune Company and, with his cousin Joseph Medill Patterson, co-editor of the *Chicago Tribune*. Their mothers Katherine Medill McCormick and Elinor Medill Patterson largely owned the Tribune Company. From 1910 onwards the *Tribune* carried the sub-title "the World's Greatest Newspaper."

Kate McCormick chose Marion Deering as an appropriate spouse for her son Robert. But he showed little interest in the daughter of William Deering. Instead, his cousin Chauncey McCormick married the wealthy heiress. Robert was more interested in Amie de Houle Irwin, then married to his cousin, Edward Shields Adams; son of Amanda J. McCormick, the youngest of the eight children of Robert and Mary Ann McCormick. Born in Rockbridge County, Virginia in 1845, Amanda married Hugh Adams, and in 1857, followed her three brothers to Chicago. Hugh Adams became wealthy as a partner with Cyrus Hall McCormick, Sr., in the firm of McCormick & Adams, grain merchants. At Hugh's death in 1880, the business went to his sons Cyrus H., Hugh l., and Edward Shields Adams. Born in 1859, Edward S. Adams married Amie de Houle Irwin in 1895.[6] Edward was twenty-one years older and was married to Amie for ten years before the 25-year-old Robert R. McCormick came to visit.

Amie (or Amy) Irwin was the daughter of general Bernard J. D. Irwin, renowned as "The Fighting Doctor" in the Apache Wars and the Civil War, and the first man to receive the Congressional Medal of Honor. By 1905, Edward Adams's business was failing and he began to drink heavily. The bachelor Bertie McCormick paid regular visits to the Adams's residences both in Chicago and at Lake Forest. McCormick began an affair with Amie, nine years his senior. She was a slim and beautiful woman, an artist, and an accomplished horsewoman. In March 1914, Amie obtained a divorce, after which Edward Adams sued McCormick for alienation of his wife's affections. In turn, McCormick sued his cousin for $38,000, alleging that Adams was "indebted to him in large sums of money." Robert and Amie made their separate ways to London and, on March 10, 1915, in front to only two witnesses, thirty-five-year-old Robert and forty-four-year-old Amie were married in St. George's Registry, Hanover Square.[7]

With World War I raging on the Continent, Robert and Amie left England on March 14, 1915, by steamer for the Mediterranean, docking at Malta and Salonika. From Salonika they traveled by train to Bulgaria, crossed into Russia and made their way to Petrograd. Robert had arranged for the governor of Illinois to appoint him a major in the Illinois National Guard. His military rank and the fact that his father served in Russia from 1903 to 1905 as the American ambassador opened doors for Robert McCormick. On April 10, wearing full evening dress, Robert R. McCormick traveled the fifteen miles from Petrograd to Tsarskoye Selo for a brief meeting with Tsar Nicholas II. "The war was very sudden and very unexpected," said Tsar Nicholas to McCormick. After a few minutes of small talk, the Tsar said, "I am very sorry but I must go now." McCormick was ushered out. The next day McCormick met 59-year-old Nicolas Nicolaiwitch [*sic*] Romanoff, standing six feet six inches, the cousin to the Tsar, and commander-in-chief of the Russian Army. "His soldiers are willing to do and die for him."[8]

The battle plan of the Russian army was to attack the Germans near Koeningsberg, and draw them away from French soil. McCormick was given permission as a journalist to follow the Russian army as it attacked at Ossowetz and Peremysl. In a series of reports that appeared in the *Chicago Tribune* and the *New York Times*, Robert R. McCormick saluted the fighting spirit of the Russian Army. "The Tsar's army is highly efficient. The Russian cavalry charges with the lance and saber, the second rank is armed with automatic pistols." McCormick was much impressed by the officer class, many of whom spoke good English or French. Unlike the French and the British who use "great motor trucks" for transportation, the Russians still used horse-drawn carts that "can go over any kind of road or no road…. The Russian infantryman is the most splendid physical specimen in the war. The Russian soldier is so very much bigger and very much more athletic than the English Tommy [because] the bulk of the Russian population is agriculture, while the English is manufacturing."[9] The Russian soldier "on average is half a head taller than other soldiers, weighs 25 pounds heavier and is more athletic." Russian army regiments were named for the towns from which their soldiers came. The towns took great pride in their regiments, sending letters, presents and praise. Each regiment had its own fete day to celebrate past victories over the likes of Napoleon or the Turks. The Russian soldier was prepared "to fight for the emperor to the death." McCormick was much impressed by the high morale of the Russian army.[10]

Robert McCormick followed the Russian army into battle against Austria-Hungary. He watched as the Russians crossed the Carpathian Mountains to attack the Austrians. In its wake, the war left ruined villages, destroyed bridges, the dead and the maimed. He observed "a Polish peasant. 60 years of age, who was shot by a Prussian officer for objecting to the burning of his house…. Better for himself he had died where he lay." His shattered arm would "keep him from the cultivation of his little farm, whereby he earns his living."[11] Robert McCormick left Russia for Chicago to write his experiences into a book, *With the Russian Army,* published in the fall of 1915. McCormick suggested that the preparedness of the Russian Army served as an example for the United States to follow. He offered a romanticized view of Russians, bound tightly by tradition, devoted to the Romanov dynasty, and still reliant on horse-pulled transportation, the sword and the bayonet.[12] McCormick's rosy assessment of the Russian Army was quickly destroyed. In August 1915, the Tsar replaced the Grand Duke as commander-in-chief. Following the Revolution, the Bolsheviks made peace with Germany and withdrew the Russian army from the war. The Tsar and his family were murdered and the Grand Duke went into exile.

The Colonel

On April 2, 1917, President Woodrow Wilson asked Congress to declare war on Germany. Four days later, Congress granted his request. In May, Wilson authorized an American

Expeditionary Force under the command of general John J. Pershing. Eager to take part in the war, Robert R. McCormick wrote to Washington, offering his services to Pershing "in any capacity." Family influence, including support from his brother, U.S. congressman Medill McCormick, gave Robert what he desired. Major Robert McCormick of the Illinois National Guard Cavalry "has been called to Federal service and detailed with major general Pershing's expeditionary force in France."[13] In July, McCormick traveled to Paris and checked in at the Ritz Hotel before joining the general staff of the newly formed American Expeditionary Force. The 36-year-old newspaperman was out of place among the West Point-educated officers and the newly trained troops of the mechanized American force. "The year 1917 closed with Germany once more successful in all fronts," wrote McCormick. "In the east Russia had gone Bolshevik and had made peace with Germany." This allowed the Germans to move their troops westwards to battle the French, English and American armies.[14]

By the start of 1918, large numbers of American troops were arriving to assist the British and French armies. McCormick took part in the May 28, 1918, Battle of Cantigny. Major McCormick commanded a battalion of the 1st Division into Cantigny, a small farming village. Led by general Pershing, Cantigny was "the first offensive movement of any importance which American troops undertook."[15] Thirty-five hundred doughboys of the U.S. Army's 1st Division attacked the Germans. "The Americans left their trenches at 6:43 after heavy artillery preparation and covered the 600 yards in ten minutes.... American troops in Picardy captured the village of Cantigny, took 200 prisoners and inflicted severe losses in killed and wounded on the enemy.... The American casualties were relatively small." The Battle of Cantigny was a boost to Pershing and the American Expeditionary Force, previously regarded as a mere "reserve addition to the forces of democracy." The American success at Cantigny "added much to the very favorable impression which the American troops already have created along the British front.... This is the sort of stuff we will give to the boche."[16] In his 1920 book *The Army of 1918,* McCormick wrote: "The morale effect of the Cantigny battle was infinitely greater than its tactical importance." Until that battle, "German troops had been winning all along the line." At Cantigny, "American troops proved they could throw back the enemy in formal battle." After Cantigny, "the first division went on to greater victories at Soissons and at St. Michiel."[17]

Robert R. McCormick (left) is seen in the trenches before the Battle of Cantigny, 1918 (courtesy Robert R. McCormick Research Center, First Division Museum at Cantigny, Wheaton, Illinois).

Pershing submitted the names of officers and men "who have been cited for bravery under fire in the operations around Cantigny." Among them were lieutenant E. D. Orreal, who showed "bravery and coolness in handling a platoon under heavy bombardment, inflicting heavy losses"; corporal Carter C. Selfe, who, though severely wounded, assisted his comrades; and private Benjamin Perill who climbed a tree to observe the approaching enemy "giving timely warning to his platoon." Also acknowledged for bravery was 31-year-old major Theodore Roosevelt, Jr., son of President Theodore Roosevelt. Major Robert Rutherford McCormick of the First Division was not included in the list of the brave and the cool. In August 1918, he was promoted to colonel. To the end of his days, Robert R. McCormick was known as The Colonel, and renamed his farm in Wheaton, Illinois "Cantigny," where he built the First Division Museum. In 1919, the French minister of war awarded his wife, Amie McCormick, the medal d'honneur for "her tireless devotion and ministry to the wounded and sick of the French army."[18] Discharged from duty at the close of 1918, colonel Robert R. McCormick and his wife returned to Chicago to live at 1529 Astor Street and spend the summers on their farm, where Amie kept a prize-winning heard of Guernseys. Amie established Chicago's Lilac Day and collected lilacs for distribution to the sick and elderly.

By September 1912, *The Chicago Tribune* had a daily circulation of 220,500 copies, with 304,325 copies sold on Sundays. Under the leadership of Robert McCormick, the paper's circulation increased year after year, reaching in 1920 a daily circulation of 457,158 and with 716,254 copies distributed on Sunday. At its peak, McCormick built the *Chicago Tribune* to a daily circulation of 892,088 and the Sunday edition to 1,392,384. With increased sales came increased advertisements and increased profits. The *Tribune* continued its boast as "the World's Greatest Newspaper" and its determination to "Make Chicago the First City in the World." Chicago generated much news and participated in the great events of the day, including the 1893 and 1933 World's Fairs, race riots of 1919, votes for women, prohibition, Al Capone, and the attempt in 1924 of Leopold and Loeb to commit the undetectable murder. Even before prohibition, organized crime was thriving in Chicago with gambling, protection rackets and prostitution. Robert R. McCormick had an early interest in radio. In 1925 his WGN radio station exclusively broadcasted the *State of Tennessee v. John Thomas Scopes*, a high school teacher from Dayton, indicted for teaching evolutionary theory. Known as the Scopes Monkey Trial, it generated tremendous interest and boosted the ratings of the radio station. Clarence Darrow, Chicago's leading defense attorney, defended Scopes. Paying $1,000 a day for a long-distance telephone line from Tennessee, McCormick's radio station captured the sound and the drama of this seminal event. John Thomas Scopes was found guilty and ordered to pay a $100 fine.

Under the leadership of Robert R. McCormick, the *Chicago Tribune* launched an "America First" platform, "Our country right or wrong," with the newspaper leading the battle for free speech, clean government and the end of corruption and waste. Through the columns of the *Chicago Tribune*, Robert R. McCormick expressed his forceful opinions on the leading issues of the times; Prohibition, Woman's Suffrage, Freedom of the Press, The Great Depression, and, especially, America's role in world affairs.

In 1916, the *Tribune* "looked upon Henry Ford as a menace to American unity and true American ideals," labeling him "an ignorant idealist" and the "anarchistic enemy of his country."[19] Claiming libel, Ford sued the paper for $1 million. In a trial that lasted 98 days, the jury awarded Henry Ford the token of twelve cents, much to the delight of the *Tribune*.

The Great Migration of black people or African Americans from the American South to Chicago began around 1910, settling mainly in the South Side. Rivalry over jobs and housing festered between blacks and the white immigrant communities. On July 27, 1919, race riots erupted in Chicago. The police were unable to stem the arson and looting. Thirty-eight people were killed and 527 injured, with blacks comprising two thirds of the victims. One thousand people, mainly black, were left homeless. Among the killed were James Crawford, "colored," Nicholas Kleinmark, white, Lee Edwards, "colored," and David Marks, "white."[20] The governor called up 6,000 national guardsmen to restore the peace. The coro-

Robert R. McCormick appears at the unveiling of the cornerstone of the *Chicago Tribune* building in 1920 (courtesy Robert R. McCormick Research Center, First Division Museum at Cantigny, Wheaton, Illinois).

The Tribune Tower, North Michigan Avenue, Chicago, ca. 1930 (private collection).

ner's jury interviewed 450 witnesses and in November, issued its report on Chicago's race riots, declaring the cause was the "invasion ... of the colored people to white neighborhoods." Believing that whites and blacks could not live peacefully side by side, the jury recommended "voluntary segregation" to remove "the cause of the unrest."[21] Aided by racially restricted covenants, this recommendation limited blacks to the South Side, making Chicago the most segregated city in America.

Prohibition

Corruption and gang warfare increased during Prohibition.[22] Several Chicago aldermen received kickbacks by selling lucrative city contracts. Bribed police officers turned a blind eye to gaming and brothel operations. The *Tribune* "endeavored to find out where the money came from [and] which corrupt legislators were paid." In Chicago there was "a tremendous amount of graft being collected for the protection of bootleggers, police, judges and the influence of state's attorneys." Three times mayor of Chicago, Boston-born William Hale Thompson was infamous for corruption and association with gangsters. *Tribune* reporter John Boettiger unearthed payments by gangsters to politicians and judges. Mayor Thompson diverted a check for $25,095 "for flood relief to political purposes."[23] In a scathing 1931 editorial, the *Tribune* editorial board accused mayor Thompson of giving his city "an international reputation for moronic buffoonery, barbaric crime, triumphant hoodlumism [and] unchecked graft.... It is unpleasant business to eject a skunk, but someone has to do it."[24]

Ever suspicious of the concentration of power, McCormick "saw in Prohibition confirmation of his worst fear; an overreaching government enacting laws that resulted in unprecedented lawlessness."[25] The Volstead Act of January 16, 1920, also known as the National Prohibition Act, banned the sale, transportation and use of alcoholic drinks. Chicago became the center for speakeasies ("speak softly when ordering"), gang warfare, corruption, and illegal distilleries. "Chicago's gangsters, crooked cops, corrupt politicians and the booze-consuming public all conspired to keep the drinks coming." By 1924, Chicago had 20,000 illegal saloons. "Scarface" Al Capone was the scourge of Chicago, with his beer and liquor rackets and his control of officials through bribes and threats. Starting in 1927, federal agent Eliot Ness and his men raided Capone's breweries, destroying thousands of gallons of alcohol and arresting mobsters. The investigations of Internal Revenue officer Frank J. Wilson showed that Capone had not paid taxes on his ill-gotten earnings. Before 1929, Capone had "never before been convicted even of a misdemeanor in his years of murderous racketeering." He was arrested after attending a peace conference of Chicago mobsters in Atlantic City, N.J.

"You're "Scarface Capone?" asked the detective.

"My name is Al Smith—call me Capone if you want to," Capone replied.

Capone allegedly "produced a roll of $20,000 cash and attempted to press it upon" the detective.[26] In October 1931, Al Capone was sentenced to eleven years in prison for tax evasion.

Thirty-eight-year-old Alfred "Jack" Lingle was a *Tribune* crime reporter investigating mobsters and the illegal liquor trade. On June 9, 1930, an assassin gunned him down in broad daylight at the corner of Randolph Street and Michigan Avenue with a single shot to the back of the head. Announcing that a "tragedy struck with stunning force," the *Tribune* believed that the murder "was to prevent a disclosure and to give warning" to other reporters. The newspaper offered a reward of $30,000 for the capture of Lingle's murderer.[27] Indignation quickly shifted to embarrassment when the newspaper learned that the $65 a week reporter was in the pay of the mob, wrote false stories and had fattened his bank account by $65,000. "There is venality in almost everyone's life,"[28] commented the publisher, colonel Robert R. McCormick.

Prohibition was a noble experiment that failed. Several months before the 18th amendment was repealed at the close of 1933, "highballs, whisky sours and other drinks of the pre–Volstead period flowed freely over bars … without interference of federal agents or police and without disorder." The *Tribune* approvingly reported that Prohibition was dead.[29]

Woman's Suffrage

After the Civil War, the *Chicago Tribune* regularly followed the debate about extending suffrage to women. In an 1870 editorial, the newspaper stated that it is the right and the duty of women to enter the political debate and to be voters.[30] The national convention of the Prohibition Party held in Indianapolis in May of 1888 linked woman's suffrage and the prohibition of alcohol. "Some say woman suffrage and prohibition cannot fret in the same class; that they might not travel at the same speed. I say, drive them in tandem and they'll go well together." The right to vote should not depend on "sex, color, race or nationality."[31] The battle for woman's suffrage was long fought. Suffragettes faced indifference, dirty looks, hostility, snowballs and physical attack. It was not until 1910 that a sitting president, William Howard Taft, publically supported the cause.[32] Robert R. McCormick's sister-in-law, Ruth Hanna McCormick, worked to ensure passage of the Illinois Equal Suffrage Act of 1913. This act permitted women in Illinois to vote for aldermen and mayor and in the presidential election, but not in the election for governor, state representatives or members of congress. "Illinois is the first state east of the Mississippi," wrote Marion Walters in the *Tribune* of June 15, 1913, "to extend the franchise to its women…. Illinois' victory will push the woman's suffrage movement forward in every country in the world where the women are working and waiting to have justice accorded them by the men." As chairperson of the Congressional Committee of the National Woman Suffrage Association, Hanna was determined to extend her success in Illinois and pressure Congressmen "from the Atlantic to the Pacific" to pass a Federal amendment in support of equal suffrage.[33] By 1916, the majority of members of the main parties—Democratic and Republican—"favored the extension of the suffrage to women."[34] World War I accelerated the move to universal suffrage in America. Canada and Great Britain had already granted votes to women. "We cannot afford to lag behind," announced President Woodrow Wilson in 1918, "to take a reactionary position on such a matter. We must be in harmony with our allies."[35] Woman's suffrage was first proposed in Congress in 1878. Forty-two years later, on August 18, 1920, the 19th Amendment of the United States Constitution finally ensured voting rights to women. The National American Woman's Suffrage Association recommended that women "should join with the two leading parties and should not attempt to form a party of their own."[36]

Near v. Minnesota—McCormick's Finest Hour

"Jay Near was a small-time journalist and political opportunist who harbored all the dominant prejudices of the period." He was anti–Semitic, anti–Catholic, anti–African American and anti–Labor.[37]

Writing in the 1920s in the *Saturday Press,* a scandal sheet, Near claimed, "It is Jewish thugs who have pulled practically every robbery" in Minneapolis. Jews "falsified the election results" and were behind every act of corruption. "Practically every vendor of vile hooch, every owner of a moonshine still, every snake-faced gangster and embryonic yegg in the Twin Towns is a Jew.... If the people of Jewish faith in Minneapolis wish to avoid criticism" it was their responsibility "to clean house" and get rid of Jewish gangsters. Near attacked the police commissioner and the country attorney. In 1927, the city fathers of Minneapolis acted to shut down the *Saturday Press* under the 1925 Minnesota Public Nuisance Bill designed to act against newspapers deemed slanderous or obscene. Seeing the gag order against the *Saturday Press* as a direct threat to all newspapers and a violation of First Amendment rights, Robert R. McCormick and his *Tribune,* together with the American Civil Liberties Union, came to the defense of Jay M. Near, claiming that government had no authority to interfere with or restrict "any citizen of the United States from printing, writing for publication ... by license, censor, tax ... or any other means to abridge the freedom of the press." The Minnesota gag rule, McCormick wrote, "would put every newspaper at the mercy of any corruptible judge and I carried the appeal to the Supreme Court of the United States." In a 1931 landmark decision, the Supreme Court ruled by five to four that the Minnesota Public Nuisance Bill was unconstitutional.[38] The ruling of the Supreme Court was "a great chapter for the freedom of the American press," gloated the *Tribune.* "The decision was a sweeping victory for the American press," which was championed by the *Chicago Tribune.*[39]

The Great Depression

The Wall Street crash of 1929 sent shock waves across America and around the world. October 24 "saw the most disastrous day in Wall Street History." Losses "were staggering, easily running into billions of dollars.... Thousands of brokerage and banking accounts, solid and healthy a week ago were wrecked in the strange debacle."[40] Prices sank, companies went bankrupt and millions were out of work. The origins of the Great Depression, claimed the *Chicago Tribune,* dated to 1914 when America "was producing more than we were consuming.... Cheap money is the most dangerous intoxicant known."[41] Banks lent the cheap money and people got heavily in debt. Soup kitchens and shantytowns sprang up to feed and shelter the dispossessed. A pundit wrote: "The great depression was not caused by the breakdown of capitalism.... The country will enjoy unbounded prosperity [only if] it again adopts the principles and practices of capitalism.... The sole cause of the great depression in every country was the excessive amount of capital wasted in government."[42]

"The homeless casual laborer is not the only or even the principal sufferer" in the Depression. Since the mid–1920s, Edith Rockefeller McCormick was paying top dollar for raw land north of Chicago with the plan to build a vast housing estate and "do great things for the community." The housing bubble burst as the streets, water and electricity of her endeavor were set down. Short of cash, Edith moved out of her vast mansion into a set of rooms at the Drake Hotel. Edith died 1932 from the complications of breast cancer, leaving her real estate venture in ruins. Her vast collection of objet d'art and jewelry was sold at auction for pennies on the dollar.

In a rousing editorial written March 1930, Robert R. McCormick announced that the "extreme optimism of the summer and fall" of 1929 had been replaced "by the pessimism of recent months." Both reactions had "been baseless." America remained "the richest country in the world" blessed with "immense national resources" and with great "economic competence." Now "we are pretty well out of the woods [and] getting back in our stride.... The period of recession is over."[43] Later that year the still optimistic *Tribune* informed its readers that a business depression was "a natural phenomenon like the coming of night" but "the outlook is far from hopeless.... There was no need for fear or hysteria," and recovery would soon follow.[44]

The Great Depression of the 1930s was the longest and deepest economic downturn of the twentieth century. By 1933, one quarter of the nation's workforce was unemployed, affecting largely the young, immigrants and blacks. America's gross national product that year was half as much as in pre–Depression 1929. "Spending for new plans and equipment had ground to a virtual halt." In 1929, business invested $24 billion, but in 1932 only $3 billion. Automobile production fell by two-thirds. The International Harvester Company, headquartered in Chicago, had a net profit in 1929 of $37 million. The first three years of the Great Depression saw substantial losses for the company. Not until 1934 did Harvester return a profit of a mere $4 million. With its deep pockets, International Harvester bought a twenty-three-story building at the corner of Michigan Avenue and Lake Street as its new headquarters and continued to pay dividends to its shareholders.[45] Shares in International Harvester reached fantastic heights in 1929 before the Wall Street crash. In 1937, the *Tribune* reported the death of Cyrus Hall McCormick, son of the founder of McCormick Harvester. He owned 237,066 shares in International Harvester. In 1933, these shares were worth only $2,453,559. At the time of his death the shares had rebounded ten-fold in value, adding $24,526,321 to his estate.[46]

Robert R. McCormick opposed government intervention in the economy and called for unfettered capitalism to solve the nation's ills. "You big businessmen," bellowed McCormick in 1921, "Many of your Armours, Swifts, Cudahys, McCormicks, Fields, Spragues etc., are the families which built Chicago. They produced the Chicago industries. They produced Chicago. They were the driving force."[47] The *Tribune* saw the New Deal as a policy of waste, with most of the money feeding bureaucracy and graft and only pennies on the dollar going to the relief of the unemployed and the poor.[48] McCormick was highly critical of his Groton School classmate, President Franklin D. Roosevelt, whose New Deal spent government money lavishly to create jobs and boost the economy. President Roosevelt and his wife Eleanor were branded as socialists. McCormick claimed, in 1936, that the Democratic Party was aligned with the Communists. "Only 97 days left to save your country," announced the *Chicago Tribune* on July 31, 1936. McCormick supported Alfred M. Landon, the Republican candidate for president of the United States. The 1936 election was a landslide for Roosevelt, with Landon winning only two states. In 1940, the *Tribune* extensively quoted Thomas E. Dewey, who accused Roosevelt of dragging the United States into a world war. "It was Roosevelt who deserved the entire blame for the nation's continued depression in business and the dangers of unpreparedness in military affairs." The New Deal and government spending were wasteful and were stifling free enterprise.[49] Both in 1936 and 1940, McCormick and his bellicose *Tribune* had little impact on the presidential vote.

America First

His diplomat father, Robert Sanderson McCormick, in 1905, proposed the establishment of a world court to settle differences between nations and to preserve peace. Robert R. McCormick vigorously opposed America's entry into the League of Nations or the World Court. His philosophy was America First, to keep America out of European conflicts and wars, get rid of Anglophile textbooks and stress American ideas and virtues, and to view opposition as disloyalty and treasonous. In September 1940, Robert R. McCormick was a founding member of the America First Committee (AFC), headquartered 141 West Jackson Boulevard in Chicago, America's leading isolationist and anti-war organization. During the tenure of the AFC, the *Tribune* gave it support, publicizing its goal to gain ten million members and put pressure on the administration not to assist Great Britain or enter the European war.[50] Support for the AFC was largely in the Midwest, with 700 chapters. Following the Japanese attack on Pearl Harbor on December 7, 1941, and Nazi Germany's declaration of war against the United States four days later, support for the AFC collapsed and the organization was disbanded.

In his impassioned America First crusade, Robert R. McCormick claimed he was following the basic principles laid down by Presidents George Washington and Thomas Jefferson. In his farewell address, Washington said: "It is our true policy to steer clear of

McCormick-Deering tractor, with disc harrow attachment, is at work in 1929 on Robert R. McCormick's Cantigny Farm (WHS Image ID 51617).

Veterans of the First Division enjoy an outing in 1941 at Robert R. McCormick's Cantigny Farm. The truck was manufactured by the International Harvester Company, led at the time by Robert's cousin Fowler McCormick (courtesy Robert R. McCormick Research Center, First Division Museum at Cantigny, Wheaton, Illinois).

permanent alliances with any portion of the foreign world." In his inaugural address, Jefferson advocated: "Peace, commerce, and honest friendships with all nations—entangling alliances with none." McCormick's commitments to America First and unbridled capitalism were evident in the early 1920s and intensified to the close of his life. In 1935, his newspaper likened the New Deal to "socialism thinly veiled." It was part of the scheming of Communists "to establish a proletarian dictatorship in the United States."[51] In a September 1941 editorial, Robert McCormick noted, "Col. Lindbergh said that the Jews of America, as a group, are working for war." Americans should not respond according to their ethnic background but "that they should think and act like Americans [and realize that] our participation in the war will bring on this nation bankruptcy and a centralized despotic government different in no essential detail from Hitler's despotism."[52] To be truly American, McCormick said, is to eschew "foreign ideologies and foreign systems of government. The New Deal-Communist war mongers will be telling us that American boys must march with Soviet Russia."[53] In America, "the New Deal party regards the Communist party ... as an ally to be encouraged and strengthened." The Communists "have made much progress" in infiltrating the trade union movement and "into the government offices ... and have found support among Mr. Roosevelt's millionaire friends.... Americans cannot count on their administration to resist communist activity in this country."[54] In 1944, McCormick charged "communists dominate our government [and] dominate the Democratic party although they number less than one percent of our population.... It is the communists who taught the New Deal the tactics of smear and vilification." Communists, declared McCormick, were concentrated in New York State, with the largest vote in the electoral college, "where there are 410,000 of them.... These communists and their abettors not only dominate the

Democratic party but are actively trying to control the Republican national convention as the New Deal did in 1940." It was time to stand up "against communists and fellow traveler abuse."[55] In his extreme isolationism, McCormick greatly understated the evils of Nazism as an attack on fundamental American values of individual freedom. Despite the xenophobic harangues of the *Tribune*, in the 1944 election, Chicago voted overwhelmingly for Franklin D. Roosevelt.

Willard Edwards started in 1925 as a reporter on the *Tribune*, based in Chicago. In 1934 he was transferred to the Washington bureau, where he reported on Communist activities; factual, alleged or imagined. Communists, he reported in 1940, "were scattered all over the nation" and have "aroused grave concerns in Congress."[56] Edwards linked the labor unions with the "Red bloc in Congress," and the New Deal into a vast Communist conspiracy to undermine the United States. Groups "active in behalf of the New Deal" were identified as "members of organizations labeled subversive."[57] In Hollywood there were "high salaried film writers" who were "associates of Communist party officials" trying to gain access to American atomic research. Among them was Charles A. Page, "a state department employee from 1928 to 1933."[58] "During the dying days of the New Deal," reported Walter Trohan, the *Tribune's* Washington bureau chief, "the administration worked desperately to stave off any investigation of the state department." The state department "is cluttered with fellow travelers and communists" who issue reports that "bear a Communist tinge [and are] slanted for the Kremlin."[59] Walter Trohan's and Willard Edwards's harangues about Communist infiltration reached a crescendo during the ascent of senator Joseph R. McCarthy.

On September 21, 1946, Joseph R. McCarthy, running for senator from Wisconsin, entered the *Tribune* building, where he "met Colonel Robert R. McCormick, the publisher, and won the support of America Action, Inc., a McCormick-controlled right-wing group."[60] McCarthy gained national prominence on February 9, 1950, with his "Enemies from Within" speech in Wheeling, West Virginia. "I have in my hand," bellowed McCarthy, "205 cases of individuals who would appear to be either card carrying members or certainly loyal to the Communist party, but nevertheless are still helping to shape our foreign policy." Early that year, Willard Edwards of the *Chicago Tribune* wrote a series of articles about Russian spies "who were under orders to control the trade unions … and establish a fifth column to disorganize the country from within in preparation for the moment when Russia might attack it from without."[61] Willard Edwards fed his newspaper articles to senator Joseph McCarthy. In later speeches McCarthy varied the number of "communists in the State Department" from ten to two hundred. When claiming that Communists had infiltrated Hollywood, the armed services and the state department, McCarthy was assisted by newspapermen working for McCormick's Chicago *Tribune,* the Washington *Times-Herald,* and by the staff of McCormick's Mutual Broadcasting System. Presidents Franklin D. Roosevelt and Harry Truman were well aware of Communist infiltration, claimed a 1950 editorial of the *Tribune*, but "sat tight and did next to nothing…. The only theory which fits the facts is that Mr. Roosevelt was himself sympathetic with the aims of the Communists [and] was a willing partner in the conspiracy directed against his own country."[62] From March to July 1950, the Tydings Committee (led by senator Millard E. Tydings of Maryland) investigated McCarthy's charges and concluded that McCarthy was a "fraud and a hoax" and there was no truth in his allegations.[63]

"Three men called a government in themselves," ran the front-page headline of the *Chicago Tribune* of May 29, 1950. Written by Walter Trohan, the article listed Felix Frankfurter, associate justice of the United States Supreme Court, Henry Morgenthau, Jr., former secretary of the treasury, and Herbert H. Lehman, United States senator and former governor of New York, as running "the secret government of the United States." These men, alleged the *Tribune*, "all have been pro–Soviet to a degree but only when the Russian position advanced the British or Zionist causes or worked toward the fall of Nazi Germany." Morgenthau was "the spokesman of the powerful Zionist groups," alleged the article. Frankfurter had "cultivated government officials, military men, members of congress and other influential people. He was considered the power behind the White House throne." In another 1950 editorial, the *Tribune* alleged a continued Communist infiltration of the state department and the army and navy dating from the 1930s, through the war years and beyond. "Charges of espionage in time of war by known soviet sympathizers," wrote the editorial, "establishes beyond doubt that the New Deal put out the welcome mat for communists and fellow travelers in positions of highest trust as commissioned officers of the army and navy."[64]

"Smear Attack is Boomerang in Wisconsin," announced the *Chicago Tribune* on its front page on September 11, 1952. The article by Clayton Kirkpatrick announced that Joseph R. McCarthy won, by a wide margin, the Republican primary in Wisconsin for re-election to the U.S. Senate. The newspaper saluted McCarthy's "extraordinary victory [by] the nation's foremost opponent of communist infiltration into the government." Most of the national press, led by "New Deal Democrats, eastern international Republicans and newspaper columnists" opposed McCarthy. "The principal paper favorable to McCarthy was the Times-Herald in Washington. The Chicago Tribune, which circulates widely in Wisconsin, led the press campaign for McCarthy in the middle west." The *Chicago Tribune* "set the tone for the defense of McCarthyism." Despite attempts at "character assassination," Joseph R. McCarthy was determined to continue his "fight against Reds [and] scores of homosexuals who had wormed their way into the state department."[65]

Walter Trohan accused the opponents of Joseph McCarthy of spreading the "most blatant falsehoods." McCarthy's opponents were "those who had something to hide in their own past and in their own association on the subject of communism."[66] Willard Edwards, of the *Tribune's* Washington Bureau, acknowledged the connection between his newspaper and Senator McCarthy. After all, McCarthy "just fitted into what we had been saying long before."[67] The *Tribune* supported McCarthy's "cause of driving the disloyal from government service."[68] The *Tribune*, wrote Edwards, gave McCarthy "complete support. We never criticized him in any way.... We just went all the way with him editorially—one of the very few newspapers that did."[69] "The *Tribune* editorializing vociferously in behalf of McCarthy." To win Robert McCormick's confidence "meant aiding Joe McCarthy at every opportunity."[70]

In October 1947, the *Chicago Tribune* congratulated the International Harvester Company on the one hundredth anniversary of Cyrus Hall McCormick's first reaper factory located on the north bank of the Chicago River. International Harvester had "contributed enormously to Chicago's prosperity" and to the prosperity of the nation. With the "modern tractor-drawn harvester-thresher ... one man does what 67 men did by hand a century ago." International Harvester's cotton pickers, hay mowers, rakes and bailers did the work that previously many men did by hand. These machines did not cause unemployment on the farm but allowed America "to produce many, many times as much wheat" and other

crops. In his editorial, Robert R. McCormick could not resist the opportunity to again crit-
icize the Roosevelt-Truman "high tax policy [that] robbed men of the fruits of their enter-
prise only to waste them on government profligacy at home and foreign adventures."[71] The
Chicago Tribune covered the opening of the Merchandise Mart, Adler Planetarium, the
Shedd Aquarium, the Century of Progress world fair of 1933, and the shooting of John
Dillinger in 1934.

Amie de Houle Irwin McCormick died August 14, 1939, aged 68 (although listed as
age 59, to hide the difference in their ages.)[72] On December 21, 1944, Robert McCormick
married Mrs. Maryland M. Hooper in the apartment of his cousin Chauncey and Marion
McCormick. She was divorced from Henry Hooper, president of the Lake Shore Fuel Company, and the mother of two daughters. McCormick delivered weekly broadcasts on the
"Chicago Theater of the Air" over his WGN (World's Greatest Newspaper) and the Mutual
Broadcasting System. On January 2, 1954, the Colonel revealed: "There were great disputes
in my family over the invention of the reaper.... With these I have no concerns. If inventive
genius is hereditary I got it from the McCormick side. None of the Medills knew a fence
from a lawn mower."[73]

Robert R. McCormick was emotionally stuck in the early 20th century, reliving the golden
years of World War I.[74] McCormick spoke daily with his editors and editorial writers and used
the *Tribune* as "a megaphone to amplify the publisher's caprices."[75] "Colonel McCormick's
xenophobic 'World's Greatest Newspaper' is one of the last anachronistic examples of muscular
personal journalism."[76] His *Tribune* was a "ferociously conservative and stridently isolationist
newspaper."[77] The *Tribune* was a "headstrong, pugnacious, trumpet-voiced" newspaper [that
was] an extension of his own strong-minded, strong-willed personality.[78]

In 1948 Henry A. Wallace, vice president under Franklin D. Roosevelt from 1941 to
1945, abandoned the Democratic Party to run for the presidency under the Progressive
Party. His platform included federal health coverage for all, the end to the Cold War and
the end to segregation. The *Chicago Tribune* tainted Wallace as a member of the "Moscow
wing ... a Stalin appeaser" and the man who filled "the government payroll [with] fellow
New Dealers and fellow travelers."[79] Where Robert R. McCormick opposed Wallace, his
great aunt Anita McCormick (Mrs. Emmons Blaine) was an outspoken supporter of the
Progressive Party. Wallace received only 2.4 percent of the popular vote. In the 1948 election,
the *Tribune* of November 3, in bold headlines, declared, "Dewey Defeats Truman," much
to the delight Harry S Truman. "That ain't the way I heard it," joked Truman.

In 1949, McCormick bought the *Washington Times-Herald* for $4,500,000 and
appointed his niece, 26-year-old Ruth "Bazy" Elizabeth McCormick Miller, as editor. She
was the daughter of his deceased brother Joseph Medill McCormick and Ruth Hanna
McCormick. Under McCormick's direction, the *Times-Herald* followed the line of the
Chicago Tribune as isolationist, anti-Communist and ultra-conservative. After the report
of the Tydings Committee, the *Times-Herald* attacked the senator with a vengeance, a factor
in Tydings' defeat for re-election. The *Times-Herald* accused the liberal columnist Drew
Pearson, a critic of Joseph McCarthy, as being a spokesman for the Communists, leading
Pearson to sue McCarthy and the newspaper. In 1951, "Bazy" and her uncle had a difference
of opinion. She held "broader Republican views" than he would permit, and she resigned
as editor of the *Times-Herald* to take up horse breeding. Three years later McCormick sold
the money-losing paper to the *Washington Post* for $8,500,000.

In 1952, at age 72 years, Robert R. McCormick announced he was leaving the Republican Party, asserting that "the time has come to organize another party," a patriotic America-First party that would oppose the "international New Dealers" and others spreading "falsehood and corruption" and advocating aid to war-damaged Europe. "Our economic stability … has been brought nearly to ruin by the New Deal." Among the candidates he supported was the senator from Wisconsin, Joseph R. McCarthy, in his campaign "to oust Communists from government posts, especially in the State Department."[80] McCormick later abandoned the idea of forming a third party to become a leader of the "extreme Right Wing" of the Republican Party opposed to general Dwight Eisenhower.[81]

Robert Rutherford McCormick was cut from the same cloth as his great-uncle, Cyrus Hall McCormick. Authoritarian and conservative, they both built big organizations: one the largest reaper company, the other the World's Greatest Newspaper. Both men coveted awards and recognition. Both were tall and lived into their mid–70s. Like his great-uncle, Bertie dressed elegantly in clothes from the leading tailors of London and Paris. They delighted in high living, moving from place to place. Robert Rutherford McCormick enjoyed luxury residences on Lake Shore Drive, Chicago, a 1,000-acre farm in Wheaton, Illinois, with a 35-room mansion, a home in Washington, and a winter home at Boynton Beach, Florida. Both men were litigious and had few close friends. From his youth, the Colonel loved polo and horse riding. Like Cyrus, Robert wished to establish a dynasty but had no children of his own. Instead he expected his nephew John Medill McCormick, his niece Ruth Elizabeth, or his grandnephew Mark McCormick Miller to enter the doors of the *Tribune* as heir apparent. This was not to be.

Robert R. McCormick returned from a trip to Europe in 1953 in poor health. He spent the winters of 1953 and 1954 in Florida. In January 1955, he underwent surgery and was found to have a severe bladder condition, "weakness in the liver" and circulatory problems. Returning to Cantigny, his condition worsened by the day. He died at his farm on April 1, 1955. Placed in an oversized coffin, colonel Robert R. McCormick was dressed in his World War I uniform. Under the headline "Carry On," his *Chicago Tribune* displayed numerous letters of tribute. One came from general Douglas MacArthur, who wrote that McCormick "was an old comrade in arms from World War I."[82] The funeral service, attended by 1,500 people, was held at the Fourth Presbyterian Church in Chicago and broadcast over his radio station, WGN. Robert Rutherford McCormick was buried on the grounds of his farm, Cantigny, in Wheaton, Illinois. Eight riflemen and a bugler from his beloved First Infantry Division saluted as his uniformed body was laid to rest.[83] The Tribune Company owned the *Chicago Tribune*, the *New York Daily News* and two radio and television stations. McCormick left the management of his company to his "trusted lieutenants" J. Howard Ward, Chesser M. Campbell and William D. Maxwell, who were long schooled in his "ideals and principles." McCormick's wife, Maryland McCormick, was already well provided for. In addition, he left her a trust fund to yield $100,000 annually for life. His home and the Cantigny farm became a "public park and a museum." The bulk of the estate, worth $55 million, largely in common stock issued by the Tribune Company of Illinois, formed the Robert R. McCormick Charitable Trust, with the income to be used for "religious, charitable, scientific, literary or educational purposes."[84]

Chapter Fifteen

Edifices

In 1859, Cyrus H. McCormick journeyed to Indianapolis to attend the general assembly of the Presbyterian Church. The church established a seminary in Indiana to train young men to spread the doctrine in the Midwest. Cyrus "looked upon the church as a great educational power into the land." Cyrus delighted the assembly by offering $100,000 to fund four professorships, on the condition that the seminary moved "within or near the city of Chicago." One of the endowed positions was named the Cyrus H. McCormick Professorship of Theology. In 1860, the Presbyterian Theological Seminary of the Northwest officially opened in Chicago. Over the years Cyrus helped the struggling seminary by funding new professorships, putting up buildings and paying down the deficits. A few years after his death, the name of the seminary was changed to the McCormick Theological Seminary. Nettie and Cyrus Hall McCormick, Jr., took the responsibility of continuing to support the Presbyterian school. In 1887, the McCormick family donated $135,000 to build Fowler Hall, a student dormitory. Cyrus, Jr., was appointed "a special and perpetual director of the seminary" in place of his deceased father.[1] Well into the 20th century, the McCormick family was the seminary's financial mainstay. In 1909, the McCormick family offered to match dollar for dollar to rebuild the Fourth Presbyterian Church on North Michigan Avenue, Chicago.

In 1866, Cyrus Hall McCormick responded to an appeal from Robert E. Lee, former general of the Confederate Army and now president of Washington University in Virginia. Cyrus donated $20,000 to endow a professorship of Natural Philosophy. Over the years, McCormick and his family donated $350,000 to the college, renamed Washington and Lee University. In 1931, as a sign of its gratitude, the university named its library in honor of Cyrus H. McCormick and erected a statue in his likeness commemorating the 100th year of the first public demonstration of his mechanical reaper.

Nearing his 70th year, Cyrus Hall McCormick began the construction of his grand house at 675 North Rush Street. It took four years to be completed. During their European visits, Cyrus and Nettie acquired costly carpets, tapestries, clocks, chandeliers and other ornaments to furnish the house. Cyrus and Nettie moved into the house in 1879. It was a house with "elegance and luxury hardly equaled by any similar one in the West." The three-story, thirty-five-room mansion covered "fully half of the block of Rush, Huron, Pine and Erie Streets.... It faces Rush Street. A large lawn extends on the north to Huron and on the south to Erie." Built of Lake Superior sandstone, the design followed parts of the Louvre that Cyrus admired on his trips to Paris. The mansion surpassed in size and elegance the great homes of other Chicago magnates such as George M. Pullman and Marshall Field. In the McCormick mansion, Aubusson tapestries covered the walls of the entrance room,

With financial support from Cyrus and Nettie McCormick, the Presbyterian Seminary settled in Chicago in 1859. After his death it was renamed the McCormick Presbyterian Seminary. Originally in Lincoln Park, the seminary moved in 1975 to Hyde Park. Virginia Hall ca. 1900 (Newberry Library, Wikimedia Commons).

The Cyrus Hall McCormick statue at Washington & Lee University was unveiled in 1931 (Carol M. Highsmith Collection, Library of Congress).

and on the floor was a large Khorassan rug "of rich texture that extends to the middle hall." Cyrus's private library was finished in walnut and ebony and furnished in the Queen Anne style, with French tapestries on the walls and a Persian carpet laid over the oak and satin-wood floor. A large fireplace dominated the room. "The window hangings are of royal crimson with a gold relief to the solid ebony.... The shelves of the library are adorned with the works of the standard authors, bound in the handsomest style of blue and gold." In the music room was an "elegant Steinway grand piano." The concert room seated 150 people with a stage 18 feet wide and 15 feet deep for the orchestra.[2]

The ceiling of the drawing room was covered with an "elaborate system of designs." Most conspicuous was a copy of the Legion of Honor awarded McCormick by emperor Napoleon III, and a relief of his original harvesting machine. The bedrooms were spacious and ornate, the butler's pantry filled with "rare china and snowy-white table-linen." The house had a telephone room "supplied with an Edison and a Bell." The small "but cozy" smoking room, with its ebony furniture, was "a very desirable place in which to puff away the post-prandial cigar." The rooms were supplied with speaking tubes "for the more direct delivery of orders to the servants in the lower portion of the house." The house was a temple to Cyrus Hall McCormick's wealth and taste. A leading New York decorator ensured that the McCormick house was "a rare display of good taste that stood near the top of the really fine houses of this or any other part of the country."[3]

Tusculum College, Tennessee: Cyrus and Nettie McCormick funded several buildings at Tusculum to signify the North-South unity of the Presbyterian Church after the Civil War (Library of Congress).

At the close of his life, Cyrus Hall McCormick chose Tusculum College in Tennessee to demonstrate his wish to unite Presbyterians in the North and the South. McCormick Hall was a dormitory for male students. After his death, Nettie continued to support Tusculum with Virginia Hall, a women's dormitory, and four other buildings. In 1915, Nettie and her sons Cyrus and Harold funded buildings for the university art department and school of architecture.

Nettie supported the Olivet Institute, a settlement house affiliated with the Presbyterian Church. In 1914, Nettie donated $140,000 to buy land in the 1400 block of North Cleveland Avenue, and in 1917 donated a further $100,000 to erect the building to serve as a community center. In 1923, McCormick Hall at Princeton University, built of brownstone from the Connecticut Valley, was officially opened. During her life and through her will, Nettie supported Presbyterian-affiliated churches, hospitals and seminaries in Asia. McCormick Hospital in Chiang Mai, Thailand, was founded in 1888 by American Presbyterian missionaries and expanded in 1920 with McCormick funds. In 1916, Nettie McCormick commissioned the firm of Perkins, Fellows and Hamilton to build her "House in the Woods" in Lake Forest, Illinois. On the grounds of the spacious home were a gardener's cottage, teahouse, powerhouse and garages for cars. Nettie lived there until her death in 1923.

The great wealth generated from harvesters and other farm implements gave the McCormick and Deering families the means to leave edifices to their lives. Cyrus Hall McCormick, Jr., lived at a four-story house at 50 East Huron Street. His Lake Forest country house, "Walden," sat on 180 acres near his brother Harold's Villa Turicum. Designed by James Hunt, "Walden" was a rich man's version of the simple life as depicted by Henry David Thoreau. The house contained twelve bedrooms, each with its own bathroom and fireplace. Elizabeth McCormick, daughter of Cyrus and Harriet McCormick, born in 1892, possessed a "warm, gay personality, so loving and lovable, so vigorously alive and full of eager, intelligent interest in so many things." Her young life was marked "by deeds of kindness to others." She had large, dark eyes, deep golden hair and lovely features that "gave promise to extraordinary beauty of which she seemed quite unaware." She loved the countryside, music, and literature, and found expression through drawing and writing. She was interested in the wellbeing of "the toiling classes." Elizabeth, the only daughter, died following surgery for acute appendicitis at age twelve in 1905. With donations of more than $500,000, her parents in 1913 established the Elizabeth McCormick Memorial Fund "for improving the condition of infant and child health in America." The fund supported the "delicate and malnourished child" through nutritional programs and an open-window program in Chicago schools. In the belief that fresh air prevented tuberculosis, the Elizabeth McCormick fund established open window classrooms in many of Chicago's schools so that children could benefit from fresh air despite the bitter cold of Chicago's winters. The fund paid to swaddle children "like little Eskimos" in freezing, open-air classrooms. A study paid for by the Elizabeth McCormick Fund claimed that formerly "limpid, placid and physically blighted children" were soon transformed by the open-air crusade into normal, alert and attentive children, with an average weight gain of four pounds.[4] The Elizabeth McCormick Memorial Fund served Chicago children for many years by sponsoring day care services and foster care programs.[5] Her parents erected nine cottages in Lake Forest to house working people and their families. These cottages were sold at cost.[6]

Harriet Hammond McCormick went about town in her small horse-driven brougham.

The Elizabeth McCormick Memorial Fund supported ways to improve the health of children, including open-window classrooms in the wintertime (Library of Congress).

In 1912, Mr. and Mrs. Cyrus Hall McCormick remodeled the stables of their city home "and finally discarded horses for motors."[7] Harriet was deeply involved in making the McCormick factory a more wholesome environment for the workers. On her first visit to the factory, she "felt thrilled and overwhelmed with the enormity of the plant," but was haunted by the weary faces of the workers. She said "something would have to be done for the vast army in our employ."[8] Harriet died on January 17, 1921, and was buried at Graceland Cemetery. In 1926, Cyrus and his sons donated $1 million to build a YWCA building at 1000 North Dearborn as the Harriet Hammond McCormick Memorial. The 10-story building offered young women individual rooms with kitchen appliances. There were soundproof rooms for music lessons, and laundry facilities, at a subsidized rate for the poorly-paid workingwomen.

Anita Eugenie McCormick was the fourth of the children of Cyrus and Nettie McCormick. She was born in 1866 in a hotel room in Vermont, where her parents were visiting the local spa. In Chicago, she attended Misses Grant's Seminary and later Misses Kirkland's Academy. Her closely regimented youth included music lessons with lots of practice time. She studied geometry, natural philosophy and Latin. Most importantly, she acquired a strict Presbyterian worldview and felt it her duty to do missionary work and bring comfort to the poor. At age twelve she accompanied her parents and siblings on a tour of Europe, with a visit to the Paris Exposition where Cyrus displayed his reaper and won the Grand Prize for agricultural machinery.

Anita McCormick was among the daughters of the "best families who were permitted by their parents" to go into the slums of Chicago and help out at the settlement houses.[9]

Harriet Hammond McCormick Memorial YWCA, built after her death in 1921 (private collection).

Cyrus Hall McCormick's White Deer Camp in Marquette County, Michigan (Library of Congress).

Her efforts to teach upper class social graces to poor and hungry immigrant children were not successful. She soon learned that giving her money rather than her time had a greater impact. Her father, Cyrus Hall McCormick, died when she was 18. Five years later, it was time to marry, but her widowed mother Nettie was reluctant to let her go. Anita McCormick "is one of the prettiest girls in Chicago society. Of medium height for a woman, slender and delicately fair.... Handsome and accomplished, Miss McCormick is also a great heiress ... to at least $2,000,000." Anita McCormick was "one of Chicago's most prominent belles [with] many personal as well as social attractions."[10] Anita's fiancé, Emmons Blaine, "is a pleasant sort of fellow, tolerable good-looking.... He is quite likely to become a very successful practitioner in that most remunerative branch of the profession, corporation law."[11] Emmons Blaine was born in 1857, a graduate of Harvard College and Harvard Law School. He served as vice president of the Baltimore & Ohio Railways. The chubby Emmons was nine years Anita's senior. He came from a distinguished Maine family. His father, James G. Blaine, served at U.S. senator from Maine, and was an early supporter of Abraham Lincoln and an advocate of black suffrage. James Blaine served as secretary of state under Presidents James Garfield and Benjamin Harrison, and was twice a candidate for the Oval Office. Emmons "could make Anita laugh, and he adored her."[12] For an engagement gift he gave her a ruby ring flanked by two diamonds. Nettie took Anita to Paris for a wedding dress of white satin, trimmed with lace. On September 26, 1889, in the Presbyterian Church of Richfield Springs, New York, 23-year-old Anita McCormick married Emmons Blaine. The wedding was the "event of the season" of the village, the McCormick's summer home. One thousand Chinese lanterns adorned the houses and hotels in the village. The Spring House was covered with red, white and blue Japanese lanterns. The church was festooned with orchids, cut flowers and palms.[13] Mr. and Mrs. James Blaine, Sr., arrived in their private railcar, "The Wanderer."[14] The union of a daughter of one of America's richest families with the son of one of its most distinguished families made news across the nation.[15] Cyrus left Anita $3 million. There were concerns over her money. An ironclad legal agreement gave her brother, Cyrus, Jr., and uncle, Eldridge Fowler, control over her trust fund, allowing her only the income.

Emmons and Anita lived in the McCormick mansion on Rush Street in Chicago. In 1884, Emmons worked feverously for his father as the Republican candidate for President of the United States, only to see him narrowly defeated by Democratic candidate Grover Cleveland. In 1892, at the Republican convention in Minneapolis, James Blaine garnered little support and the nod went to Benjamin Harrison, who was running for re-election. "Young Mr. Blaine was a notable figure in the exacting convention scenes in Minneapolis that resulted in his father's defeat. He took the result greatly to heart."[16] Returning to Chicago, Emmons had abdominal pains and was diagnosed with intussusception of the bowel. With the rupture of the bowel he developed septicemia. Emmons died on June 18, leaving Anita a widow at age 26, after only 33 months of married life, with a two-year-old son, Emmons McCormick Blaine. The deaths of Emmons's brother and sister in 1890, and now Emmons, left the family bereft.

After her husband died, Anita, now known as Mrs. Emmons Blaine, opened her increasingly heavy purse to support her special interests, especially progressive education. Working with Professor John Dewey, she funded the University Elementary School (later named the Laboratory School), where she sent her son Emmons Blaine, Jr. In 1898, she donated $750,000 to the School of Education at the University of Chicago, followed by an additional $2 million in 1901.[17] Anita donated $500,000 to build a college to train school principals and superintendents. She opened the Chicago Institute, Academic and Pedagogic with "a model school for children in a poor district of Chicago."[18] In 1904 she donated $395,000 to build the Emmons Blaine Hall at the University of Chicago, to serve as its school of education and home of the Laboratory School.

Through her interest in the education of children, Anita befriended Jane Addams, who with Ellen Gates Starr, founded the Hull Settlement House in 1889 in Chicago's Near West Side. Jane Addams's ideas and compassion for immigrants motivated Anita to provide funds to house and feed homeless men and vagrant boys.[19] Anita mobilized her wealthy friends, including her sister-in-law Mrs. Cyrus Hall McCormick, "to improve the physical conditions of life in the more thickly settled districts of Chicago."[20] Anita funded Chicago's first sanitary inspector. She was a member of the city's playground association and served on Chicago's board of education. She established the Juvenile Protective Association, aimed to keep children out of the adult prison system. Together with Jane Addams, Anita McCormick Blaine served on the national board of the Child Labor Commission. Anita appeared on the platform of the NAACP meeting of 1912, "immediately bestowing new legitimacy to the fledgling organization in Chicago.... She developed a report, albeit slightly patronizing, for the aspirations of black people."[21] In 1904, Anita advocated the use of "dramatic acting in the classroom as a means of educating children in history, literature and ethical truths." Her theories were tried out by the education department of the University

Emmons Blaine Hall opened in 1904 as the University of Chicago's school of education. Blaine died in 1884 of septicemia. With an interest in education, his widow Anita McCormick Blaine funded the building in his memory (private collection).

of Chicago "which Mrs. Blaine has endowed to the extent of nearly one million dollars."[22] Anita McCormick Blaine imposed her social values on other members of her family and friends to share a portion of their wealth to those in need. The noblesse oblige of Mrs. Emmons Blaine and her kin was sporadic. In contrast, Jane Addams remained the indefatigable champion of immigrant integration, workers' conditions, child welfare, woman's suffrage, and world peace, and in 1931, was awarded the Nobel Peace Prize.

Trade unions demanded the eight-hour day for factory workers. In 1900, Anita McCormick Blaine applied this standard to her household. "To better meet the conditions of household servants ... her cooks, maids, butlers, laundresses, coachmen, grooms and gardeners worked no more than eight-hour days.... Those whose duties began at 6 o'clock in the morning were relieved at 2 o'clock in the afternoon by a force that remains on duty until 10 o'clock at night." Anita's experiment proved "highly successful [and was copied by other] society and club women" of Chicago.[23] With her brothers Cyrus and Harold, she established the McCormick Historical Association to protect their father's reputation as the inventor of the reaper. Anita could not forgive anyone "who sought to show my father's life to be a lie."[24]

Anita's son, Emmons Blaine, Jr., was sickly as a child. Despite doing poorly at school, he was admitted to Harvard and then the Massachusetts Institute of Technology, studying engineering. Emmons, Jr., did not join the family harvester business. After he married Eleanor Gooding, daughter of a New Hampshire Unitarian minister, he planned to settle on a farm in Wisconsin. World War I stirred Emmons, Jr., but he was rejected by the United States army as physically unfit. Instead, he moved to Philadelphia to work for the American Shipbuilding Company. The "influenza epidemic transformed Philadelphia into a plague city."[25] In October 1918, Emmons Blaine, Jr., died of influenza, leaving a pregnant wife. Anita brought her daughter-in-law Eleanor to live with her in Chicago. The widowed Eleanor gave birth to twins; the boy child was stillborn, the girl healthy.

Mrs. Emmons Blaine had an eccentric side to her personality. She engaged in spiritualism in an effort to communicate with her deceased husband and son. She kept a diary, wrote many letters and employed three secretaries. One of America's richest women, she enjoyed great privileges but worried about the immigrant poor. She supported the formation of the League of Nations. She had a habit of calling Western Union to send messenger boys to deliver her presents. One afternoon in May of 1922, Anita called the Western Union office, saying, "I'd like a messenger boy to Alabama."

"Surely," replied the manager, "I'll send one right up." Turning to Thomas Enck, his star messenger boy, the manager asked if he wanted to go to Alabama.

"Sure," said Enck, "I can pack up and be all ready to start tomorrow morning."

"Tomorrow morning? You're going right now."

Young Enck set out to the Blaine residence to pick up a painting to take to Huntsville, Alabama as a gift to Anita's mentally ill sister Mary McCormick.[26]

During 1928–29, Mrs. Emmons Blaine was heavily involved in decisions regarding the care of her schizophrenic brother Stanley, and engaged in bitter legal battles against her sister-in-law Katharine Dexter McCormick over the control of Stanley's ever enlarging trust fund. In 1937, seventy-one-year-old Anita McCormick Blaine set out for a tour of Europe, accompanied by 43 pieces of luggage, two maids, two butlers, a chauffeur and her physician. In 1941, 75-year-old Anita openly and boldly supported sending military aid to Great Britain.

The war in Europe, she wrote, was a battle of "the forces of aggression" against those "defending freedom." America must be on the side of freedom and prevent "the domination of men by men [and] the triumph of falsehood." In stark opposition to her isolationist great-nephew Robert R. McCormick, Anita McCormick Blaine announced: "the United States should now declare war ... against the forces of aggression ... and help those free people now holding the line of freedom."[27]

In 1948, 82-year-old Anita McCormick Blaine gave $1 million to establish the Foundation for World Government. In the Presidential election of 1948, Mrs. Emmons Blaine supported the Progressive Party candidate Henry Wallace, who campaigned on a platform to end segregation and conciliation with the Soviet Union. Wallace was "completely controlled by the communalists," announced the *Chicago Tribune*, and Anita's foundation would "only mean added income for Moscow propaganda."[28] In 1949, the high-minded Anita funded *The Compass*, a New York City tabloid newspaper edited by Theodore Olin Thackrey, only to see it fold two years later.

Mrs. Emmons Blaine celebrated her 80th birthday with friends and family who discussed "the old Rush Street days."[29] Throughout her adult life, Anita supported progressive political candidates. In her lifetime she gave away 8 million dollars. During her last years, her memory began to fail and her speech became incoherent. Anita McCormick Blaine died on February 12, 1954, at age 87, of bronchial pneumonia.[30] She left an estate of $38 million. Three hundred thousand dollars went to Yenching University (then a Christian university in China) for a memorial to her mother, Nettie Fowler McCormick. Anita sent $100,000 to Madame Chiang Kai-shek to care for Chinese orphans. One third of the estate went to her granddaughter, Mrs. Anna Elaine Harrison, with smaller gifts to relatives, her secretaries, her butler, and to other household employees.[31]

Before the discovery of antibiotics, infectious diseases like tuberculosis, diphtheria, and syphilis were the main causes of death. At the close of the 19th century, one hundred and ninety out of every 1,000 American children died before reaching age one. In 1880, Alphonse Laveran isolated the parasite of malaria. In 1882, Robert Koch identified the tuberculosis bacillus and in 1884 Edwin Klebs isolated the germ causing diphtheria. Laboratories established by Louis Pasteur and Robert Koch attracted scientists from all over Europe. The United States lagged far behind Europe in the discovery of illness-causing bacteria and parasites. Before 1901 there were no funds in the United States to support scientific work in the medical fields.

After the death of their first-born child, by scarlet fever on January 2, 1901, his parents Harold Fowler McCormick and Edith Rockefeller McCormick established the John Rockefeller McCormick Memorial Institute of Infectious Diseases, housed at Rush University. John D. Rockefeller had long considered funding an institute for medical research. With the death of his beloved three-year-old grandson, his idea saw action with the establishment of the John Rockefeller Institute of Infectious Diseases in New York City. Modeled on the European research institutions, the John Rockefeller Institute aimed to lead America away from quack medicines and into the scientific age. In 1910, The Rockefeller Institute Hospital opened alongside the research institute. With Rockefeller and McCormick money, researchers isolated the bacillus that causes scarlet fever. George and Gladys Dick discovered the antitoxin to the disease. Over time the John Rockefeller Institute evolved into a postgraduate research center, expanding from infectious diseases into cancer, heart disease,

THE ~~MEMORIAL~~ *McCormick* INSTITUTE FOR INFECTIOUS DISEASES, CHICAGO

Following the death in 1901 of their three-year-old son, Harold and Edith McCormick funded the McCormick Institute for Infectious Diseases in Chicago (private collection).

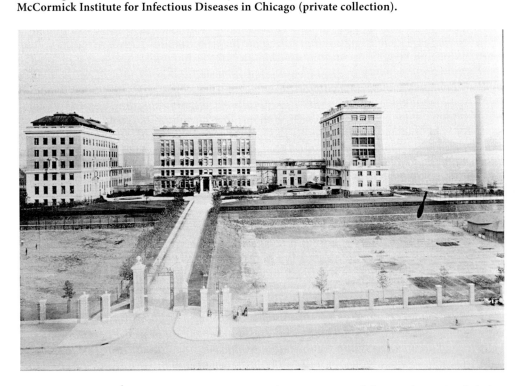

The John D. Rockefeller Institute, Avenue A and 66th Street, New York (ca. 1917), was funded after the death by scarlet fever of his three-year-old grandson John Rockefeller McCormick in 1901 (Library of Congress).

564.

McCormick Building,
Chicago

The McCormick Building, 330 S. Michigan Avenue, was built in 1911 by R. Hall McCormick, trustee of his father Leander James McCormick's estate (private collection).

and diabetes research. The Rockefeller Institute served as a model for dozens of other research centers, giving the United States leadership in medical research.

Stanley Robert McCormick was the youngest son of Cyrus Hall McCormick. On the day of his marriage, Stanley wrote: "I hereby bequeath my entire estate to my wife, Katharine Dexter McCormick. I also make her executrix of my estate." This brief note had extraordinary consequences. Incarcerated for forty years as mentally incompetent, Stanley died on January 19, 1947, at age 72. His estate, made up of Chicago real estate and shares in International Harvester, was valued at $35 million.[32] Stanley's wife, Katharine Dexter McCormick, was seventy-two years of age when she, as primary beneficiary, received Stanley's bonds, stocks, cash and private property together with half of his real estate holdings. The remaining half of the real estate went to his sister, Mrs. Emmons Blaine, his three nephews, Fowler, Cyrus III, and Gordon McCormick, and his nieces Muriel Hubbard and Mathilde Oser.[33] It took a further five years to deal with the Internal Revenue Service and liquidate the estate to cash. Katharine was already rich, having inherited $10 million from her mother's estate in 1932. At age seventy-seven, Katharine was one of America's wealthiest women and ready to spend the money on a worthy cause; a pill to prevent unwanted pregnancies.

With Mary and Stanley McCormick both diagnosed as schizophrenic, Katharine concluded that the disease was inherited. Women with a family history of schizophrenia needed

This 1930s postcard shows Chicago as the center of the worldwide International Harvester Company with Harvester House at 600 S. Michigan Avenue, the McCormick Works at Blue Island and Western Avenue, the Deering Works at Fullerton Avenue on the city's North Side and Wisconsin Steel in the South Side (private collection, Joseph and John Barry owned a varnish company in Chicago).

help to avoid pregnancy. Around 1920, Katharine met the birth control activist Margaret Sanger of the Planned Parenthood Federation and wholeheartedly backed the cause of birth control. After inheriting Stanley McCormick's estate, Katharine shifted her interest away from mental illness to the control of unwanted pregnancies. In 1953, in her chauffeur-driven Rolls Royce, Katharine, in the company of Margaret Sanger, traveled from her home in Boston forty miles west to visit Dr. Gregory Goodwin Pincus at his Worcester Foundation for Experimental Biology. For years, Pincus, with his colleague Dr. Min Chueh Chang, researched the use of steroids to treat arthritis. Sanger shared with Pincus "the misery and suffering of women and said it was time to have an effective contraceptive pill." Experimenting on rabbits and rats, Pincus showed that progesterone could stop ovulation. Could it do the same in humans and lead to a safe contraceptive pill?

Katharine Dexter McCormick agreed to fund the research of the Worcester Foundation with an immediate check for $15,000, with $150,000 more to follow by the end of the year. Each year for the next decade, McCormick backed the work of the Worcester Foundation with $100,000 to $150,000, giving in all $2 million.[34] In 1957, the United States Food and Drug Administration approved the sale of Enovid as a treatment for menstrual disorders and in 1960 as a contraceptive pill.[35] In 1947, Katharine gave $5 million to Stanford University Medical School.[36] In 1962, Katharine provided the money for the Stanley McCormick Courtyard at the Art Institute of Chicago. An Alexander Calder sculpture graces the center of the garden. In 1964, she funded the Stanley McCormick Hall to house women students at the Massachusetts Institute of Technology. Katharine Dexter McCormick died age 92 on December 28, 1967, and left the bulk of her remaining $30 million to her alma mater.

In 1870, Leander J. McCormick promised a telescope and observatory to the University of Virginia in his native state. The Great Fire of Chicago caused a delay in funding the gift. In 1880, Leander finally donated $50,000 to build the telescope and $18,000 more to construct the observatory to house the telescope. In 1882, the Leander J. McCormick Observatory was completed, housing "the largest refracting telescope in the world, at the time of donation."[37] Alvan Clark & Sons of Cambridgeport, Massachusetts, then the leading American lens-maker, built the 26-inch telescope. A descendant of Cape Cod whalers, Alvan Clark established his firm in 1846. The company built the U.S. Naval observatory in 1862, and thirty years later, built the 40-inch Yerkes telescope that was displayed at the 1893 World's Columbian Exposition held in Chicago, and later donated to the University of Chicago.

In 1889, three years after the wrenching strike at the McCormick Reaper Works that led directly to the Haymarket Massacre, Leander James McCormick "disposed of his entire stock in the company to his nephew and retired from the business." Leander used most of the $3,250,000 from the sale of his shares to invest in Chicago real estate. Leander was "a firm believer in the great destiny of Chicago [and became] one of the largest individual owners of centrally located business properties."[38] His investment portfolio included the Victoria Hotel, Roanoke Building, Ceylon Building, Essex Building, the Atlas Block, the McCormick Block, a stock farm, and a summer residence at Lake Forest, Illinois. The pride of the Leander McCormick real estate empire was the 450-room Virginia Hotel built at the corner of Ohio and Rush streets on the site of their burned-out former home. Opened in 1891, in time for the World's Columbian Exposition, the $600,000 ten-story hotel was an "absolutely fire-proof building and a finished hotel second to no other."[39] Situated in a fashionable area of the city, the hotel offered excellent service and cuisine with a separate ladies entrance, a ladies dining room and a men's smoking room. The cost was $3.50 a day and upward, with special rates for families or for extended stay guests.

Robert Rutherford McCormick owned a 1,000-acre farm and houses in Chicago, New York, Washington and Florida. In 1920, Colonel McCormick and his cousin Captain Patterson laid the cornerstone to the new printing plant of the *Chicago Tribune*. Two years later, on its 75th anniversary, the *Tribune* offered a prize of $100,000 for the architectural design for its new headquarters at 435 North Michigan Avenue. The winning design came from the New York firm of John Mead Howells and Raymond Hood. Colonel McCormick asked that rock and relics collected from the Taj Mahal, Palace of Westminster, the Great Wall of China, Angkor Wat and other grand places the world over, be incorporated into the lower façade of the building. Tribune Tower, thirty-six stories and built of Indiana limestone at a cost of $8,500,000, was completed in 1925. Robert McCormick occupied a forty-five-foot-long office on the topmost floor. Sitting behind his marble-topped desk, he was ready to make his newspaper and his WGN radio station the bastion of Midwestern conservatism, preaching America First and with a visceral distaste for government control and foreign entanglements.

Chicago's McCormick Place conference center is named in honor of Robert Rutherford McCormick, as are McCormick Hall at Northwestern University Law School, and the Robert R. McCormick School of Engineering and Applied Science at Northwestern University. Robert supported the Medill School of Journalism at Northwestern University. His beloved

McCormick Place, billed as the world's largest convention center, opened in Chicago in 1960. It was named in honor of Robert Rutherford McCormick, great-nephew of Cyrus Hall McCormick and publisher of the *Chicago Tribune* (private collection).

farm in Wheaton, Illinois is still maintained as public park and museum to honor the First Infantry Division, which saw action at the village of Cantigny, France during World War I.

Charles and James Deering worked for their father in his Deering Harvester Company. After Deering merged with the McCormick harvester company, Charles served as chairman of the board of International Harvester until 1910. Having amassed great wealth, the Deering brothers set about to establish fine art collections and build grand homes. Charles owned a castle in Sitges, Spain where he kept his collection of El Greco and Diego Velasquez paintings. In Florida he bought a 444-acre estate at Cutler along the edge of Key Biscayne, on which he built a large home. In 1914, James Deering, with his partner Paul Chalfin, began planning Villa Vizcaya on Key Biscayne. When completed, the house cost him $10 million. James spent December to May at Vizcaya where he entertained lavishly and kept two yachts. When not in Florida, James flitted between his Chicago home, a New York townhouse and his Paris apartment. He enjoyed this affluent life for only a decade, dying in 1925 of pernicious anemia. At his death, he willed his estate and his art collection to his nieces Marion Deering McCormick and Barbara Deering Danielson. When Charles died two years later his daughters inherited his art collection as well. In 1932, Charles Deering's daughters commissioned the Charles Deering Library at Northwestern University. When completed a year later, the building served as the university's main library.

Chauncey and Marion McCormick owned the St. James Farm, Warren, in DuPage County, Illinois. Medill and Ruth Hanna McCormick owned the 2,500-acre Rock River Farm near Byron, Illinois. After Medill died, Ruth bought a 250,000-acre ranch in New Mexico. Anna Rubeania (Ruby) McCormick, daughter of William Sanderson McCormick

The Charles Deering Library at Northwestern University, Evanston, Illinois, opened in 1934 (courtesy Northwestern University Archives).

The Charles Deering estate at Cutler, Florida, was decorated with the works of El Greco, Diego Velázquez, Rembrandt and other notable painters. After his death in 1927, the estate went to his daughters (Elisa.rolle, Wikimedia Commons).

JAMES DEERING'S RESIDENCE, MIAMI, FLORIDA.

James Deering had the opulent Villa Vizcaya, Key Biscayne, Florida (author's collection).

The Glessner House at 1800 S. Prairie Avenue, Chicago, was designed by Henry Hobson Richardson for the family of John and Frances Glessner. John Glessner was the owner of Warder Bushnell and Glessner, one of the smaller harvester companies in the International Harvester merger. He served as vice president and later as chairman of the executive committee of IHC. The Glessner House is now a museum depicting Chicago's Gilded Age (Library of Congress).

and her husband Edward Tyler Blair, built 1516 N. Lake Shore Drive in 1917. Designed by McKim Mead & White, the 4-story French-chateau style 12,000-square-foot residence overlooked Lake Michigan. The grand house was sold during the 1960s to serve as the headquarters of the International College of Surgeons. Fowler McCormick owned the vast McCormick Ranch in Scottsdale, Arizona. Several members of the family built their grand homes along or close to Rush Street, in an area named McCormickville. Decay set into Rush Street after 1910 with the once-grand homes deteriorating and later torn down.[40]

Chapter Sixteen

Successors to International Harvester
Case IH and Navistar

Early in the 20th century the International Harvester Company was by far America's largest farm implement company. Its harvesters and other farm implements found ready markets around the world. From the American Midwest to Australia, the versatile Farmall tractor reduced the farm labor force and ended the dependence on draught animals. International Harvester grew so big that the United States government accused it of monopolistic practices and tried to split it up. Competition soon came. John Deere set up his plow company in Moline, Illinois, expanding into a full-line agricultural implement maker determined to "compete with the monster of Chicago," the International Harvester Company. In 1912, Deere entered the tractor business.[1]

After World War II, competition came from other domestic as well as from foreign farm machine companies. On January 8, 1986, the International Harvester Company, once the leader in farm implements and still "the nation's leading producer of heavy-duty trucks," announced that it was getting out of the farming business and changing its name to the Navistar International Corporation. The clear collapse of International Harvester was part of a general loss of manufacturing jobs that hit America in the 1980s. The loss was particularly severe in Chicago with the closing of Wisconsin Steel, Western Electric, Sunbeam and numerous smaller tool companies and steel fabrication shops. Between 1979 and 1989, Chicago lost 128,986 manufacturing jobs. With the loss of manufacturing jobs went restaurants, lunch wagons, barrooms and workers' neighborhoods.[2] The company gave up its name and sold its farm equipment and tractor business to Tenneco, which merged it with its own farm implement subsidiary to form Case International, later named Case IH. Harvester continued its trucking business under its new computer-generated name, Navistar.

Jerome Increase Case was born in 1819 in Oswego County, New York. In his early twenties he moved west, first to Chicago, then settled in Racine, Wisconsin, where he designed, fabricated and sold threshing machines. With business growing, in 1847 Case built a large factory in Racine, the same year Cyrus Hall McCormick opened his harvester works in Chicago. After the Fire of 1871 destroyed the McCormick's factory, Jerome I. Case offered to build the McCormick harvester in Racine, but McCormick refused. Case expanded to plows and steam-powered traction machines. Lacking propulsion, the Case machine was pulled by horses, and when stationary, connected by belting to the threshing machine. In 1880, he formed the J. I. Case Threshing Machine Company. Jerome I. Case

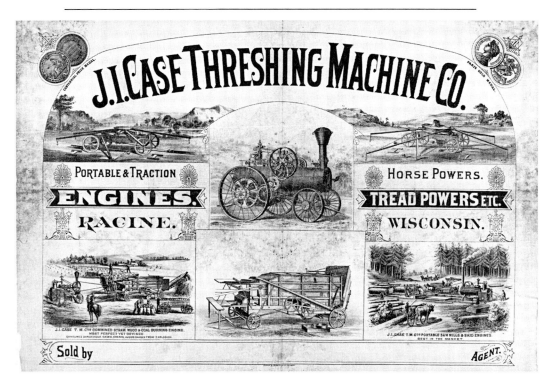

A J.I. Case Threshing Machine Company advertisement, ca.1895, shows its stream engines and machines for threshing grain and for logging (Library of Congress).

A stationary Case steam engine attached by leather belting to a threshing machine is depicted on a postcard circa 1910 (private collection).

died in 1891, aged 72 years. J. I. Case was one of America's largest builders of steam engines. Early in the 20th century, the Case Corporation built gasoline-powered cars and tractors, competing with Deere and International Harvester. The gasoline-powered J. I. Case thresher "separates and cleans the grain, weighs it and delivers it into bags." Using the J. I. Case thresher, "one man accomplishes more than thirty men did in the days of the flail and the work is performed better and with less waste of grain."[3] In 1967, Houston-based Tenneco bought the Case Corporation to specialize in tractors and combines. When Tenneco bought the agricultural division of International Harvester, it was already a large conglomerate with 91,500 employees and interests in oil, pipelines, paper manufacturing, automotive parts, chemicals and shipbuilding.

Case IH gained Europe-wide recognition from Harvester's Neuss and Doncaster-built tractors. In the United States, the combination of Case and Harvester gave Case IH thirty-five percent of the tractor market. Case's 94 series tractors replaced those of Harvester. In 1989, Case International came out with its 195-HP Magnum tractor. In 1998, Case IH introduced the QuadTrac, weighing a massive 43,700 pounds, and powered by a 360-HP engine. To our day, Case IH manufactures a wide range of farm machines, including tractors, harvesters, combines, mowers, rakes and loaders.

The International Harvester Company was considered "a sleepy Midwest giant." In 1986, it re-emerged under the new computer-generated name of Navistar to herald "a progressive, dynamic company ... to navigate to the stars, to a rosy future."[4] To avoid bankruptcy, the company shrank from a worldwide maker of farm equipment, tractors and trucks to a smaller American-based maker of medium and heavy trucks. Harvester's workforce in 1979 numbered 97,700 in forty-two plants. Navistar was International Harvester reborn, smaller and more nimble, with only 14,137 employees in seven plants. Navistar cut its management by a quarter. The company had 2.5 retirees for every employed worker. Annual costs to support retirees and pay health benefits were $225 million. Japanese truck imports were 25 percent cheaper than American made trucks, even including transportation costs. To achieve its goal of commanding a quarter of the nation's truck business, Navistar cut costs, raised cash and brought out new lines "for the city pick-up and delivery markets." In April 1986, Navistar sold 48.8 million shares to raise $624 million, which it used to retire high-interest debt and reduce its debt-load from $736 million to a manageable $222 million. Two hundred banks and insurance companies acquired Navistar stock in a "debt-for-equity swap." Tenneco assumed responsibility for much of International Harvester's retiree benefits, lifting the burden from Navistar. Navistar reduced employee health benefits by requiring co-pays and increased deductibles. Navistar's 4000, 8000 and 9400-model trucks proved successful. Navistar contracted to supply diesel engines for the Ford Company's pickup tracks and vans.[5]

Donald D. Lennox, formerly with the Xerox Corporation, "steered the Navistar International Corporation away from the brink of bankruptcy." In October 1986, the 67-year-old Lennox stepped down as chairman and chief executive officer. James C. Cotting replaced Lennox. Forty-eight-year-old Neil A. Springer, "who won praise for cutting costs," was promoted to chief executive officer of Navistar's truck and engine subsidiary.[6] Cotting spent three years in the navy before entering Ohio State University. He joined International Harvester in 1979. Under the leadership of Lennox, Cotting and Springer, Navistar was on the road to become a profitable truck and school bus company. Navistar showed steady growth,

A Navistar truck is shown at the Panama Canal, 2014 (courtesy Navistar International Corporation).

and in 1990 took a stake in Dina Camiones, a Mexican truck builder. In 2000, Navistar departed Chicago to establish its headquarters in Lisle, Illinois. In 2003, Navistar re-entered the defense industry with Navistar Defense, to secure Pentagon contracts and agreements with foreign governments to build small trucks, personnel carriers, delivery vehicles and mine-resistant, ambush-protected vehicles. Navistar Defense's International military trucks were used in Afghanistan and in Iraq.[7] In 2016, Volkswagen of Germany brought a stake in Navistar, with the intent to enter the American truck market. In our time, Navistar makes a wide range of trucks, school buses, military vehicles and diesel engines.

Early 19th century America had a few cities and many villages with three-fourths of the workforce on the land. When Cyrus Hall McCormick began his harvesting machine factory in Chicago, fully two-thirds of the American population was engaged in farming. Farm machines have steadily eroded the proportion of the population living on farms. In 1920, at the cusp of the invention of the gasoline-powered tractor, thirty-two million people, 30 percent of the American population, were still on the land. Between 1981 and 1987, the American farm population fell by 2.5 percent annually. By 1987, only five million people, 2 percent of the population, were on the farms.[8] At the time of writing (July 2018), the population of the United States exceeded 328 million, with less than 2 percent of the people engaged in farming.

John Deere's horse-pulled plow and Cyrus Hall McCormick's horse-pulled harvester advanced agriculture during the second half of the nineteenth century. The increasingly powerful farm tractor pulled agricultural implements through the twentieth century and beyond. Trucks, railroads and ships carried the farm products to the markets. In the 21st century, agriculture is primed for its next revolution, with computer-operated, self-driving tractors and machinery for precision planting, pruning, fertilizing, watering and harvesting. With global positioning system (GPS) technology, these machines can work around the clock, be controlled remotely and work in tandem to save gasoline, seed, water and labor costs. Self-guided machines will harvest grains and pick fruits and vegetables. Machines will package farm products and self-driving vans and trucks will carry the goods to markets near and far. In 2018, the population of the world passed seven and a half billion people, with a projected 9.8 billion by 2050. It will take a revolution in farming methods to feed the rapidly growing population and its animal stock.

Chapter Notes

Chapter One

1. Sir Astley Cooper was the wealthiest surgeon of his time. He owned an ostentatious chariot. When he first meet George IV, the king exclaimed: "I have seen you in your little chariot." Bransby Blake Cooper. *The Life of Sir Astley Cooper, Volume 2.* London: Parker, 1843, p. 226.

2. *Times of London*, May 1, 1851.

3. United States Congress. *The Congressional Globe,* Volume 23, Part 3, for 1854, pp. 1901–1902.

4. *Illustrated Cyclopaedia of the Great Exhibition the Great Exhibition of the Industry of All Nations.* London: Clark, 1852.

5. *The American Farmer*, Volume VII, No. 8, pp. 293–294. Baltimore: Samuel Sand, 1852.

6. From a letter by Horace Greeley, editor of the *New York Tribune*, reported in the September 1851 issue of the *Knickerbocker, or, New York Monthly Magazine*, Volume 38, p. 375.

7. John Tebbel. *The Inheritors: A Story of America's Great Fortunes and What Happened to Them.* New York: Putnam's Sons, 1962, p. 211.

8. William T. Hutchinson. *Cyrus Hall McCormick: Seed-Time, 1809–1856.* New York: Century, 1930, p. 21.

9. Cyrus McCormick (grandson). *The Century of the Reaper.* Boston: Houghton Mifflin, 1931, pp. 1–2.

10. Follett L. Greeno. *Obed Hussey, Who, of All Inventors Made Bread Cheap.* Rochester: Rochester Herald Publishing Company, 1912.

11. *Mechanics' Magazine*, Volume 3, Number 4, April 1844, p. 192. Printed by Minge and Challis, Wall Street, New York.

12. Cyrus McCormick. *The Century of the Reaper*, p. 20.

13. Hutchinson. *Cyrus Hall McCormick: Seed-Time, 1809–1856*, p. 93. Cyrus McCormick. *The Century of the Reaper*, pp. 26–27.

14. Salem G. Pattison. *The McCormick Extension Case of 1848.* Chicago: Donnelley, 1900.

15. Cyrus McCormick. *The Century of the Reaper*, pp. 26–27. *Chicago Daily Democrat*, December 23, 1851.

16. Theodore Dreiser. *A Book About Myself.* New York: Boni and Liveright, 1922, p. 2.

17. *Chicago Daily Democrat*, December 23, 1851.

18. Hutchinson. *Cyrus Hall McCormick: Seed-Time, 1809–1856*, pp. 308–323. Sir James Caird. *Prairie Farming in America.* New York: Appleton, 1859, pp. 37–38.

19. Cyrus McCormick. *The Century of the Reaper*, p. 33.

20. Henry Ellsworth was a Yale-educated lawyer and son of the chief justice of the United States Supreme Court, Oliver Ellsworth. After leaving the Patent Office, Henry Ellsworth became president of the Aetna Insurance Company.

21. Salem G. Pattison. *The McCormick Extension Case of 1848: And Other Matter Relating to the Invention of 1834.* Chicago: Donnelley, 1900.

22. Craig Canine. *Dream Reaper.* Chicago: University of Chicago Press, 1997, p. 39.

23. Pattison, *The McCormick Extension Case of 1848.*

24. *Ibid.*

25. *Genesee Farmer*, 1864.

26. John McLean, Reports of the Cases Argued and Decided in the Circuit Court, Seventh Circuit, Volume 6. Cincinnati: Derby, 1856, pp. 539–559.

27. Brian Dirck. *Lincoln the Lawyer.* Urbana: University of Illinois Press, 2009, p. 88.

28. John McLean. *Reports of the Cases Argued and Decided in the Circuit Court, Seventh Circuit, Volume 6.* Cincinnati: Derby, 1856, pp. 539–559.

29. William T. Hutchinson. *Cyrus Hall McCormick: Harvest, 1856–1884.* New York: Appleton-Century, 1935, p. 145.

30. *New York Times*, June 6, 1861. Alan L. Olmstead. "The Mechanisation of Reaping and Mowing in American Agriculture, 1853–1870." *Journal of Economic History*, Volume 30, No. 2 (January 1975), pp. 327–352.

31. Herbert N. Casson. *Cyrus Hall McCormick: His Life and Work.* Chicago: McClurg, 1909, p. 96.

32. Report of the Committee on Awards of the World's Columbian Commission. Washington, D.C.: Government Printing Office, 1901, p. 458. The National Agricultural Society (of America)'s "high appreciation" of McCormick and his reaper was reported in the *Chicago Tribune* of May 7, 1856.

33. Herbert H. Casson. *Cyrus Hall McCormick: His Life and Work.* Chicago: McClurg, 1909, p. 103.

34. Cyrus McCormick. *The Century of the Reaper*, p.62. Salem G. Pattison. *The McCormick Extension Case of 1848.* Chicago: Donnelley, 1900. Charles Benjamin Norton. *World Fairs from London 1851 to Chicago 1893.* Chicago: World's Columbian Exposition, 1983, 1890, p. 28.

35. Hutchinson, *Cyrus Hall McCormick: Seed-Time, 1809–1856*, pp. 103–105.

36. *Ibid.*, pp. 105–106.

37. *Ibid.*, p. 107.

38. Leander J. McCormick. *Memorial of Robert Mc-*

Cormick: Being a Brief History of His Life, Character and Inventions. Chicago: Barnard & Gunthrop, 1885. Norbet Lyons. *The McCormick Reaper Legend: The True Story of a Great Invention.* New York: Exposition Press, 1955.

39. Leander James McCormick. *Family Record and Biography.* Chicago: 1896, pp. 301, 320. Oren F. Morton. *A History of Rockbridge County, Virginia.* Westminster, MD: Heritage, 2007, p. 310.

40. *Memorial of Robert McCormick: Being a Brief History of His Life, Character and Inventions.*

41. Gilbert A. Harrison. *A Timeless Affair: The Life of Anita McCormick Blaine.* Chicago: University of Chicago Press, 1979, p. 165.

42. Guide to the Depositions of Manuscript Collections in Illinois. Chicago: Illinois Historical Records Survey Project, 1940, pp. 10–14.

43. Cyrus McCormick. *The Century of the Reaper,* pp. 1–2.

44. Ibid., p. 2.

45. Harrison. *A Timeless Affair,* p. 167.

46. Hutchinson, *Cyrus Hall McCormick: Seed-Time, 1809–1856,* p. 125.

47. Casson. *Cyrus Hall McCormick,* pp. 140–142. John F. Steward offered a detailed account of the controversy regarding the invention of the mechanical reaper in *The Reaper: A History of the Efforts of Those Who Justly May Be Said to Have Made Bread Cheaply.* New York: Greenberg, 1931.

48. Hutchinson. *Cyrus Hall McCormick: Harvest, 1856–1884,* pp. 109–110, 749.

49. Stella Virginia Roderick. *Nettie Fowler McCormick.* Ridge, NH: Richard R. Smith, 1956.

50. Hutchinson. *Cyrus Hall McCormick, Harvest, 1856–1884,* p. 521.

Chapter Two

1. Roderick. *Nettie Fowler McCormick,* pp. 45–47.

2. Frank Abial Flower. *Edwin McMasters Stanton: The Autocrat of Rebellion, Emancipation and Reconstitution.* Akron: Saalfield, 1905, p. 113.

3. Alfred Theodore Andreas. *History of Chicago: Ending with the Year 1857.* Chicago: Andreas, 1884, pp. 312–313.

4. *Chicago Daily Tribune,* Saturday, October 31, 1857.

5. Jonathan Blanchard and Nathan Lewis Rice. *A Debate on Slavery.* Cincinnati: Moore, 1846. Jonathan Blanchard was the pastor of the Sixth Presbyterian Church in Cincinnati and Nathan Lewis Rice was pastor of the Central Presbyterian Church.

6. Breckenridge was born in Kentucky in 1821 and ran on a pro-slavery platform. He obtained the votes of the slave states. During the Civil War, he actively served the Confederacy and in 1865 was its secretary of war.

7. *Chicago Tribune,* October 27, 1860.

8. *Chicago Tribune,* September 16, 1864.

9. James A. Rose. *Blue Book of the State of Illinois, 1907.* Springfield: State Printer, 1908, p. 542.

10. Eugene M. Lerner. "Investment Uncertainty During the Civil War: A Note on the McCormick Brothers." *The Journal of Economic History,* Volume 16, Number 1 (March 1956), pp. 34–40.

11. *Chicago Tribune,* October 27, 1864.

12. *Chicago Tribune,* May 14, 1884.

13. Hutchinson. *Cyrus Hall McCormick: Harvest, 1856–1884,* pp. 96–97.

14. Mary Ann McCormick to L.P. Grigsby, Hickory Hill, Virginia, August 10, 1858.

15. Hutchinson. *Cyrus Hall McCormick: Harvest, 1856–1884,* pp. 103–104.

16. *Ibid.,* p. 468.

17. *New York Times,* September 26, 1931.

18. Leander James McCormick. *Family Record and Biography.* Chicago: 1896, p. 920. Jerome Increase Case of the J. I. Case Threshing Machine Company, Racine, Wisconsin, offered to build the McCormick harvester but Cyrus McCormick refused and undertook to build a new factory.

19. Hutchinson, *Cyrus Hall McCormick: Seed-Time, 1809–1856,* p. 508.

20. *Chicago Tribune,* October 9, 1872.

21. Hutchinson, *Cyrus Hall McCormick: Seed-Time, 1809–1856,* pp. 519–521.

22. *Ibid.,* p. 331.

23. *Chicago Tribune,* December 11, 1876.

24. *Chicago Tribune,* June 27, 1879. Reports of the McCormick success in British harvester competitions are recorded in the *Journal of the Royal Agricultural Society of England,* Volume 18. London: John Murray, 1882, pp. 299–300, and Third Series, Volume 4, 1893, p. 703.

25. Hutchinson. *Cyrus Hall McCormick: Harvest, 1856–1884,* p. 673.

26. *Prominent Democrats of Illinois.* Chicago: Democratic Publishing Company, 1889.

27. Julius Fuchs was born in Germany in 1836. He came to Chicago as a teacher of piano and organ. In his youth he knew Liszt and Wagner and introduced their music to the New World.

28. *Chicago Tribune,* May 28, 1880.

29. *Chicago Tribune,* May 16, 1884, and *New York Times* May 14, 1884.

30. *Chicago Tribune,* May 20, 1884.

31. Roderick. *Nettie Fowler,* p. 137.

32. *Ibid.,* p. 200.

33. *Ibid.,* p. 233.

34. Frank T. Wheller. *Tusculum College, Tennessee.* Charleston, SC: Arcadia, 2000.

35. *New York Times,* December 22, 1913.

36. *Chicago Tribune,* March 25, 1925.

37. *Chicago Tribune,* August 8, 1923.

Chapter Three

1. The estate was sold after Reuben's death. In 1928, Robert Rutherford McCormick and Chauncey McCormick, grandsons of William and Mary Ann, bought the grand house and surrounding acreage.

2. Hutchinson, *Cyrus Hall McCormick: Seed-Time, 1809–1856,* p. 101.

3. *Ibid.,* p. 81.

4. Mary Katharine Frost. *William Sanderson McCormick: A Biography.* Master's thesis, Graduate School of Creighton University, Omaha, Nebraska, 1961.

5. Hutchinson, *Cyrus Hall McCormick: Seed-Time, 1809–1856,* p. 273.

6. Hutchinson. *Cyrus Hall McCormick: Harvest, 1856–1884,* p. 108.

7. William Henry Egle. *Pennsylvania Genealogical: Scotch-Irish and German.* Harrisburg, Pennsylvania, 1886, p. 477.

8. Andrew McFarland. *The Escape.* Boston: Mussey, 1851.

9. Hutchinson. *Cyrus Hall McCormick: Harvest, 1856–1884,* p.129.

10. A good description of the life of William Sanderson McCormick comes from the Master's thesis presented to Creighton University in 1961 by Mary Katharine Frost.

11. Allen D. Spiegel. *A. Lincoln, Esquire: A Shrewd, Sophisticated Lawyer in His Time.* Macon: Mercer University Press, 2002, p. 125.

12. Obituary of Dr. Andrew McFarland. *Chicago Tribune,* November 24, 1891.

13. Jason Emerson. *Mary Lincoln's Insanity Case: A Documentary History.* Urbana: University of Illinois Press, 2012.

14. Leander J. McCormick. Memorial of Robert McCormick. Chicago: Barnard & Gunthorp, 1885.

15. Letter in the *Ohio Cultivator* [Columbus], Volume 1, No. 6, p. 47.

16. Thomas S. Dicke. *Franchising in America: The Development of the Business Method: 1840–1980.* Chapel Hill: University of North Carolina Press, 1984, pp. 18–23. David Hounshell. *From the American System to Mass Production, 1800–1932: The Development of Manufacturing Technology in the United States.* Baltimore: Johns Hopkins University Press, 1984, pp. 151–153.

17. Caroline Kirkland. *Chicago's Yesterdays: A Sheaf of Remembrances.* Chicago: Daughday, 1919, pp. 35–40.

18. Leander James McCormick. *Family Records and Biography.* Chicago, 1896, p. 820.

19. Henrietta Hamilton McCormick. *Genealogies and Reminiscences.* Chicago, 1894.

20. *Ibid.* Frederick and Edward Bauman also designed the new McCormick Reaper Works on 24 acres on the south branch of the Chicago River at Blue Island and Western avenues.

21. *Chicago Tribune,* January 25, 1914.

22. Hutchinson. *Cyrus Hall McCormick: Harvest, 1856–1884.*

23. *Ibid.,* pp. 518–519.

24. *Chicago Tribune,* Friday, June 27, 1879.

25. *Chicago Tribune,* June 11, 1879.

26. Hounshell. *From the American System to Mass Production, 1800–1932,* p.178.

27. John W. Klooster. *Icons of Invention: The Makers of the Modern World from Gutenberg to Gates.* Santa Barbara: ABC CLIO, 2009, p. 142.

28. *Chicago Tribune,* January 1, 1881.

29. Hounshell. *From the American System to Mass Production, 1800–1932,* pp. 153–185.

30. Henrietta Hamilton McCormick. *Genealogies and Reminiscences,* p. 87.

31. *Chicago Tribune,* November 27, 1899.

32. *Chicago Tribune,* obituary, February 21, 1900.

33. *Chicago Tribune,* February 24, 1900.

34. *Chicago Tribune,* March 10, 1932.

Chapter Four

1. Letter of William Deering, March 9, 1845. William Deering Family Papers, Northwestern University Archives, Evanston, Illinois.

2. William Berry Lapham and Silas P. Maxim. *History of Paris, Maine From its Settlement to 1880.* Paris, ME, 1884. L. E. W. Johnson. "Before William Deering Came West." *The Harvester World,* Volume 11, November 1920, p. 4.

3. Chaim M. Rosenberg. *Yankee Colonies Across America: Cities Upon the Hills.* Lanham, MD: Lexington Books, 2015.

4. *Chicago Tribune,* July 20, 1863.

5. *William Deering, Born in Maine, 1826, Died in Florida 1913.* Chicago, 1913. Decision of the commissioner of patents, August 9, 1872, on the Marsh brothers application to extend their patent.

6. Herbert Newton Casson. *The Romance of the Reaper.* New York: Doubleday, 1908, pp. 48–49.

7. *The Harvester World,* Volume 11, June 1920, p. 14.

8. *Chicago Tribune,* November 16 and 18, 1880.

9. *Chicago Tribune,* January 1, 1881.

10. *Chicago Tribune,* January 1, 1880. Hutchinson. *Cyrus Hall McCormick: Harvest, 1856–1884,* p. 531.

11. *Chicago Tribune,* November 7, 1901.

12. *Chicago Tribune,* December 21, 1901.

13. Randy Leffingwell. *Farmall: The Red Tractor that Revolutionized Farming.* St. Paul: MBI, 2005.

14. Letter of James Deering to Dr. Charles J. Little, March 28, 1910. From the Chauncey McCormick Papers, Newberry Library, Chicago.

15. Telegram from Chauncey McCormick to Charles and James McCormick, December 20, 1913.

16. *New York Times,* December 29, 1913.

17. Letter from William Deering to his son Charles, November 10, 1861. William Deering Family Papers, Northwestern University Library Archives.

18. Letter of William Deering to his son Charles, July 27, 1862. William Deering Family Papers, 1845–1983, Charles Deering Library, Northwestern University.

19. Walter Dill Scott and Robert B. Harshe. *Charles Deering 1855–1927: An Appreciation Together with His Memoirs of William Deering and James Deering.* Boston, 1929.

20. J. P. Packard. *Grant's Tour Around The World.* Cincinnati: Forshee & McMakin, 1880.

21. Portrait now in the collection of the Art Institute, Chicago.

22. *New York Times,* February 6, 1927.

23. *Chicago Tribune,* August 19, 1902.

24. *Chicago Tribune,* May 10, 1902.

25. *Chicago Tribune,* January 13, 1932.

26. *New York Times,* December 1, 1943.

27. *Chicago Tribune,* August 12, 1919.

28. *New York Times,* May 19, 1924.

29. *New York Times,* November 16, 1926.

30. *New York Times,* January 29, 1937.

31. Althea McDowell Altemus. *Big Bosses: A Working Girl's Memoir of Jazz Age America,* ed. Robin F. Bachin. Chicago: University of Chicago Press, 2016, p. 10.

32. *Ibid.,* pp. 30–32.

33. *New York Times,* September 22, 1925. Pernicious anemia is caused by a deficiency of Vitamin B12. Drs. George R. Minot, William P. Murphy and George Hoyt Whipple discovered the cause and cure of pernicious anemia and were jointly awarded the 1934 Nobel Prize in Medicine. The Whipple family in America stems from Matthew Whipple who arrived from England in 1638.

William Whipple was one of the signers of the Declaration of Independence. Charles Deering's wife was a Whipple. Her distant relative Dr. George Hoyt Whipple discovered the cure for the illness that earlier killed her brother-in-law.

Chapter Five

1. Marjorie Warvelle Bear. *A Mile Square of Chicago.* Oak Brook, IL: Tirac, 2007, pp. 93–98.

2. Roderick. *Nettie Fowler McCormick*, pp. 116–117.

3. *Ibid.*, p. 127.

4. *Ibid.*, p. 132.

5. Cyrus McCormick. *The Century of the Reaper*, p. 90.

6. Roderick. *Nettie Fowler McCormick*, p. 137.

7. *Chicago Tribune*, June 2, 1884.

8. *Chicago Tribune*, April 10, 1895.

9. *Chicago Tribune*, February 17–18, 1886.

10. *Chicago Tribune*, February 26, 1886.

11. *Chicago Tribune*, March 5, 1886.

12. *Chicago Tribune*, March 5, 1886.

13. *Chicago Tribune*, March 16, 1886.

14. *Chicago Tribune*, May 4, 1886.

15. *Chicago Tribune*, May 9, 1886.

16. *The Great Anarchist Trial: The Haymarket Speeches of August Spies and Albert R. Parsons.* Chicago: Chicago Labor Press, 1886.

17. "A Hellish Dee," *Chicago Tribune*, May 5, 1886.

18. Elizabeth Stansbury Kirkland's school was situated at 275 E. Huron Street. She came from a highly educated family and was a noted authoress in her own right.

19. *Chicago Tribune*, September 14, 1889.

20. *Chicago Tribune*, June 10, 1897.

21. John Miller Cooper, Jr. *Woodrow Wilson: A Biography.* New York: Random House, 2009, p. 68.

22. Arthur S. Link. *Wilson, Volume 1: The Road to the White House.* Princeton: Princeton University Press, 1967, p. 405.

23. Robert Ozanne. *Wages in Practice and Theory.* Madison: University of Wisconsin Press, 1968, pp. 32–33.

24. *New York Times*, September 22, 1919.

25. James Howard Gore served as professor of mathematics at George Washington University.

26. *Memoriam to Harriet Hammond McCormick.* Chicago, 1921.

27. *New York Times*, December 31, 1924, and January 1, 1925.

28. *Chicago Tribune*, April 25 and May 4, 1927.

29. *New York Times*, September 20, 1935.

30. *New York Times*, June 5, 1936.

31. *New York Times*, August 28, 1937.

32. *Chicago Tribune*, June 2 and 19, 1936. *New York Times*, April 6, 1937.

Chapter Six

1. Hadley Winfield Quaintance. "The Influence of Farm Machinery on Production and Labor." *American Economic Association*, 3rd Series, Volume 5, No. 4 (November 1904), pp.1–106.

2. Gordon M. Winder. *The American Reaper: Harvesting Networks and Technology, 1830–1910.* London: Routledge, 2016.

3. *Chicago Tribune*, November 20, 1890.

4. "To Fight the Harvester Trust," *New York Times*, January 7, 1891.

5. Cyrus McCormick. *The Century of the Reaper*, pp. 108–109.

6. *Chicago Tribune*, January 10, 1891.

7. The International Harvester Company, Report, March 3, 1913. Department of Commerce and Labor, Bureau of Corporations. Washington, D.C.: Government Printing Office, 1913, pp. 58–59.

8. Roderick. *Nettie Fowler McCormick*, p. 208.

9. Chaim M. Rosenberg. *America at the Fair: Chicago's 1893 World's Columbian Exposition.* Charleston, SC: Arcadia, 2008.

10. *A Week at the Fair.* Chicago: Rand McNally & Company, 1893.

11. John Moody. *The Truth About the Trusts: A Description and Analysis of the American Trust Movement.* New York: Moody, 1904.

12. Cyrus McCormick. *The Century of the Reaper*, p. 109.

13. Gordon M. Binder. *The American Reaper.* London: Routledge, 2016.

14. *New York Times*, September 17, 1912.

15. John William Leonard. *History of New York City, 1609–1909.* New York: Journal of Commerce, 1910.

16. *Chicago Tribune*, July 23, 1902.

17. *Chicago Tribune*, August 14, 1902.

18. *Chicago Tribune*, October 10, 1904.

19. Hearings before the Committee on Investigation of the United States Steel Corporation, Volume 2. House of Representatives. Washington, D.C.: Government Printing Office, 1912,pp. 829–832.

20. *New York Times*, October 18, 1903.

21. Robert Ozanne. *A Century of Labor-Management Relations at McCormick and International Harvester.* Madison: University of Wisconsin Press, 1967, pp. 38–55.

22. Ron Chernow. *Titan: The Life of John D. Rockefeller Sr.* New York: Random House, 1998, p. 419. "Harvester Deal Now Worldwide." *Chicago Tribune*, August 14, 1902.

23. *New York Times*, April 29, 1903.

24. The International Harvester Company, March 3, 1913. Department of Commerce and Labor. Washington, D.C.: Government Printing Office, 1913.

25. *Chicago Tribune*, December 18, 1906.

26. Alfred Henry Lewis. "The Opportunity of the Newly Formed Trust and Its Far Reaching Implications." *Cosmopolitan Magazine*, Volume 38, May 10, 1906, pp. 666–672.

27. *Harvester World*, Volume 3, No. 6, August 3, 1912, p. 3.

28. *Chicago Tribune*, August 18, 1907.

29. *New York Times*, June 11, 1908, and July 24, 1911.

30. Rondo Cameron and V. I. Bovykin. *International Banking, 1870–1914.* New York: Oxford University Press, 1991, pp. 507–515.

31. Cyrus McCormick. *The Century of the Reaper*, pp. 145–146.

32. *Chicago Tribune*, October 12, 1947.

33. Randy Leffingwell. *International Harvester Tractors.* St. Paul: Motobooks International, 2004. Patrick Foster. *International Harvester Trucks: The Complete History.* Minneapolis: Quarto, 2013.

34. John Kimberley Mumford. "The Heart of the Soul-

less Corporation." *The Shepherd's Criterion*, Volume XVIII, No. 19. Chicago: October 1908, p. 14.

35. United States Steel Corporation. Congressional Hearings No. 12–20. Washington. D.C.: December 1912, pp. 829–839. Congressional Debate, April 26, 1912, Debate of the 62nd Congress, Second session, Volume XLVIII, Washington, D.C.

36. *Chicago Tribune*, August 11, 1911.

37. "Harvester Trust Report Suppresse," *Pilot*, May 15, 1912. Geofrey Cowan. *Let the People Rule: Theodore Roosevelt and the Birth of the Presidential Primary*. New York: Norton, 1916.

38. *New York Times*, September 21, 1911.

39. "Missouri Ousts Harvester Truss," *Chicago Tribune*, November 15, 1911.

40. *New York Times*, November 30, 1912.

41. *New York Times*, August 14, 1912.

42. Lothar Conant, Jr. *The International Harvester Company*. Washington D.C.: United States Bureau of Corporations, March 3, 1913.

43. *New York Times*, April 30, 1912.

44. *New York Times*, May 1, 1912.

45. *New York Times*, March 3, 1913.

46. *New York Times*, March 13, 1913.

47. "Harvester Trust Divides Itself," *Chicago Tribune*, January 28, 1913.

48. Conant. *The International Harvester Company.*

49. *New York Times*, August 14, 1914.

50. *Chicago Tribune*, May 8, 1916.

51. *Chicago Tribune*, May 1, 1916.

52. *Chicago Tribune*, August 5, 1918.

53. *New York Times*, September 20, 1918.

54. *Chicago Tribune*, June 18, 1923.

55. *New York Times*, October 27, 1926.

56. *Chicago Tribune*, June 27, 1927.

57. Cyrus McCormick. *The Century of the Reaper*, p.182.

58. C. H. Wendel. *150 Years of International Harvester*. Osceola, WI: Motorworks, 1993, p. 250. By the year 1955, International Harvester had built its three millionth Farmall tractor, rising to a powerful 265-horsepower engine. First published in 1981, Wendel's book offers an extensive account of International Harvester's agricultural machines, engines, tractors and trucks. Randy Leffington's *International Harvester Tractors* is another source of information on the Harvester products.

59. *New York Times*, March 15, 1926.

60. *Memorrium to Harriet Hammond McCormick*. Chicago, 1921.

61. John R. Commons. "Social Work in a Great Industrial Plant." *American Monthly Review of Reviews*, Volume 18, July 1903, pp. 79–80.

62. *Chicago Tribune*, April 3, 1903.

63. Nikki Mandel. *The Corporation as Family: The Gendering of Corporate Welfare, 1890–1930*. Chapel Hill: University of North Carolina Press, 2002, pp. 14, 50.

64. Christopher J. Cyphers. *The National Civic Federation and the Making of a New Liberalism, 1910–1914*. Westport, CT: Praeger, 2002.

65. *Chicago Tribune*, October 10, 1904.

66. *Chicago Tribune*, January 19, 1906.

67. *Chicago Tribune*, April 14, 1910.

68. George H. Ramsey. "Employees Benefit Association of the International Harvester Company." *Bulletin of the United States Bureau of Labor*, Issue 208. Washington D.C.: Government Printing Office, 1918, pp. 480–490.

69. C. W. Price. "Employees' Benefit Association of the International Harvester Company." *The Annals of the American Academy of Political and Social Science*, Volume 33, No. 2, March 1909, pp. 22–33.

70. Cyrus H. McCormick. *Harvester World*, Volume 10, No. 12, December 1919.

71. Lisbeth Cohen. *Making a New Deal: Industrial Workers in Chicago, 1919–1939*. Cambridge: Cambridge University Press, 2014.

72. Cyrus McCormick. *The Century of the Reaper*, p.272.

73. *New York Times*, June 3, 1936.

74. Jennifer Delton. *Racial Integration in Corporate America, 1940–1998*. New York: Cambridge University Press, 2009, pp. 133–137. *Extra Compensation and Stock Ownership Plan for the Employees of the International Harvester Company*. Chicago: November 1, 1920.

75. Ozanne. *A Century of Labor-Management Relations at McCormick and International Harvester*, p. 195.

Chapter Seven

1. Hutchinson. *Cyrus Hall McCormick: Harvest, 1856–1884*, pp. 643–683.

2. *New York Times*, August 1, 1880.

3. Rondon Cameron and V. I. Boykin, eds., *International Banking, 1870–1914*. New York: Oxford University Press, 1991, p. 507.

4. *Chicago Tribune,* June 7, 1902.

5. *Farm Implements*, Volume XXIII, No. 5, May 31, 1909, p. 34.

6. *New York Times*, December 6, 1908.

7. The International Harvester Company, March 3, 1913. Washington, D.C.: Government Printing Office, 1913.

8. In 1935 McAllister became president of International Harvester, serving six years in that position.

9. *The Harvester World*, Volume 12, No. 9, September 1921, p. 19.

10. Hutchinson. *Cyrus Hall McCormick: Harvest, 1856–1884*, p. 411.

11. *Oxford Times*, January 20, 1910.

12. William D. Rubinstein, Michael A. Jolles and Hilary L. Rubinstein. *The Palgrave Dictionary of Anglo-Jewish History*. London: Palgrave Macmillan, 2011, p. 58.

13. *The Illustrated Farm and Garden Almanac*. London: Simpkin and Marshall, 1979, pp. 176–177. The records of the International Harvester Company of Great Britain are kept at the University of Reading.

14. Fred V. Carstensen. *American Enterprise in Foreign Markets*. Chapel Hill: University of North Carolina Press, 1984, p. 118.

15. Katharine A. S. Siegel. *Loans and Legitimacy: The Evolution of Soviet-American Relations, 1919–1923*. Lexington: University Press of Kentucky, 1996.

16. *New York Times*, December 4, 1904.

17. Fred V. Carstenson. *American Enterprise in Foreign Markets: Singer and International Harvester in Imperial Russia*. Chapel Hill: University of North Carolina Press, 1988.

18. *New York Times*, October 3, 1911.

19. Cyrus Hall McCormick. *The Harvester World*, Volume 5, No. 1, February 1911, p. 20.

20. *Chicago Tribune*, August 5, 1918.

21. Leo J. Bacino. *Reconstructing Russia: U.S. Policy in Revolutionary Russia, 1917–1922*. Kent, OH: Kent State University, 1999.

22. Paul R. Josephson. *Would Trotsky Wear a Bluetooth? Technological Utopianism under Socialism, 1917–1989*. Baltimore: Johns Hopkins University Press, 2010, p. 27. "International Harvester In Russia, 1850–1972," from the International Harvester Archives, prepared by Elizabeth Cowan Pickering and J. D. Henn, 1972.

23. Alan M. Ball. *Imaging America: Influence and Images of Twentieth Century Russia*. Lanham, MD: Rowman & Littlefield, 2003, p. 124. Thomas P. Hughes. *A Century of Invention and Technological Enthusiasm, 1870–1970*. Chicago: University of Chicago Press, 2004, p. 272.

24. *Chicago Tribune*, May 24, 1931.

25. *Chicago Tribune*, October 14, 1942.

26. Robert W. Clawson. "An American Businessman in the Soviet Union; The Reimer Report." *The Business History Review*, Volume 50, No. 2 (Summer 1976), pp. 203–218.

27. *Chicago Tribune*, March 4, 1945.

28. Lee Klancher. *The Authoritative Guide to International Harvester and Case-IH Farm Tractors in the Modern Era*. Austin: Octane Press, 2013.

29. *Tractor and Gas Turbine Review*, Volume 11, No. 11, November 1918, p. 20.

30. Herbert Bonin and Ferry De Goey, eds., *American Firms in Europe: Strategy, Identity, Perception and Performance*. Geneva: Librarie, 2009, p. 562.

31. Graeme R. Quick. *International Harvester Tractors and Equipment in Australia and New Zealand*. Sydney: Rosenberg, 2007.

32. Tom Clark, "Post WWII Soviet & Chinese Copies of IH Trucks." *Harvester Highlights*, pp. 24–25.

33. *Chicago Tribune*, March 9, 1984.

Chapter Eight

1. *Chicago Tribune*, November 27, 1895. In 1863, John D. Rockefeller established the Standard Oil Trust to become the world's largest oil company and make him the world's richest man. Legal troubles began with the passage in 1890 of the Sherman Antitrust Act, eventually forcing the company to break up into several smaller companies, each with its own board of directors.

2. *Chicago Tribune*, June 14, 1895.

3. *New York Times*, November 27, 1895.

4. John W. Boyer. *The University of Chicago: A History*. Chicago: University of Chicago Press, 2015, p. 44.

5. *Chicago Tribune*, November 27, 1895.

6. The International Harvester Company. Washington, D.C.: Department of Commerce and Labor, Bureau of Corporations, Government Printing Office, 1913, pp. 163–164.

7. *Chicago Tribune*, May 10, 1902.

8. *Chicago Tribune*, June 30, 1903.

9. George W. Corner. *A History of the Rockefeller Institute: 1901–1953*. New York: Rockefeller Institute Press, 1954, pp. 310–31.

10. *New York Times*, November 24, 1907.

11. George W. Corner. *History of The Rockefeller Institute: 1901–1953, Origins and Growth*. New York: Rockefeller Institute Press, 1965.

12. *Chicago Tribune*, March 6, 1906.

13. James Langland. *Chicago Daily News Almanac and Year Book*, Volume 20, p. 390.

14. *New York Times* February 7, 1906.

15. *New York Times*, August 15, 1909.

16. Robert C. Marsh. *150 Years of Opera in Chicago*. DeKalb: Northern Illinois University Press, 2006.

17. *Chicago Tribune*, August 14, 1966.

18. *New York Times*, August 4, 1910.

19. *New York Times*, July 31, 1913.

20. *Chicago Tribune*, August 4, 1913.

21. Gary Lachman. *Jung the Mystic*. New York: Penguin, 2010, p. 106.

22. Richard Noll. *The Aryan Christ: The Secret Life of Carl Jung*. New York: Random House, 1997, pp. 200–233.

23. Deidre Bair. *Jung: A Biography*. New York: Back Bay Books, 2003, pp. 265–275.

24. Frank McLynn. *Carl Gustav Jung: A Biography*. New York: St. Martin's, 2014.

25. Ronald Hayman. *A Life of Jung*. New York: Norton, 1999, p. 202.

26. Otto Luening. *The Odyssey of an American Composer: The Autobiography of Otto Luerning*. New York: Scribner, 1980.

27. Richard Ellmann. *James Joyce*. New York: Oxford University Press, 1959, p.435.

28. June and Gerhard Adler, eds., *Letters of C.G. Jung, Volume 2, 1951–1961*. London: Routledge, 1975, pp. 348–349.

29. Deidre Bair. *Jung: A Biography*. Boston: Little, Brown, 2003, p. 303.

30. Marsha Shapiro Rose. "The Legacy of Wealth: Primogeniture Among the Rockefellers." *Journal of Family History*, Volume 27, No. 2, April 2002, pp. 172–183.

31. Harold F. McCormick. *Via Pacis: How Terms of Peace Can Be Automatically Prepared While the War Is Still Going On*. Chicago: McClurg, 1917.

32. *Chicago Tribune*, June 19, 1922.

33. *Chicago Tribune*, June 19, 1918.

34. *Chicago Tribune*, December 27, 1918.

35. *Factory: The Management Magazine*, Volume XXIV, No. 1, January 1920, p. 264, and *Automotive Industries: The Automobile*, Volume 40, March 15, 1919, pp. 565–568.

36. Cyrus McCormick. *The Century of the Reaper*, p. 272. "C.H. McCormick Gives Up Post with Harvester," *Chicago Tribune*, September 20, 1935.

37. *Musical America*, Volume XXXIII, No. 24, April 9, 1921, p. 2.

38. *New York Times*, September 28, 1921.

39. John Davison Rockefeller. *Dear Father/ Dear Son: Correspondence of John D. Rockefeller and John D. Rockefeller Jr.* Ed. Joseph W. Ernst. New York: Fordham University Press, 1994, p. 119.

40. "McCormicks Live Apart in Chicago," *New York Times*, October 4, 1921.

41. *New York Times*, October 19, 1921.

42. *New York Times*, April 22, 1922.

43. *New York Times*, January 26, 1922.

44. *New York Times*, March 21, 1922.

45. *Chicago Tribune*, December 30, 1921.

46. *New York Times*, January 1, 1922.

47. *Chicago Tribune*, January 15, 1922.

48. *New York Times*, January 15, 1922.

49. *Chicago Tribune*, August 26, 1932.

50. *Chicago Tribune*, December 6, 1956.

51. *Chicago Tribune*, May 7, 1966.

52. *Chicago Tribune*, May 22, 1922.

53. *Chicago Tribune*, May 19, 1947.

54. *Chicago Tribune*, February 20, 1922.

55. *New York Times*, February 20, 1922.

56. *New York Times*, May 1922.

57. *New York Times*, June 3, 5, 1922.

58. *Chicago Tribune*, June 8, 1922.

59. Ozanne. *A Century of Labor-Management Relations at McCormick and International Harvester*, p. 91.

60. Letter dated February 14, 1921, from John D. Rockefeller to his son. *Dear Father/Dear Son: Correspondence of John D. Rockefeller Sr., and John D. Rockefeller Jr.* New York: Fordham University Press, 1994, p. 119.

61. Ozanne. *Wages in Practice and Theory*, p.49.

62. *Chicago Tribune*, June 3, 1922. *New York Times*, June 3, 1922.

63. *New York Times*, November 5, 1922. Alexander Legge served as president of Harvester from 1922 until 1933.

64. Robert Ozanne. *Wages in Practice and Theory*, p. 49.

65. *New York Times*, August 4, 8, and 12, 1922.

66. *New York Times*, May 19, 1941, and *Chicago Tribune*, May 19, 1947.

67. *Chicago Tribune*, September 21, 1947.

68. *New York Times*, June 18, 1922.

69. *New York Times*, June 19, 1922.

70. *Chicago Tribune*, July 14, 1922.

71. *New York Times*, June 23, 1922.

72. In 1928, Dr. Serge Voronoff published his book *Rejuvenation by Grafting*, showing before and after pictures of dozens of his rejuvenated patients.

73. *New York Times*, May 2, 1922.

74. *Chicago Tribune*, July 26, 1922.

75. Cochran died of pulmonary tuberculosis June 20, 1929, leaving Ganna $3 million and a mansion at 14 Rue Lubeck in Paris. *New York Times*, June 22, 1929. "She's Mrs. Harold F. McCormick Now." *Chicago Tribune*, August 12, 1922.

76. *New York Times*, October 18 and November 26, 1922.

77. *Chicago Tribune*, September 9, 1922.

78. *New York Times*, December 3, 1922.

79. *Chicago Tribune*, December 18, 1922.

80. "Harold F. McCormick and Ganna Walska Marry Again," *Chicago Tribune*, February 14, 1923.

81. *New York Times*, February 20–21, 1923.

82. *New York Times*, June 27, 1923.

83. *New York Times*, June 25, 1924.

84. *New York Times*, January 29, 1925.

85. *Chicago Tribune*, May 3, 1925.

86. *New York Times*, January 17, 1926.

87. *New York Times*, November 11 and 13, 1927.

88. *New York Times*, February 1, 1928.

89. *New York Times*, October 30, 1928.

90. *Chicago Tribune*, February 8, 1929.

91. *New York Times*, January 19, 1929.

92. *Chicago Tribune*, February 21, 1929.

93. *Chicago Tribune*, October 11, 1931.

94. *New York Times*, October 10, 1931.

95. *Chicago Tribune*, April 19, 1935, and April 19, 1933.

96. *Chicago Tribune*, September 20, 1935.

97. *Chicago Tribune*, April 11, 1937.

98. *Chicago Tribune*, January 16, 1910.

99. *Chicago Tribune*, October 2, 2009.

100. *Chicago Tribune* October 26, 1965.

101. *Chicago Tribune*, September 18, 1925, and August 27, 1932.

102. *New York Times*, May 2, 1926.

103. David Rockefeller. *Memoirs*. New York: Random House, 2003.

104. *Chicago Tribune*, June 20, 1929.

105. *Chicago Tribune*, September 1, 1945.

106. *Chicago Tribune*, September 20, 1932.

107. *Chicago Tribune*, August 27, 1932. Stephen Birmingham. *The Grande Dames*. Guilford, CT: Lyons, 2016.

108. *Chicago Tribune*, September 20, 1935.

109. *Chicago Tribune*, August 26, 1932.

110. *New York Times*, August 26, 1932.

111. *New York Times*, August 28, 1932.

112. *Chicago Tribune*, August 26, 1032.

113. *New York Times*, January 7, 1934.

114. *New York Times*, November 4, 1932.

115. *Chicago Tribune*, September 19 and December 28, 1965.

116. *New York Times*, February 28, 1932, and March 32, 1933.

117. *New York Times*, May 24, 1937, and *Chicago Tribune* May 26, 1937.

118. *New York Times*, November 16, 1932. During World War II Major Young was in charge of the venereal disease services of the American army in Europe. He worked hard to remove prostitution near American army bases.

119. *New York Times*, January 20, 1933.

120. *New York Times*, October 25, 1933.

121. *New York Times*, October 5 and 6, 1935.

122. *New York Times*, May 14 and June 1, 1938.

123. *New York Times*, December 4, 1938, and January 4, 1939.

124. *New York Times*, June 27, 1939.

125. *New York Times*, October 17, 1941, and *Chicago Tribune* June 20, 1953.

126. *New York Times*, October 30, 1941, and July 30, 1942.

127. Paul G. Hackett. *Theos Bernard: The White Lama*. New York: Columbia University Press, 2012.

128. Ganna Walska. *Always Room at the Top*. New York: Ronald R. Smith, 1943.

Chapter Nine

1. *Chicago Tribune*, November 25, 1914.

2. *Chicago Tribune*, June 7, 1914.

3. *Chicago Tribune*, February 14, 1915.

4. *New York Times*, June 26, 1926.

5. *Chicago Tribune*, June 30, 1926.

6. *New York Times*, February 6, 1931, and *Chicago Tribune* February 10, 1931.

7. *New York Times*, March 15, 1931.

8. *New York Times*, August 10, 1941.

9. *New York Times*, April 1, 1970.

10. *Chicago Tribune*, February 26, 1939.

11. *Chicago Tribune*, September 21, 1906.

12. *New York Times*, June 20, 1921.

13. *Chicago Tribune*, March 29, 1925.

14. *New York Times*, April 3, 1925.

15. *New York Times*, November 1, 1925.

16. C.G. Jung. *Memories, Dreams, Reflections*. New York: Vintage, 1989, pp. 247–248.

17. Deidre Bair. *Jung: A Biography*. New York: Back Bay Books, 2003, p. 351.

18. *Chicago Tribune*, May 2, 1926.

19. Headline in the *Chicago Tribune* of June 8, 1931, reads: "Fowler McCormick Weds Fifi Stillman as She Gets Divorce—Al Capone Indicted by U.S, Surrenders." *New York Times*, June 7, 1931.

20. Barbara Marsh. *A Corporate Tragedy: The Agony of International Harvester Company*. Garden City, NY: Doubleday, 1985, p. 95.

21. *Chicago Tribune*, March 4, 1939.

22. *Chicago Tribune*, December 15, 1933.

23. *Chicago Tribune*, April 26 and September 25, 1935, and April 16, 1940.

24. *Chicago Tribune*, June 3, 1937.

25. Bair. *Jung*, p. 426.

26. *Chicago Tribune*, July 1, 1938.

27. *Chicago Tribune*, April 25, 1938, and *New York Times*, April 25, 1940.

28. *New York Times*, March 1, 1941.

29. *New York Times*, March 23 and 24, 1941.

30. *New York Times*, March 27, 1941.

31. Ozanne, *A Century of Labor-Management Relations at McCormick and International Harvester*, p. 201.

32. *New York Times*, April 4, 1941

33. *Chicago Tribune*, May 13, 1941.

34. *Chicago Tribune*, November 30, 1942, and *New York Times*, November 29, 1942.

35. *New York Times*, April 21, 1943.

36. *The Strong Shall be Free: International Harvester During World War II* (film).

37. *New York Times*, January 18, 1944.

38. *New York Times*, April 13, 1944.

39. *New York Times*, August 31, 1944.

40. *Chicago Tribune*, December 9, 1945.

41. *Chicago Tribune*, May 10, 1944.

42. *New York Times*, October 18, 1945.

43. *New York Times*, June 30, 1946.

44. *New York Times*, January 22, 1946.

45. *New York Times*, May 17, 1946, and *Chicago Tribune* May 17, 1946.

46. *Chicago Tribune*, March 7, 1946.

47. *Chicago Tribune*, October 12, 1947.

48. Ozanne, *A Century of Labor-Management Relations at McCormick and International Harvester*, pp. 188–189.

49. *Opportunity: Journal of Negro Life*, Volume 22, (January–March 1944), p. 15.

50. *Monthly Labor Review*, Volume 17, No. 1. (January 1954), pp. 16–23.

51. *Chicago Tribune*, November 22, 1948.

52. *Chicago Tribune*, November 22, 1946, and December 24, 1950.

53. *Chicago Tribune*, October 10, 1947.

54. *Chicago Tribune*, October 1, 1947.

55. *New York Times*, May 12, 1950.

56. *New York Times*, November 5, 1950.

57. *Chicago Tribune*, June 27, 1947.

58. "Antitrust Suits Filed Against Case, Deere, Harvester," *Chicago Tribune*, September 10, 1948.

59. *Chicago Tribune*, May 30 and June 23, 1951.

60. *Chicago Tribune*, June 22, 1951.

61. *New York Times*, February 23, 1952.

62. *New York Times*, May 13, 1956.

63. *Chicago Tribune*, November 17, 1951.

64. *Chicago Tribune*, June 20, 1858.

65. *Chicago Tribune*, January 20, 1958.

66. *New York Times*, June 4, 1922.

67. *New York Times*, April 17 and 19, 1922.

68. *Chicago Tribune*, September 6, 1944.

69. *New York Times*, December 23, 1947.

70. *Chicago Tribune*, December 14, 1944.

71. *Chicago Tribune*, January 30, 1959.

72. *Chicago Tribune*, December 6, 1962.

73. *New York Times*, May 12, 1965.

74. *New York Times*, October 4, 1952.

75. *New York Times*, April 4, 1961.

76. Bair. *Jung*, p. 286.

77. *New York Times* January 7, 1973.

Chapter Ten

1. Harriet Hammond McCormick to Chauncey McCormick, June 6, 1906. Chauncey McCormick Papers, Newberry Library, Chicago. Boutwell Dunlap. *The Kappa Sigma Book: A Manual of Description, Historical and Statistical*. Nashville: Cumberland Press, 1909.

2. Son of the owner of an evangelical printing house in Chicago.

3. *Chicago Tribune*, October 8, 1906.

4. Letter of Cyrus Hall McCormick to Chauncey McCormick, October 9, 1906. Letters from the Chauncey Brooks McCormick Papers, Newberry Library, Chicago.

5. Letter from Harold Fowler McCormick to Chauncey McCormick, October 12, 1906.

6. Letter from Cyrus H. McCormick to Chauncey McCormick, October 11, 1906.

7. *Chicago Tribune*, October 8, 1906.

8. Letter from William Grigsby McCormick to his son Chauncey, February 26, 1909.

9. On May 7, 1915, a German U-boat sank the *Lusitania* off the coast of Iceland, with the loss of 1,198 passengers and crew. The attack on the 44,000-ton ship turned American public opinion against the Germans.

10. Letter of Marion Deering to Chauncey McCormick, September 11, 1912.

11. *Chicago Tribune*, June 21, 1914.

12. *New York Times*, July 7, 1914.

13. *Chicago Tribune*, August 23, 1914.

14. Letter from James Deering to Robert Bliss, June 19, 1917; Cyrus H. McCormick to Major General Hugh L. Scott January 24, 1918, and Major General Scott to Cyrus Hall McCormick, January 29, 1918. Chauncey Brooks McCormick Papers, Newberry Library, Chicago.

15. Letter from James Deering to Chauncey McCormick, June 11, 1917.

16. Letters from James Deering to Chauncey McCormick, June 23, June 27 and October 16, 1917.

17. Letter from Chauncey McCormick in France to his wife Marion Deering McCormick, August 23, 1917.

18. Letter from Chauncey McCormick in France to Marion Deering McCormick, September 5, 1917.

19. Letter from Chauncey McCormick to Marion Deering McCormick, August 5, 1918.

20. Letter from Edith Rockefeller McCormick to Chauncey McCormick, September 28, 1918.

21. *Chicago Tribune*, May 21, 1933.

22. Herbert Hoover, *Freedom Betrayed*. Ed. George H. Nash. Stanford: Hoover Institute Press, 2011.

23. *Chicago Tribune*, September 4, 1954.

24. *Chicago Tribune*, July 21, 1929.

25. *Chicago Tribune*, September 10, 1954.

26. *Chicago Tribune*, January 13, 1965, and *New York Times*, January 14, 1965.

27. *New York Times*, January 9, 2000.

28. *Chicago Tribune*, May 11, 1944.

29. *Chicago Tribune*, February 20, 2017.

30. *New York Times*, November 14, 1968.

31. *Chicago Tribune*, July 24, 1951, and August 16, 1954.

32. *Chicago Tribune*, July 20, 1968.

33. William R. Haycraft. *Yellow Street: The Story of earthmoving equipment Industry*. Urbana: University of Illinois Press, 2002, p. 241. *Chicago Tribune*, June 19, 1972. The developments of the International Harvester Company were covered in the *Chicago Tribune*, March 22, 1958, July 10, 1960, January 21, May 6, May 9, 1962, January 19 and September 17, 1971. Roger Amato. *International Harvester, Hough and Dresser: Construction and Industrial Machines.* Clarence, NY: Buffalo Road Imports, 2016.

34. *Chicago Tribune*, May 18, 1975.

35. *Chicago Tribune*, July 11, 1979.

36. Marsh. *A Corporate Tragedy*, p. 130.

37. *New York Times*, November 12, 1978.

38. Eric G. Flamholtz and Yvonne Randle. *Changing the Game: Organizational Transformations of the First, Second and Third Kinds*. New York: Oxford University Press, 1998, p. 102.

39. *New York Times*, August 30, 1980, and *Chicago Tribune*, June 6, 1979.

40. *Chicago Tribune*, November 17, 1980.

41. Marsh. *A Corporate Tragedy*, p. 241; *New York Times*, June 11, 1983.

42. *New York Times*, May 4, 1982; *Chicago Tribune*, July 4, August 10, October 2, 192; January 8, 1983, and March 9, 1984.

43. An optimistic report by Donald D. Lennox appeared in the *Christian Science Monitor* on April 4, 1984. On November 27, 1984, the *New York Times* reported on the closing of the company's farm implement division. *Chicago Tribune*, January 29 and June 22, 1984.

Chapter Eleven

1. *Chicago Tribune*, December 30, 1894.

2. *Chicago Tribune*, April 25, 1915.

3. *Chicago Tribune*, March 21, 1917.

4. *Chicago Tribune*, March 28, 1940.

5. *Chicago Tribune*, June 23, 1932.

6. *Chicago Tribune*, December 4, 1938.

7. *Bulletin of the Museum of Fine Arts*, Volume 41, #246 (December 1943), p. 60.

8. *New York Times*, April 1, 1945.

9. Hannah Freece. *The Gift of a Museum to a Museum: Elizabeth Day McCormick Textile Collection at the Museum of Fine Arts, Boston.* Master's thesis, University of Delaware, 2011.

10. *Chicago Tribune*, August 14, 1957.

11. Letter sent by L. Hamilton McCormick to his aunt, August 4, 1876.

12. Essay written by L. Hamilton McCormick, 1887. Leander Hamilton McCormick Papers, University Archives and Special Collections, Loyola University, Chicago.

13. Frank Henry Parsons. *Thirty Years After: Amherst College Class of '81*. New Haven: Tuttle, 1911, pp. 125–26.

14. L. Hamilton McCormick Catalogue of Pictures. Loyala University Archives, Chicago.

15. L. Hamilton McCormick. *What the Ability to Read Character Will Mean to You*. Chicago: Rand McNally, 1923.

16. Leander Hamilton McCormick. *Characterology: An Exact Science, Embracing Physiognomy, Phrenology and Pathognomy*. Chicago: Rand McNally, 1921.

17. *New York Times*, February 3, 1934.

18. *Chicago Tribune*, October 16, 1917.

19. *Chicago Tribune*, October 8, 1917.

20. *New York Times*, May 15, 1929.

21. *Chicago Tribune*, April 3, 1929.

22. *New York Times*, July 4 and 13, 1933.

23. *Chicago Tribune*, September 7, 1939.

24. *Chicago Tribune*, April 29, 1960.

25. *New York Times*, January 31, 1964, and *Chicago Tribune* January 31, 1964.

26. *New York Times*, January 3, 1922.

27. *Chicago Tribune*, April 1 and 8, 1956.

28. *New York Times*, October 15, 1923.

29. *New York Times*, April 30, 1928.

30. *Chicago Tribune*, February 19, 1933.

31. Isabel Coll Mirabent. *Charles Deering and Ramon Casas: A Friendship in Art*. Evanston, IL: Northwestern University Press, 2012.

32. At time of writing this section of the book I visited the John Singer Sargent exhibit at the Art Institute of Chicago. On display were portraits of Charles and his wife Marion Whipple Deering painted by John Singer Sargent in 1885 and a painting of Charles Deering done during Sargent's visit to the Deering brothers in Florida in 1917.

33. Stephanie L. Herdrich, Metropolitan Museum of New York, August 18, 2015.

34. Altemus. *Big Bosses*, p.20.

35. *New York Times*, March 15, 1953.

36. *Chicago Tribune*, December 18, 1927.

37. *Chicago Tribune*, November 18, 1906.

38. *New York Times*, October 4, 1941, in 1948,

39. *New York Times*, December 22, 1973.

Chapter Twelve

1. Roderick. *Nettie Fowler McCormick*, p. 121.

2. Harrison. *A Timeless Affair*, p. 43.

3. Roderick, *Nettie Fowler McCormick*, p.137.

4. Mary donated $5,000 to build the hospital for black patients in Huntsville. *Journal of the American Medical Association*, Volume 66, No. 8, February 19, 1915, p. 585.

5. *New York Times*, May 26, 1941.

6. *New York Times*, May 15, 1942. *Chicago Tribune*, May 14, 1942.

7. *Chicago Tribune*, July 18, 1945.

8. Roderick, *Nettie Fowler McCormick*, p. 179.

9. *Ibid.*, pp. 193–194.

10. John W. Leonard, ed., *Who's Who in Finance*. New York: Joseph & Sefton, 1911, p. 146.

11. Papers of Katharine Dexter McCormick. Special Collections (MC 148), Massachusetts Institute of Technology.

12. *New York Times*, October 15, 1962.

13. Armond Fields. *Katharine Dexter McCormick: Pioneer for Women's Rights*. Westport, CT: Praeger, 2003, pp. 60–65.

14. Roderick, *Nettie Fowler McCormick*, pp.232–233.

15. *New York Times*, November 3, 1929.

16. *Chicago Tribune*, April 9, 1909.

17. Fields. *Katharine Dexter McCormick*.

18. *New York Times*, November 29, 1929, and September 25, 1930. Dr. Edward Kempf later served as president of the Psychopathological Association and vice-president of the New York Academy of Sciences. He left $500,000 to Yale University to hold international conferences on the science of human social organization. *New York Times*, December 14, 1971.

19. Dr. Hoskins's research at Worcester State Hospital showed that schizophrenics as a group had some abnormalities in their endocrine function, but treatment with glandular extracts yielded very disappointing results. R.G. Hoskins. *The Biology of Schizophrenia*. London: Chapman and Hall, 1946.

20. *New York Times*, November 27, 1929.

21. *New York Times*, June 16, 1929.

22. *New York Times*, November 19, 1932.

23. *New York Times*, December 18, 1940.

24. *New York Times*, January 20, 1947.

25. *Hampton's Magazine*, Volume 23, December 1909, pp. 851–853.

26. *Chicago Tribune*, February 26, 1925.

27. Stacy A. Cordery. *Alice: Alice Roosevelt Longworth from White House Princess to Washington Power Broker*. New York: Penguin, 2007, p. 191.

28. George E. Condon. *West of Cuyahoga*. Kent, OH: Kent State University Press, 2006, pp. 137–144.

29. Richard Norton Smith. *The Colonel: The Life and Legend of Robert R. McCormick, 1880–1855*. Evanston, IL: Northwestern University Press, 197, p. 51.

30. Christie Miller. *Ruth Hanna McCormick: A Life in Politics, 1880–1944*. Albuquerque: University of New Mexico Press, 1992, p. 27.

31. *New York Times*, June 11, 1903.

32. Miller. *Ruth Hanna McCormick*, p. 35.

33. Amanda Smith. *Newspaper Titan: The Infamous and Monumental Times of Cissy Patterson*. New York: Knopf, 2011, pp. 174–175.

34. Richard Norton Smith. *The Colonel*, p. 127.

35. Bair. *Jung*, pp. 157–158.

36. Ronald Hayman. *A Life of Jung*. New York: Norton, 1998, pp. 116–117.

37. Amanda Smith. *Newspaper Titan*, p. 223.

38. *Chicago Day Book*, August 9, 1913.

39. *Chicago Tribune*, September 10, 1918.

40. Anna Y. Reed. "Child Labor Legislation." *The Elementary School Journal* Volume 23, No. 4 (December 1972), pp. 276–282.

41. Medill McCormick, *Congressional Digest*, Volume 11, No. 1 (October 1922), p. 138.

42. Richard Norton Smith. *The Colonel*, pp. 250–251.

43. *New York Times* February 26, 1925.

44. Miller. *Ruth Hannah McCormick*, p.151.

45. Cordery. *Alice*.

46. *Chicago Tribune*, July 2, 1938.

Chapter Thirteen

1. Ervin L. Jordan Jr. *The University of Virginia during the Civil War*. Virginia Foundation for the Humanities. On-line.

2. *Chicago Tribune* June 14, 1940.

3. L. U. Reavis. *St. Louis and the Future Great City*. St. Louis, Missouri: Barns, 1878, p.81.

4. History of the *Chicago Tribune*. Chicago: *Chicago Tribune*, 1922, pp.29–31.

5. Amanda Smith. *Newspaper Titan: The infamous Life and Monumental Times of Cissy Patterson*. New York: Knopf, 2011.

6. *Ibid.*, p. 45.

7. Jason Emerson. *Giant in the Shadows: The Life of Robert T. Lincoln*. Carnondale, Illinois: Southern Illinois University Press, 2012, pp.304–327.

8. Chaim M. Rosenberg. *America at the Fair: Chicago's 1893 World's Columbian Exposition*. Charleston, S.C: Arcadia, 2008.

9. *New York Times*, June 27, 1902.

10. Papers Relating to the Foreign Relations of the United States. Washington, D.C: Government Printing Office, 1903, pp. 25–72.

11. *New York Times* June 3, 1903.

12. New York Time April 25, 1903.

13. Peter Wienik. *History of the Jews in America: From the Period of the Discovery of the New World to the Present Time*. New York: The Jewish Press, 1912, p.354.

14. United States Congress, House Committee on Foreign Affairs, December 11, 1911. *Termination of Treaty of 1832 between the United States and Russia*. Washington, D.C: Government Printing Office, 1911, pp.216–223.

15. *New York Times* June 3, 1903.

16. Papers Relating to the Foreign Relations of the United States, December 6, 1904. Washington, D.C: Government Printing Office, 1905.

17. Report submitted by ambassador Robert Sanderson McCormick to the secretary of state John Hay on January 31, 1905.

18. *New York Times* March 28 and 30, 1905.

19. *Chicago Tribune*, May 3, 1905.

20. *New York Times* March 18, 1907.

21. Richard Norton Smith. *The Colonel: The Life and Legend of Robert R. McCormick, 1880–1953*. Evanston, Illinois: Northwestern University Press, 2003, p.141.

22. Megan McKinney. *The Magnificent Medills: America's Royal Family of Journalism during the Century of Turbulent Splendor*. New York: Harper Collins, 2011.

23. *New York Times* July 5, 1932, and *Chicago Tribune* July 17, 1932.

24. *New York Times* July 28, 1932.

25. *Washington Post* Obituary December 10, 2015.

Chapter Fourteen

1. John Terrel. *An American Dynasty: The Story of the McCormicks, Medills and Pattersons.* Garden City, NY: Doubleday, 1947, p. 208.

2. *Ibid.*, p. 208.

3. *Chicago Tribune*, November 2, 1910.

4. Message of President Robert R. McCormick. The Sanitary District of Chicago, 1909.

5. Dudley Paine Lewis, ed., *History of the Class of 1903, Yale College.* New Haven: Yale College, 1913.

6. Leander James McCormick. *Family Record & Biography.* Chicago, 1896.

7. *New York Times*, March 11, 1915.

8. *Chicago Sunday Tribune*, August 1, 1915.

9. *New York Times*, June 22, 1915.

10. *New York Times*, July 12, 1915.

11. *New York Times*, July 25, 1915.

12. Robert Rutherford McCormick. *With the Russian Army: Being the Experiences of a National Guardsman.* New York: Macmillan, 1915.

13. *New York Times*, July 11, 1917.

14. Colonel Robert R. McCormick. *The Army of 1918.* New York: Harcourt, Brace and Howe, 1920.

15. *New York Times*, June 9, 1918.

16. *New York Times*, May 29, 1918.

17. Colonel Robert R. McCormick. *The Army of 1918*, p.89.

18. *Chicago Tribune*, July 16, 1919.

19. "Ford as an Anarchist," *Chicago Tribune*, June 23, 1916.

20. *Chicago Tribune*, August 1, 1919.

21. *Chicago Tribune*, November 5, 1919.

22. John J. Binder. *Al Capone's Beer Wars: A Complete History of Organized Crime in Chicago during Prohibition.* New York: Prometheus, 2017.

23. *Chicago Tribune*, February 8, 1931.

24. *Chicago Tribune*, April 9, 1931.

25. Richard Norton Smith. *The Colonel*, p. 279.

26. *Chicago Tribune*, May 18, 1929.

27. *Chicago Tribune*, June 10, 1930.

28. *Chicago Tribune*, October 2, 2011.

29. *Chicago Tribune*, November 9, 1933.

30. *Chicago Tribune*, April 10, 1870.

31. *Chicago Tribune*, June 1, 1886.

32. *Chicago Tribune*, April 14, 1910.

33. *New York Times*, January 14, 1914.

34. *Chicago Tribune*, June 17, 1916.

35. *Chicago Tribune*, February 25, 1918.

36. *Chicago Tribune*, August 20, 1920.

37. Samuel Walker. *Hate Speech: The History of an American Controversy.* Lincoln: University of Nebraska Press, 1994, p. 29.

38. Fred W. Friendly. *Minnesota Rag: The Dramatic Story of a Landmark Supreme Court Case That Gave New Meaning to Freedom of the Press.* New York: Random House, 1991.

39. "Free Criticism Held Nation's Safeguard," *Chicago Tribune*, June 2, 1931.

40. *Chicago Tribune*, October 25, 1929.

41. *Chicago Tribune*, October 2, 1930.

42. *Chicago Tribune*, October 23, 1932.

43. *Chicago Tribune*, March 7, 1930.

44. *Chicago Tribune*, October 25, 1930.

45. David M. Kennedy. *The American People in the Great Depression: Freedom from Fear, Part One.* Oxford: Oxford University Press, 1989. *Chicago Tribune*, April 26, 1935.

46. *Chicago Tribune*, June 2, 1937.

47. *Chicago Tribune*, October 20, 1921.

48. *Chicago Tribune*, October 25, 1936.

49. *Chicago Tribune*, June 23, 1940.

50. *Chicago Tribune*, March 30, 1941.

51. *Chicago Tribune*, August 28, 1935.

52. *Chicago Tribune*, September 13, 1941.

53. *Chicago Tribune*, May 19, 1942.

54. *Chicago Tribune*, September 7, 1942.

55. *Chicago Tribune*, February 16, 1944.

56. *Chicago Tribune*, April 1, 1940.

57. Willard Edwards in the *Chicago Tribune*, October 4, 1944.

58. *Chicago Tribune*, October 31, 1947.

59. *Chicago Tribune*, June 26, 1947.

60. Edwin R. Bayley. *Joe McCarthy and the Press.* Madison: University of Wisconsin Press, 1981, p. 16.

61. "The Spies' Best Friend," editorial, *Chicago Tribune*, February 12, 1950.

62. *Ibid.*

63. Robert Griffith. *The Politics of Fear: Joseph McCarthy and the Senate.* Amherst: University of Massachusetts Press, 1987, pp. 10, 63.

64. *Chicago Tribune*, June 14, 1950.

65. Clayton Kirkpatrick, *Chicago Tribune*, September 11, 1952. Years later Kirkpatrick became editor and moved the *Chicago Tribune* to a centrist position.

66. Walter Trohan writing in defense of Joseph R. McCarthy in the *Chicago Tribune*, April 4, 1954.

67. Donald A. Ritchie. *Reporting from Washington: The History of the Washington Press Corps.* New York: Oxford University Press, 2005, p. 79.

68. *Chicago Tribune*, March 1, 1954.

69. David M. Oshinsky. *A Conspiracy so Immense: The World of Joe McCarthy.* New York: Oxford University Press, 2005, p. 182.

70. Robert Norton Smith. *The Colonel*, p. 502.

71. *Chicago Tribune*, October 28, 1947.

72. *New York Times*, August 15, 1939.

73. *Chicago Tribune*, January 3, 1954.

74. Megan McKinney. *The Magnificent Medills, America's Royal Family of Journalism During a Century of Turbulent Splendor.* New York: Harper, 2011, pp. 224–242.

75. Robert Norton Smith. *The Colonel*, p. 502.

76. *Time Magazine*, cover, November 2, 1938.

77. *New York Times*, July 13, 1997.

78. *New York Times*, April 1, 1955.

79. *Chicago Tribune*, December 31, 1947.

80. *New York Times*, August 24, 1952.

81. *New York Times*, March 18, 1954.

82. *Chicago Tribune*, April 2, 1955.

83. *New York Times*, April 6, 1955.

84. *New York Times*, April 3, 1955.

Chapter Fifteen

1. Leroy James Halsey. *A History of the McCormick Theological Seminary of the Presbyterian Church*. Chicago: Published by the Seminary, 1893.

2. Cyrus H. McCormick, "A Grand Fashionable Gathering to His New House Last Night," *Chicago Tribune*, May 25, 1880.

3. *Ibid.*

4. Sherman C. Kingsley. *The Open Air Crusade: A Story of the Elizabeth McCormick Open Air School*. Chicago: United Charities of Chicago, 1911.

5. *The Elizabeth McCormick Memorial Fund: The First Forty-Five Years*. Chicago, 1954.

6. *Chicago Tribune*, October 12, 1905.

7. *Chicago Tribune*, January 20, 1912.

8. *New York Times*, January 24, 1926.

9. James Webber. *Jane Addams: A Biography*. Urbana: University of Illinois Press, 2000, p. 115.

10. *New York Times*, July 20, 1889.

11. *New York Times*, July 29, 1889.

12. Harrison. *Timeless Affair*, p. 51.

13. *New York Times*, September 26, 1889. Clayton Lodge designed by McKim, Mead & White, was built for Cyrus in 1882, two years before he died. The grounds were designed by Frederick Law Olmsted.

14. *Chicago Tribune* September 27, 1889.

15. Gilbert A. Harrison. *ibid.*, p.61.

16. *New York Times* June 19, 1892.

17. *New York Times* February 24, 1901.

18. *New York Times* June 4, 1899.

19. *New York Times* June 20, 1900.

20. *The Common*, Volume VII, #74, September 1901, pp. 2–3.

21. Christopher Robert Reed. *The Chicago NAACP and the Rise of Professional Leadership, 1914–1966*. Bloomington: Indiana University Press, 1997, pp. 23–24.

22. *Chicago Tribune*, April 5, 1904.

23. *New York Times*, March 16, 1900.

24. Daniel Off. "Producing a Past." *Agricultural History*, Volume 88, No. 1 (Winter 2014), pp. 87–119.

25. *Chicago Tribune*, October 10, 1918.

26. *New York Times*, May 4, 1922.

27. Open letter by Edith McCormack Blaine in the *Chicago Tribune*, May 17, 1941.

28. *Chicago Tribune*, September 15, 1948.

29. *Chicago Tribune*, July 5, 1946.

30. *Chicago Tribune*, February 20, 1954.

31. *New York Times*, February 20, 1954.

32. *New York Times*, August 28, 1953.

33. *Chicago Tribune*, January 22, 1947.

34. Jean H. Baker. *Margaret Sanger: A Life of Passion*. New York: Hill and Wang, 2011.

35. Jonathan Eig. *The Birth of the Pill: How Four Crusaders Reinvented Sex and Launched a Revolution*. New York: Norton, 2015.

36. *New York Times*, June 16, 1947.

37. *Chicago Tribune*, May 24, 1872.

38. Leander James McCormick. "Family Records and Biography." Chicago, 1896, p. 320.

39. *Industrial Chicago*. Chicago: Goodspeed, 1891, p. 618.

40. *Chicago Tribune*, January 17, 1954. John W. Stamper. *Chicago's North Michigan Avenue: Planning and Development, 1900–1930*. Chicago: University of Chicago Press, 1999.

Chapter Sixteen

1. Ralph W. Sanders. *Ultimate John Deere: The History of the Big Green Machines*. Stillwater, MN: Voyageur Press, 2001.

2. David Ranney. *Global Decisions, Local Collisions, Urban Life in the New World Order*. Philadelphia: Temple University Press, 2003, pp. 71–90.

3. 1920 instruction manual of the threshing machine made by the J. I. Case Threshing Machine Company.

4. *New York Times*, January 8, 1986.

5. *New York Times*, January 7, 1986, and *Chicago Tribune*, February 21, April 11, 1986. Thanks to Thomas of Navistar for data on the move from International Harvester to Navistar.

6. *New York Times*, October 17, 1986

7. *Chicago Tribune*, February 6, 2001, and October 26, 2007.

8. *New York Times*, July 20, 1988.

Bibliography

Adler, June, and Gerhard Adler, eds. *Letters of C. G. Jung, Volume 2, 1951–1961.* London: Routledge, 1975.

Altemus, Althea M. *Big Bosses: A Working Girl's Memoir of Jazz Age America.* Ed. Robin F. Bachin. Chicago: University of Chicago Press, 2016.

Andreas, Alfred T. *History of Chicago: Ending with the Year 1857.* Chicago: Andreas, 1884.

Bair, Deidre. *Jung: A Biography.* New York: Back Bay Books, 2003.

Baker, Jean H. *Margaret Sanger: A Life of Passion.* New York: Hill and Wang, 2011.

Ball, Alan M. *Imaging America: Influence and Images of the Twentieth Century Russia.* Lanham, MD: Rowman & Littlefield, 2013.

Bayley, Edwin R. *Joe McCarthy and the Press.* Madison: University of Wisconsin Press, 1981.

Bear, Marjorie W. *A Square Mile of Chicago.* Oak Brook, IL: Tirac, 2007.

Binder, John J. *Al Capone's Beer Wars: A Complete History of Organized Crime in Chicago During Prohibition.* New York: Prometheus, 2017.

Blanchard, Jonathan, and Nathan L. Rice. *A Debate on Slavery.* Cincinnati: Moore, 1848.

Bonin, Herbert, and Ferry De Goey, eds. *American Firms in Europe: Strategy, Identity, Perception and Performance.* Geneva: Librarie, 2009.

Boyer, John W. *The University of Chicago: A History.* Chicago: University of Chicago Press, 2015.

Cameron, Rondo, and V.I. Bovykin. *International Banking, 1870–1914.* New York: Oxford University Press, 1991.

Canine, Craig. *Dream Reaper.* Chicago: University of Chicago Press, 1997.

Carstensen, Fred V. *American Enterprise in Foreign Markets: Singer and International Harvester in Imperial Russia.* Chapel Hill: University of North Carolina Press, 1984.

Casson, Herbert Newton. *Cyrus Hall McCormick: His Life and Work.* Chicago: McClurg, 1909.

_____. *The Romance of the Reaper.* New York: Doubleday, 1908.

Chernow, Ron. *Titan: The Life of John D. Rockefeller Sr.* New York: Random House, 1998.

Cohen, Lizbeth. *Making a New Deal: Industrial Workers in Chicago, 1919–1939.* Cambridge: Cambridge University Press, 2014.

Cooper, John M. *Woodrow Wilson: A Biography.* New York: Random House, 2009.

Corner, George W. *A History of the Rockefeller Institute, 1901–1953.* New York: Rockefeller Institute Press, 1954.

Cowan, Geoffrey. *Let the People Rule: Theodore Roosevelt and the Birth of the Presidential Primary.* New York: Norton, 2016.

Cyphers, Christopher J. *The National Civic Federation and the Making of a New Liberalism, 1900–1915.* Westport, CT: Praeger, 2002.

Delton, Jennifer. *Racial Integration in Corporate America, 1940–1998.* New York: Cambridge University Press, 2009.

Dicke, Thomas S. *Franchising in America; The Development of the Business Method, 1840–1980.* Chapel Hill: University of North Carolina Press, 1984.

Egle, William. *Pennsylvania Genealogical: Scotch-Irish and German.* Harrisburg, PA, 1888.

Eig, Jonathan. *The Birth of the Pill: How Four Crusaders Reinvented Sex and Launched a Revolution.* New York: Norton, 2013.

Ellmann, Richard. *James Joyce.* New York: Oxford University Press, 1959.

Emerson, Jason. *Giant in the Shadows: The Life of Robert T. Lincoln.* Carbondale: Southern Illinois University Press, 2012.

Fields, Armond. *Katharine Dexter McCormick: Pioneer for Women's Rights.* Westport, CT: Praeger, 2003.

Flamholtz, Eric G., and Yvonne Randole. *Changing the Game.* New York: Oxford University Press, 1998.

Flower, Frank A. *Edwin McMasters Stanton: The Autocrat of the American Rebellion, Emancipation and Reconstruction.* Akron: Saalfield, 1905.

Foster, Patrick. *International Harvester Trucks: The Complete History.* Minneapolis: Quarto, 2015.

Friendly, Fred W. *Minnesota Rag: The Dramatic Story of a Landmark Supreme Court Case That Gave New Meaning to Freedom of the Press.* New York: Random House, 1991.

Greeno, Follet L. *Obed Hussey, Who, of All Inventors Made Bread Cheap.* Rochester: Rochester Herald Publishing, 1912.

Griffith, Robert. *The Politics of Fear: Joseph McCarthy and the Senate.* Amherst: University of Massachusetts Press, 1987.

Halsey, Leroy J. *A History of the McCormick Theological Seminary of the Presbyterian Church.* Chicago: Published by the Seminary, 1893.

Harrison, Gilbert A. *A Timeless Affair: The Life of Anita McCormick Blaine.* Chicago: University of Chicago Press, 1979.

Haycraft, William R. *Yellow Steel: The Story of the Earthmoving Equipment Industry.* Urbana: University of Illinois Press, 2002.

Hayman, Ronald. *A Life of Jung.* New York: Norton, 1999.

Hoover, Herbert, and George H. Nash. *Freedom Betrayed.* Stanford: Hoover Institute Press, 2011.

Hoskins, R. G. *The Biology of Schizophrenia.* London: Chapman & Hall, 1946.

Hounshell, David. *From the American System to Mass Production, 1800–1932. The Development of Manufacturing Technology in the United States.* Baltimore: Johns Hopkins University Press, 1984.

Hutchinson, William T. *Cyrus Hall McCormick; Harvest, 1856–1884.* New York: Appleton-Century, 1935.

_____. *Cyrus Hall McCormick: Seed-Time, 1809–1858.* New York: Century, 1930.

Josephson, Paul R. *Would Trotsky Wear a Bluetooth? Technological Utopianism Under Socialism, 1917–1989.* Baltimore: Johns Hopkins University Press, 2010.

Jung C. G. *Memories, Dreams, Reflections.* New York: Vintage, 1989.

Kennedy, David. M. *The American People in the Great Depression: Freedom from Fear, Part One.* Oxford: Oxford University Press, 1989.

Kingsley, Sherman C. *The Open Air Crusade: A Story of the Elizabeth McCormick Open Air School.* Chicago: United Charities of Chicago, 1911.

Kirkland, Caroline. *Chicago's Yesterdays: A Sheaf of Remembrances.* Chicago: Daughaday, 1919.

Klancher Lee. *The Authoritative Guide to International Harvester and Case-IH Farm Tractors in the Modern Era.* Austin: Octane Press, 2013.

Klooster, John W. *Icons of Invention: The Makers of the Modern World from Gutenberg to Gates.* Santa Barbara: ABC-CLIO, 2009.

Lachman, Gary. *Jung the Mystic.* New York: Penguin, 2010.

Leffington, Randy. *International Harvester Tractors.* St. Paul: Motorbooks, 2004.

Leffingwell, Randy. *Farmall: The Red Tractor that Revolutionized Farming.* St. Paul: MBI, 2005.

_____. *International Harvester Tractors.* St. Paul: Motorbooks, 2004.

Leonard, John W. *History of New York City, 1609–1909.* New York: Journal of Commerce, 1910.

_____, ed. *Who's Who in Finance.* New York: Joseph & Sutton, 1911.

Lewis, Dudley P., ed. *History of the Class of 1903, Yale College.* New Haven: Yale College, 1903.

Link, Arthur S. *Wilson, Volume I: The Road to the White House.* Princeton, New Jersey: Princeton University Press, 1967.

Luering, Otto. *The Odyssey of an American Composer: The Autobiography of Otto Luering.* New York: Scribner's, 1980.

Mandell, Nikki. *The Corporation as Family; The Gendering of Corporate Welfare, 1890–1930.* Chapel Hill: University of North Carolina Press, 2002.

Marsh, Barbara. *A Corporate Tragedy: The Agony of International Harvester Company.* Garden City, NY: Doubleday, 1985.

Marsh, Barbara. *A Corporate Tragedy: The Agony of International Harvester Company.* New York: Doubleday, 1985.

McCormick, Cyrus. *The Century of the Reaper.* Boston: Houghton Mifflin, 1931.

McCormick, Harold F. *Via Pacis: How Terms of Peace Can Be Automatically Prepared While the War Is Still Going On.* Chicago: McClurg, 1917.

McCormick, Henrietta M. R. *Genealogy and Reminiscences.* Chicago, 1894.

McCormick, Leander H. *Characterology: An Exact Science Embracing Physiognomy, Phrenology and Pathognomy.* Chicago: Rand McNally, 1921.

_____. *What the Ability to Read Character will Mean to You.* Chicago: Rand McNally, 1923.

McCormick, Leander J. *Family Record and Biography.* Chicago, 1896.

McCormick, Robert R. *The Army in 1918.* New York: Harcourt, Brace and Howe, 1920.

_____. *With the Russian Army: Being the Experiences of a National Guardsman.* New York: Macmillan, 1915.

McFarland, Andrew. *The Escape.* Boston: Mussey, 1851.

McKinsey, Megan. *The Magnificent Medills: America's Royal Family of Journalism During the Century of Turbulent Splendor.* New York: Harper, 2011.

McLynn, Frank. *Carl Gustav Jung: A Biography.* New York: St. Martin's, 2014.

Miller, Kristie. *Ruth Hanna McCormick: A Life in Politics, 1880–1944.* Albuquerque: University of New Mexico Press, 1992.

Mirabent, Isabel Coll. *Charles Deering and Ramon Casas: A Friendship in Art.* Evanston, IL: Northwestern University Press, 2012.

Moody, John. *The Truth About the Trusts: A Description and Analysis of the American Trust Movement.* New York: Moody, 1904.

Morton, Oren F. *A History of Rockbridge County, Virginia.* Westminster, MD: Heritage, 2007.

Noll, Richard. *The Aryan Christ: The Secret Life of Carl Jung.* New York: Random House, 1997.

Oshinsky David M. *A Conspiracy So Immense: The World of Joe McCarthy.* New York: Oxford University Press, 2005.

Ozanne, Robert. *A Century of Labor-Management Relations at McCormick and International Harvester.* Madison: University of Wisconsin Press, 1967.

_____. *Wages in Practice and Theory.* Madison: University of Wisconsin Press, 1968.

Packard, J. P. *Grant's Tour around the World.* Cincinnati: Forshee & McMakin, 1880.

Parsons, Frank H. *Thirty Years After: Amherst College Class of '81.* New Haven: Tuttle, 1911.

Pattison, Salem G. *The McCormick Extension Case of 1848.* Chicago: Donnelley, Canine, Craig, 1900.

Quick, Graeme R. *International Harvester Tractors and Equipment in Australia and New Zealand.* Sydney: Rosenberg, 2007.

Ranney, David. *Global Decisions, Local Collisions, Urban Life in the New World Order.* Philadelphia: Temple University Press, 2003.

Reavis, L. U. *St. Louis and the Future Great City.* St. Louis, 1878.

Reed, Christopher R. *The Chicago NAACP and the Rise of Professional Leadership, 1914–1966.* Bloomington: Indiana University Press, 1997.

Ritchie, Donald. A. *Reporting from Washington: The History of the Washington Press Corps.* New York: Oxford University Press, 2005.

Rockefeller, John D. *Dear Father/Dear Son: Correspondence of John D. Rockefeller Sr., and John D. Rockefeller*

Jr. Ed. Joseph W. Ernst. New York: Fordham University Press, 1994.

Roderick, Stella V. *Nettie Fowler McCormick*. Rindge, NH: Smith, 1956.

Rose, James A. *Blue Book of the State of Illinois, 1907*. Springfield: State Printer, 1908.

Rosenberg, Chaim M. *America at the Fair: Chicago's 1893 World's Columbian Exposition*. Charleston, SC: Arcadia, 2008.

_____. *Yankee Colonies Across America: Cities Upon the Hills*. Lanham, MD: Lexington Books, 2015.

Rubinstein, William D., Michael A. Jolies, and Hilary L. Rubinstein, Hilary L. *The Palgrave Dictionary of Anglo-Jewish History*. London: Palgrave Macmillan, 2011.

Sanders, Ralph. *Ultimate John Deere: The History of the big Green Machines*. Stillwater, MN: Voyageur Press, 2001.

Scott, Walter D., and Harshe, Robert B. *Charles Deering, 1855–1927: An Appreciation together with His Memoirs of William Deering and James Deering*. Boston: Privately Printed, 1929.

Siegel, Katharine A. S. *Loans and Legitimacy: The Evolution of Soviet-American Relations, 1919–1923*. Lexington: University Press of Kentucky, 1996.

Smith, Amana. *Newspaper Titan: The Infamous and Monumental Times of Cissy Patterson*. New York: Knopf, 2011.

Smith, Richard N. *The Colonel: The Life and Legend of Robert R. McCormick, 1880–1953*. Evanston, IL: Northwestern University Press, 2003.

Spiegel, Allen D. *Lincoln, Esquire: A Shrewd, Sophisticated Lawyer in His Time*. Macon: Mercer University Press, 2002.

Tebbel, John. *The Inheritors: A Story of America's Great Fortunes and What Happened to Them*. New York: Putnam's Sons, 1962.

Terrel, John. *An American Dynasty: The Story of the McCormicks, Medills and Pattersons*. Garden City, NY: Doubleday, 1947.

_____. *Farmall: The Red Tractor that Revolutionized Farming*. St. Paul: MBI, 2005.

Walker, Samuel. *Hate Speech: The History of an American Controversy*. Lincoln: University of Nebraska Press, 1994.

Walska, Ganna. *Always Room at the Top*. New York: Ronald Smith, 1943.

Webber, James. *Jane Addams: A Biography*. Urbana: University of Illinois Press, 2000.

Wendel, C. H. *150 Years of International Harvester*. Osceola, WI: Motorbooks, 1993.

Wheller, Frank T. *Tusculum College, Tennessee*. Charleston, SC: Arcadia, 2000.

Wienik, Peter. *History of the Jews in America: From the Period of the New World to the Present Time*. New York: The Jewish Press, 1912.

Winder, Gordon M. *The American Reaper: Harvesting Networks and Technology, 1830–1910*. London: Routledge, 2010.

Index